Soldier Saint

By the same author

A HUNDRED YEARS' WAR

Soldier Saint

GEORGE SCOTT RAILTON
William Booth's
first Lieutenant

by

BERNARD WATSON

HODDER AND STOUGHTON

Printed in Great Britain for Hodder and Stoughton Limited,
St. Paul's House, Warwick Lane, London, E.C.4. by
Willmer Brothers Limited, Birkenhead.

Foreword

GOOD MEN have often had their differences.

'I withstood him to the face,' said Paul about his fellow apostle Peter at a time when the very foundations of the Christian church were being laid.

The subject of this biography was one in mind and spirit with William Booth when the foundations of The Salvation Army were being laid but, as the work grew, his Franciscan spirit revolted against those commercial involvements with the world which, for better, for worse, became necessary to a Movement which aimed to save the world. And Railton withstood his venerated leader to his face.

There were incipient elements of tragedy in this tension, but the situation was redeemed because Railton himself always paid the price of loyalty to his ideals, and the other protagonist in the story, the then Chief of Staff, Bramwell Booth, could say to him with affection which triumphed over passing exasperation: 'I love you, but you are a worry to me at times!'

The author has enhanced his accepted reputation as a Salvationist writer by the life which he has breathed into this unusual story, into the making of which has gone a considerable amount of original research.

FREDERICK COUTTS

Author's Note

I WISH to express my gratitude to General Frederick Coutts, for giving me permission to embark on the undertaking, and to General Wilfred Kitching for information and valuable papers relating to Railton. The Railton family were kind and co-operative: Miss Esther Railton, the surviving daughter, gave me wise counsel and corrected my notes; Dame Ruth Railton (wife of Cecil King), a grand-daughter, and Mr. Andrew Railton, a grandson, read the manuscript and corrected errors. They also gave me access to valuable family papers.

Aid with research came from Miss Peggy Beels and Mrs. Captain Banks. Lieut.-Colonel Harry Dean assisted with the details on Railton's contribution to the Army's holiness teaching. Lieut.-Colonel Cyril Barnes, of the Literary Department, was a mine of information. Brigadier John Waite spent valuable time in the Public Record Offices searching for light on Railton's one-man expedition to Morocco, and Brigadier Christine McMillan, of New York, travelled to St. Louis for background to Railton's attempt upon that city. Colonel Wilhelm Kiesel checked the chapters on Germany, as did Commissioner Gilbert Abadie on France. Major Elizabeth Balshaitis assisted with translating from Raoul Gout's life of Blanche Peyron.

Numerous people who remembered Railton, or had family association with him, wrote giving information. Some of this was used; all of it was helpful. Those who assisted with the typing of the numerous rewritten drafts deserve much praise. I am grateful to Commissioner Catherine Bramwell-Booth for permission to quote from the letters of her father.

Any errors in the record will be mine.

London, 1970   BERNARD WATSON

Contents

1
The General's Lieutenant

THE REVEREND DAVID RAILTON, in France as a Church of England chaplain in World War I, was seized with the idea that one of the countless fallen British soldiers, anonymous, unhonoured, alone with his glory, should be taken to London and buried in the nation's shrine. In due time, as a result of Railton's suggestion, the Unknown Soldier was buried in Westminster Abbey.

The padre's father had been an unknown soldier in a different regiment, The Salvation Army. Though his life was being written as the war was being fought, though many eulogistic obituaries had been published, and many words spoken, not half had been told. It was part tragedy and partly a clash of personalities. George Scott Railton had been William Booth's first Lieutenant, his right-hand man, an inspired tactician, originator of some of the brilliant ideas that made The Salvation Army. He had lived in the Booth home for eleven years. The Army's founder and his wife, both twenty years older, looked upon him as a son. He was a big brother to the Booth children and a mentor for Bramwell Booth, elder son, and successor to the Generalship. The Booths loved him and relied upon him. It is doubtful whether The Salvation Army would have come into existence without George Scott Railton's guidance in the crucial years 1873 to 1880.

In the climate of the early twentieth century the record could not reveal that the same Commissioner Railton who was revered for his saintly life—'the St. Francis of The Salvation Army'—had publicly protested against Army policies, fallen from the General's favour and persisted in disapproval of new methods adopted by his son Bramwell, the Chief of the Staff. As the Reverend David Railton, and the Reverend Nathaniel Railton, also a Church of England chaplain in France, read the proof sheets of their father's biography they noted many omissions. There was no mention of Railton's startling public protest in the Queen's Hall, in a meeting led by General William Booth. His long, courageous campaign to save what he regarded as the soul of the Army was not recorded. His years 'in the wilderness' were not explained. It was a one-sided story.

But Railton had died in 1913, a year after William Booth, and the writers of his life, not without skill, and certainly sympathetic towards Railton, had to tread warily among delicate susceptibilities of many yet alive who were concerned in the Railton story. Bramwell Booth was now the General. So the full story of Railton, the saintly individualist, did not see the light of day. The motives of those concerned were not discreditable. Bramwell Booth differed strongly as to the methods by which The Salvation Army might achieve its aims but it was a problem of interpretation: how best can one save souls? How hasten the coming of the Kingdom of God? Bramwell Booth thought it possible one way; Railton another. It is a dichotomy as old as Christianity itself.

The official records show Railton as the Army's first Commissioner, better educated than the norm among his colleagues, a linguist, a prolific writer, and leader of the Army's first official invasion overseas — to the United States. He is known to have framed many of the movement's *Orders and Regulations,* to have helped to set out its first doctrines and to have made radical and highly successful contributions to Salvationist tactics.

But this is by no means the sum of Railton's contribution to the making of The Salvation Army. Doctor John Kent, of Bristol University, states that Railton was the most important formative influence in the Army, after the Booths themselves.[1] Rowland Robertson, of Essex University, describes Railton as 'the Army's first Chief of Staff'.[2] Except on a technicality this is true, and it in no way detracts from Bramwell Booth's tremendous contribution to add that in some important respects Railton was the most influential 'Chief of the Staff' the Army has had to date.

Officially the Army does not say this but in effect Bramwell Booth did. He wrote, 'Next to the Founder and the Army Mother the leading personal force in that decade from 1872 to 1880 was George Scott Railton, our first Commissioner.'[3] As Bramwell well knew, those crucial years saw the development of the Army in its disciplined structure, internationalism, unconventional methods, female ministry and the omission of the sacraments. As William Booth's first Lieutenant, Railton had a leading part in framing these policies; some of them he initiated.

Railton was the first to think of the Christian Mission as an Army. His idea was accepted by William Booth after a period of about six years. The full story is published here for the first time but if confirmation were needed then Bramwell Booth supplies it. In Railton's obituary the General wrote:

'From the earliest days, and even, I think, before the idea had taken possession of any other mind, Railton's conception of the future embraced the idea of a world-wide war.'[4]

Elijah Cadman has been credited with the conception of the military analogy that gave rise to the name, The Salvation Army. Salvationist writers have accepted this view of what happened and non-Salvationists have not unnaturally followed suit.[5] But Cadman found the Mission an Army in all but name when he joined it in 1876. He was largely drilled by the General Secretary, Railton, who for three years before Cadman arrived on the scene issued a stream of military metaphors and a number of war songs as William Booth's right-hand man from 1873.

Railton was a leading protagonist, perhaps the decisive influence, in causing William Booth to give women equal place with men in Salvation Army commands. The documentation for this claim is ample but again Bramwell Booth confirms:

'The Army Mother herself never quite contemplated placing women in positions which would involve their authority over men. This would be going further than anything recorded even in the Early Church. The Founder delayed for a considerable time before making his decision. Commissioner Railton, who was always ready for new departures, favoured entrusting women with the responsibilities and authorities which we had given to the men.'[6]

Indeed, in the 1870s, long before female suffrage, the liberation of women and their entry into the professions and into industry, George Scott Railton, the Secretary of the Christian Mission, was writing that he did not see why women should not have equal pay. In conceding that principle, as recent-day newspapers show, Railton was about a hundred years before his time.

The planet round which Railton's satellite revolved was William Booth. Railton led the *coup d'état* which allowed the General Superintendent to become the General—the *Supremo*—of The Salvation Army.

Though William Booth had to work through committees, he often acted as if they did not exist and abhorred them. His take-over took place in January, 1877, having been delayed by Railton's attack of smallpox. *The History of The Salvation Army* thus describes the purge:

'Railton, Bramwell Booth, Dowdle, Ridsdel, Corbridge and other ardent spirits grew tired of the futility of attempted government by Conference and the slowing down of progress consequent on the lack of effective leadership inherent in that system. Headed by Railton and Bramwell Booth, they waited upon William Booth and protested: "We gave up our lives to work under you and those you should appoint, rather than under one another".'7

At this time William Booth was forty-eight years of age, an old man as life expectancy went in those days. He was often ill, angry and frustrated. But henceforth he never looked back, he looked like a phophet, roared like a lion, acted like a General and lived to the age of eighty-three.

Railton's influence was also decisive on the General's policy in abandoning the use of the sacraments in The Salvation Army. When he joined, both baptism and the Lord's Supper were observed but were becoming focal points of misgiving. Catherine Booth feared that the converts from the dark satanic mills, the sweat-shops, the beer-houses of the East End would not be able to comprehend the mysteries of the broken bread that was Christ's body, or the wine that was His Blood.

In the words of Bramwell Booth she feared 'that our people, most of whom were very ignorant and simple, might come in time to lean upon some outward ceremonial, instead of the work of the Holy Spirit, as witnessed in the change of heart and life'.8 Bramwell confessed that he came round to the idea of abandonment with 'considerable hesitation, not to say reluctance'. He admitted that he sprinkled as many as thirty in one service and believed that he may have been the last Salvation Army officer to administer the sacraments.

Many of the converted drunkards could not be offered fermented liquors without hazard to their new-found teetotalism. Some who had been sent to the churches fell away because of the peril in the cup. Many objected to the 'diluted jellies' which well-meaning people concocted to overcome the danger in liquor. There were bickerings in newly-formed, immature congregations as to who should administer the sacraments—some would not have it, wrote Bramwell Booth, unless 'offered by the regular preachers'.

But the greatest stumbling-block was the possibility that women should administer the sacraments. Railton's policies called for the acceptance of women in full ministry. William Booth was pragmatic: 'Will it help?' he asked of any proposed change. Subject to that his instinct was conservative. Railton tipped the scales towards abandonment. Bramwell wrote:

'We were led, therefore, to make an examination of the whole subject. Railton, from the beginning, was in favour of abandoning all ceremonials which were prominently associated with the rest of the religious life of the world. He argued with great cogency that if, as we all admitted, participation in the Supper was not necessary to salvation, it became merely a question of its value, as one method of helping the people; and he claimed that the freedom which was purchased by Jesus Christ was a freedom from all that belonged to the old dispensation, including the whole ceremonial principle. My mother, although not feeling so strongly as Railton on the subject, at once grasped the seriousness of anything which might mislead or divide our simple people.'[9]

Railton had much to do with the framing of Army doctrines, and particularly the definition of New Testament holiness as he saw it.

Some Salvationists think of him as the St. Paul of the Army, as well as the St. Francis. He was, next to Catherine Booth, the first of the Army's theologians, and played a vital part in making The Salvation Army, to some extent, a holiness movement.

Doctor John Kent has written:

'After 1857 there was no further serious division in British Methodism from an institutional point of view. It is often forgotten, however, that The Salvation Army was created by ex-Methodists. George Railton, the most important formative influence in the movement after the Booths themselves, had, like them, been Wesleyan Methodist. But The Salvation Army also drew some of its early support from Methodists who had become discontented with the comparative respectability of late nineteenth-century Methodism. The holiness revivalism of the early Army was a conscious throw-back to an allegedly "primitive Methodism".'[10]

Present-day Salvationists would be reluctant to agree with the past tense in reference to the Army's 'holiness revivalism'. But certainly Railton came to William Booth strongly indoctrinated with the idea of Wesleyan holiness, and his life was consistent with the doctrine. In his eleven years in the Booth home he was exposed to Catherine Booth's ardent and eloquent exposition of holiness. As the General Secretary of the Christian Mission it fell to him to move, at the 1876 Annual Conference, the following resolution:

'1876. Resolved: that the following definitions of the doctrines numbered 9 and 10 in our list of doctrines be printed and issued to all our members. That is to say:

'We believe that after conversion there remain in the heart of a believer inclinations to evil or roots of bitterness, which, unless over-powered by divine grace, produce actual sin, but that these evil tendencies can be entirely taken away by the Spirit of God, and the whole heart thus cleansed from everything contrary to the will of God, or entirely sanctified, will then produce the fruits of the Spirit only. And we believe that persons thus entirely sanctified may by the power of God be kept unblameable and unreprovable before Him.'[11]

The phrase 'the roots of bitterness' ran into theological stormwaters in later years, although John Wesley had used the analogy of a 'rotten tooth removed'. It suggested a superhuman condition for which there seemed to be no New Testament warrant. William Booth may have had reservations about it; he was never one to overlook a man's humanity, being ever conscious of his own frailties. The Railtonian definition of holiness was not included in the all-important Parliamentary 1878 Foundation Deed Poll which constituted William Booth as General of the newly-formed Salvation Army.

But in 1881 it was written by Railton into a booklet entitled *The Doctrines of The Salvation Army* and was carried forward into the *Handbook of Doctrine*, where it remained until 1927. A later edition made it a recognizable interpolation and in 1935 it became a footnote. But it was removed from the *Articles of War* in 1959, and from the revised *Handbook of Doctrine* in 1969.

Railton was not, despite his Bible knowledge, his Latin, Greek and Hebrew, a theologian in the sense that research and scholarship make a theologian. The faith he had when he came to William Booth was the faith he had when he was 'promoted to Glory'.[12] His tremendous contribution to the Army was not theology but tactics. He was a man of daring, original ideas, unequalled in Salvation Army history and, as we shall see, his great work was accomplished in his first ten years. He was a Commissioner at thirty-one and after that the story is marked by pain and frustration, differences with his General and with Bramwell Booth and the sacrifice of his own position and happiness for what he regarded as his struggle to save the soul of The Salvation Army.

2

The Making of a Soldier

THE AUSTERE, sacrificial pattern of Railton's life was largely determined by the events of his childhood and youth. He was born on July 6th, 1849, at Arbroath in Scotland, and his parents had been Wesleyan missionaries in Antigua in the West Indies, where they had met and married. The Reverend Launcelot Railton was a stern, withdrawn father. Margaret (née Scott), his wife, though affectionate towards both her sons, was haunted by other people's poverty, afflicted by their pain. She sometimes stripped the blankets from her beds to give to those in greater need. In the various Wesleyan manses, where the Railtons lived in Scotland and the North of England, the diet was frugal, discipline spartan, religion severely evangelical.

Launcelot Railton and his wife died within six hours of each other, on the night of November 8th, 1864, at Peel on the Isle of Man, probably of cholera. An epidemic was raging in the district and the devoted couple were nursing those who were too poor to afford professional care.

When the disease swept them away, grateful townspeople, whose descendants have not forgotten the Railtons to this day, erected a memorial at the entrance to the Peel Methodist Church where it can still be seen. The inscription reads:

Erected by many friends in memory of a faithful pastor and his devoted wife whose remains together wait the Resurrection of the blessed.[1]

As the Railtons' were evangelical it is not surprising that young George was 'saved' at the age of ten. It happened at Wigton in Cumberland where an epidemic of 'flu had carried off numerous local inhabitants. The boy, having contracted the malady, was left alone in the house one Sunday night and became convinced that he was about to die. He prayed hard and confessed his sins. Fifty years later he remembered:

'I have never had the slightest reason to doubt that Jesus Himself set my soul free in that little room, that Sunday evening on February 19th, 1860.'[2]

At Woodhouse Grove School, Leeds, then open to the sons of Wesleyan ministers only, young Railton's religious instincts and alert mind were well nourished. He rose at seven in the winter and six in the summer. There were prayers before and after breakfast and a forty-five-minute prayer meeting after tea. Besides two compulsory Sunday services the weekly Bible-study class was attended by about sixty boys.

In addition some of the older boys formed themselves into praying bands. Of these J. T. Slugg, in his history of the school, writes:

'The Reverend J. W. Denham (who entered the school as a boy in 1858), says, "A remarkable revival took place in 1862, John Wesley Whitehead, George Scott Railton, a scholar named Jones and myself spending a whole holiday afternoon in prayer more than once. This was the beginning and the work spread mightily".'[3]

Railton left Woodhouse following the death of his parents for he had already passed the normal age limit, which was fourteen years. His education would not have amounted to much if he had gone to a university and then into one of the professions. But among those who were to be lifelong comrades it made him unique. He acquired a grounding in Greek and Latin, stimulus for the flair for languages which he possessed. He learned to endure hardness. Key words at Woodhouse were 'work' and 'duty' The Reverend John Farrar, D.D., was the governor. Of him Railton wrote that he accepted Wesley's purpose for the school, that all his preachers' sons should turn from the world and its follies and follow in their fathers' footsteps.[4] Wesley did not approve of fun and games for the young and Dr. Pritchard, the present Headmaster, agrees that the regime in Railton's time was severe:

'Till after the 1860s discipline could not be helped by the prefectorial system, as was becoming normal in boarding schools of the time, because pupils left at fourteen. As a result the discipline at Woodhouse Grove was too repressive and autocratic ... There was little opportunity of getting out of the monastic atmosphere of a small community.'[5]

Railton knew few of the joys of childhood. But there were compensations. He lived in exciting times. Christian missionaries were conquering Africa and Christian soldiers, India. John Nicholson, a hero of

Delhi, died a General at thirty-four, in the moment of his triumph, having saved India as a jewel for Victoria's crown. He had also killed many Indian tribesmen but the England that wept over his glorious death thought little of that. Railton read that Nicholson loved his Bible, said his prayers and walked not in the paths of the ungodly. An incurable romantic, Railton glimpsed at Woodhouse Wesley's vision of one parish, the whole world: 'Red and yellow, black and white, yet all precious in God's sight.' With that vision he helped transform an East End London mission into a world-wide Salvation Army.

Apart from a few pounds, proceeds of the sale of his father's library, Railton was now penniless, orphaned, homeless and jobless. He was fifteen years of age, but he never lacked confidence. The recently published Smiles's *Self-Help* was a best-seller and Railton had many of the virtues lauded in that Victorian classic. His elder brother, Launcelot, a Wesleyan minister, found him a place in a London shipping firm where he soon astonished his employers, and himself, with the ease with which he learned Spanish. Soon he was able to take over much of the correspondence in that language.

He was lonely in London, bored by parlour conversation, unattracted by the opposite sex, indifferent to prospects of promotion and better salary. He was in the world but not of it. Like his dead hero, John Nicholson, he preferred his lonely lodgings and the consolations of his Bible to the concerts and music halls. His job was soul-destroying. He wrote to clients to say that the wines had arrived, the fruit had been badly packed, the olives were not of the stipulated grade. Sometimes he had to write letters that were 'white lies', statements of the 'business is business' kind which did not square with Wesleyan holiness, for then as now many businessmen acted according to Lord Melbourne's well-known dictum that religion should not interfere with a man's private life.

Railton could not separate the one from the other. He now had a call to be a minister and sometimes visited Wesley's chapel, only to be disappointed at what he considered to be the formal, cold services. He sat in at Guildhall trials to learn eloquence from the barristers, and at the Palace of Westminster in the hope that he could learn from Palmerston, then Prime Minister, who had been ready to wage war at the drop of a hat and paint the map with the red of empire. Railton was already dreaming of a greater conquest, in the religious imagery of his time, 'through the Blood of the Lamb'.

Round about Limehouse he tried out his new-found skill on seamen from the Spanish ships, distributing tracts and trying to convert faithful children of the Pope to Protestantism. He had no success. In 1868 he tried an even more forlorn hope. The British were acquiring large slices of Africa for the Queen; de Lesseps's Suez canal was being built to bring East and West together. Railton, aged nineteen, with twenty pounds in his wallet, decided to journey to Morocco to win the Moors for Christ. Had he known that Francis of Assisi had tried this, and failed, it would not have stopped Railton.

To him office was always a prison and there were those dubious letters he had to sign. Railton didn't believe a lie could be white. After refusing to put his name to one outrageous example he was dismissed, greatly to brother Launcelot's distress. Possibly Railton engineered the whole affair. He hoped never to sit at a city desk again.

Tangiers was an international city. The formidable Sir Drummond Hay was ambassador there from 1844 to 1885. He cared not for British visitors, who lost themselves in the desert, were stabbed to death in back streets, or fell victim to drink and women. Pepys had been miserable there. Railton was even more so. The Moors were more obdurate against Christianity than the Catholics against Protestantism. Railton tramped alone through Morocco and Tunis, carrying a flag inscribed, REPENTANCE—FAITH—HOLINESS.[6] At least this was less incendiary to the Arab mind than the Union Jack.[7]

When his money was gone and his mission a failure, Railton had to go to the British consul.

'Why did you come here?' that worthy asked.

'Because God sent me,' replied Railton, who was always simple and direct in speech.

He was allowed to work his passage home as a steward and the elder brother Launcelot had to provide for 'the prodigal son' back from the far country. It all seemed to be a fiasco but Railton claimed in later years, 'I had passed unscathed through physical and moral dangers and learned many lessons from which I am still profiting.'[8]

The mines in Siberia would have been as attractive to Railton as another stint in the City and as he could not continue to impose upon his brother he walked to Cornwall, where there was work to be had in the lead mines. On the way, by the roadside and in common lodging houses, he made his first close acquaintance with the rising, militant 'lower orders', who had formed themselves into trade unions and, in the case of the engineers, ship-builders, miners and farm workers, had recently demonstrated their new-found strength in strikes.

Railton always showed a complete unawareness of social distinctions and this brief contact with the Cornish mining community, their hardships, prejudices and religion, were to stand him in good stead. For them Methodism was brotherly love:

'On arrival at Bridport I sank exhausted by the wharf, every penny gone, and no idea how to get any further. Then I remembered that I still had a pawnable overcoat, and the proceeds of it carried me to a lead-mining village not far from Exeter. Here I learned that manual work could be got and I had time to discover how much kindness can be shown to a tramp, how much patience with his incapacity, how much readiness to help him in every way.'[9]

If the social impact of life among the poor mining families was useful to Railton he gained from their brand of Methodism even more so. Those he worshipped with were Bible Christians (or Free Methodists), one of the early breaks from the parent tree of Wesleyan Methodism, established by John Wesley, to which Railton belonged. The great Jabez Bunting, who ruled the Wesleyans with a heavy hand in the first part of the 19th century, gave ample excuses for schism. 'Democracy is a sin,' he said.[10] Though reform was in the air he had little sympathy with it and refused to conduct the funeral of a Wesleyan shot during the Luddite riots. His remedy for dissent was simple: 'It is no sin for a man to think our discipline is wrong, provided that he quits us.'[11] He gave the platform excessive authority, did not favour conference discussion, and frowned on interventions by the laity. 'The whole Methodist Conference is buttoned up in a single pair of breeches,' one critic asserted. The Bible Christians of Cornwall taught Railton the value of lay participation, of eccentric and sensational tactics, and the worth of women preachers. He learned that it was possible for the unlettered man to be a successful revivalist as witness Billy Bray, a Bible Christian, who though hardly literate was a most effective preacher. 'If the devil put me in a barrel I'd shout hallelujah through the bunghole,' Bray declared. While among the lead-miners Railton began service as a local preacher, walking as many as fourteen miles to a service which would be held in a chapel built by Bray.

The Cornish interlude ended when his brother Launcelot found him 'more suitable' employment, this time in the North East where, at Stockton-on-Tees, at the age of twenty-one, Railton began work for an uncle who ran a shipping agency. The Stockton area was to be one of the first provincial battlefields of the Christian Mission, a direct result of Railton's years there.

Soon he was promoted to the larger Middlesbrough agency, but

office life was still unattractive and Railton now had his heart on the
Wesleyan ministry. After appearing before a board of examiners to
expound a trial sermon he became a local preacher. Though the Wesleyans required higher scholastic standards than the New Connexion, the
'Prims' or other offshoots of the Wesleyans, Railton's chances of joining
his brother Launcelot were good. A fellow Wesleyan wrote:

'We made him Secretary of our Mission Band Committee. He was a
good preacher, well educated, with a fine voice and an attractive style.
He was also courageous and pushing, and loved to address a crowd on
the street. He went into his work with all his heart.'[12]

He sang Baring Gould's new song, 'Onward, Christian soldiers', and
felt that this was what he wanted—a fight. In him the jingoism of the
time was transmuted into a militant evangelism. He was weary of pale
and quiet religion. Edward Cardwell's controversial changes of the
British Army took place at this time. The crux of his reform was that
he made it the army of the ordinary man. One of Railton's heroes, John
Lawrence, had reformed the Army of India during his term as Vice-
roy (1864–69). There had been much to-do about this in the papers.
Now, after the Franco-Prussian War of 1870—when German peasant
conscripts routed France's professional army—and with the memory
of the Crimean debacle in their minds, Mr. Gladstone's government
hastened to put the British military house in order. The purchase of
commissions was abolished, promotion established on merit and short-
service enlistment allowed. The high command was improved.[13] This
all caused a nation-wide furore in press and Parliament. There now
existed a people's army, an army of the common man, the rank and
file together. It soon won for itself a high reputation, adding numerous
colonies to the Queen's possessions. Railton was no lover of militarism,
yet Cardwell's reform of the British Army inevitably influenced him.
It could well have been one of the factors that transformed the Christian Mission into The Salvation Army.

3

Holy War!

IN 1872 Launcelot Railton visited a hydro at Matlock, in Derbyshire, a place frequented by Methodist ministers with health problems. There he met the Reverend William Booth, who was suffering from nervous exhaustion. Booth had been a minister with the Methodist New Connexion but was now engaged in leading a mission in the East End of London. The man who was to found The Salvation Army listened with interest to the account of the exploits of young George Railton, particularly his single-handed invasion of Morocco. There had been both audacity and failure in Booth's career.

Booth's ill-health was dyspeptic in origin, a condition aggravated by years of frustration. Forty years of age, ripe in experience, rich in talent, he was wholly committed to his task of reaching the godless masses of London with the gospel. But he was not a good organizer, and was irascible by temperament, often falling victim to melancholy and doubt. Intolerant of anyone or anything that kept him from his impassioned quest for souls, he was found by his subordinates to be a hard taskmaster. His interests were among the people who responded to his preaching: his deep, husky voice, the Hebraic nose, the large compelling eyes, the love for erring mankind which burned in him and which made him a John the Baptist in a Victorian wilderness of doubts and conflicts. He needed a manager of details, a chief of staff for the business for which he had neither time nor inclination.

Launcelot told his brother of his meeting with the leader of the East London Mission and indicated that Booth needed an assistant. Railton sent for *How to Reach the Masses with the Gospel,* a sixpenny booklet in which Booth described his work in the East End. For Railton the book was a trumpet call to action. He ceased to think of the Wesleyan ministry, and had no further doubts as to what he should do with his life. Straightway, he hitched his waggon to Booth's star and through all the heartache, sacrifice and privation that followed, even when it seemed that his leader had treated him harshly and unjustly, he never regretted his decision. He came to have doubts about certain

Salvation Army policies and some Salvation Army people but the Founder retained Railton's affection and loyalty to the end.

The close association of the two men, the young idealist Railton with the seasoned campaigner Booth, which began in 1872 was the beginning of the metamorphosis of the Mission into the Army. Railton, living in a militaristic, jingoistic England, instantly promoted Booth to the rank of General and was the first to address him so by letter— a form which embarrassed Booth. But the imagery was understandable. In the American Civil War cameras had recorded the lives and deaths of heroes and earlier, at the Crimea, Russell, of *The Times,* the first great war correspondent, had clothed ugliness, blood and death in superlative prose. American patriots of Federal persuasion gave the church a new sort of battle hymn, based on real war incidents, such as 'Hold the Fort, for I am coming!'

Yet Booth's first reaction to young Railton's request to join forces was cautious. Let the young man come up to London and see the Mission at work. It would be unwise to give up his job and lodgings without first-hand knowledge. In October 1872, therefore, Railton journeyed to London, where he became a guest in the Booth home. He seems to have decided at once; his brother was grieved by the speedy and drastic severance of his ties with Methodism.

'Take time, consult with your friends,' Launcelot advised. But Railton, who had returned to Middlesbrough to settle his affairs and make his final departure was sure:

'Even since 1868 I have been declaring my views of trading and have declared myself bound in duty and honour to enter the first door God should open to me ... Mr. Booth and I are so much one that I cannot separate myself from him and his work. He says that when I left him after my visit both he and Mrs. Booth felt they had lost one who had become a pleasure and a power to them. I hope the grand man is making no mistake.'[1]

Though Railton soon became as a son to Mrs. Booth—they were both by Salvationist standards 'intellectuals'—it was William Booth who was the magnet.

'I was specially pleased to find the Mission under the leadership of one man, and that man in the vigour of his days, instead of the venerable being I had imagined. He is full of desire for all that is most heavenly yet talking about everything in the language of the street and the shop. He seemed to me the ideal leader.'[2]

The Mission itself excited Railton. The meetings were crowded, the missioners, though often crude and uneducated, dynamic and eloquent. All was alive and vital, full of wonderful potential. From the North he wrote to tell William Booth that he had made up his mind. Again he saw the Mission as an army:

'Though nearly everyone seems capable of leading, all seem glad to be led ... I expected to see a company of powerful but irrepressible volunteers, whereas I found myself in the presence of a battalion of trained male and female soldiers, quite as remarkable for their steadiness as for their readiness.'[3]

The next letter, January, 1873, shows Railton's conception of the Mission as an army in even more explicit terms. For the first time Booth is called General in the military sense. (It is possible that he had earlier been called 'General' as an abbreviation of General Superintendent by members of his family):

'My dear General,
    Please tell me your new office address as I think of sending a box ... Everything I read about you and your people reawakens and refreshes my love for you all ... I shall arrive at the right moment and all is well for ever!
        Your ever-to-be faithful Lieutenant,
                                        George Scott Railton.'[4]

Within a year of joining the Mission he was writing articles which made full use of the military analogy. One was entitled *Holy War!* and, in February, 1874, he published the Mission's first war song. Indeed, he may have written it. The fact that it is unsigned and uncredited supports Railton's claim. All his life he was diffident about signing articles. He sometimes 'ghosted' for William Booth and frequently used the simple letter 'R' at the foot of his contributions. Often he wrote anonymously. But whoever wrote the song Salvationists still sing it. It is Railtonian in its sentiment, style and spirit. The probability that it is Railton's is strong; with typical disregard for religious conventions he used a secular tune, *Men of Harlech*. Here is the first verse and chorus:

Christian, rouse thee! War is raging,
God and fiends are battle waging;
Every ransomed power engaging,
Break the tempter's spell.
Dare ye still lie fondly dreaming,
Wrapped in ease and worldly scheming,
While the multitudes are streaming
Downwards into hell.

Through the world resounding,
Let the gospel sounding,
Summon all, at Jesus' call,
His glorious Cross surrounding.
Sons of God, earth's trifles leaving,
Be not faithless but believing;
To your conquering Captain cleaving,
Forward to the fight.

Railton was soon acting editor of *The Christian Mission Magazine* and, probably quite unconsciously, indoctrinating the missioners with his ideas for the waging of Christian war. Meanwhile the Booths were influencing Railton. He had been homeless and orphaned before his fifteenth year and the Booth home at Hackney was to be the nearest approach to a permanent dwelling he was ever to know; in days to come Railton's wife and children would see less of him than did the Booth children. Catherine Booth tried to make him pay more attention to his food, his clothes and his health, about which he was recklessly indifferent. William Booth probably saved him from becoming a hopeless crank. Railton had an inbuilt inability to compromise; he was ascetic by nature; unable to relax; a pleasant sort of fanatic if that is possible.

Booth had been reared an Anglican. This perhaps gave him a tolerance which sometimes shocked his wife Catherine, who had the puritanical zeal of a *Mayflower* pilgrim. The Founder would take brandy for medicinal purposes until his sweetheart put a stop to such licence.[5] He took a gun to go hunting in Lincolnshire, a relaxation of which she did not approve. Dutifully, he always gave way to her strong opinions, though seeking ways to modify them later if opportunity arose. He bought gay, lilting tunes for his sweetheart, and suggested, knowing her abhorrence of anything 'worldly', that she write religious words to justify their use. Perhaps this was why Railton after one year in the Booth home, would say of music what some people credit William Booth with saying, 'Let us rescue this precious instrument from the clutches of the devil, and make it as it may be made, a bright and lively power for good.' There is no reliable record that William Booth ever said 'Why should the devil have all the best tunes?' a remark often attributed to him.[6]

Railton's coming to London marks the beginning of an international emphasis in the Mission which was to grow until all were seized by it, chanting Railton's own words in a world-wide rallying cry:

> Salvation Army, Army of God,
> Onward to conquer the world with Fire and Blood.

The youth whose parents had wed in the West Indies, who had been reared in the Methodist missionary tradition, who had become multilingual and journeyed alone to seek to win the Arabs for Christ, is the father of the Salvationist missionary spirit. It is no discredit to William Booth that he was, at first, something of a 'Little Englander'. He had never been outside Britain. For a time the task confronting him in Britain was so mighty that he could not see beyond it. But he would one day. His teacher was George Scott Railton. William Booth was a highly teachable man.

One thing both men agreed upon: the way to save the world was to save souls, to get men converted religiously. Neither was interested in the new cult of salvation by science, by better health and better homes —the humanitarian 'gospel' of Charles Booth, Chadwick, Huxley, H. G. Wells and the rest. The General and his first Lieutenant took it for granted that 'we needed only to bring the prodigal back to his Father and then all would be well with him'.[7] This common ground of William Booth and George Scott Railton should be noted, for the General's departure from it, by which The Salvation Army later added world-wide social service to evangelism, was to cause the rift by which Railton's career was adversely affected and the relationship between the two men severely strained.

4

Behind the Lines

IN SEPTEMBER 1873, Railton's appointment as General Secretary to the Christian Mission was announced thus:

General Superintendent—Reverend William Booth
General Secretary　　　—George S. Railton[1]

He was not just a secretary and never, as some have suggested, William Booth's secretary. He was soon thrown into close contact with Bramwell Booth, who, though aged about sixteen years, had already shown ability as manager of a small chain of food shops run by William Booth:

HOT SOUP DAY OR NIGHT THREE-COURSE DINNERS FOR 6d.—
though these were closed down shortly after Railton's arrival.

As yet Bramwell, who was to be the Army's second General, was sickly and indeterminate about his future, not enthusiastic about the 'blood and fire' evangelism espoused by his parents. At the age of nineteen he wrote to his father:

'In my present condition the burden of fatigue of preaching positively unfits me to do anything else much, at any rate compared with what I might do without it ... The present state of things, coupled with the fact that I do not achieve anything—if it was anybody else they would have to resign—is unbearable ... I do not feel I am called to preach.'[2]

Indeed, his reservations lasted until he was twenty-one years old.

'It was in 1874, when I was eighteen years of age, that I came thus definitely into the Mission service. I did not consider that my entrance into that service pledged me to a life of public ministry ... I was in the midst of a great controversy with myself, which continued for at any rate three years.'[3]

General Secretary Railton soon exerted wide influence. One can see in his letters precedents which bind The Salvation Army to this day.

The ban on commercial advertising in the Army's press has caused it to forfeit hundreds of thousands of pounds. At first William Booth allowed it, subject to conditions. Railton wrote to a would-be advertiser:

'We are sorry to find that one of the advertisements sent for the Magazine this month with a block relates to hair dye. This we really could not accept as it seems so repugnant to the notions of religion adopted by the vast majority of our readers that it could scarcely produce any benefit to the advertiser, and might damage us.

Yours faithfully,

G. S. Railton, Secy.'

In this letter to William Booth one can see the impatience of Booth's right-hand man with the casual and 'churchy' ways at some Mission stations:

'Whitechapel is more "chapelified" in its preaching arrangements than ever. They had 120 last night, no souls—D. M. in the chair—a speech night, no doubt, if the truth were known. Mrs. Reynolds is, I am certain, one of the most parsonic people in the concern. No amount of slaving can hide from me the fact that these folk simply tolerate our presence. I wonder if you have been told that they are trying to raise £15 for gas stoves to warm the hall?'

Railton could be a hard man when the cause demanded it:

'As to Whitby and Cadman, if after all his letters there is next to nothing, for pity's sake never let his name be mixed up with us, above all not as a pioneer, much less to lead any other men in the Black Country or any other new district. If after past reports he does not do at Whitby I cannot conceive of an excuse for him. It is possible that good and willing as he is he may even yet not be incapable of drill and training, if Bramwell would undertake the job, but, if he fails at Whitby, I shall be satisfied that he is utterly incapable of taking charge of a work ... It is no kindness to be so far overcome by people's goodness as to encourage them in an attempt they were never made for.'

By 1876 he was already accepting women Missioners but not making it easy for them as witness Miss Woodcock:

'All we hear of you is perfectly satisfactory. Would you please, when you write, say whether you will give a pledge not to marry for some fixed period. I do not know whether you know the amount we give our female preachers: 15/- per week.

'What practice have you had in public speaking lately? Could you come up here for a few days if desired for us to see and hear you and could you arrange so as to stop and at once enter upon the work if we then wished it? If so, how soon could you come?'[4]

He wrote to Bramwell:

'Hammersmith Allen again wiring in about the number of members reported at confr., says he has had to drop 67 out of 140 and is prepared for an investigation as to Stockton! Your pa really should hold an investigation with him alone and a castigation also. He was well off last night. By his own account it was a speech of Miss Parkins in the open-air that did it. The women who are in the background would revolutionize our concern fairly brought out and led.'

To Missioner Garner, who had a strong preference for chapels, Railton, who loathed them, wrote:

'We are glad to hear that you have had such an abundant entrance into Middlesbro, and hope you will revolutionize the whole place. Why not go in for the Exford Music Hall? It is amongst the lowest of the people, but old Imeson ought to let it cheap for that reason and then the Middlesbro folk could be taught to fight like we poor Londoners have to. If you go in for the Cleveland or any other chapel of your own I hope they'll make you pay a heart-breaking price for it.'

Railton, who had climbed aboard the Booth chariot in a blaze of heroic ardour, possessed by visions of glorious Christian war, could hardly have forseen that he would have to write letters such as this to a delinquent Missioner:

'We find that the landlord fully understands that the house you occupy was taken for the agent of the Mission and will not allow that arrangement to be evaded. I am sorry you should have made it

necessary for me to warn you not to interfere in any way with the property of this Mission either in the house or in the hall if you do not wish to bring upon yourself most serious consequences.
Mr. George Mace,
Hackney.'

This unofficial Chief of Staff recruited the most unlikely material. There was Brother P. who

'leaves Paddington tomorrow at noon ... he wears a city missionary billycock, a little funny moustache and nothing more, looking a decided doggy bloke.'

The young Secretary had hardly taken office before he attacked Disraeli, the Prime Minister, for the customary motion in the House of Commons that there should be an adjournment for Derby Day:

'The Chief Minister of the British Government has once more moved, and the House of Commons consented, to lay aside the business of the country in honour of—the Derby Day! Again have the streets of the Metropolis been thronged with the giddy multitude hastening to and from that scene of damnation. More young people demoralized, more characters blasted, more young converts borne back by fierce temptation, into the seething, eddying tide of the world around them; more families ruined, more suicides, and yet again the Christians of England have next to nothing to say on the subject.'[5]

The pages of *The Christian Mission Magazine* became less sedate and it is chiefly Railton's voice which is the summons to that noise and extravagance that was to be part of Salvationism:

'Men are dead in sin, and none but fools should dream of awakening them without sensation. Millions of sinners have been appealed to for many a long year, and have become so callous and indifferent, that a very earthquake of sensation alone can suffice to arouse them.'

At Poplar, where Railton was temporarily in charge of the Mission station, it could be seen that the sedate Mission was giving way to the dynamic Salvation Army. Railton commented:

'The old Society and congregation are almost gone. As our life increases they will fade away I fancy still more. I am very sorry. God knows I have spared no love or pains over them; but they will not have my Jesus and so the publicans and sinners are getting into their places. I have already an army of navvies superior to all the old men and we are gaining every day. We are now feeling the financial pinch of the change from a comparatively respectable to a poor lot, but never mind. We shall not want.'

Still in his early twenties Railton was as strong as an ox and as physically insensitive. He worked until late at night and far into the morning. Once when he returned home, all the Booth family being sound asleep, and finding himself locked out without his key, he crept in through a back window, and slept in the kitchen.

Railton rarely hesitated to seize upon a new idea that would further the cause. As soon as he saw that women were successful Missioners he was advocating that they should have equal place with men. No Missioner received a salary, in the legal sense, but an allowance which they could take only if they could raise it and when other liabilities had been met. A Railton letter survives from 1876 which states, 'If women can do the work and can raise the money they should have the same as men.' 'Rachel Agar had twenty-two souls at Felling last Monday night' and, he went on, 'they have an all-night of prayer to-night also.' Miss Agar was doing better than some men in the Mission and that being so nothing was too good for her in Railton's eyes.

It is no coincidence that the tide of battle began to turn in favour of the Mission soon after Railton joined it. One thing he brought was optimism. Genius though the Founder was, he had waited so long and taken so many knocks that he sometimes came near to despair. A year after Railton's arrival Booth wrote to his wife:

'You must not be discouraged—get your will to help your faith. A little bit of Railton mixed up with our anxious temperament would do us a world of good.'[6]

A colleague remembered:

'He was a lion in strength and energy. I have often known him work all day Sunday from 6 a.m. till 11 p.m. Then, because he had to be early in the office, and would not ride on public conveyances on Sundays, he used to walk a few miles till twelve o'clock, find the nearest railway station, and wait there until the first train came along to take him to his office, where he began work immediately.'[7]

C

Railton's ardour enthused many of the sedate members of the Mission and encouraged those who were already addicted to off-beat religious behaviour. It was all part of an Army in the making.

Well acquainted with Spain and Morocco, he used two bones as clappers (or castanets) and became known as the 'bone man' as he used them in meetings.

He had been to hear Charles Haddon Spurgeon, the renowned Baptist preacher, at the Tabernacle by the Elephant and Castle. He was full of admiration for the mighty work being done, and had a desire to emulate it on something like the same scale. He wrote to William Booth:

'But if I could set to and build up a concern in some central spot, say near the Eagle, I cannot see why in the course of years we might not build up a really big concern that would keep a whole houseful of young chaps to be made real soldiers of ... There is nothing like piling up people year after year like bricks to make a good organization capable of all sorts of enterprises. Why not try?'[8]

The Eagle public house (in which Marie Lloyd was to sing, 'My old man said, follow the van') and the adjacent royal Grecian music and dance halls had fallen on bad days. Macdermott had sung his ditty there:

> We don't want to fight;
> But by jingo if we do,
> We've got the men,
> we've got the ships,
> We've got the money too.

and gave the word 'jingosim' to the English language.

Railton pressed home his case to William Booth:

'There is a superbly central spot—the Eagle—with a splendid artisan neighbourhood E.; black heathendom W.; and a stream of the finest young fellows in the kingdom passing continually. Why not try to form a drill hall there? ... We might in the course of years build up a really huge affair that would strike all London.'[9]

He wrote later:

'I find that the Grecian theatre—next door to the Eagle, and one of the most notorious in London—which I had coveted for eventual head-quarters on Sundays, instead of holding only 800 has been rebuilt and professes to hold 5,000. Still that shows how far ahead we must look.'[10]

When, later, William Booth acted on Railton's suggestion and ac-quired a lease on the Eagle public house with its adjacent theatre, the Grecian, it provided all the sensation that Railton could have wished for. The buildings were the headquarters for dubious characters of all sorts. There had been fights and allegations of a 'haunt of vice', as Railton put it without originality. The well-known song went:

> Up and down the city road,
> In and out of the Eagle;
> That's the way the money goes,
> Pop goes the weasel.

'Pop goes the weasel' meant putting goods into the pawnshop for money to buy beer or other indulgencies, and that was how many of the poorer patrons lived. The place cost about £16,000. Railton was given command. On the opening day at six o'clock in the morning, a thousand Salvationists, headed by a band, marched down the City Road to the Eagle, and Salvationism was soon advancing in the area on the wide front. But already an appeal had been made in the Chancery Court. The Eagle was a licensed premises and William Booth was using it for his far, far different purpose: to get people converted. In a few weeks a thousand people knelt at the penitent-form.

To some people this was much, much better than the liquor traffic and Mr. Justice Kay refused the first plea for an injunction. He could not see that the licensing authorities would withdraw or refuse to renew the licence because The Salvation Army held religious meetings in the Grecian; he would not prejudge the case.

The second legal action was fought round the Army's contention that there was an option for establishing the Eagle as a temperance hotel, which it did. With seventy beds, good food and soft drinks the Eagle Tavern was a public-house, at least that was William Booth's case.

Queen Victoria, the Archbishop of Canterbury, the Bishop of London and many other famous people supported the General. This action came up before Mr. Justice Fitzjames Stephen at the court of the Queen's Bench. He decided against William Booth: the Army could not operate a new order under an old lease. Railton's great centre must be re-established as a proper, wet, alcoholic public house within a month, the judge ruled. The decision went to appeal and meanwhile William Booth had to become the licensee of a public house where beer was on sale.

Their Lordships of the Appeal Court decided they could not allow any nonsense about temperance and religion being fit substitutes for a good old British pub. Yet the Army was left in possession of the Grecian until September 1898, by which time thousands of people had been influenced by the work and many had been converted.

5

The Apex of Authority

THE PERIOD up to 1880, when Railton asked to be sent to the United States in charge of the Army's first official overseas invasion, is the apex of his authority and influence. These are the days when he drafted *Rules and Regulations*, made crucial suggestions regarding the tactical changes which marked the transformation of the Mission into an Army, and compiled for the approval of Catherine and William Booth the doctrines which were part of the parliamentary Deed Poll and which are substantially unchanged to this day.

A letter, hitherto unpublished, from Railton to the General dated November 10th, 1877, shows something of the position the General Secretary held:

'I do hope you will not mention our training scheme in any definite way to anybody. It can only be for some time a station with no more show of training about it than any other—and the host of events and emergencies that must come upon us before, long before anything we can point to is arrived at, may ten times over render further progress impossible. I have a dim prospect of the number of times Bramwell, and even you, will have set down the attempt as useless before it has accomplished anything ... I cannot at all understand your paragraph about the Report.[1] You speak of "filling up with incident" a thing which I fear is much too long already and which so far as I recollect is nearly all incident in most chapters, another you doubt as to the commencement being as effective as later parts. I shall be able to write better about it when I have carefully read it all again. But I have not a hope of getting done in time except upon the principle of altering nothing except for grave reason, because I see already such an enormous field for discussion in my own mind as to the insertion or omission even of whole chapters ... All well at home. Love to all.

Yours affectionately,

G. S. Railton[2]

The tone is not that of a mere secretary, or subordinate; the Army's Founder took none of Railton's forthright letters amiss. In the same year Railton could write to Bramwell Booth in this strain:

'You seem, upon further reflection, to see that the training question demands a solution. But you do not appear, nor does your ma, to understand me. I shall always I trust continue dead against any approach to a college sort of thing which cannot ever be justified from scripture experience, and can never produce anything but parsons. We want to train men to be like us, without time for self, always at it, and yet always being fed and stoked up as they fly.

'It would unquestionably be most satisfactory to train a lot whose whole time could be used. But that could only be done with a lot of money and I am dead against any scheme in the direction of needing subscribers. All our policy should aim at becoming more and more Apostolic free from the slightest tie to anything but our Mission ... A year's training whilst in secular employment and then a year at a London station should turn out men in our mould. If we could raise a concern that would keep a lot of men so much the better. But whatever we do we must not be in a hurry, and we must not be in a hurry to talk about the matter to anybody, because a breakdown will help to discourage the very folks we want to help and to encourage.'[3]

But looking ahead to the time when Bramwell Booth is Chief of Staff of a rapidly growing Salvation Army a different note is heard and Railton's changed status is clear. The Chief writes from the new headquarters in Queen Victoria Street on October 18th, 1884:

'My dear Railton, I do protest against the tone you adopt in speaking about the Training Homes. It appears to me to be both uncalled for, and unlikely to help the particular views you seem to have adopted. I think Johnson, the ex-Bobby, is vastly improving lately. I should not wonder that if he had some villages or islands or something of that sort to look after, he might make something out of them.

'You are mistaken; the General does not lean towards Ballington staying in Australia. He has written him most positively by this mail. And with regard to Horsley, we have simply answered all their talk, by a reference to their "Instructions" which say that we won't have Horsley at all, whether he is a good man or a bad one; and that being convinced that he is good has nothing to do with it.

'I am really concerned about you. Would to God there were some

means by which I could get you cured. Yours affectionately, as ever
W.B.B.'[4]

In 1876 one of the Booth girls, Lucy, went down with smallpox. A
servant also contracted the disease and died of it. While she lay in
hospital Railton visited her and fell victim to a most virulent form of
the malady. Aged but twenty-seven years he was ready to welcome the
final summons regarding it as 'promotion from the infantry of the earth
to the cavalry of the skies!'[5]

'I knew what was the matter with me and fully expected to die,' he
said later.

Mrs. Booth remarked that her husband 'had felt Railton's illness and
danger to an extent she had never known him affected by any other
threatened bereavement'. That their young crusader should be taken
from them now, was a dreadful thought.

The Booths always had great faith in hydropathic treatment. Years
later Bramwell Booth recalled:

'He was terribly ill, and had been given up by the doctors, when I
brought the late Mr. Metcalfe, the hydropathist, to him. I remember
that morning his hands and feet were already cold, and the nurse had
got a hot-water bottle to try and bring some animation into them. Railton himself thought the end had come. "It's no use, Nurse," he said
feebly, "it's no use trying to warm up Jordan with hot-water bottles!"
But hydropathy saved him, to the amazement of all.'[6]

He had refused to go to bed during the onset of his illness and when
they hid his boots to make it impossible for him to leave the house, he
went off to his Poplar Mission station in his carpet slippers, his face
hidden like the women of Tangiers, for he was covered with the repul-
sive, scaly eruptions which are the aftermath of smallpox.

His illness gave him time to write *Heathen England,* a book which
must rank with William Booth's *In Darkest England and the Way
Out* as among the most important of all Salvation Army publications.
It was an appeal to the public for understanding of the aims of William
Booth, a description of the plight of the poor in the East End, and an
explanation of the methods adopted.

Before the name for the movement existed the idea of The Salvation Army leaps at one from every page. Railton used the term
'Volunteer Army', and one can sense the inevitability of the metamorphosis of the Mission from such phrases as 'street-fighting', 'soldiers

marching' and such sentences as: 'Half-a-dozen people, linked arm-in-arm, look anything but contemptible marching along an ordinary street; three or four, walking silently in single file, as policemen do, attract as much attention as a large band.'

The book is notable for its emphasis on the working man—not the poor man. It is clear that Booth and Railton saw them as members of trade unions, able to buy drink, clothes, pork pies, Sunday newspapers. Of the East-Enders Railton wrote: 'Their houses are thoroughly respectable in position, construction and appearance as any man could wish.' It was the organization of their lives that was lacking, not their material content. The children went to buy father's liquor and tobacco and all avoided places of worship as if they were plague houses. Young men and girls sang 'shameless songs' and some were promiscuous. Like Charles Booth, Sims and Mayhew, Railton was there among them and he knew. His account is not objective, but it was substantially accurate of that section of the populace amongst which he worked.

All through *Heathen England* we see that General Superintendent, William Booth, and General Secretary, George Scott Railton, had an army on their hands. On pages 143 and 144 Railton has a paragraph which foretells all:

'But we deny that we are in any proper sense a sect. We refuse to settle down into places of worship such as might be agreeable to our people and their families, but insist upon the open-air stand and the place of amusement where there may be little comfort, but where the most good may be done. We refuse to allow evangelists to stay very long in any one place, lest they or the people should sink into the relationship of pastor and flock, and look to their mutual enjoyment and advantage of others. The whole Mission is kept in its course by the direction of one controlling will ... We are a corps of volunteers for Christ, organized as perfectly as we have been able to accomplish, seeking no church status, avoiding as we would the plague every denominational rut, in order perpetually to reach more and more of those who lie outside every church boundary.

'Owing to our adherence to this rigid military system, we are losing almost every year evangelists, as well as people, who, having lost their first love, begin to hanker after the 'rights', 'privileges', 'comforts', 'teaching', or 'respectability' of the churches. The Mission will always remain under the direction and control of an earthly Commander-in-Chief, called the General Superintendent.'

These are the years also of Railton's unconfined writing. His pen ranged over a wide area, introducing new and arresting dimensions into arid Mission literature. He wrote on *Revolution* in *The Christian Mission Magazine*.[7] The word and the idea lay like a dark shadow all over Europe although the *Communards* in Paris had brought blood and light into it by being the first to use petrol as a weapon with which to burn a city. About 20,000 of them paid with their lives. Christ was the greatest revolutionary, declared Railton, and salvation and conversion was the ultimate revolution.

This was strange and strong meat for the magazine readers. But they were even more bewildered when the young acting editor took on a great poet in a leading article: 'About Culture—The Gospel According to Arnold'.[8] It was a riposte to *Culture and Anarchy,* in which humanitarianism was uplifted: 'Culture indefatigably tries to draw ever nearer to a sense of what is beautiful, graceful and becoming.' Arnold seemed to be saying that men could improve themselves into what they should be. He attacked in *Culture and Anarchy* Booth's way of salvation:

'Look at the life imaged in such a newspaper as the *Nonconformist* —a life of jealousy of the establishment, disputes, tea-meetings, openings of chapels, sermons, and then think of the ideal of human life completing itself on all sides aspiring with all its organs after sweetness, light and perfection!'

For Railton Arnold was far off the mark when he thus raised up Oxford as the essence of perfection:

'Steeped in sentiment as she lies, spreading her gardens in the moonlight, and whispering from her towers the last enchantments of the Middle Ages, who will deny that Oxford by her ineffable charm, keeps ever calling us nearer to the true goal of all of us, to the ideal, to perfection?'

It may have been this argument that prejudiced Railton against the university for, as we shall see, he was incensed when both his sons chose to become students there. For Railton, Wordsworth knew more of the truth when he wrote:

> ... there indeed
> Love cannot be, nor does it thrive with ease

> Among the close and overcrowded haunts
> Of cities, where the human heart is sick,
> And there feeds it not and cannot feed.

One can decide for oneself whether time has vindicated Arnold, or Railton, in the near-century that has passed since Railton wrote:

'Even supposing that culture were a great success in the case of individuals, it is manifestly impracticable for the mass ... How many Bethnal Green Museums, how many National Galleries, how many conversations and lectures would be necessary to "culture" the people of East London? ... But is there no possibility of making that great rough fellow over the way a gentleman? Thank God! there is. The culture of God can fit that man to sit down at the table of the King of kings. In this Mission are hundreds of ladies and gentlemen by the grace of God. Here are men and women, who might once have been addressed as the 'brutish among the people', who are developing faculties and powers they never imagined they possessed when they were under the culture of the devil. Godliness is the true culture.'

6

California, Here I Come!

BY 1880 there was an element of disenchantment in Railton's life. He was thirty-one years old, yet unmarried, still living with the Booths and conscious that young Bramwell was about to step into his place as number two in the Army hierarchy—Bramwell's first directive as Chief of Staff was published in *The War Cry* of 1881.

The now officially named Salvation Army was sweeping all before it and the waves of emigrants from Britain included converts who wanted Salvationism to be available for export. Particularly was this true of the United States where there had already been an abortive attempt to begin operations. Railton was filled with desire to stretch his wings. Though in Britain the Army was opening new corps and winning converts all over the land Railton did not agree with some of its tactics. The training of officers and uniform policy were issues on which he differed from the Booths, father and son. The 'Dear General' and 'Your ever-to-be-faithful Lieutenant' relationship had become complicated by the arrival of capable converts with high potential for leadership and above all by the precocious development of the gifted Booth children. Emma became the leader of the first training home; Ballington and Herbert talented and authoritarian young officers in the Booth Army. Railton now asked William Booth to let him lead the first official contingent overseas to undertake the invasion of America. The Founder was not enthusiastic. He did not share Railton's 'imperialist' visions. But Railton had not lived with the Booths for seven years without learning that the dominating personality was the wife and mother, Catherine. He sought her support in winning William Booth's consent to his departure for America. There were strong reasons for the move. James Jermy, a Christian Mission convert, had opened the Mission in Cleveland as early as 1872, but it died out when he returned to Britain in 1876.

In April 1878 Amos Shirley of Coventry sailed for the United States. He was a deeply religious man and a member of the Booth Mission. He left his wife and daughter behind. The girl became an enthusiastic Missioner. Amos Shirley wrote to his daughter from Philadelphia:

'Come, if the Lord wills, and we will start a work in America something like The Salvation Army.' By now, seventeen-year-old Eliza
Shirley was a Lieutenant and with the audacity of youth she wrote to
her General. To him it seemed like a letter of resignation. He would
have no control over operations in Philadelphia, where Amos Shirley
was now a factory foreman. Yet, as was usual with him, Booth's reply
to the girl was sympathetic. He concluded: 'We are not prepared to
commence operations so far away ... but if your letter is the final decision, if you must go, and if you start a work, start it on the principles
of The Salvation Army, and if it is a success we may see our way clear
to take it over.' It was a timid letter and did not show William Booth
at his best. But the year 1878 was full of change and stress for the Army
in Britain, and it was part of Booth's nature to move cautiously. He
sent his son Herbert to visit the young Eliza, and the cautious note is
again evident: 'Dissuade her if you can, but if she will go tell her to
be careful about the principles of the Army: to start right. She may
call it The Salvation Army and if she succeeds, report.'

But Eliza was of the stuff that made the *Mayflower* Pilgrims, the
Jamestown settlers, the hordes of immigrants who could not be stopped
by all the obstacles between the Old World and the New. With her
mother she sailed for the United States and, as a gay, attractive but
militant Christian, was soon in demand as a speaker and singer at holiness and temperance meetings. As a true Salvationist Eliza resisted
excess of such claims in order to find a place where she could launch
The Salvation Army in the United States—to serve the 'unloved, un-
reached masses, of which there were some millions'. She found her citadel,
an old chair-factory at six dollars a week, and on October 5th, 1879,
Eliza and her mother 'opened fire'. The posters announced:

BLOOD AND FIRE!
THE SALVATION ARMY
Two hallelujah females will speak and
sing for Jesus in the old Chair Factory
at Sixth and Oxford Streets, October 5th
at 11, 3 and 8 o'clock.
ALL ARE INVITED!

Foreman Amos Shirley, who was paying the rent of the factory out
of his own pocket, went about the town sticking the posters on bill-
boards. Success was slow in coming until a notorious drunk was con-

verted, and then things began to move. Soon there were numerous converts in Philadelphia and a second corps was opened in Forty-Second and Market Streets. The *Philadelphia News* published a long report on the work. Eliza sent this to William Booth who was pleased indeed and promoted her to the rank of Captain. Amos was told by his firm that he must either give up the Army, which was absorbing too much of his time and energies, or lose his job. He chose the latter and became a full-time missioner. The Army had a bridgehead in Philadelphia. This made William Booth give way to Railton's repeated pleas, for he did not want a Salvation Army which he could not control. Railton gave utterance to this fear in a letter to Catherine Booth:

'I feel sure that our own affair in Philadelphia will go with such a sweep that unless we get hold of it, and lead, and go in at full speed at once, I doubt if we should ever be able to get the reins at all ... I do not see why they should not let me go.'

William Booth dithered for a short while. 'The General seemed almost for it last night but is not so today,' reported a disconsolate Railton. William Booth later explained, 'We were anxious to avoid this a little longer, seeing how much remains to be done for all the millions who remain in utter darkness even in this land of light.'[1] He clarified his attitude to the unofficial opening—'We refused to authorize the Shirleys formally to inaugurate our work in the States, but we cannot blame the love and zeal which has driven them, without waiting for us, to open the attack.'

Railton asked for 'sisters' as his invasion force. He had no lack of confidence in himself or in God. He felt that he could conquer America single-handed. But 'sisters' were in relatively plentiful supply and he wanted to use every favourable factor to induce William Booth to make up his mind. He expected to get men officers from American converts. It would not occur to Railton that it might seem a little odd for a young bachelor to wish to command a force of young women none of whom was married. At the official farewell in February 1880 at Whitechapel Mrs. Booth gave Railton two flags, one for the already established corps at Philadelphia, the other for the corps Railton was to open in New York. Before the large crowd Mrs. Booth looked with pride at the contingent of seven young women and their leader, all dressed in full Salvationist regalia. Railton was the first man ever to wear full Salvation Army uniform. Mrs. Booth said: 'I hand these flags to you praying that God may give you, young as you are, strength to fight heroically under His banner, and to lead tens of thousands to the Cross.' Two days later Catherine Booth went down to the Albert Docks to see Railton off, she wrote the following in a letter to a friend:

'The getting off of dear Railton and the sisters was a scene! Hundreds of people walked with the procession to Fenchurch Street. They sang all the way, and vehicles of all sorts stopped and lined the roads to see them pass. They marched from Tidal Basin to the ship. We had half an hour there, during which time a ring was formed and a meeting held. The crew and passengers on the ship seemed quite struck!

'It was a grand sight. The women's hats looked capital, having a broad crimson band with gold letters. Three of our flags were flying on board. Dear, devoted Railton looked well in his uniform, and appeared as happy as an angel.'[2]

Early in the morning William Booth and his first overseas emissary had had their private farewell. Years later Railton remembered it:

'There is at the corner of Victoria Park Road, London, an old horse-omnibus halting-place that I always look at as I go past with peculiar thankfulness. The General and I often caught the omnibus there together to go to the old Whitechapel Headquarters, before the days of the Aldgate horse-tram, let alone the fine electric cars. We used to ride to the corner of Brushfield Street, Shoreditch, and thence walk to 272 Whitechapel Road through the Spitalfields Market.

'And so from that corner, thirty-one years ago, I reckon I started for America on that omnibus. We had a little time at Headquarters together before the public march of our party, thence to Fenchurch Street Station.

'But a word from the General as we stood at that corner waiting for the bus has never faded from my memory or lost any of its weight.

' "Never forget that it is not what you do yourself so much as what you get others to do in the meetings that will be the making of the Army".

'It might have been a humbling remark if I had aspired to being thought a great orator. I took it rather as the expression of a fear that America might turn my head and create in me some such tendency. And I do praise God after all these years, that He kept me all along unchanged in the great purpose we both had that day in mind—to make everywhere an Army every soldier of which should stand up and fight instead of sitting still to listen to any "sacred oratory".[3]

They sailed that same day on s.s. *Australia* and Railton was displeased because the conventions of the day separated him from his seven female officers. He wanted to use the voyage for a series of briefing sessions, to hold services and canvass the passengers about the state of their religious life. The idea of propriety, because he was unmarried, or deference because he was the leader of the party did not enter Railton's head. For the most part he ignored his allocation to the better class section of the ship and went forward where the 'sisters' were among passengers who were 'a godless set of Italians and other emigrants'.

Railton was possessed by the desire to capture America for God. 'California, here I come!' never more ardently expressed the will to conquer; the gold at Sutter's Creek was not sought with greater dedication. He did have his briefing sessions and was given permission to hold services—he would probably have held them anyway. He prayed for the passengers, while they drank and played cards. This was just as well for the ship broke down and tossed hither and thither with its two engines out of commission. There was some talk of turning back, as the *Mayflower* had done. But Railton's prayers seemed to be more efficacious and the repairs were effected at sea. The voyage was prolonged from ten days to a month, food ran out and potatoes and other supplies had to be transferred from another vessel in mid-Atlantic. The women were wretchedly seasick and miserable at times, but there were brighter interludes. In one of these a young man emigrant was converted. Like Cabot, Raleigh and many others, through peril the Salvationists arrived. Columbus, that wretched unrewarded man who had begun it all, had said, 'I have opened the gates and others will enter at their pleasure!' But there would be little pleasure for Railton. That was an indulgence which usually eluded him. On landing they sang the 'Song of The Salvation Army', written two years earlier by William Pearson, officer in charge at Bradford, who often heard the time churned out by the town hall clock. It was an invitation all Americans would hear and many thousands heed:

> Come, join our Army, to battle we go,
> Jesus will help us to conquer the foe;

Fighting for right and opposing the wrong,
The Salvation Army is marching along.

The tune was American: 'Ring the bell, watchman'.

7

'The Splendid Seven'

THE GREAT days of the American frontier were passing when Railton arrived. Though immigrants were settling in hundreds of thousands most went to swell the growing city and urban population: the wide open spaces of the West were not open to them. A repetition of the British Industrial Revolution, on a much vaster scale, was taking place. Children were leaving the farms and farmers their land, exchanging the hard life of the soil for the worse conditions of the cities.

As Eliza began the Army in Philadelphia, Woolworths began to span the country with its popular ten-cent stores. William Booth had hinted that America was a land in need of light; just before Railton landed Edison invented the incandescent lamp. Bell had already put the telephone into use; the typewriter was clicking away furiously. All this made work and created social problems. The American giant was suffering excruciating growing pains. Not all her immigrants were self-reliant types like Amos Shirley and his family. Particularly towards the end of the boom period, by 1880, many immigrants joined the under-privileged.

Conditions which favoured the commencement of Salvation Army work were a result of the passing of the frontier. It would not be much use Horace Greeley saying now, 'Go West, young man', for there was little of the West left excepting desert, Indian country, or disputed territory. So the cities grew and the slums multiplied. Vanderbilt and others joined the Atlantic to the Pacific and the Great Lakes to the Mississippi with railroads. This filled up the country, brought tremendous economic development and the inevitable percentage of human failure.

New York, when Railton arrived, had 10,000 children adrift in the streets, many of them weeping outside 8,000 saloons. On East Side there were about 300,000 people in conditions that Shaftesbury, Barnardo and William Booth would have found reminiscent of London's East End at its worst. The East Side death rate was three times that of New York as a whole.

D

Professor Herbert A. Wisbey, in his excellent history of the Army in the United States, writes:

'The United States in the last two decades of the nineteenth century offered a fertile field to the Church of the Poor, as The Salvation Army was sometimes called. American Protestantism had largely failed to meet the needs of the urban working class. Changes were taking place in American churches that reflected the vital economic and social changes of the times. It was a period of great material wealth. As a leading religious historian observed, "The most significant single influence in organized religion in the United States from about the year 1880, to the end of the century and beyond, was the tremendous increase in wealth in the nation." This increase in wealth helped a more easy-going intellectual religion to replace the hard, emotional religion which had characterized the American frontier. Poorly dressed workingmen felt out of place in the smaller, more costly churches where professional robed choirs and quartets substituted for simple music and congregational singing.

'Not only the physical surroundings but the attitude both of the clergy and of the congregations of the Protestant churches discouraged poorer people from attending church. They found no sympathy or understanding for the problems of the poor or of labouring people. Many Protestants persisted in believing that human sufferings were "the penalties of idleness, disease or other similar causes, in a great measure the fault of the sufferers". Yet others were observing that "the suffering poor had rejected this view and along with it the Christianity which championed it".'[1]

Henry Ward Beecher, one of America's leading clergymen, whose later inglorious fate suggests that wisdom was not all he lacked, thundered with characteristic eloquence:

'Is the great working class oppressed? Yes, undoubtedly it is ... God had intended the great to be great and the little to be little ... I do not say that a dollar a day is enough to support a working man! ... Not enough to support a man and five children if a man would insist on smoking and drinking beer ... But the man who cannot live on bread and water is not fit to live.'

Railton with his apostolic indifference towards money was a worthy Lieutenant of his beloved William Booth, and an inspired choice as leader of the first Salvationist overseas offshoot. Had he been an Englishman in the narrow sense, ultra-patriotic, a sponsor of the superiorities of Britain over the still developing Republic, it would have been different. But Railton was a citizen of the world. He did not have a long term in the United States but by the time of his departure the American Salvationists had taken him into their hearts and he is still their 'patron saint'.

The present strength and efficiency of the Army in America, its relevance to the nation's needs, stems in great part from those beginnings in the days of young Eliza Shirley, and Railton and his band of seasick women on the storm-battered, long-delayed s.s. *Australia* which docked at Castle Garden, the immigrant station at the Battery, New York City on March 10th, 1880.

Booth had given Railton £200 and with that, his seven females, and those who could be 'captured' as converts, he was to engage in this 'spiritual buccaneering expedition', as William Booth described it at the farewell meeting. A solicitor read out the commission:

'TO ALL WHOM THESE PRESENTS SHALL COME, I, GEORGE SCOTT RAILTON, of No. 272, Whitechapel Road, in the County of Middlesex, send greetings:

'WHEREAS, it has seemed good to the Reverend William Booth, the General of The Salvation Army ... to extend to America the operations carried on by the said Salvation Army in England, it has seemed to the said General desirable and necessary to appoint a person who shall represent him as his Commissioner to act for him and on his behalf in all matters connected with the said Salvation Army in the various States and countries of North and South America and the Islands adjacent thereto AND WHEREAS it has seemed fit to the said General and he has deemed it desirable to appoint me to be such Commissioner as aforesaid.

'Now I, the said George Scott Railton, do here accept the appointment by the said General of myself as Commissioner to act in the name of the said William Booth, and on his behalf in all matters whatsoever and relating to or connected with the said Salvation Army in all parts of North and South America and Islands adjacent thereto, AND I engage to the utmost of my power to extend the operations of the said Salvation Army to, and to carry on the same in, parts of America and the Islands adjacent thereto.'[2]

Columbus hardly had a larger mandate while Penn's, Baltimore's,

Orglethorpe's and the rest of the proprietors were trivial by comparison. One check on Railton reflected the anxiety of Booth about a particular American problem. Denominations proliferated and schism followed schism. The Mormons had settled in Utah and made a rich state in a short time out of an inhospitable wilderness, but they soon had their offshoots. Methodists, Anglicans, Baptists, Moravians, Mennonites and other sects multiplied and divided like grass on the prairie. Booth wanted his Army to be one, all loyal to original principles, although from the first he was aware that there must be indigenous qualities, allowances for the independence and differing culture of his overseas segment. The terms of his protective clause read out in public by his solicitor were:

'AND I hereby agree that I will continue to be, and to act altogether at all times, under the command of the said William Booth, and to carry out in spirit and to the letter the *Orders and Regulations of The Salvation Army,* and all General Orders issued from time to time from the application of which it is not expressly declared that America shall be exempt.

'AND I hereby further agree to suffer only such persons as will accept to act under the same conditions as aforesaid to be connected with the carrying on of the said Salvation Army operations in America, AND I further agree that all directions that I shall give to any officer or officers or any person or persons whomsoever over whom I shall exercise any control in pursuance of the functions delegated to me as such Commissioner as aforesaid shall be subject to the absolute direction countermanded and veto of the said William Booth.

'AND I hereby declare that all real and personal property whatsoever which shall come to or be held by me in anywise howsoever as such Commissioner as aforesaid or otherwise, as representing the said William Booth or The Salvation Army, including all books, plates, moulds, casts, and other things used in connection with the said operations as aforesaid, whether protected by copyright or as designs or otherwise, shall at all times be held for and on behalf of and at the disposal of the said William Booth or other the General of The Salvation Army for the time being.'

This seemed to take care of everything but as King James found, and Cromwell and Lord North, English legal phrases tend to lose their force when they cross the Atlantic. William Booth saw two of his American leaders leave the ranks—one of them his own son Ballington.

For all Railton's faith it seemed at one time that the operation in New York might fail. The reception was respectful but city folks were apprehensive; the customs officials at the Battery asked for an open-air meeting there and then; they wanted to hear this Army about which they had been reading in the newspapers. But the Mayor was afraid of riots and the churches were antagonistic.

At the Battery they unfurled one of Mrs. Booth's flags, knelt on the ground and prayed, rose up to sing, then, as one of the newspaper reports put it, asked the startling question 'Are you bound for hell or heaven?' On the flag was inscribed the words, 'New York No. 1—Blood and Fire', though as yet that salvation citadel existed only in the minds of the party, which had already grown to nine, for the young lad convert won on board ship held the flag during the service.

But if Railton thought this cordial reception was to be typical of New York, he soon learned differently. General Burgoyne had cause to lament that his smooth-bore muskets were no match for American rifles, nor the marksmanship of his men equal to the rebels' fire. Railton was to 'attack' and 'capture' a teeming city with little money, no accommodation and seven women, only one of whom was an officer and none of whom had been formally trained.

The newspapers poked fun at the provincial accents of the sisters, and their habit of dropping their aspirates. They were described as 'English peasant women of very limited intelligence', and 'wholly without grace or ease'. As to intelligence the newspapers were wrong. The girls lacked education and their want of poise was due to inexperience and nervousness. Time was to remedy these deficiencies and show that even without aspirates Railton's Splendid Seven, his own term for them, would make a worthy contribution to the growth of the Army. Within one month a newspaper reported: 'None of them can aspirate the letter "h" but they manage to get on the inside track with a good many hardened sinners who would listen to some of our pulpit orators with deaf ears.'

Much depended on the first full day of Sunday meetings, and here Railton came up against unexpected difficulties. Most of the low theatres were in use on Sunday, whilst others could not be rented because their owners were afraid of tumult, damage and loss of their good name. Then one Harry Hill, attracted by the newspaper publicity, offered Railton the use of his 'theatre' in Houston and Crosby Streets. It was a respectable place, not like some, a client told Railton. 'A man could drink until he passed out without having to worry that his watch and money would be gone in the morning.' A minister friend, however, said to Railton, 'It is the most disreputable den in the country! In the worst slum in the city! Go there and your reputation will be lost at once and for ever!' This made Railton all the more willing to begin the Army work in Harry Hill's theatre.

Hill thought that Railton's party was a sort of minstrel troupe, jubilee singers, a good act for his stage. It was not easy to get him to understand what it was all about. As they sung hymns to 'Swanee River' and 'My old Kentucky Home' his uncertainty was understandable. He asked how much, and Railton told him there would be no charge; the Army would take up a collection. That Harry had to be told this, indicates the extent of his ignorance about Salvationists. He let Railton know that he thought him a fool. This dismayed Railton not at all. But in the end, though Hill refused to forego his admission of 25c, he agreed to let Railton take up a collection. So the work in New York began on the right lines.

Herbert Wisbey, in his previously mentioned book, wrote of this event:

'The day of the attack was "cold, damp and foggy and the slimy mud seemed to ooze up out of the sidewalks" as the small army left their headquarters on Liberty Street. All were in uniform. Railton, described as "a man of medium size with dark moustache and whiskers thinly distributed", wore a "dark blue suit trimmed with yellow cord about the collar upon which was embroidered the letter 'S'." A patrol cloak and helmet-shaped hat with a crimson band bearing the words "Salvation Army" in gold completed the uniform. The women were dressed in plain black dresses with red cord on the collar, and wore black straw hats with crimson bands similar to that of the Commissioner. Dividing his force into two parts, Railton sent one down each side of Greenwich Street, stopping at the barber-shops and barrooms that were open, and addressing customers. In nearly every instance they were treated with courtesy and respect—a circumstance that caused Railton to compare the civility of everyone they met with the ruffianly conduct they had been used to in England.

'After lunch in their lodgings, they walked more than three miles in the mud to hold a short service at the Hudson River Mission Hall at West Twenty-ninth Street and Ninth Avenue. It was against their principles to use the 'trains' on Sundays. After this service they tramped back downtown to Harry Hill's variety theatre.

'The house was crowded, and people were standing three deep in the galleries when the meeting began. Out of deference to the Salvationists no liquor was sold during the service, but the usual mottoes lined the wall. Harry Hill had offered to pay the Salvationists for their appearance, and when Railton refused payment Hill expressed his opinion that they were "a set of——fools". Railton, however, was very satisfied with the bargain. He had what he wanted: "As compact a crowd of thoroughly ungodly men and women as could have been hoped for, with perfect liberty to do as we liked whilst we were before them."

'Railton led the service, following a familiar Salvation Army practice of singing a hymn and exhorting between the verses, taking a line or two for his text. He knelt for prayer, the "female Lieutenants" kneeling in a semicircle behind him "in various and curious positions". Each of the women prayed in turn, while the Commissioner, who remained on his knees, "his body swaying to and fro, first one arm working and then the other, continually ejaculated 'Amen!' and 'Hallelujah!'" One of the young women "intoned a hymn in a high tremulous voice, dropping her 'h's' and inserting 'ahs' with a rising inflection as she raised herself on her toes in a manner that made the irreverent audience laugh. The hymn as she read it invited the ''appy pilgrim' to go to Eden above, and the concluding refrain, 'We will go', sung by the whole army was applauded with energy." The audience became restless as the meeting went on. No one answered the call to the Penitent-form, and when the Salvationists marched from the theatre at nine o'clock and the "panorama of 'Uncle Tom's Cabin'" went on, the meeting might have been counted a failure.'

But outside that meeting Jimmy Kemp was waiting, an incorrigible drunk. He had been arrested, not for the first time, only to appear before a weary judge who thought up a different sentence. 'I'm tired of sending you to jail. The Salvation Army is holding a service at Harry Hill's theatre. I'm ordering you to go along.' He was the first of countless judges in the United States who have passed on their problems to The Salvation Army.

Jimmy did not go to prison again. Instead he became a Salvationist, a convert who helped to turn the tide for Railton, and in due course a Salvation Army Captain. Because of the newspaper publicity given to Jimmy Kemp's conversion the crowds began to flock to Railton's meetings and he was able to rent a hall on Seventh Avenue, where the first New York corps was opened with one of the Splendid Seven, Captain Emma Westbrook, in command.

8
Philadelphia in the Morning

BUT THE Mayor of New York would not allow Railton to hold open-air meetings and that was tantamount to refusing an army a battlefield. No open-air meetings meant no future in the United States. This Railton knew, and if America would not have him, what were the chances in Canada, Mexico, Chile, Argentina, all the way indeed from Alaska down to near Antarctica, at Punta Arenas? The Army battle-line stretches all that distance today but the story might have been different if William Booth had sent the wrong man to take charge in America at the beginning—as he was to do later.

Railton had something in common with Cortes and Pizarro; he did not know when he was beaten. When Mayor Edward Cooper refused to allow the Army to conduct open-air meetings in Union Square on the grounds that only ministers and licensed clergymen were permitted, Railton did not point out that he was well grounded in theology and could read his New Testament in Greek—as well as give his aspirates their proper place. William Booth's commission was as authoritative to him as a Bishop's laying on of hands. But he would not argue his own credentials. Instead, he marched to the City Hall, accompanied by the prayers of his followers and smiling newspaper men. He then read out an ultimatum in the manner of Cromwell before Drogheda. It was aimed over the Mayor's head at the people of New York and showed the naïve quality that often marked Railton. He ought to have known that City politicians are not averse to transferring their problems to other cities. Part of Railton's ultimatum read:

'To his Honour the Mayor and the Corporation of the City of New York, I, G. S. Railton by the grace of God and by the appointment of William Booth, General of The Salvation Army, Commissioner for the various States and countries of North and South America, send greetings.

'Whereas, under the authority granted to me I have appointed certain officers to carry on within this city such operations as may be necessary to cause those who are at present in rebellion against God to submit to Him, that they may be saved from sin and hell, and may be made righteous and happy in life, in death and for ever.

'And whereas it is an essential part of such operations that the people who habitually avoid entering places of worship should be followed in the public thoroughfares, and should, by means of services held there, be made willing to attend meetings indoors. Which can only be accomplished by using everyone who places himself or herself under our direction to testify publicly for Christ, or, in other words, by making every Saul of today who is converted under our ministrations a Paul of tomorrow.

'Now therefore I hereby most respectfully request and require in the name of the Lord God of Hosts that before six o'clock on the evening of Thursday next the eighteenth day of March 1880 an engagement to be delivered to me at the above address from the government of this city to permit any person acting under my direction to proclaim salvation in the streets upon the same terms and conditions under which permission to do so would be granted to any other citizen whatsoever.

'And I hereby further give you notice that failing the delivery of such an engagement before the above named time I shall forthwith remove the headquarters of this Army in America to some city where equal privileges are enjoyed by all citizens ordained or not.'

It is doubtful whether the very busy Mayor Cooper ever read the long and fantastic document. But New York newspapers printed it and it helped to ensure the eventual establishment of the Army in New York in great strength for it was valuable publicity.

Mayor Cooper was not intimidated and heartily wished Railton and his people would be off to Philadelphia in the morning. Railton threatened the Mayor with prayers, which caused *The Daily Graphic* to print a cartoon headed PAST PRAYING FOR, and showing Mayor Cooper with a group of Salvation Army lassies kneeling around him.

The same newspaper made an unkind reference to Tammany Hall but Mayor Cooper was no Boss Tweed of infamous memory. There was an ordinance which he had to enforce; the technical definition allowing Salvation Army officers the privileges and status of ministers in the United States was not conceded until 1917. Railton was impatient as always.

So Railton went to Philadelphia, 'The City of Brotherly Love', where there were two corps, 200 Salvationists with red hat-bands, and the Shirleys. He cabled Booth, in May 1880, that the forces now totalled sixteen officers, forty cadets, 412 soldiers. A huge notice spanned the length of 45 South Third Street, Philadelphia, which proclaimed the 'Headquarters of The Salvation Army'. It was a brave front, but those who went to investigate found Railton in a basement where he lived, worked and slept, subsisting on twenty-five cents (1/-) a day. He was always on duty—the brass 'S' of the Army uniform was fastened even on his nightshirt collar. He travelled with all his worldly goods in a small Gladstone-bag and often skipped his meals, sometimes because he was too busy to eat and sometimes because he was too poor. He was lonely—he was always lonely—but not unhappy. Indeed few men have lived lives more serene than he. He prayed long but not too long, read his Bible, but also the newspapers and always retained his sense of humour.

At Newark, near New York, the Mayor had also refused permission for Railton to hold open-air meetings. But the newspapers were friendly. One reporter wrote of an opening campaign in the Odeon Theatre:

'At the Theatre door flies a red and blue flag, the banner of a "Salvation" Army which has invaded the city. The show tonight will be put on by the uniformed officers of this strange group, in our midst, so they say, to save our souls.'

Railton's 'show' was a decided success. The Odeon had been a house of dubious reputation, its former proprietor had been prosecuted and it had been empty for a year. It was dirty and dilapidated. A prescient newspaper man wrote, 'There are sinners of the worst kind dwelling in the immediate neighbourhood so the building will probably be filled for all the meetings.' Three of Railton's 'sisters' helped him and the pressman's hunch was sound. The place was packed and the police had to control the crowd that could not get in. It is on record that almost everyone contributed to the collection but more significantly that 'sinners were saved'.

As in Britain Railton found that religious papers were generally hostile to the Army. Of the secular press the worst that Railton could say about it, years later, was that it poked fun at him.

'We made the acquaintance of everybody in America who reads the newspapers. New York looked with all its eyes at the Army that had come to invade the country. It heard a single message of half-a-dozen ignoramuses about sin and salvation, heaven and hell—especially hell. It realized that these English girls had come believing that God was going to use them in the salvation of multitudes of sinners. And it lifted its vast head and laughed one great laugh whose echoes have not yet died away from the Northernmost to the Southernmost recesses of the great continent.'[1]

But one Methodist paper—surely the cruellest blow of all—hurt Railton by contemptuous remarks because 'we did not speak grammatically'. He added, 'a terrible fault this for Methodists to comment on.' He might have invoked the memory of Billy Bray, and countless wonderful Wild West frontier Methodist preachers who built a mighty church in America without benefit of grammar.

Railton also remembered the *New York Observer,* which featured 'Fanaticism and Crime', mentioning the Army in highly critical vein. He need not have taken it so seriously. Both the fun and the hostility helped him to achieve his great victories. The one thing that might have defeated him was for him to have been ignored. In New York where his lassie officers were fighting bravely, and converts were being won, it was difficult to find halls large enough to hold the crowds. In the hot summer Captain Westbrook had catcalls and other hooliganism to contend with in New York and much ungentlemanly mimicry of her broad English accent. All this she could take and when things got too hot she complained to the police, something of which Railton would not have approved. But the people kept coming, the collecting box was well patronized, and by the end of the summer New York No. 1 was out of debt. Best of all, native-born Americans had become soldiers of Booth's Army.

At New Jersey the Odeon was living down its former dubious reputation. As the Salvation Army citadel it was constantly crowded, and within a month the lassie Captain in charge reported about seventy converts, seven of them women, the rest young men 'mostly of the rougher classes'. This disproportion among the converts suggests that the marvel of a young woman leader was not without effect on impressionable New York males. Railton, who had pressed for woman assistants for the United States assignment, and who had been a strong advocate of female ministry in the Army, had no reason to be ashamed of the work of his party even though there were casualties among them.

In view of the stand Railton later took on colour in other parts of the world, it is significant that he insisted on a non-segregationist policy in the United States, though he knew the colour problem could be an acute one. At the farewell in London William Booth had given an optimistic account of the options open to Railton and had concluded:

'Last but not least there are the blessed negroes.' At which point a converted negro was pulled to his feet to take up the collection and give Brother Railton £200 for the work.

But London was not New York. It is difficult to know whether Railton at this stage was just guileless or recklessly defiant. A *New York Herald* reporter had written of seeing 'impudent young negresses' in the Army's meetings down in Baxter Street, where the meeting was held in a former brothel. He went on, 'A 170-pound drayman-looking negro came in and posed himself forward in prayer as unctuous as would a young lady in a 300,000 dollar Episcopal church.'

But Railton was convinced that in this matter he had begun on the right lines: 'We have the honour today to be the only white people to whose company, to whose platforms, to whose operations, coloured people have had the same welcome as others.'

He had time to ponder on American women. He wrote to Mrs. Booth in London:

'Those English may stick to their men as hard as they like, but I am certain it is the women who are going to burst up the world generally, especially American women. I am sorry my poor officers have not stood the climate, though I cannot help feeling relieved to see them go home to England. They have done nobly—but they are nowhere beside people like——' who is only a seamstress, and yet has intelligence and grasp to take in and carry out my ideas.'[2]

In the light of what is written of the supremacy of the American woman, the matriarchal society, his later comment is percipient:

'American ladies are rapidly getting the first front places in the world. Yet no person has the wit or the diligence to make more of them ... There will be one day a rising of these women again, as rapid and incontestable as the other.'

He was, however, chronically short of funds. He complained of having to pay heavily for cases from the New York Customs House—where not long before there had been grave scandals, and proof of extortion and embezzlement. This was the era of the great money-barons, so there is a particular irony in the fact that London sometimes had to send Railton money to pay his bills in New York and Philadelphia, the meagre printing expenses of his campaigns, his rail fare, the bare subsistence allowance of his lassie officers and his own few dollars a week.

Time would come when Federal, State, City and County support would substantially finance the Army's tremendous work in America but there was hardly a cent for Railton.

For one thing he was British and that was no commendation in America in 1880. There had been a decade of Anglo-United States strain from the time of British alleged intervention in the Civil War, her sympathy with the South, and refusal to pay compensation for sea losses. Afterwards there were Fenian plots said to be hatched in New York which led to attacks on Canada and ill-will and damage for which the United States refused compensation. For years, lasting to the time Railton arrived, there had been resentment between Britain and the United States. Britain's mid-19th century treatment of the Irish, who formed a large part of the poorer immigrant population of the Eastern cities, had created anti-British feeling.

Also, the country's tremendous political and social and economic problems made it necessary for immigrants, whether individuals or religious groups, to solve their own problems. As yet the door was wide open to the millions from Europe but they entered a land of free enterprise. If they could make good by their own efforts there was hardly any limit to what they might achieve, but there were no featherbeds for failures, one of whom, a demented frustrated office seeker shot President Garfield in July 1881, an event which caused the newspapers to give Railton a rest from notoriety.

9

Expedition to St. Louis

RAILTON'S SINGLE-MINDED evangelical approach cut him off from the financial support he could have expected if he had conducted social welfare work. Frank Smith, Ballington Booth and Booth-Tucker, who followed him, gave welfare work high priority and then the American public unloosed its purse strings. Today The Salvation Army in the United States is most generously supported and its Salvationist social work is the largest in any country by a big margin. Yet the spiritual dedication and abandonment shown by Railton and his small band was the foundation upon which all Salvation Army work in America was built.

After the opening of a German-American corps in New York he wrote: 'The first German corps had a most promising start in one of the worst neighbourhoods outside hell. A drunkard was saved and a brother had his eyes almost knocked out at the first service. Now, it is impossible for us to fight our way without winning; therefore how grand must be the future before us!'

That might be, but the present was bleak. Railton journeyed thousands of miles looking for openings and trying to win converts and goodwill, always alone, and all for small apparent reward. For many of the nights in transit he slept on straw, railroad benches and chairs. He travelled with the poorest people, in the cheapest seats. He could hardly fail to make some headway but it was slow, too slow for him.

Like many other pioneers in America he had romantic notions about the Mississippi: he wanted to get the Army's flag west of the great river, so he went to St. Louis:

> To the West, to the West, to the land for the free,
> Where the mighty Missouri rolls down to the sea ...

It was, in those days, regarded as the heart of America and some had suggested that it should be the capital. But if he thought the city fathers, far away from the sea, were going to be more understanding and accommodating than the New Yorkers he was soon disillusioned. Of course he had all the optimism of the true settler:

'I shall never forget the cool November morning when the train slowly pulled into my headquarters city. As I looked into the long line of streets, while the cars were creeping over the Mississippi bridge, I involuntarily asked myself, "Who shall bring the light into this big city?" and I had a glorious realization that through God we shall do valiantly. But I had no idea how long it would take to do it.'

That was November 1880. In January 1881 the first issue of his *War Cry* was on the streets. He rented halls to lose them at once when it was found that his clientele spat on the floors, broke the windows, and perpetrated other enormities. The city authorities, who may have been reading the London *Times,* forbade open-air meetings. Everywhere it seemed that he faced a blank wall. 'If ever providence did its level best against anybody and anything, it is against me and this expedition,' he said, which is by no means Railtonian language. He tried to evade the city ordinance against open-air meetings by going on to the frozen Mississippi; towards the Illinois side, where the St. Louis writ would not run. He gave bills and tracts to the men cutting ice and then stood to sing to the skaters.

St. John Ervine wrote of this incident:

'Is not the picture of this indomitable, ill-clad, impoverished man, who probably had not had a proper meal that day, singing for the salvation of the plump and well-clothed people on the frozen Missisippi, immensely moving? There is no saint in the calendar of the Roman Catholic Church, neither Francis of Assisi nor Ignatius Loyola, to both of whom he was spiritually related, more worthy of a halo than this singular Scot who thought it no hardship to starve for Christ.'[1]

Week after week he made one sortie after another without much success, until January he secured a hall with a balcony that he could use for legal 'open-air' meetings—he could get at the passers-by without breaking the letter of the law. He had an ambitious handbill printed and people were attracted to the meetings. But the sad truth had to be faced: his single-handed attack on St. Louis was a failure.

He launched *The War Cry* from a cellar. To this day it has a large sale, in four separate editions, all over the United States. But at first Railton had to be his own newsboy on the side-walks, and in the saloons and clubs. Publication was intermittent and so many unsold copies accumulated in his cellar-office that he was able to use them to sleep on when long days and exhaustion made it impossible for him to go to his lodgings with the Parker family. Railton had met Mr. George Parker, a building contractor and English immigrant, in a book shop. The two men became friends and Railton made the house his home.

Railton was still doing literary work for William Booth. One task was a draft of the 1881 Annual Report of The Salvation Army. It was in the form of a letter to William Booth:

'With regards to the fight on our side, I have had my say. I wish to say no more at present, although when I compare the results achieved by the little handful of English lassies landed in New York last March with those—if there are any—of the great Afghan Expedition, which I hear has cost England £17,500,000 as against our £450, I venture to say we have made a better page of English history, 1880, than the government of the Empress of India anyhow ...

'The Army has had to endure opposition such as it never before encountered. The persecutions that have been so joyously endured are themselves tokens of the rightness of your cause. Looking across from this country, where government and people (except in New York and a few other localities) will insist upon freedom of speech for all, I would not tolerate open opposition. But we can realize what it is for you to go out expecting, at the least, showers of filth at every step. It was in 1880 that a sister was first seriously wounded in the West End of London whilst singing in your hall. It was in 1880 that a little sister was all but trampled to death in the cathedral city of Carlisle and that a Bishop fast joined his voice to the voice of the rabble which would away with you. It was in 1880 that in Portsmouth and in Chatham and in Sheerness "the people and their rulers" combined as never before against you. It was in 1880 that in Aberdeen and in Jersey professors of religion and haters of religion unitedly strove to drive you away. But like the Iron Duke and his glorious squares you stood firm, the enemy was everywhere hurtled back in confusion and you became a great and growing power.

'It was in 1880, whilst the troops of France were chasing away from their seclusion the monks and nuns of Rome, that you gathered into their several homes the first band of men and women who gave themselves to training as officers. So far from being disheartened by the ferocity of the conflict there was found a readiness utterly beyond all previous

E

experience on the part of the people to take the very foremost places
in the line ...

'During 1880 I can recollect but one distinguished officer who has
resigned, and in only one neighbourhood I believe has there been any
great attempt to create mutiny or division!

'Considering the material of which the Army is composed, and the
almost unbearable demand so often made on the courage, endurance
and discipline of both officers and men, especially in the continual tearing from corps of their beloved commanding officers, to an extent
which in the hottest fight of other armies scarcely ever occurs, this
unbroken unity, this ceaseless fellowship of all with all, is simply a
spiritual miracle, a realization of the prayers "that they all may be one"
such as the world never saw before. Remembering the thirty attempts
at division in 1878, all of them thank God foiled, I cannot but look
upon this enormous improvement in union and discipline as glorious.'[2]

He wrote this in his St. Louis cellar. The fact that he had to write it,
that Booth, for all his successes depended on him to do it, shows how
indispensable Railton was. The Army, advancing with Napoleonic
élan, was in need of a skilled propagandist, the leader of a 'Ministry
of Information'. Someone must answer the libels in the press, the denunciations from the pulpit, the distortions and attacks from all quarters
which might injure morale and poison public opinion. No one was
able to do this but Railton and in January, 1881, William Booth ordered him to return to London.

Railton was shocked and as near to insubordination as he ever came.
He felt that his mission had hardly begun. He knew that the conquest
of America was only a matter of time; advances had already been
considerable. He tried to parley with William Booth. His letter in part
reads:

'We are all, no doubt, outrageously overtaxed and had no idea—
though God had—what it would amount to. But the simple truth
is we cannot avoid the apostolic price. We are paying the price in full,
I firmly believe, and if so, God cannot fail to supply all our need ... I
hope you will not fancy I am preaching to you. I am just telling you
the lesson I got here all alone, yesterday morning, so that you may
understand how I can be so hard-hearted as to grasp in your letter

an assurance that I may dismiss all calculations of return and plan accordingly.'

Yet on New Year's Day he received a peremptory telegram, 'Come along!' Disconsolate, but always a good soldier, he packed his small bag and left cold, unfriendly St. Louis, which would one day change its mind about the Army and give it a worthy place in its affairs. Railton went into one of those emotional, self-pitying moods, tinged with melancholy, which often spurs a man towards poetry or at least verse. He chose the setting, 'Ole Man River', writing his verses on James Eads's great new steel bridge across the Mississippi, a landmark in world engineering, Railton's rubicon between 'East and West', the New World and the Old. His lines were a fitting anthem for a Salvationist tramp, a homeless wanderer, a follower of One who said, 'Foxes have holes, and the birds of the air hath nests; but the Son of man hath not where to lay His head'. It began 'No home on earth have I'. This was literally true and would always be so. The Salvation Army sings the song to this day. It is so much the epitome of Railton's life that it is his epitaph (see pages 240-241).

While waiting for a boat Railton had one more try to persuade William Booth to relent:

'Of course, as I said before, no conceivable circumstances could be of importance as compared with your health, and rather than risk a breakdown of any of you, I can come gladly, however terrible consequences it may produce as to this Army ... The spiritual tide is rising every hour. It is only a question of time. It is the chance of a generation ... The West, and by it the States, will be in our power in 1881, whereas my going away now would shake their expectation as to us, and injure us perhaps irreparably ...

'If indeed I *must* go, I should hope it will be only for a while and then back. Do not let us be short-sighted ... Railton.'

Possibly Wisbey's explanation of why Railton's appeals fell on deaf ears is correct:

'It was part of the genius of William Booth that he could remain unmoved by the piteous appeals of a man he dearly loved. Booth knew the needs of his Army better than anyone else, and put its needs before all things. Railton's recall was not an arbitrary and capricious act. The General shared Railton's belief that God would provide for

His own, and felt that if the United States was to be saved the United States must do the saving. The Salvation Army was rapidly becoming an international force, and Booth desperately required Railton's help at home. The Army had begun operations in France and Australia and other nations were calling to be invaded. Catherine Booth was failing in health. The Salvation Army was still persecuted in England. Never before had the General needed Railton's unique assistance so much.'[3]

Major Thomas E. Moore, who succeeded Railton in 1881, had been in charge of Army work in London. He soon began to shake in the strong winds of New York: the occasional anti-British outburst, the trend to nationalism and resentment at London's alleged despotism. Some of his problems were technical and inescapable, having to do with American laws on ownership of property, and the firm distinctions between American citizens and aliens. Moore became an American citizen, which helped him tremendously as regards America, but created grave problems between him and his General in London. Eventually it led to Moore's breaking away from the international Army in London in 1884, taking with him more than 100 officers and most of the forces, properties and finance.

Yet in the end the Army of William Booth, Eliza Shirley and Railton triumphed. Major Frank Smith, who was appointed to take over the remnants of the Army after Moore seceded, soon rebuilt the Army. When William Booth visited the country for the first time in 1886 there were 238 corps in the Union, under the leadership of 569 officers, mostly Americans. He wrote home to his son Bramwell:

'I shall soon love this country. I am not sure that if there were to be a quarrel between your herdman and my herdman, as with Abraham and Lot, and you were to have the choice of countries and you chose the Old One—I am not sure—whether I should not very thankfully take this, but we must have them both.'[4]

On Railton's reluctant way home his ship called at Halifax and the lonely, melancholy man walked the streets and felt the urge to hold an open-air meeting. He is therefore credited by Canadians with being the first fully-uniformed Salvationist to visit their shores and the first officer to hold a meeting. It was not until two years later that Salvation Army work began in Canada.

One did not talk of the sub-conscious mind in those days but perhaps it existed. The man who did not want to leave America became so engrossed in his open-air meeting that he forgot the passing of time. He had no watch; he did not want to go home. The ship sailed without him. For the ten days before there was another vessel leaving for England he engaged in a salvation campaign, finding Christian sympathy and hospitality in the home of the Saunders family like to that he had found among the Parkers of St. Louis. Converts were won. Railton wrote in the autograph book of one of the Saunders girls:

'The life of a soul-saver is the grandest, merriest, strangest life that can be lived on earth—the life of Jesus lived over again in us. It will cost you all, but it will be a good bargain at that!'[5]

This Franciscan theme, the paradoxical equation of sacrifice with 'merriment', is often found in Railton's life.

10

Maid Marianne

MISSING THE boat at Halifax, which must have seemed to be slip-shod conduct, if not deliberate, combined with his argument about coming away from the United States did not improve Railton's position at Headquarters. He felt that William Booth did not fully trust him. Young Bramwell, about to step into second place as the Chief of Staff, was already tightening disciplinary procedure in ways Railton was to find irksome.

He arrived in London in April 1881, having been away rather more than a year: but it seemed like an age. The military system which he had encouraged the Booths to adopt was being developed. Railton was put to work framing regulations which were an attempt to put his own romantic, idealistic vision into cold print. But the father did not love the child. 'Railton, who believed in doing things until he was told not to,'[1] was hoist by his own petard. He would dangle for the rest of his life.

The Salvation Army was already beginning its march across the world—Booth's older daughter Katie, in France, was winning for herself comparisons with Joan of Arc as a dauntless fighter—*la Maréchale* the French dubbed her. There had been spontaneous outbreak of Salvationist activity in Australia through the activities of immigrants and a Captain and Mrs. Sutherland had been sent to change the guerilla warfare into officially declared hostilities.

Soon after his return from the United States Railton, acting Editor-in-Chief of *The War Cry,* was writing to Colonel Arthur Clibborn, who was to marry one of the Booth daughters:

'How can I once for all convince you that your reports are never delayed avoidably? Some good report of you goes in every week. You cannot expect to have addresses on the Army in *The War Cry*. We are so completely at our wits' end for space for 555 corps and 246 outposts that even the General's Easter Sunday report had to be delayed, and we cannot put in long reports of addresses which simply repeat what he has said so often. As to speeches by the Revd. so-and-so and the Mayor and such-like we cannot put in more than the briefest possible account of what they say.'[2]

He even seized the opportunity to lecture the Colonel on faulty tactics. Railton was opposed to all lectures, displays and public relations ventures.

'I do hope your time is not going to be wasted in demonstrations. There will be no possibility of demonstrations soon if a lot of spiritual work is not done, and I thought this was to be your speciality. All the talk of the immense advantage of there being an explanation of our work has been proved fifty times over to be bosh. The more we follow Christ the better we shall get on and the worse we shall be despised and hated.'

But this officer shared a human weakness for publicity and Railton's next rebuke is harder. There is a touch of the irony at which he became an expert practitioner:

'I hope you will be now content on finding that you have a column of *War Cry* space next Wednesday, all the long speeches omitted, but the entire list of your dates to May 22nd included.
'You will see the enclosed also, from the General's speech, which makes any more speeches about the Army quite needless for at least twelve months.
'What distresses me, however, is not to have one line about your Sunday meetings, or any other real salvation war, especially as almost your last words to me led to hope you were going about to pray with the people.
'I'm certain the Army is being crushed by the perpetual series of meetings to extol it to the skies, and I dread the effect of these reports showing the introduction of these genteel horrors of magistrates and celebrities to our platforms.
'Let us see to salvation, and God will see to us! We had two proper officers' meetings at Clapton yesterday. Plenty of tremendous praying such as will do more for us than all the Exeter Halls we ever held ...
'Do make a salvation report in a Salvationist way about a warlike Sunday and hang these wretched newspapers and the local bigwigs!'[3]

In 1882 Railton noted that 1,600 tambourines had been sold in six weeks. Far and wide Army women were learning to make a joyful jingle on them with ever-increasing skill. Railton exhorted them to sing as they beat, while William Booth suggested that bones, clappers, fifes and banjos should be used for balance. Railton used the bones himself. But he married a tambourine girl, Marianne Parkyn, socially a cut above the average salvation lass of the time, to her family's horror a sergeant in The Salvation Army in genteel Torquay. The Booths often urged Railton to marry. He was so feckless regarding food, clothing and care of his health that his survival to date was to be marvelled at. He was still a lodger at the Booth home, though now thirty-five years of age. If he did not marry they foresaw that he would be a permanent guest and that was not now so pleasurable a prospect.

Marianne was perhaps not as gay as the hallelujah lass is reckoned to be, or should be. Her father, who was a Free Church minister and a man of property, was a stern man, something of a snob, and in the Torquay of that time this would be snobbishness of considerable degree. This, coupled with intense religious fervour, made her a girl in the Brontë tradition, sombre, insular, possessed with strong feminist feeling. When she confined her charities to Sunday-school work her father did not object, but an 'Association for the Care of Friendless Girls', poor girls, some of them of most dubious character, was much too much; the Rev. Mr. Parkyn reacted in the manner of Mr. Barrett of Wimpole Street.

But the young lady had also something of the Brontë obstinacy. Miss Ellice Hopkins, a well-known social worker, with Josephine Butler and others, was persuaded to visit Torquay to give the girls' rescue home her blessing. Lady Mount-Temple, a local aristocrat, became the President and at that the class-conscious Rev. Mr. Parkyn had to subside. But the poor man's troubles were just beginning. Marianne went up to London to visit a brother and there heard about The Salvation Army. She attended some of their meetings and induced the Army to go down to Torquay and 'open fire'. To most people's astonishment, and to her father's explosive anger, the new Army corps at Torquay got off to a flying start. Police were needed to control the crowds, the hall was packed and the converts numerous. Marianne attended some of the meetings but, although her heart was telling her to join up, her discretion was dictating a less hazardous action. What would dear Papa say?

She adopted a devious course, went up to London again and attended one of the frequent 'All Night of Prayer' gatherings arranged by the Army, which must at this time have been suffering from acute lack of sleep. It was in one of these praying marathons that young Marianne was 'saved': she went out to kneel at the Penitent-form, confessed her sins and was forgiven. In due course she became a Salvation Army soldier. Indeed, more than that, she was soon the timbrel sergeant of a bevy of Army lassies who enlivened the streets of Torquay by beating the tambourine, as did the Biblical Miriam in olden times. She became the Army's first timbrel sergeant and the first Salvation Army lassie to wear a red ribbon on her bonnet.[4]

Booth, who did not have enough educated soldiers, suggested that Marianne should come up to London to assist in training women officers, some of whom needed assistance with elementary reading and writing, to say nothing of the Queen's English. But Marianne's father raised so many strong objections to this proposal that Booth dropped the idea and Marianne worked in the corps and helped occasionally at a home for 'sick and wounded' officers that Booth had opened in Torquay. It is, of course, a peculiarly Victorian phenomenon that Marianne, who was in her early thirties, should have been treated in such a tyrannical fashion by her father, and even more Victorian that she should submit to it. There was nothing a respectable girl could do in face of parental opposition.

About this time Railton came back from America. He was something special in the Army. 'Have you seen Mr. Railton?' 'Have you heard him?' Marianne was asked. 'You do not know The Salvation Army until you have met him.'

When Marianne was in London she learned that Railton was to lead an 'All Night of Prayer' at Woolwich. She arrived at 10 p.m. to find the citadel practically deserted, with an old caretaker fussing about. He stopped to address the young lady from Torquay: 'They're all out on a march, drumming in the sinners for the prayer meeting. Commissioner Railton is a-leading them. I suppose you be the Commissioner's missus?'

Instead of regarding this error as prophetic Miss Parkyn jumped to the conclusion that this young, much-admired Mr. Railton was a married man. She has not left any record as to whether this caused her any sense of disappointment. There was no sign of a wife when Miss Parkyn found herself very early in the morning in the same carriage as Railton on the way back to the city. But in some way, she does not tell us how, she had learned he was in fact unwed. He was soon asleep; thin, exhausted and, as she said, 'singularly apart from the others'. Then it was, after a night spent in prayer, that she fell in love with George Scott Railton.

We do not know how deeply Railton slept. He had the ability to take cat-naps; he may well have opened his eyes at some point in the short train journey home to take a longer look at the girl sitting opposite. At any rate, as she was alone and it was very early, he offered to walk part of the way home with her. Their courtship began with that 'part way' walk.

They would be happy, true lovers to the end; but she could hardly have allowed herself to love him and marry him had she known how much of him was set apart for Booth, for the Army, for the salvation of sinners. If there is a case for Christian celibacy Railton is part of it. Often, after tears, heartache and long, long months of separation, Marianne was to ask herself whether she had married a man with too many masters because he was, in God's name, a servant of all.

They were sure they were in love, but hurried marriages were frowned on by the Booths. Besides, the reverend gentleman down at Torquay seemed determined to re-enact Mr. Barrett's role and prevent the match. He would not have his only darling daughter ally herself to any one of 'these outrageous people'. He refused to have a Salvationist in his home and he believed most of the libels and scandals about the Army current in gossip and in the press of that time.

Unlike Robert and Elizabeth, elopement was no solution—the Booths did not favour that either—though it is possible to imagine the highly romantic Railton contemplating it. Poetry did not serve, but prayer did, both the lovers having faith enough to move mountains, leave alone one adamant paternal heart.

Marianne wrote of her lover: 'I almost worshipped him. I never thought that any human being could be like him. I know no two people who were nearer to each other than we.' Railton left nothing on record of poetry or prose regarding his courtship. But the man who had braved the Riffs in Morocco and Mayor Cooper in New York was not going to accept defeat at the hands of one doting father. He somehow broke down the Rev. Mr. Parkyn's resistance and was allowed into the house to ask for Marianne's hand. Marianne waited outside prayerful yet fearful as her beloved pleaded his cause before the ogre. Her father was surprised by Railton. The man was a gentleman and that was the last thing one would expect a Salvationist to be. He had imagined them to be raucous, semi-literate ranters, singing and shouting about the Blood of the Lamb and asking people that absurd question, 'How are you in your soul?', as if the soul were subject to neuralgia.

After long consideration the old man gave his consent to the marriage but only on condition that Railton withdrew from the Army. It was the wrong place for a man of his education and refinement. Papa would provide Marianne with adequate income and a home. He did not know his Railton. All the gold of the Rand, the undiscovered diamonds of Kimberley, could not have bought him. He would have his Army, his Christian poverty and his Marianne too. But she must be a soldier, a hallelujah lass, his 'continual comrade in the war', as his Salvationist marriage service puts it.

That last ominous sentence was prophetic to a degree that the love-dazed woman could not have anticipated by the most realistic assessment. She had other warnings as their 'courtship' proved to be quite unlike anything that even the most staid restricted Victorian couples would regard as tolerable. When he might have been with her he was at the *War Cry* offices 'putting the paper to bed', or in conference with William Booth and Bramwell, travelling here and there, conducting meetings, dealing with recalcitrant officers as the General's trouble-shooter. He wrote to a friend, John Roberts, who had congratulated him on his engagement:

'I am already finding out the good of this engagement in opening up communication with comrades I have loved in my own silent way for years but whom I fear I have not helped as I might have done with sympathy, for want of knowing how ... Be assured that I marry with a view to more than redoubled fighting. So don't suppose I am going to be trained into a domestic animal. We must be lions and tigers more than ever!'[5]

The home of General Booth was not a good place for courtship—the headquarters tent of General Garnet Wolseley quelling rebellion in the Egyptian desert could hardly have been worse. But Mrs. Booth, always concerned about Railton, did try. She invited Miss Parkyn to London. Railton had told Mrs. Booth: 'We are both, I think, completely gone and matched.' That was as near to lovesick rhapsody as Railton could get, but Mrs. Booth's assurance to Marianne, 'Then you will be able to see more of him,' proved to be chimerical. By now the salvation war was a veritable blitzkrieg on many fronts. Booth and Railton would arrive home about ten at night after a hard day at headquarters, have a light supper—Booth was a vegetarian and extremely faddish about his food, while Railton regarded the necessity for eating as a misfortune and refused to take any interest in the matter— then the General would say 'Now Railton, let's get those letters done', and the men would work far into the night.

Catherine Booth could only remind the girl that that was how it had been with William when he courted her. Yet all had come right in the end. Booth thought that one day a month, or half a day a week, was ample time for the pleasures of courtship and he made rules to that effect which Railton drafted without any qualms. So that, apart from being sure that she loved him, Marianne did not get to know her sweetheart before the wedding. She had to take him on trust. Railton put it into the words of a soldier, such words as the rising young Kitchener might have uttered had he any time for women or thought of marriage. 'It is no use,' the young Commissioner said to the young lady from Torquay, 'we shall never get any time together but I think we know enough of each other. If you can trust me I can trust you.'

She did, and ten weeks later, January 17th, 1884, they were married by the General himself at the Exeter Hall in the Strand, a public occasion, with tickets, a packed house, hundreds of tambourines, many concertinas, a full brass band and a large, noisy drum. The first impression of a stranger might well have been that it was a popular variety show.

There was a group of newspaper reporters present and W. T. Stead's *Pall Mall Gazette* reported the event at length. By now, 1884, Railton's status in the Army was clearer: as one newspaper put it, 'The third member of the triumvirate by whom the Army is governed'. Stead in the *Pall Mall Gazette* paid him high tribute:

'For a dozen years Mr. Railton has lived and moved and had his being at headquarters, apparently consumed from first to last by an all-absorbing zeal to generate enthusiasm in the service of the Army. When he slept, or whether he ever ate, are mysteries to most of those about him. All that was known was that early or late he was always to be found overwhelmed with work, which could never be postponed for anything short of reading at a prayer meeting or conducting a convention.'

After giving its own version of Railton's work in the United States the *Gazette* went on:

'General Booth would be the first to admit how much the Army would have come short of its present position but for the untiring energies of her Commissioner Railton. In the familiar dialect of the Army Railton "was in for everything" and was always "on the go" ... Considerable surprise was excited among those familiar with the interior workings of the Army when it was announced that Mr. Railton was going to marry. It seemed just as probable that one of the dynamo machines generating electricity for the illumination of Queen Victoria Street would think of matrimony ... In every way he is one of the most remarkable members of The Salvation Army and the only surprising thing is that, so far as is known, he had never succeeded in making the acquaintance of the treadmill.[6]

'His bride, Miss Parkyn, like Mr. Railton, is the child of a Nonconformist minister and had been conducting evangelistic services at Torquay, at the head of a band of sisters, for several months before the Army entered the town. She then joined its ranks, and became a devoted private in the 248th Corps. Her rank in the Army is now that of a sergeant of a tambourine band, and of the little soldiers' corps. In his way Mr. Railton is quite as unique as General Booth himself. It was, therefore, only natural that the announcement of his marriage should occasion great interest throughout the ranks; an interest which showed itself this morning in the crowd which filled Exeter Hall. Admission was by ticket only, and the competition for tickets was very eager.'[7]

Stead referred to 'a far away look' in Railton's eyes, giving one the impression that 'he is not altogether of this world'.

This Marianne would learn amid tears because of long lonely vigils waiting for the post from Russia, from Turkey, from Spain, India, China, Japan, anywhere, everywhere there were souls to be saved, the Army flag to be raised. It can be said in Railton's favour that he never misled the leader of the timbrelists who dared to join her life with his, and she always had the knowledge that wherever he was she was never far from his thoughts. She was the only woman in his life; he loved her until his last breath.

For the honeymoon at Felixstowe Railton had made arrangements through the divisional officer of the Army, which ought to have been warning to the bride that hers would be no ordinary marriage. Railton had already signified his intention of giving her language lessons in Spanish, French, German, all three during ten days' honeymoon and others later as the need arose so that she could speak to godless mankind. But she hoped for quiet and her dear Railton for herself. He was thin, underfed and neglected. She wanted just to love and cherish him as she had promised. No man needed it more. She was herself exhausted. The speech she had made in the Exeter Hall, with the redoubtable Booths eyeing and judging her, was in fact pronounced a very good one. But it had been an ordeal.

They arrived at Felixstowe in the dark, to be met by their host, Mr. Gardner Frost, a man after Railton's own heart, but no man for a honeymoon. Actually he had been taken aback by the idea of 'Saint' Railton getting married and he soon showed that he was making no allowance for any romantic conventions. Railton and his new wife were soldiers. Railton had helped to start this war. War it would be. As they sat down in the little cottage Frost said: 'You won't mind taking a meeting tomorrow night?' It was not a question. 'We have already announced it to the people,' he added.

Before breakfast on that first morning the visitors began to arrive. Railton was a celebrity. He was a great man for prayer and the teaching of holiness. The tiny cottage became a mecca. If they went for a walk uninvited third persons fell into step beside them; if Frost took them for a ride along the sea front he talked about the Bible, the Army, General Booth, religion generally.

Marianne would have loved something more to her mood. What Miss Rossetti had written was just right for the young lady from Torquay:

> My heart is like a singing bird
> Whose nest is in a watered shoot;
> My heart is like an apple-tree
> Whose boughs are bent with thickest fruit;
> My heart is like a rainbow shell
> That paddles in a halcyon sea;
> My heart is gladder than all these
> Because my love is come to me.

But nothing so idyllic entered Railton's head. 'Don't worry dear,' was his reply to her lament; 'it is such a lovely beginning to a married life.' He led services and many converts were won in the chapels around and in the little cottage room. Marianne found that she had to take it and take it until she became hardened to it. She learned fast. 'Are you in a hurry for a house?' he asked her. As a Commissioner he was entitled to reasonably furnished quarters, a small suburban home with a garden and a front gate, the sort of accommodation in which one would expect to find a bank clerk or a lower grade civil servant. But when unwittingly Marianne indicated that she was content to leave such a matter to Railton, he informed London that 'a couple of rooms somewhere' would serve. Headquarters, never averse to encouraging Christian self-denial in its officers, obliged with two—situated near to the General and his son Bramwell.

These dismayed the young lady from Torquay when first she set eyes on them.

Two rooms in a poor street did not quite match her dreams, yet Railton had no knowledge of what might be passing in the mind of his young wife, reared in affluence in Torquay and knowing that her father owned numerous houses in the area. Railton sometimes sang:

> A tent or a cottage, why should I care?
> They're building a palace for me over there;
> Though exiled from home, yet still I may sing:
> All glory to God, I'm the child of a King.

It was all Christian discipline that Mrs. Commissioner George Scott Railton would have to learn. She learned the hard way.

11

The First Crisis

THE YEAR of Railton's marriage saw the first of his mysterious health breakdowns and also his first serious clash with the Army high command. Usually Railton's health and his relationship with William Booth were inter-dependent. His removal from the Booth home brought about a diminution of his special relationship with William Booth and Catherine. This had lasted for eleven years and its close inevitably affected him adversely.

His changed status vis-à-vis Bramwell Booth was even more a cause for concern and tension. The youth who had been in many respects Railton's pupil was now his superior and showing a distinct flair for administration and the exercise of authority. Railton, who had been the General Secretary of the Christian Mission and second-in-command of the Army had now taken third place. By the end of the year he was even lower on the hierarchical ladder.

He was never a mere place-seeker and he tried hard not to show his hurt. His concealment of his distress probably aggravated his plight, for it is clear that though overwork contributed to his breakdown there were deeper psychological causes. The precious 'Captain and Lieutenant' relationship with William Booth had passed away. This was inevitable, as new men were advanced to one or another command in the Army's ever-widening battlefield. The first and only Commissioner had become one of a number.

His first major clash over Army policy arose from the growth of 'diversionary operations'—as Railton viewed them. At the Army's trade centre there was a boot and shoe department, the sale of tea, toilet requisites, towels, combs for women Salvationists, dressing tables stamped 'Salvation Army', and tablets of 'best ruby glycerine soap' in the centre of which would be placed a photograph of one or other of the following: 'The General, Mrs. Booth, Miss Emma Booth, Miss Eva Booth, Colonel Booth, the Chief of the Staff, Miss Charlesworth and a number of other Majors.' The photo would remain intact until the soap tablet was washed away.[1]

One notices that Railton's photograph was not on offer. He would have taken a very poor view of any such idea. It is doubtful even whether Marianne would have been allowed to use these 'worldly' baubles, three for a shilling. Railton was already out of step with this trend in the Army he had helped to make. He did not want soap, tea, cutlery and did not understand the Booth dilemma: if the Army was to do its work, take advantage of the tremendous opportunities now opening up all over the world, it simply must have money. Railton did not approve of the Army's development of social welfare schemes and public relations techniques. His persistent and outspoken objections, both to Bramwell Booth and the Founder, became a strain upon their patience though their affection for Railton withstood all tests.

It is the great paradox of Railton's life that having willed the Army into being, a movement deliberately and brilliantly analogous to the army of Wolseley and Roberts, the military legends of Railton's day, he shrank from the natural consequences of his act. He too, wanted a spartan discipline, but self-administered: he was no man for courts martial or any severe sanctions. For him the way to deal with an offender was to pray with him until the erring one repented and confessed and promised to mend his ways. In practice Bramwell Booth found that by this method some defaulting officers and soldiers merely went their ways to sin again. There had to be penalties. There were many good reasons for this but the good name of the Army and public opinion were chief among them. In a movement motivated by Christian principles and amid a watchful Victorian society it was unthinkable that any sexual or financial offences should not be treated with severity. Railton, with all the travail of the idealist, wanted it both ways. He wanted holiness in conduct but he wanted the sinner, too. Bramwell Booth was a realist who saw that sometimes you cannot have it both ways, and Railton's pleas for mercy were at times thrust aside.

Yet Railton was to look back upon his first year of married life as being idyllic. It was the one complete year when he lived at home with his wife—'That happy year when you never left me,' he remembered. This was hardly fair to Marianne because all the leaving was on his part. But she understood it was the one year when he was based in London, before the wide, wide world seized him.

Marianne warned the Booths that her husband was overworking. She had been in charge for a while of the officers' rest home at 20 Bath Terrace, Torquay. But the Booths, father and son, were also experts at health breakdowns. You had them and you got better, or you didn't, and if the latter—sudden death, sudden glory. Mrs. Booth, who had a special place in her heart for Railton, was failing in health but all the Booths' including the sufferer, were calm and resigned about it.

Marianne never claimed to possess Salvationist devotion of that quality. To her it seemed more like self-immolation, but she tried to understand that she had joined herself to a saint, and there is no evidence that she ever tried to divert him from his course.

Sometimes Marianne went campaigning with her husband, as the wives of officers are expected to do. She tried at these times to ensure that her husband had intervals for rest, decent meals and a modicum of care. A visit to Bristol, when Marianne was with him, included three days of officers' councils, a task arduous enough of itself. But they were met at the station, on the Saturday, by an enthusiastic young officer who said: 'I have fixed a Sunday for you, Commissioner, just after your own heart.'

Mrs. Railton's heart sank. She had hoped that her husband could spend the Sunday at worship with rest in the intervals, but the matter was aleady decided.

'We start at six in the morning,' the Major continued in a tone of triumph, 'with a meeting till seven, outdoor meeting till eight, indoor meeting till nine, and so on alternately all day. You are not to go in for meals all day, Commissioner.'

'How about food?' inquired Mrs. Railton.

'Oh, we'll have some sandwiches and eat as we go,' was the somewhat vague answer.

Mrs. Railton was in despair, but gave in to her husband's whispered plea, 'Don't say anything to stop him!'

At the end of the programme of open-air services, indoor meetings, officers' councils, the ardent young Major had arranged a 'Half Night of Prayer', continuing until 2 a.m. Spent and limp from this ordeal Railton and his wife walked to their lodging and were caught in a shower which drenched them both. Railton was always an optimist, and in the morning he remarked to his anxious wife: 'You see, my dear, I am all right. We are going to have a great day at Bath!'

So they did. But when Railton reached London he was very ill and was found unconscious slumped over his office desk at Headquarters. The doctor pronounced his condition to be serious.

12

African Interlude

ON NEW YEAR'S DAY, 1885, the Railtons sailed for Natal. The old year had been a disaster; the Commissioner was a broken man physically. Young David, two months old, was left behind much to Marianne's distress, but she had to choose between her child and her husband. William Booth wrote in *The War Cry*: 'Commissioner Railton is in South Africa and although his health is improving he has little hope of ever being strong again.' The biography of Railton published in 1920 ends an account of his breakdown with the words: 'His extraordinary strength had succumbed at last, and he never regained his early vigour.'

But it was not as simple as that. Two events had affected Railton so profoundly that he was not able to adjust to them. The first was his return from the United States to find Bramwell Booth about to become the second-in-command of the Army. The other was his marriage to Miss Parkyn, of Torquay.

That she was not an officer did not much matter; this procedural point was soon corrected by regulation. That she was a lady who would soon inherit a small fortune and who soon showed that she had a mind of her own was of considerable importance. An officer's wife must be his 'continual comrade in the war'. Marianne's love of domesticity and the frequent sicknesses of her children prevented her from fulfilling this role. More to the point, she soon began to fight Railton's battles for him. Like many who strive after holiness, Railton would accept rough treatment from others, turning the other cheek. He cultivated self-sacrifice and hid his grief. Marianne was less restrained.

Nowadays even laymen are aware that such repressions as Railton practised can have adverse psychological consequences. Any rift between the Booths and Railton had to be secret for the Army's sake. There could be only one Chief of Staff and William Booth had to work through him. In the differences between Bramwell and Railton he sided with Bramwell. Railton felt that he was out in the cold. Compared with earlier days this was so, but it had to be. By no stretch of the imagination could Railton be seen as a possible Chief of Staff. So the results of overwork and stress combined to cause the man who had shown the strength of ten to become as a child.

On the long voyage the sick man kept a journal. Mrs. Railton later wrote that it was 'destroyed by order of General Booth'. The Railtons were the only passengers. There was no doctor. The little schooner dawdled and Railton grew worse. The food was suited to sailors of the toughest description, and the elderly Dane who was both cook and steward told Marianne: 'Your poor gentleman ought never to have come aboard this ship. He is exactly like one who came on my first voyage and who died the day after we reached port.'

The only Salvationist activity Railton seems to have been able to undertake was to remonstrate with the crew, some of whom drank much more than was good for them, or the safety of the ship. The carpenter replied: 'That's all right, sir, when I sees I've had a drop too much I just goes to bed and says to God: "Now God, you see I'm drunk, so take care of me".'

They arrived in Natal on March 8th, after sixty-seven days at sea. Only Marianne's unremitting care kept Railton alive. The Salvation Army had not commenced operations in Natal Colony, although work had begun at Cape Town in 1883. Railton hoped to arrange the opening, but at first Marianne would not let him wear uniform. Her fears for his well-being were not unfounded. They had no reservations for accommodation and no friends awaiting them in Durban. They were directed to an inn by eight Africans who each seized an item of luggage and ran off with it, much to Marianne's dismay. But they were all waiting at the inn and all expecting to be paid.

It was Sunday and at night, after tea, Railton felt strong enough to go to the nearest chapel. It was used by Africans. This non-observance of the European customs was to make him notorious.

They found a home at last—'Ocean View', a lovely place, far too delightful a spot in which to die, for the Durban air was not helping Railton and Marianne became alarmed at his seeming lack of will to live. Some of the ships out in the bay had come round the Cape where the new Salvation Army was digging in and extending its operations to Port Elizabeth, Grahamstown and other parts inland. Railton seemed indifferent even about the Army.

Later that year *The War Cry* of London reported:

'Commissioner Railton is pleading for officers for Kaffraria and Zululand and is busy translating our songs into the languages of both these countries ... Mrs. Railton is preaching in Natal to the Dutch, who are crying for mercy in the meetings. Officers must be sent there immediately.'

Railton began to look about him. A Durban paper reported that: 'Chief Commissioner Railton has arrived in Durban to commence hostilities.'

The Zulu War had not long since been fought, partly in Natal, and the subject came up in conversation with visitors and acquaintances. Railton thought that the English had treated the Zulu nation with great injustice, and said so. Marianne was hard put to on occasions to preserve amiability though privately she shared Railton's indignation. He was making progress with the study of Zulu which to Marianne seemed to be full of extraordinary 'click-clicks'. She felt she could never learn it, but she was soon accepting invitations to speak here and there to those who spoke English, and became a local celebrity as one of the Salvation Army lassies so frequently mentioned in the London papers.

At Easter Railton had a relapse and the doctor suggested a move inland. They made the train journey in easy stages and Railton indulged his eccentricity, buying the cheapest ticket, 3rd class, used, so Marianne said, 'by natives and coolies. The ticket collector could hardly believe his eyes, and everyone stared as we took our seats in what is really an open cattle truck with planks across, among Africans. I liked the novelty of an open carriage'. The scenery was delightful and they had plenty of time to take it in as the train puffed slowly between the foothills which would rise at last to merge into the Drakensberg Mountains.

They stayed the night at an hotel where the son of the host was one of the soldiers who captured Cetshwayo, the last of the great Zulu kings. There was a military camp in the area. Soldiers went by singing a most inappropriate song, 'Sailing, sailing'. Marianne noted, 'Papa tried to learn it for the Army.' Salvationists did in fact use the tune for many years afterwards.

There were lovely walks all around but Railton could not walk, so they persuaded him to mount a most docile horse and walk that. Marianne who had a little experience of riding was permitted to gallop. They went to a Presbyterian chapel with about thirty people present. Marianne was asked to preach and Railton scandalized everyone by singing during the prayers. To add to the horror, writes Marianne, 'three members of one of the worst families in the place rushed out for salvation in regular Salvation Army style'.

Next day Railton was too ill to continue his journey so Marianne rode out to visit a nearby Trappist monastery where groups of kaffir boys and girls were being cared for. As a woman would she asked questions about domestic matters, and the prior disclosed a system that appealed to Railton:

Seven hours a day for prayer.

Rise at 2 a.m.

Breakfast 7 a.m. if we work extra hard but if only ordinary work breakfast at 12 noon.

No dinner.

Supper at 6, Soup, vegetables from the garden. We never eat meat.

'Poor wretches!' Marianne wrote afterwards. Yet she felt sometimes that she was living with a Trappist.

Railton's malaise was proving obstinate. One doctor diagnosed pleurisy but treatment was not successful. Railton waited for letters from London but mail was long delayed, and little when it came. The Army was expanding like the hordes of Ghengis Khan. There were new men, new places, new methods but he felt out of it—a forgotten soldier. Perhaps this was his sickness.

Continuing by train they went on from Pine Tree to Half Way House, fourteen miles. It was only a request halt with a solitary inn, and the guard did not stand on ceremony, dumping the luggage of the two 'poor whites' who were travelling third among the Africans. They were farther up among the hills now, and cold, when a solitary Zulu took pity on them and shouldered their luggage as he led the way to the inn. There were no fires, and they were too cold to sleep. Later they proceeded towards the capital, Pietermaritzburg, stopping once at a Boer farmhouse where Railton was kept awake all night with raging neuralgia, said to be of nervous origin. For the last fourteen miles to Pietermaritzburg—Railton was so ill that he hardly noticed—the stationmaster put them in the relative comfort of a second-class carriage. In so far as Railton thought at all on that weary ride he fumed at the arrogance of a farmer they had met who, said Marianne, had 100 acres for £30 per annum; no rent or rates; but who treats his workers as 'black animals'.

It was here, now at the capital of Natal, on May 6th, 1885, that the idea of Salvation Army Red Shield Work for men in the Forces came into being. As with many other of the Army's tactics it arose almost by accident. Natal was crowded with soldiers of the Queen. Neighbouring Transvaal had been annexed in 1877 and later fabulous quantities of gold had been discovered there. Kimberley's diamond fields proved to be the richest in the world. The Zulu War had been fought in 1879; the 'first Boer War', called by some 'the great insurrection', in 1881. There were soldiers everywhere.

When Marianne led a service in the YMCA, the day after arriving at Pietermaritzburg, the building was full of military men including a general and a chaplain. Marianne got a cheer from the soldiers and a polite greeting from the general. She spoke up, and left after half an hour as any Victorian lady should. Later, she and Railton learned of the needs of servicemen: their lack of suitable recreation and the absence of a place where they could spend leisure hours without being cajoled into drunkenness and fleeced by harpies. This need stimulated the Railtons to suggest the commencement of the Naval and Military League. Indeed the first Salvation Army hut near a battlefield was put up at Pietermaritzburg, at the Estcourt Camp, Natal, where Mrs. Railton had spoken to the soldiers fifteen years earlier.[2] At the service at the mission there were many penitents and Marianne insisted on a penitent-form, not an inquiry room.

The Wesleyan Superintendent minister called to ask Marianne would she do an evangelistic service at his church—not at his own desire, Marianne thought, but in response to the wishes of his congregation. 'We begin to think the Army should come here at once,' Marianne wrote. Railton was able to do a little work occasionally. He persevered with the learning of Zulu and the translation of Salvation Army songs into that language.

At the Wesleyan service a number of penitents came forward to kneel at the front; most of the congregation disapproving of such innovation. When one of those who walked forward, in the Queen's uniform, and the worse for drink, began to loosen his clothing prior to kneeling, the horror of the respectable folk may be imagined. But what else could be expected from this dreadful Salvation Army?

Marianne encountered another military problem of the utmost seriousness and delicacy which was confided to the Railtons by a soldier in a Highland regiment: 'We want to come out for salvation but we cannot kneel at your penitent-form in the kilt.' She wanted to settle the matter by having the men kneel facing the congregation, but the minister who was not an advocate of the penitent-form, took the men to the inquiry room, much to Marianne's displeasure.

Railton's health was improving, possibly because of the treatment of a Doctor Allen at Pietermaritzburg, 'a sort of genius' Marianne wrote. That he was getting back to normal can be gathered from Marianne's comment: 'Papa is busily searching for a Salvation Army hall.' He was advised by an expert, 'The Army must not go into Zulu-land unknown beforehand, for your position would not be safe.' The Boers, 'whose influence is enormous among the Zulus would only have to say "The people are bad, your cattle will die", then your officers would be thrown out or perhaps massacred.'

This curb to Railton's impetuosity proved to be well founded. Though attempts to get into Zululand were made in 1888 they had scant success for the very reasons put to Railton. When in 1891 the Acting Commissioner for Zululand was persuaded to give his support the work began to prosper.

Railton arranged the opening of salvation work in Natal for June 1885. He engaged a theatre for the first day's work. Marianne's activi-ties as an evangelist had whetted the people's appetite for the full-scale 'invasion'. When she visited a Wesleyan Sunday-school the chapel went into united session, no classes, and about fifty of the pupils knelt at Marianne's novel penitent-form.

In London Railton had been more or less written off by now. His illness was obstinate and mysterious. Besides, the Booths had other things to occupy their minds. Josephine Butler and Members of Parlia-ment were allied with the Army, and W. T. Stead in his sensational *Pall Mall Gazette* was agitating to compel Parliament to protect young girls and raise the age of consent to sixteen years. In a packed Prince's Hall, Piccadilly, Mrs. Catherine Booth told a horrified audience that

'A lustful beast may get hold of your little daughter, cajole her, and coax her into any place with the promise of a wax doll or a fine feather, obtain her consent to an act of which she is totally ignorant and thus accomplish her ruin for life; and there is no law in the English statute book to give you redress. I say it is time we women had some voice in choosing our lawmakers when they consign our helpless daughters to such a fate as that.'[3]

Near Richmond, Marianne addressed her first Zulu meeting—the men one side of the chapel, the women the other. Most of the women had babies strapped to their backs. Railton was present. Unsuspecting, Marianne gave the appeal to the penitent-form and what followed un-nerved her for days afterwards.

'In a few moments the whole space around the communion rail was filled with penitents, screaming, yelling, wailing, more like the lost in hell than anything else I could imagine. The place seemed to be filled with the power of God but I was powerless.'

An effort to commence singing and some sort of control failed entirely. Railton had to leave the meeting. This went on for half an hour and in the end some sort of order was obtained when a converted African went to each excited Zulu in turn and shook him by the shoulder until there was calm, though the tears did not cease.

Railton's host was a missionary of the old paternal sort: well-to-do; six well-bred horses for his own use; a herd of cattle. The Methodist Missionary Society which sent him there left him to his own devices. Marianne said he was more like an African king, an absolute ruler. 'His outlook and speech,' wrote Marianne, 'is that of a rich landowner.' Of course this missionary did not approve of Marianne's effort to *convert* Zulus. His family, noted Marianne with disapproval, played tennis and the missionary even had a valuable prize bull which followed him about like a pet, which seemed to suggest that the missionary could not have been wholly bad. None the less Marianne was sure that Wesley could not have approved of him.

Railton sang a song, 'I am saved', in Zulu at the next meeting for the excitable converts. The interpreter present commended Railton's translation and said that his short speech could be understood by the Zulus. But after Marianne's sermon all the converts of the previous evening came out to the penitent-form again. This is not the done thing, and Marianne was dismayed. The tears and wailing went on for a longer period than before, at least an hour, while the strapped babies looked up at the ceiling with philosophic calm. Marianne was told that the 'hysteria' would go on for a fortnight and after that many of the Zulus would have the right idea and be real Christians. It was all very confusing and un-English. But at their last meeting at Richmond a number of men of the Zulu nation were genuinely converted and the Railtons had other evidence that their visit had been worthwhile.

On June 22nd they returned to Durban to welcome the Salvation Army contingent from the Cape Colony which was to begin work in the Natal capital, Pietermaritzburg. This consisted of Mrs. Major Rose Simmonds, two lassie Lieutenants and two children of Mrs. Simmonds, one an infant of a few weeks old. The other child, 'named Railton, after papa, is only eighteen months'. Marianne, who recorded these facts, was full of admiration for Mrs. Simmonds, a veritable amazon who had won fame as Captain Rose Clapham before marriage. Her intrepid exploits in Africa do not belong to this story except to say that the work at Pietermaritzburg and Durban, though encountering fierce initial opposition, afterwards flourished exceedingly. Boers and Englishmen, Zulus, Kaffirs and Indians, she encountered them all. Mobs and policemen were all alike to her. She was a Queen Boadicea in a chariot of heavenly fire.

The Railtons were at the opening meeting in Durban and Marianne was able to assess the matronly Mrs. Simmonds who 'seemed to electrify the quiet chapel folk with her declaration that leaving her husband and endangering her children were nothing to her if she could save some of the perishing souls of Natal'. Mrs. Simmonds and her party left for Pietermaritzburg early the next day. Despite the Railtons' previous work, they had a hot reception—bricks thrown through the windows, benches smashed and complaints from the canteen keepers that the Salvationists were ruining the trade by getting the drunks converted. The police found rifles under the floor of the hall and hoped to make something of it. What Mrs. Simmonds could do with guns was not clear. It transpired that they were relics of the war days when the building had been a drill hall.

On July 1st Marianne and her husband left on the s.s. *Melrose* for the Cape, where Railton had official business to transact for the General. Railton travelled among the noisy and drunken section of the passengers but Marianne's principles did not prevent her modifying Christian poverty and Railton's rigid principles, by allowing the first-class steward, a Salvationist, to bring trays of fruit and other occasional luxuries.

A Jew tested Railton's Hebrew on this voyage and refused to believe he was not an Israelite. 'Ah,' he said cynically, 'it sometimes pays to change one's religion.' They reached Port Elizabeth on July 3rd, and on July 5th Marianne and Railton held their first Salvation Army meeting. Marianne found her tambourine and Railton gave a ten-minute talk. Marianne said that the effect of such odd dress, mixed nationalities and behaviour was to make things sometimes 'like a circus'. Among the Cape's polyglot population Railton's linguistic skill was useful.

Railton became convinced that white and coloured work should be operated separately. Marianne wrote in her diary:

'July 5th, 1885: Experience is proving that we cannot with advantage mix coloured and whites in the same corps. It is not good or happy for either. In fact they do not mix. We found *two* groups of soldiers waiting for the open-air meeting on different sides of the road, talking to each other separately. One was of differing shades of colour, the other white. When the sharp order rang out, 'Form up!' or 'Fall in!' they did so, and mixed to that extent, but there was not much real union in that.'

Railton reported to this effect to William Booth. He insisted that the coloured people should have corps of their own where they should have unhindered opportunity of developing their full powers and of seeking to save their own people.

On July 6th Railton was thirty-six years of age and The Salvation Army twenty. Marianne gave him a Revised Version of the Scriptures; they prayed for young David, about whom there was no news. Marianne's love for her absent child and her invalid husband springs up from every page of the diary she kept at this time. 'Papa' she called Railton. The term signified spiritual authority, wisdom, patience, a strong rock-like quality encased in that frail physique. It also indicated the Victorian woman's conventional attitude towards her lord and master—as in George Eliot's *Middlemarch* and Dorothea's attitude to her sickly lover, Casaubon. But Railton was never pedantic and he loved Marianne with all his heart.

At Port Elizabeth at an All Night of Prayer Marianne was astonished to see that 'the blacks' were first out to the holiness table—a sort of penitent-form for Christians already converted. Blacks and whites would not kneel in prayer together. As the coloureds, like the Zulus, were apt to linger over their prayers and tears they were 'cleared away to allow the whites to come'. Many of these, Marianne noted with particular satisfaction, were young and were offering themselves as candidates for officership—'there are not nearly enough white officers here'. The meeting went on until five a.m.

Railton had to miss all this. He was hardly able to lift his head and could walk only with difficulty, slowly and for short distances. A talk to a group of officers made him ill for the following three days. In the end Marianne had to get him away from Port Elizabeth before the salvation war killed him. She departed for Grahamstown, about 120 miles away, but halted at Alicetown, half way along. Railton was 'quite done up'. Here the Hottentots were not forbidden to buy liquor, as in Natal. Marianne wrote, 'They were nearly always drunk.'

While Railton regained enough strength to continue, they stayed at the only hotel and watched the ostriches and Marianne appreciated the masses of wild flowers—a pleasure denied to Railton who was at present unresponsive to the beauties of nature. But he reacted against the trade in ostrich feathers, a fashionable finery at that time and one for which Salvationists in Britain kept scissors handy, so that a frivolous girl seeker at the penitent-form, if she became converted, had the feathers snipped off her hat as a sign that she was beginning a new, unworldly life. The pulling of the plumes from live male birds— worth about £100 each when demand was high—made him highly indignant. Yet poor Marianne had thought that nothing in Alicetown could upset him—no Army, one small hotel, a river and a vast carpet of flowers.

They were met at Grahamstown by Captain Pascoe, from Cornwall, England, her German Lieutenant, Lirbusch, and a fine 'Cape cart' with an excellent pair of horses. Railton went straight to bed, but gentle careworn Marianne must perforce attend the open-air meeting, where a large number of Salvationists had gathered: 'All white—a splendid corps. Their first Captain, and everybody's pet.'

Marianne liked Grahamstown: 'Wide streets, avenues of trees, hand-some buildings and meat in the daily market from 1½d to 4d a pound.' There were 400 people present at the Friday night holiness meeting. Something of the bourgeois stamp of Torquay survived in Marianne's comment on the crowd: 'All of a very respectable class.' But such an audience made a nice change from mobs which spat in the aisles, threw bricks through the windows and shouted obscenities at the lassies. Marianne was struck in the face with a stone, 'which made my nose bleed very much', while standing in the open-air meeting at Grahamstown. The diarist noted another way with sinners—not all found peace with prayer and tears at the penitent-form.

'The citizens sometimes take it into their own hands to punish those who do not come within reach of the law. One of them was the wife of the Dean of Grahamstown and last night the mob, mostly women, dragged her out of her lodging, beat her, then tarred and feathered her! She appealed to the magistrates today and her companion was seized in the court, driven round the town, tarred and feathered and then driven through the streets by a fierce mob which beat and threw stones at him until he was nearly dead. There were only eight police-men in the city altogether and they knew better than to interfere when the roughs begin. It makes us realize what a time The Salvation Army might have here if it should offend the mob.'

It was time to move on but Railton made another sortie in the sal-vation war and was then prostrated for days. Marianne had time to try to 'get the Captain's love affairs' happily settled. The plural would be a slip of the pen, for Salvation Army officers are allowed love affairs only in the singular. Some ring-leaders of the tar and feather brigade knelt at the penitent-form in a meeting led by Marianne and the Captain, who was 'full of earnestness and love'.

On July 21st they returned to Port Elizabeth, Railton being too weak to demur when Marianne insisted that they travel second-class. The new Captain was a lassie and the soldiers were delighted with her. The girl officer at East London was also doing well whereas men officers 'did but little'. Railton, who had played the vital part in encouraging the use of women as officers, must have found pleasure in this, particularly seeing that some South African corps had 'made a fuss about having to accept women as commanding officers and looked down on them'.

They sailed for the Cape on July 25th, Railton very ill and the local druggist confessing himself to be baffled. Outside the bay the vessel began to roll alarmingly and Marianne was soon violently sea-sick. Railton, however, contrary as usual, was helped by the strong sea winds and had his first decent sleep for many a day. They anchored in Table Bay on July 27th and when ashore made for the headquarters: a coffee bar, profits for the Army; offices, quarters for officers and a hall for meetings. Railton worked at interviews of officers, options for new openings, helping with some of Major Simmonds's problems, for without his wife the command was really too much for him. Railton also met various civic personages, editors and ministers. He worked hard at the Zulu hymn book and dreamed dreams of imperial glory for the Salvationists—building a New Jerusalem on the veld among the Boer farmers, the Kimberley diamond miners, the Rand gold-seekers, the Kaffirs, Malays, and all who were coming to this land of promise. Here at the Cape, Rhodes also had his dwelling and his dreams. One quirk he had in common with Railton, the sick, indigent neighbour he was never to meet—both men were indifferent to money for its own sake. Railton wanted Africa for God; Rhodes wanted it for the Queen. But Rhodes, who like Railton was the son of a minister, had lost faith.

Railton never lost his faith and his vision of what might be; he could infect others with his grand design. Emma Murray, daughter of one of the great Cape families, met the Railtons at Wellington, went back to the Cape with them and became in due course a Salvation Army Major. Her father was head of the Dutch Reformed Church. Murray, who had himself known a serious breakdown, told Railton that rest and an abundance of sleep were his only chance of cure.

Marianne and Railton boarded the *Roslin Castle* on August 19th. In about an hour they were in heavy seas and Marianne, again wretchedly ill, saw her invalid husband get much better—indeed she was of the opinion that he was the only passenger aboard who was not seasick.

The sailors blamed the rough seas on the Railtons—Salvationists were always Jonahs, they said. The Captain told the Railtons not to worry about this; the men were fond of a joke. Most of the conversation was in Dutch or German, which cut Marianne off from the talk. Railton could take part when he felt inclined but Marianne said the passengers were interested mainly in drink, cards and reading novels.

They crossed the line in suffocating heat. The ship's engines were new and she was therefore not allowed anything like full speed. At one time Marianne was so ill from the incessant pitching of the ship that she thought the prospect of collision, or any other catastrophe, could be deliverance. But of course this was a phase. She had a few curls of young David's hair in her bag, sent from England with the news that he was fat and flourishing. Railton was finishing off his report on South Africa for the Chief of Staff and looking forward to meeting William Booth again. When at last they came to Lisbon, steaming up the Tagus, Railton pointed out the Custom House, where as a youth eighteen years previously he had worked for the London export firm. They went ashore and he showed Marianne the Square where he had munched his meagre, lonely lunches. Journeying on the Bay of Biscay sent Marianne wretched to her bunk while Railton was one of the few passengers who could stay on his feet.

Very early, on September 9th, Marianne left the ship at Plymouth; Railton went on by water to London. Marianne had high hopes of getting to Torquay in time for breakfast with her father and—more important—to hold her precious David in her arms. Her final entry was: 'Goodness and mercy has followed us every day and every hour since we left the English shore.' In all her journal there is not one word of self-pity or complaint. Her husband's ill health, the separation from her child, the sneers of the ignorant, the stones of the mobs all came alike to her. She was a true salvation lassie and one may wonder to what height she might not have risen if events had not removed her from the scene, for she was to become henceforth a watcher in the war.

13

Not the Police, but Prayer

THE GENERAL was apprehensive about public reaction to the Maiden Tribute case which had been a national sensation and which it was feared would injure the Army's good name. Railton wrote an apologia of the Army's action—for details one can turn to various accounts, notably Ann Stafford's *The Age of Consent*,[1]; or Madge Unsworth's *Maiden Tribute*.[2]

There was a great rally at Clapton Congress Hall, the largest citadel, on September 15th, at which various notabilities took part and where the new pattern of Salvation Army leadership was in evidence. There was Major Frank Smith, the United States leader. The Major was a go-getter with no Franciscan love of poverty—he was later to part company with William Booth and become a business tycoon and a Member of Parliament. An excellent administrator, he told the audience at Clapton that in the United States it was not a matter of getting converts to sacrifice their fine feathers but to get 'bad men to give up their revolvers and become men of peace'. Emma Booth was there from Switzerland. The Chief of Staff who was being prosecuted at the Old Bailey was not present, but the people rose and applauded at the mention of his name. Railton sat in an ante-room while the lengthy preliminaries were completed. Then he spoke briefly, seated, and his words, inaudible to all except a minority in the vast hall, were repeated sentence by sentence by a young officer with a stentorian voice. Marianne spoke hopefully of the Boers, their interest in the Army, their oft-repeated kindnesses; she told of the Zulus and their tears and prayers at the mercy-seat. The Zulu nation was still a problem to the colonial administrators. But William Booth knew the answer. 'I have always felt that The Salvation Army would have to settle the Zulu difficulty,' he told the meeting.

For a time after this Railton occupied himself with writing but he felt more and more out of the picture. A second son was born to the Railtons, Nathaniel. Like David, he became an Anglican minister, who at the time of his death was Archdeacon of Lindsey.

The long, painful illness of Catherine Booth, so good a friend to Railton, became serious at this time. This cut her off from Railton, as a counsellor and mediator. He was now but one in the hierarchy of Commissioners round the General, leading Salvationist forces in world-wide expansion. One star in the firmament was Frederick St. George de Lautour Tucker, formerly an Assistant Commissioner in the Indian Civil Service, member of a British family resident in India. He married Emma Booth and changed his name to Booth-Tucker. Railton had been 'a failure' in the United States; Tucker was a dramatic success in India. He was a colourful figure, with a flair for winning newspaper headlines. Whereas Mayor Cooper ignored Railton in New York, the Governor of Bombay, Sir James Ferguson, put Tucker in prison, thereby giving him wide publicity and public sympathy. Railton's stay in the United States was brief, and seemingly ephemeral; Tucker stayed long in India and led the Army in great advances.

There were other new men, 'characters' in the sense beloved of Victorians, who made up an Army leadership far different from a decade before, when the 'Army' was William and Catherine Booth, George Scott Railton, Bramwell Booth and a group of missioners. For months while he was ill Railton could only watch and pray, while new pioneers went to the far boundaries of the globe. He was given 'back room' tasks. The exisiting French translations of Salvation Army songs, from the English, were unsingable. Could he do something about this? This enabled him also to look into the matter of a Dutch song book for use in South Africa among the Boers.

The idea, strongly held in Holland and by the Boers in South Africa, that the Dutch were a godly people, above the need for evangelistic missions, did not carry Railton's judgment. He learned that of 70,000 people at The Hague only 7,000 attended a place of worship. The General agreed to Railton's suggestion to open the work and officers were sent.

Railton was present for the opening in Amsterdam. Staff-Captain and Mrs. Joseph Tyler, the officers in charge, had been given £5 to cover all expenses and the police soon became uneasy because they associated the red guernseys of Railton and the rest with the red flag of the Socialists. Dutch friendliness had often been abused—by the Pilgrim Fathers from England, Communists from Paris and Anarchists from Russia. But Railton's Dutch song book sold well and there was no sign of anarchy or any sort of disorder, unless you counted sixteen people weeping and praying in a sort of pandemonium at the penitent-form. A preacher who had seen the Salvationists in England, at the Exeter Hall, said that 'they were a vile group of comedians, who whistle and dance and sing in a most abominable manner'.

Railton afterwards declared that he never found a people so prepared for *Het Leger des Heils* as were the Hollanders. One of the leading theologians, Professor Gunning, attacked the Army in *The Church Times*. Railton wrote a reply which caused the Professor to change his mind about the Salvationists and Gunning became a life-long friend of the Army and occasionally host to William Booth, when that worthy visited the Netherlands.

Two Dutch Salvationists, Colonel and Mrs. Ferdinand Schoch, remembered an Army meeting in Amsterdam led by Railton. 'It was so rough that I asked him to let the police come in and close it down,' recalled the Colonel.

'No!' Railton replied. 'Let Mrs. Schoch sing:

It was for me that Jesus died
On the Cross of Calvary.'

She did, and a silence followed. After that the need was not for the police but prayer. Six people came forward to kneel at the penitent-form.

Mrs. Railton helped with some of the meetings in Holland but she seemed not typical—too much the lady, 'failing a little on the holy fire expected', as one newspaper reported. But the Army was not all blood and fire, drums and trumpets, preaching and prayer. One girl convert, who became a Lieutenant, said she could not become a Salvationist 'unless the Army believed in music and flowers'. The Army passed muster by that criterion. Every now and again, all through her life, Marianne was to remember the veld at Richmond and its carpet of flowers after the rain. Sometimes from afar Railton would send her leaves or blossoms, crushed between sheets of papers on which he had written his love for her. Some of these love tokens exist still.

It was about this time, the years of sickness and heartache, that Railton made his will, part of which reads as follows:

This is the last Will and Testament of George Scott Railton now residing at Hadley Wood in the county of Middlesex, England.

I the said George Scott Railton hereby revoke and annul all former wills, and I hereby give and bequeath to my dear wife the whole of my estate and effects whatsoever now or at any future time to be mine or to become due to me to be used at her absolute discretion. Should my dear wife not survive me then I hereby commit my children to the care of the Lord Chancellor of England in order that after suitable provision for them all my estate effects as aforesaid may pass to my friend William Booth General of The Salvation Army or to the General of The Salvation Army for the time being.

I leave my children without any sort of qualification to the care of my dear wife who understands and will I am sure carry out my wishes with regard to those perfectly during her lifetime. But in the event of her death then I hereby constitute the Lord Chancellor of England for the time being the sole Guardian of my children with all my powers on them until they attain their majority that he may carry out my wishes with regard to them as follows:

1. They are to be brought up altogether according to the engagements made by their dear mother and myself when we presented them to God in the Salvation Army form contained in the volume of *Orders and Regulations for Officers,* pages 600–1–2.

2. It is therefore my wish that they should never possess any money or goods of their own; but should recognize themselves and all they at any time possess as being the property of God and The Salvation Army, to be used as the General for the time being may direct.[3]

3. And I do not wish them to receive any education or to come under any influence whatever but such as the General for the time being may think proper.

Nevertheless I hereby charge my children and all whom it may concern to read and consider my writings and especially those entitled *Heathen England, Twenty-one Years Salvation Army* (the first 21 chapters only) and *Fight it Out* and to devote their lives to the work of The Salvation Army as therein explained. I do not wish my children to remain connected with any organization calling itself The Salvation Army which does not answer the descriptions and carry out the purposes described in those books.

Upon her return from Africa Marianne had resumed the secretaryship of a discharged prisoners' home—one of the Army's first social work experiments in Britain; the idea was first tried out in Australia. But Railton wanted Marianne by his side when he travelled and they knew that travel on Army missions was better for him than a succession of back-room tasks, annual reports, newspaper articles, translations, which piled up on his desk. He wrote to Marianne:

'It is true that I am not feeling so well as when you were here, but

I shall resign myself if you will give up your prison-gate work and be just my comrade. It is very evident my travelling days are done for the present.'

He was wrong. One of the most heroic adventures of his life was about to begin.

14

The German War

TO MANY Englishmen in the 1880s Germany was a nightmare: a rival in trade; a potential rival at sea; a growing colossus, whose army had obliterated that of the French in 1870–71. Her Chancellor, 'blood and iron' Bismarck, had fought three wars and won them decisively.

But Railton coveted for The Salvation Army the country whose traders were on the heels of the British all over the world, and whose science and industry were advancing rapidly. He met friendly Germans in the German-speaking part of Switzerland and took up the language with the intuitive facility he had for any language. From Zürich in 1887 he wrote to Marianne:

'This journey will do me no end of good. As for the money you sent, I shall give it away to help here, I think, just to relieve my mind of any anxiety about my bag and robbers!

'The great news is that I am in for Germany full speed. I was astonished at the facility with which I learned to give my experience and to lead choruses at the soldiers' meeting last night, and am confident that it would come easily enough to you too. I am delighted to think that you are getting things all so straight at home. We will soon be able to leave David, anyhow, for days together; we will rig Nat up in that Zulu holder on our backs and march.'

It must be admitted that Railton's ideas of Germany were naïve. After having written the following of a proud, highly religious country, it is not to be wondered at that he should be received without warmth:

'Their comparative respectability and knowledge make them harder to deal with than English working people; but that only means that they are a greater danger of being lost. Oh that The Salvation Army may have the strength and courage to say: "This shall not be. By the power of God we will force the door, and get at these millions of German hearts who are today abandoned to unbelief and drink." '

Railton did not commence the work in Germany but he saved it from dying soon after birth. The invasion was launched from Zürich and the officer who led the attack was a German Salvation Army officer who had been converted in New York, Staff-Captain Fritz Schaaff. He suffered much at the hands of hecklers and hostile newspaper reporters. Policemen took the names of people who wrecked his meetings but did not prosecute them, and in the end forbade meetings after 5 p.m. on weekdays and noon on Sundays. This prevented the sort of people the Army wanted from attending the meetings. The police chief answered the complaint of the Salvationists as follows:

'Your peculiarities cause one part of the people to be amused and another part disgusted. They cause the police excessive demonstrations against you. Therefore the police do quite right, in the interest of order, to stop your holding meetings at times when those who would disturb can attend.'

For Railton's first meeting at Stuttgart his audience was the Director of Police, an official of the Ministry of the Interior, a plain clothes detective, two men, two women and two boys.

At Kiel the Chief of Police was not pleased to see Railton, who disarmed opponents more successfully than belligerent people. Railton confessed afterwards that he had difficulty in refraining from laughing at the Police Chief's apprehension. Bismarck had just declared that 'we Germans fear God and nothing else in the world'. Why then, asked Railton was there such a to-do about the coming of a few hallelujah lassies?

The police were under no obligation to answer such questions, especially from an Englishman. They had a copy of *All about the Salvation Army* and that sufficed. They read out to Railton the following:

Let it be known to the said George Scott Railton that he is expelled from the entire German Empire by order of the Government, such expulsion to have effect from noon tomorrow.

They added that they would treat, in the same way, any other officers General Booth sent from abroad. But a few days later Railton was leading his first meeting in Berlin. At this there were reporters, pastors, detectives, various 'ladies and gentlemen' as Railton put it, about 600 in all. They listened respectfully and were somewhat astonished to find that the Englishman had some knowledge of their language and was not the ignoramus they had been led to expect all Salvationists to be. But they could not stomach Railton's leading premise—that they, the Germans as any other people, needed to be saved. As one reporter put it:

'The way The Salvation Army people try to convert others is really against all manners and customs, and if they could only keep before themselves the example of our Lord and Master, who did not call His disciples "saved", they would not go to such extravagances. One could only think what a pity if this sect should gain ground in our country, for it does not represent a quiet and sober, and serious Christianity, but encourages self-righteousness and spiritual pride.'

After Railton's visit to Luther's battlefield the Army was ordered to be 'silent for ever in the entire circuit of Worms'. Though he had no intention of obeying, Railton saw the German point of view.

'Naturally enough the German authorities concluded from what they had heard of riots in Switzerland, and perhaps of somewhat similar circumstances that had occurred years previously in England, that the commencement of our work anywhere must needs involve scenes of great disorder. And it must never be forgotten how serious was the effect of the unfriendly attitude of the authorities upon the mind of every decent citizen in a country where all regard opposition to the Government as naturally allied with extreme socialism, unbelief and vice.'[1]

He wrote to tell Marianne that he would be going back to Worms —like Luther, to put his neck into a noose. But he was not a whit dismayed:

'I go back to Murrhardt tomorrow, Esslingen on Sunday, and then back to Worms till ordered away. You need not have any concern about my comfort, as I dropped into clover at once. My quarters are dirty, it is true, because I am with a blacking dealer with a family of five. Moreover, if we even happen to get into prison we shall be all right, for I find from those who have been in several times for *War Cry* selling that it is a very different affair from England.'[2]

But Bramwell Booth in London could see a possible diplomatic incident boiling up. This would only embarrass German Salvationists, and increase their hardships, so Railton was ordered home for the time being. As always Bramwell Booth hoped to regularize matters and get the Army in Germany accepted officially—he was never one for guerilla warfare and he was well aware of Railton's death-wish.

But before he returned to London Railton had time to set up pockets of resistance, to brief German converts on tactics and to show German officers how to sell the German *War Cry* and thereby raise enough to keep body and soul together. Some of the officers had a hard time finding bread and rent.

Railton stayed in charge of Germany, secretly. Officially expelled, he entered and re-entered the country, keeping in the background, vanishing like the Scarlet Pimpernel whenever necessary. Some accounts of his visits survive. In 1889, at Murrhardt, he found that the girl officers paid the equivalent of 3s. 6d. a week for board and lodging; at another place three men had 'betaken themselves to a garret, managing their own cooking very well over a small stove'. He ate with these three spartans: 'Potatoes mixed with caraway seed, when fried, make a superb repast. Such absurd luxuries as tablecloths and saucers would be out of place in these romantic abodes of victory.'

During these years 1886–1890 'the German War', as Railton usually termed it, was fought in the face of official opposition and arrogant attitudes from a minority of the people—who regarded the Army as necessary only in a depraved society, such as London, England. There was always extreme financial stringency, for William Booth expected his Army to live off the country, however hostile. At Kiel, where Railton dare not visit, four officers were subsisting on about 5s. each per week.

But Railton and his 'underground Army' of Christian soldiers were bound to win. German Salvationists loved the Fatherland none the less because they also 'loved souls' as Railton oft exhorted them. The German people, suspicious of anything English, gradually accepted *Die Heilsarmee*. The aged Bismarck, coming to the end of his long voyage as the pilot of the German ship of State, making the country rich, powerful and united, mellowed considerably in his last years and greater tolerance was allowed the police.

In 1888 the old Emperor died, he whom Railton had petitioned unsuccessfully for the lifting of the expulsion order. In 1890, when his grandson, the Kaiser Wilhelm, let Bismarck go, Railton was appointed officially as Territorial Commander of The Salvation Army in Germany. By now it was clear that this was one British Army Germany was not afraid of; nearly all the officers were German and the soldiers entirely so. Railton had taken the trouble to learn the language, he was discreet and well spoken of at the Ministry of the Interior. A national decree of expulsion for such a man was like using a Krupp hammer to crack an insignificant English nut. Railton found that, for the most part, the police were content merely to keep a watchful eye on him.

Marianne and the children—there were three now, for a girl, Esther, had been born in 1886—were admitted into the country and another attempt to enjoy normal family life began. But it had the usual outcome. At Stuttgart Railton led his first officers' councils from his sick bed—the officers sat in the outer room while he spoke, and prayed with them from the adjoining bedroom. The new tolerance was of slow growth. The soldiers of the 'contemptible little Army' were forbidden, if in uniform, to walk two abreast in the streets. Anything like a crowd at the meetings brought police intervention. A policeman stood up in a meeting in Berlin at which Marianne noticed nothing that would have been thought unusual and declared 'this meeting is now closed' and meetings were banned for four weeks.

Then Railton was joined by Staff-Captain Jakob Junker, who was the reverse of all that his name might bring to mind. He had the conventional Junker qualifications: military training and service in the Franco-Prussian war, some wealth, good family background and excellent education. He opposed Sunday labour and taught children at Sunday-school. After buying a copy of the German-Swiss *War Cry* he went to Basle, in Switzerland, and saw a Salvation Army lassie officer control a meeting of 400 in which there were many who wished to cause a disturbance. The singing, the joy of the girls in blue impressed Junker, who was in effect a Salvationist from that moment. He had found what his heart had been seeking for years.

Though the Army was now established in various parts of Germany there was as yet no school for officers, so Junker came over to London to be trained. Before finally committing himself he went to hear Spurgeon, at the Baptist Tabernacle, Hugh Price Hughes, the great Methodist, and Dr. Parker, the renowned Congregationalist. Junker's attitude to money endeared him to Railton. He severed all connection with his businesses, disposing of shares and signing away rights he held in a valuable brick-making invention. As he put it: 'To take part in any undertaking carried on in a worldly spirit would cripple my spiritual life and also limit my usefulness.'

He retained enough of his savings to support himself, and the Army college in London found itself with a most unusual cadet on its hands. Having been part of the Prussian military machine he knew more about drill than any of his superiors, who avoided embarrassment by making him the Drill Sergeant. He took the idea of an Army literally, and when told to lead a 'raid' on the Elephant and Castle area of South London, planned the affair as if he were back in Bismarck's war machine leading his forces to their destination quicker than those who knew their London well and who used the main thoroughfares.

After his brief English term he went to Germany where Railton was the guiding spirit. Their service together was to be fruitful for the Army. The two men had much in common.

In 1890 Railton wrote:

'And, first of all, let me say thank God I am a German and belong to the Heilsarmee. Excuse me for feeling that this is the most beautiful country under heaven, and that our government is the strongest, wisest and best with which God has blessed mankind.

'Whatever ideas I had received during previous visits, unfavourable to our police, have been more than swept away be the experiences of the past few weeks; for I am satisfied that, with such exceptions as one must expect in every land, the police are our best friends, but for whose powerful and watchful care we should have sorry chance to do any good at all.'

If these seem to be words from cloud-cuckoo land, it is because we have hindsight. Railton was the most unworldly of men. He had written: 'No home on earth have I—no nation owns my soul.' This did not mean he did not love his native land, but that as a true Salvationist a greater love made him feel that 'Every land is my fatherland, for all lands are my Father's', as Bramwell Booth was fond of saying.

The other German army was a competitor for manpower. 'We live under the sound of the drum,' he wrote, and mourned that some of his best officers were being called up for their three years' military service. However, 'they will return to us if God spares them, in 1893, greatly improved leaders in the fight.' In this belief, he was not, as a rule, mistaken. Junker was by no means the only Salvation Army officer who learned lessons of discipline, self-sacrifice, endurance and dedication first of all in the German army. All that Railton asked of such a man, in the armed forces of any country, was that he add to it all 'the whole armour of God'.

It seemed to Railton sometimes that The Salvation Army in Germany would sweep all before it. There was in the town of Elberfeld, typical of many, only nine churches for 130,000 people. 'Yet on Sunday evening and every night of the week the Protestant churches are shut ... You may form some idea of the state of things when it gets noised abroad that two of the "Salvation Army amazons" are having meetings in some small hall.' Instead, Railton noted the people sat under the trees all sociably together and drank beer, sang songs, but did not get drunk. They would also buy *The War Cry*. There was a mixture of patronage, pride and curiosity about the 'Englanders'.

Some Germans shared Railton's confidence. One newspaper commented:

'The Salvation Army will soon be the plague of Württemberg. In spite of all the hindrances that have been put in the way, it spreads itself out more and more and strengthens its agitations.'

After five months Railton reported that there were 50 officers. One was an ornate character with 400 books and many woodcarvings. Railton thought it best to wean him from his indulgences by sending him into hard country among villagers who were said to be 'hopeless' and where money was in very short supply. 'No Württemberger ever gives more than one tenth of a penny to the collection,' it was said. The officer, with a taste for books and woodcarvings amassed eight shillings from a week's collections. He and a fellow-novice put most of this into their reserve fund, retaining only 2s. 6d. a week on which to live. They had such food as the villagers could give, for the country-folk were generous with kind, if not with cash.

As yet Railton was not officially established in Berlin. He made unobtrusive visits, but as an Englishman and leader of a movement originating in London, it would have been bad tactics for him to become anything of a public figure. He had been for some years the German leader *in absentia*; now he was to some extent the leader from behind. The German authorities used a kind of 'cat and mouse act' on him. They allowed Railton entry to Prussia, and then when it seemed expedient they expelled him again. Some of it was to do with the Anglo-German political barometer, which was usually 'stormy'.

He was still needed in London. William Booth never lost the habit of demanding that Railton should do this or that, and that no one could do it as well as Railton—it did not matter where Railton was. In 1890, the year Railton was officially named leader of the German forces, Mrs. Booth succumbed to the long illness which she had borne with such heroic fortitude. Railton was the obvious choice for the funeral. It was October, and a fine day, as Mrs. Booth had said it must be. Her delicate daughter, Emma, must not catch cold. A veteran inspector of police said that there had not been a funeral like it in London since that of the Duke of Wellington, and the reporter added—'Only soldiers win such honours.' William Booth, the Patriarch, stood tall, gaunt, head bowed, in his open carriage, a lonely figure. In a sense this was the end for him also. His Army was branching out into new fields of endeavour. 1890 was the year of *In Darkest England and the Way Out,* a blue print of social service on a scale which was to make The Salvation Army a world force in that field. It was not William Booth's *forte* but the public expected it of the Army even though Railton detested it. The old Founder wanted the simple gospel, the emotion-charged message, the responsive crowds and, most of all, the tears, the prayers of repentance at the penitent-form. More and more henceforth William Booth would give himself to this and leave the evermore complicated administration of the Army to Bramwell.

Railton opened the funeral service and uttered the committal, which was followed by a vow which a Roman Catholic could be forgiven for misunderstanding:

'Blessed Lord—We do solemnly promise ... That we will be true to our cause—And valiant in Thy service—That we will devote ourselves to the great end of saving souls—That we will be faithful to Thee—faithful to one another—and faithful to a dying world—Till we meet Our Beloved Mother in the morning.'

Then the General led them out—the Booths unto the third generation. They made their vow with all their hearts, in prayerful sincerity, but time was soon to show that the promises of men, of one name and blood, sons and daughters, promises made with prayers, can none the less be dissolved by the alchemy of time and distance, discord and obstinacy. There was not one weakling in William Booth's brood, not one nonentity, not one without high talent. But the passion which found expression in the old man's *How to Reach the Masses with the Gospel* could also be expressed in passionate differences of opinion. Soon, Herbert, Ballington and Catherine, William Booth's gifted children, were to clash with Bramwell and part company with the Army. There were other rocks ahead, as Railton was soon to find. And there would be no influential 'Army Mother' to help him now.

15

'Berlin's Booth Day'

BACK IN Germany, Railton wrote of being 'in the German trenches' and added:

'The German Salvationists can only come through the winter of 1890 by endurance, perseverance, and devotion such as the winter of 1870, before Metz and Paris, never called for. But in fighting for the Fatherland, with no ill-feeling towards any man, we can claim and expect all the grace we need, whether God sees fit to give us public entry into Berlin in 1891 or no.'

The red band on the caps of the men Salvationists caused them to be confused with German porters and they were often asked 'Are you a *dienstmann?*' which Railton translated as serviceman. When the cholera struck Hamburg, where Railton could live in relative freedom because of its status as a free city, his small but growing band of helpers had their chance to prove that they were indeed servants of all.

Like his parents, Railton encountered cholera because he worked among the poorest, and could not draw back, even from the nauseating symptoms which make cholera as great a test of compassion as any malady known to men. He was still considered to be a sick man and he was therefore advised to leave Hamburg. This he would not do. Marianne, who worried about him and had said that she should join him, had remained in Berlin with the children. It was impossible for her to take her family to Hamburg. The bodies lay piled up in the hospitals, and carts went through the city, as in the Great Plague in London, their attendants crying 'Bring out your dead!'

Railton wrote to her: 'It is no use your coming to me. If you hear I am ill—by then it will be all over, or I will be better. So there will be nothing you can do. Leave it alone.'

Marianne wrote that the graveyard men, who had to fill in the pits where the cholera victims lay, were refused admission to the beer-houses and some places of worship, and that they began to attend the Army meetings led by Railton and his people—only there were they welcomed.

Yet despite all this 'God wonderfully preserved our people and none of them were taken with the disease'.

Railton was driving himself beyond reasonable limits. When Marianne visited him in Hamburg, she remembered:

'I fairly wept with perplexity. The only possible bit of warmth in his tiny sitting room was an oil-stove on which all the cooking had to be done.'

He shared this room with other officers of his secret headquarters. Marianne asked to see his private room. The distressed wife saw that he had:

'A bedstead and one chair. There was no mattress. It was covered with one thin rug; nothing else. If I bought blankets I could not be sure he would use them—he was certain to find some other person, probably one of his officers, who was more in need. However, he gave way to my insistence that he accept one thick rug on the understanding that it would enable him to sleep in 4th class rail carriages by spreading it on the floor.

Marianne discovered with dismay that in East Prussia he had learned to eat raw bacon and fish and had 'laid aside any prejudice he might have had in favour of cooking'. Sauerkraut and potatoes were main items in his diet, and the lady from Torquay was certainly shocked at his ability to sleep in the one room with all the rest of the household, parents, children, in-laws and guests, as was also the custom in East Prussia. After all, he was merely carrying out Booth's—and Bismarck's —dictum, and living off the country.

These are the memories of his wife and the recollections of fellow officers. Railton was never a man to tell of what he suffered for Christ's sake. But one can sense in the uncharacteristically strident, apocalyptic note that he was carrying burdens he was not strong enough to bear; physique and nerves were overloaded. He raged against the churches of Hamburg because they closed down their services at the height of the cholera epidemic. He cited one thousand deaths in a week as a God-given warning to 'the new science' which was emphasized in the city whereas the Bible was neglected. He chided the preacher in 'one of the largest churches' who declared that 'God, the deliverer at Sedan, was capable of delivering Hamburg in this time of need', for not calling his congregation to repentance.

In 1891 the Army's Founder made his first visit to Germany. By
this time William Booth was a world figure. The loss of his wife had
aged him, and added a quality of pathos to him, a sense of loneliness,
a *mystique,* which increased the personal magnetism he always possessed and the affectionate regard in which he was held by the people
—not only the people of The Salvation Army.

He was always excellent at delegating authority and had created a
discipline control, or allowed his son Bramwell to create it, which was
efficient and world-wide. The Salvation Army of peace had a central-
ized staff system years before Her Majesty's War Office. The protocol
of a William Booth visit was an exercise in organizational skill. It could,
indeed, become something of a nightmare, because of the old man's
alleged short temper, food fads, pronounced likes and dislikes. No
one will ever know whether he would have displayed Christian for-
bearance in the complete absence of the formula for campaign prep-
aration, because no one ever put him to the test. It is likely that he
would have risen to the occasion for some of his reputation as a tyrant
rests on dubious evidence.

The obsequiousness which sometimes surrounded him was not to
his liking, or his making. He hated flattery. But he had become a legend
in his lifetime, someone larger than life, and some of his officers made
it their duty to ensure that the cold winds should not blow upon him.

As he grew older—he was sixty-two when he first visited Germany—
he took the red carpet treatment for granted. He liked a degree of privacy, suitable buildings, good acoustics, proper ventilation and a vegetarian diet. These, his personal staff insisted, were essential require-
ments, though proof that William Booth himself could dispense with
the full treatment and live to tell the tale is provided by his German
visit. Railton asked for permission for the great man to visit Kiel. But
the land Bismarck had made loved the Salvation General as little as
any other British General:

'Police Authority,
City of Kiel, J.No.42.   Kiel, Feb. 14th, 1891
With regard to yours of the 12th February, 1891, you are most re-
spectfully informed that it cannot be permitted for your General
Booth to deliver addresses here—unless he brings evidence that he
belongs to the German Empire.

                                                    The Police Authority, Herey.

'To Die Heilsarmee,
Berlin, S.W., Friedrichstrasse.'

Booth could have supplied such evidence, but not to the satisfaction of a policeman. With his first Lieutenant Railton he belonged to all the world. But such an idea would not easily be understood in Germany, or in Victorian England for that matter.

By now the General was accustomed to addressing officers by the hundred; Railton provided him with eleven and the old man addressed them with as much love and care as if they had been a thousand. He was used to great auditoriums, the Lord Mayor, big brass bands, and a civic welcome. Railton gave him forty people, of whom nineteen were policemen. The other twenty-one had to get a ticket from the police before being admitted. A Ministry of Interior official sat on the platform, just behind Booth, taking down every word he said, just in case . . .

But the General's reception elsewhere was more friendly. It became a welcome event. Berlin newspapers later described his visit to that city as 'Berlin's Booth Day': *Busstag-Boothtag*. To keep out vandals and rowdies there was a shilling charge for admission—not a typical Salvation Army procedure for an evangelistic meeting, but the police favoured it. The audience was 'variously estimated in the papers from 600 to a thousand'. Railton, proud of the way his General stood up to a hostile press reception and captivated the crowd and won friends and penitents, could not attend the meeting. His constant reappearances after numerous expulsions, made him unwelcome to the Berlin police.

But this did not excuse his 'Railtonian arrangements' for Booth's personal comforts. An old timetable was used, with chaotic results. At one place it was considered that a tram would be adequate—it was in order for Railton, who travelled fourth-class in trains. After all, William Booth was also reared in the tradition of Christian poverty. True as this was, the members of Booth's staff were horrified. In fact, the old man was accommodated with the driver, in the front of the tram, and all the others had to scramble on behind, as best they could. John Lawley, Booth's ADC and to become a Commissioner, never forgot that German campaign. He remembered that the building used for the next meeting was the living quarters of the officers, whose children were all down with scarlet fever. Booth was not a whit dismayed but only Railton would have permitted such an arrangement. Lawley wrote, 'The building was so low, so hot, so crowded, and as a consequence we perspired so much that there could be no fear of infection and all was well.'

In fact, William Booth was ill upon his return from his Continental campaign but Railton was never blamed for it and does not mention

it. He was far too busy pushing on with the war in Germany. He had
to tell his Salvationists to cease from clapping their hands—the police
objected to the habit as profane and likely to cause disorder.

A German naval officer told William Booth, 'The Germans regard
your Army as a caricature of religion.' In this, of course, they were not
alone. Professor Thomas Huxley was making the same point in the
correspondence columns of *The Times*. In 1892 Marianne was struck
by a stone. Stink bombs and sneezing powder were thrown into the
halls, bricks were hurled through windows. In Berlin a 'humorist'
rode on his horse into the Army hall and out to the penitent-form.

The War Cry from London told Railton of new advances in many
countries, new Commissioners winning victories, trying out new tactics,
giving utterance to views with which Railton did not agree. From the
'Foreign Office' of International Headquarters, in London, came a stream
of directives and requests for returns and proposals and information
on this and that. Railton did not care for this at all.

In the Army of the 1890s the battle was so furious that it was to a
great extent a case of every man for himself. Whether one fell or went
forward the cause was greater than any individual. There was a high
rate of recruitment; always another man to step into the place of one
fallen. There was no turning back. Railton sang, all Salvationists
sang:

> Stand like the brave,
> With thy face to the foe!

Yet he felt that 'system' was over-emphasized; he was over-worked and
over-wrought.

Junker conspired with Marianne to prevent Railton from leaving on
his long journeys without the price of a meal.

'As the train was moving Junker would draw a packet of letters
from his pocket. "You are going without these papers," he would cry,
and the Commissioner, imagining something important had been forgotten, would snatch the packet. Junker would then turn to Mrs. Railton with a smile of triumph observing, "There's money in that packet.
He would not let me give him even ten pfennigs for a cup of coffee,
but he has now at least a few marks from which he cannot escape." '[1]

The fourth-class unheated carriages were for 'seven horses or forty
men'. This was enforced. There were no seats. Railton explained

H

to the distressed Marianne that his idea was not merely economy, but 'to mix with the people'. One can safely assume that on Railton's journeys the other occupants were not horses, for the officer who travelled with him remembered long afterwards the impromptu meetings he and Railton led in the carriages.

Railton's breakthrough came when the Berlin police sent a morally derelict girl to the Army Headquarters 'to be rescued'. Prohibitions were withdrawn in one after another of the German cities. Catholics were among those who gave money to help establish social work. Railton saw no English-style slums in Germany, or ragged, barefooted children, but there was illegitimacy and prostitution, and the Germans began to believe in the Army's ability to deal with such problems. As one German put it, 'You try to bless people—no schnapps, no tobacco, no beer. Only get people to repent.'

The police at Stuttgart suddenly withdrew all restrictions and Railton began to serve ha'penny meals for the poor, three times weekly. In Berlin, which had remained adamant for so long against Railton's prayers the death of a child gave him his opportunity. The first Salvation Army march in that great, proud city was behind the coffin of the two-year-old daughter of Adjutant and Mrs. Carl Treite, German pioneer officers. Railton led, in the Army way, not a mournful procession, but a march of triumph, the celebration of a promotion to Glory. The police here and there cleared a way for the marchers. At the cemetery Army flags and uniformed marches were barred and audible prayers were not allowed. 'Eleven lewd fellows of the baser sort', as one paper reported, knelt at the penitent-form in the meeting which followed at the citadel. Railton reported that the Kaiser, Wilhelm II was a godly man and that there were signs of religious revival in Germany. The Emperor was indeed liberalizing Germany, if only to prove to the dismissed Bismarck, watchful on his estate, waiting, licking his wounds, bored, that the ship of state could sail without the man who had built it. Railton's efforts were helped by a general relaxation of tension following the resignation of 'the Iron Chancellor'.

Asked to write in aid of the Army's annual Self-Denial Appeal— and no officer was better qualified—Railton gave examples of German austerity, which might have made relatively affluent Salvationists in Mr. Gladstone's England squirm in their easy chairs. German officers were allowed seven shillings a week but most of them did not get it, three shillings was a more usual sum. Carpets were practically unknown and bedsteads often dispensed with, a custom Railton had accepted. 'It had never occurred to me before that all the advantages of a bed are

above the framework which supports it. With a little practice I am confident that those who really need to go to bed, that is those who get
tired enough to sleep, would rest just as well without as with bedsteads.' He went on to compare the simplicity of German dress with
the more sophisticated British, greatly to the detriment of the latter,
and suggested soup as a more frequent item for those well-fed people
who wished to save money for a good cause. 'Pies and puddings are
practically unknown to our officers here'—which may have been true
of German Salvationists, but it was surely not true of the Germans
generally in that heyday of their prosperity.

16
Farewell from the Fatherland

THE WAR was hard on Railton. Family life was practically non-existent and his health indifferent. London intimated that he would be expected to show an increase in the number of converts, in soldier-making, in Self-Denial income. All territorial leaders received the same exhortations toward yearly advances but Railton never liked this statistical assessment of Salvationist success.

His feeling of alienation shows through a letter which reads as if he is feeling sorry for himself:

'As for visiting England, I really hope not this year, and I am inclined to add, "not next", pleasant as it would be to see you and many other comrades. But, somehow, I get to feel more and more a foreigner, and if anybody needs explanation, I say let them come over and spend a week in this war. I cannot write or say anything approaching what I feel about it all, especially after Hamburg.'

But he pressed on. One sortie was directed at Berlin University, whence a Professor of Theology had fired a broadside at the Army. A Berlin newspaper reported:

'So *Die Heilsarmee* is taking trouble permanently to widen the sphere of its influence, even in the capital. They will now gain the students for their purposes, and one must say they are up to the level of the times. The red-band-hatted men are giving out handbills of a fiery hue, which say, in Latin—"The Salvation Army and the Apostolicum. Students and Unionists! You are kindly invited to hear the explanations of The Salvation Army as to their relation to the Apostles' Creed in Kutcher's Concert Hall, on Wednesday at 3 p.m." '

Railton reported that they had a purely student audience which 'heard all we had to say with the profoundest attention'. But the venue for the gathering was the Prussen Kneips (the Prussian Nipp-house), which had a female brass band and a bevy of pretty waitresses, which gave the place 'no very fair reputation' as Railton put it. At Darmstadt, in the splendid Schützen Hall, he set out to prove that though The Salvation Army might have odd ways of behaving its adherence was to the truths set forth in the Apostles' Creed.

In North Germany, where unorthodoxy was a monstrous offence, Railton's efforts among the intelligentsia did much to win over acceptance of the Army. His German was excellent; he was no dunce; he had none of the jingoism which Prussians looked for in an Englishman. Some of the university students became Salvationists.

Characteristic optimism comes through his impressions of the Copenhagen Congress, the first of such events, at which the Territorial Commanders and staff of eight Continental countries gathered to be counselled by the Booths, father and son. They represented 896 corps and 1,800 officers of Europe. Railton gave this impression to a reporter:

'The Copenhagen Congress was undoubtedly by far the most important event in the Army's history to date. For the first time Headquarters came away from England to confer in a foreign capital with the Army's leaders in Europe. May the de-insulization progress! Saving love was, of course, the all-pervading theme. That my dear German comrades should come back from Denmark above all impressed with the love shown them at every turn, is a triumph for the Army that no English reader can fully appreciate. This Army alone can abolish war!'

The comment on Headquarters and 'the de-insulization progress' is significant. Railton was probably alone among leading officers who thought in this way at this time, and only he would have dared to express such a view in print.

In the summer of 1893 William Booth made his second visit to Germany. He began with a public meeting in Stuttgart, the very first allowed by the authorities, the culmination of six years of pleading. By William Booth's standards most of the gatherings were small but, as Railton put it, 'we have a General who is still able to appreciate beginnings'. In Germany the going was still hard. One of Railton's officers was threatened with imprisonment because he allowed music in his meetings on Easter Monday. An additional penalty resulted from the discovery that people had been found in his citadel without police tickets of admission. There was no appeal in law so Railton appealed to the Kaiser. Railton wrote: 'It is impossible to think that the new King

William will allow this persecution to continue if only it can be brought to his personal notice. But that is the difficulty.'

William Booth had mixed feelings following his visit. Happy ones included tea as the guest of converts who had rented a hall to the Army, and relinquished their proprietorship of a beer-hall because of the Army's total abstinence regulation. In Baden the Army was allowed to march with banners and music through the street, a marvellous victory.

But between Frankfurt and Barmen they had timetable trouble again.

'From Frankfurt to Barmen was a long enough ride in any case, but alas, it was to be prolonged by our missing the quick train. I had saved sixpence, as I supposed, by not buying a new timetable for the new month, and that sixpence cost the poor General a long slow ride in the heat of the day, and cost the Barmen audience which had assembled to hear him in the splendid Central Hall, a very long wait.'

But if Railton fell short in such details he had a mighty and deep concern for the things that mattered most. This William Booth knew full well and even when Railton put him in a crowded smoking compartment from Cologne to Ostend, an all-night ride after a cruelly crowded day, the General took it all in his stride. He knew his Railton as no one else in the Army. Numerous converts had been won in Germany; candidates were coming forward for officership; official opposition was diminishing and influential support was gaining ground.

One of Railton's last tasks in Germany was to establish an Army on the Rhine. He had little difficulty in renting halls adjacent to beer-houses, for the proprietors knew so little about Salvationists that they thought they would attract large crowds to drink beer and smoke cigars. The Rhineland press had been hostile, and crowds of students at Bonn, who had to face a charge of 2d. designed to keep out irresponsibles, were disconcerted because there was so little to jeer at. They had been led to believe that the Salvationists gave vent to 'incoherent shoutings and ravings', but, apart from Railton, the three officers who took part were Junker, the former industrialist, an intelligent and lucid speaker; Schoch, a former officer in the artillery; and Staff-Captain Ehrhard, a woman who had been mistress at a high school. Converts, who included a farmer, nurse and factory worker, also won a respectful hearing. Bonn was a triumph.

At Andermach, a mainly Catholic town, a policeman town-crier toured the streets with a bell announcing: 'Salvation Army meeting in the Bell tonight at eight o'clock.' The hall was full of Catholics, 'very heavy drinkers', wrote Railton. But they knew how to carry it, for there was 'a silent and orderly demeanour, and anyone who sought to break this was checked by a neighbour immediately'. Rich and poor were present and Railton felt that having eighteen million Catholics in his 'diocese' he ought to study to get along with them all. One thing at least they had in common, he wrote, a knowledge of and reverence for the Bible. But there were no penitents at Andermach. The Catholics in Germany, as in many other parts of the world, regarded the Army as a social-service movement and were ready to fraternize with it on those terms.

Junker, whose arithmetic could be relied upon, estimated that there had been 3,700 converts in Germany during the past twelve months. But now the 'cat and mouse' expulsion order was once more put into effect and Railton had to leave the country for a while. There was a ferment of political agitation and the Army was getting masses of working-class people to its meetings. The Reichstag was showing democratic tendencies and the Emperor, Chancellor Caprivi, and the Government did not want too much popular freedom, especially any fostered from outside. Of course, to connect The Salvation Army with anything of the sort was nonsense, but as part of a general tightening of restrictions Railton had to go and, late in 1893, he was in New York.

While he was there an article appeared in *All the World*, written by Railton and approved by Bramwell Booth. It is generally accepted Christian doctrine yet, by a sad irony, action in the spirit of it was to involve him in a serious rift with William and Bramwell Booth. He titled the article 'Jesus Christ's 10,000 per cent' and because of what followed, and the fact that he used it in his own defence, it is necessary to give extracts from it:

'The word "securities", in its ordinary commercial use, has always amused me very much. Money is lent very often in consideration of the deposit of "securities", and these "securities" have often consisted of pieces of paper representing so many shares in a company, shares which not only proved worthless, but which actually obliged their holder to pay more money just in the time of need when they were supposed to "secure" him against loss.

'But a more common class of "security" consists of the deeds of property, representing apparently a value far greater than the amount of the loan made. But, alas! in the very time of urgent need, when some general crisis has left the lender without hope of repayment, that very state of things has so lessened the value of all the property that the only chance of its being any use at all lay in keeping it, and expending more money upon it year after year, that it might be sometime saleable! Well, we can afford to laugh at such "securities" of the world, because the Army has often just out of those circumstances been able to buy or rent some property more cheaply than would otherwise have been possible.

'It remains, however, a painful fact, that eighteen hundred years after Jesus Christ's plain declarations on this subject, those who profess to believe Him are just as ready with any others to hear about the "security" with which they can "lay up treasures on earth". Every new crash and disappointment, instead of opening their eyes to the truth of His word, only send them off on a new hunt after somebody who will assure them that his particular cistern is not broken and will hold water ...

'Will you, anyhow, just allow me for a while to draw your attention to Jesus Christ's securities? How positively He speaks about the prospect of those who really give up something for Him! Do you really believe that He to whom all belongs, and who has all power in heaven and on earth, said, *Every one that hath forsaken houses or lands for My name's sake shall receive an hundredfold, and shall inherit everlasting life?*'[1]

Railton lived up to this hard Christian standard, a literal acceptance of New Testament teaching, in his own life. So did many of his German people, whose Salvationism to this day is of the austere sort. London Salvationists should not therefore have been so surprised by what happened at the Queen's Hall, in the Strand, in 1894.

All mention of Railton's departure from Germany in 1893 and his visit to the United States is omitted from the trouble-prone sketch of Railton's life, published with a preface by Bramwell Booth in 1920. The authors are given as Eileen Douglas and Mildred Duff. The latter was given the delicate task of revision of Eileen Douglas's manuscript after her death during long delay caused by World War I and also by differences of opinion with the Railton family, who wanted what they considered to be the whole truth.

In the literary world of those days the convention survived that biography must be hagiography. Justifiable, perhaps, while relatives or involved contemporaries were still living, this method could be carried to extremes. The story had to be written again with the warts painted in—as with Wordsworth, Dickens, Palmerston, Disraeli, Ruskin and a host of others. So eager were the reading public for the whole truth that Lytton Strachey, an early and major operator in the new 'both sides of the story' industry, awoke one morning to find himself rich and famous following the publication of his brilliant *Eminent Victorians*.

The faultless convention gave way to reaction which resulted in faults and vices being emphasized and even invented. Thus, when Strachey could find no follies in Miss Nightingale or Newman, he imagined them. With Railton there were no vices of even the General Gordon size—alleged addiction to the bottle; while not an iota of Cardinal Manning's alleged worldliness and pride could be found in him. Yet there were 'skeletons in the cupboard'. The excised portions of Railton's 'life' dealt with strong differences of opinion between Railton and the Booths.

All through the years of rapid Salvation Army growth, the 1880s and 1890s, Railton had given voice to his disapproval of some of the methods adopted. When he could make these protests to William Booth it was the continuation of a long partnership during which Railton's dissent had been amiably tolerated, even welcomed. As Chief of Staff Bramwell Booth had brilliantly organized the Army's world-wide involvement in missionary and social work in numerous countries, often with Government approval and, in some countries, with financial aid. Railton deplored this but now the Army was becoming so big, and Bramwell so busy, that he could not, apart from temperamental disinclination, pause for argument.

Fund-raising as such became an art and a department of Salvation Army operations. It is all very well to send officers to India and Africa, to teach in schools or work among lepers, but such officers must be fed. However saintly, they had not wings to fly to their destinations, being as yet mere mortals. Their fares must be paid, basic equipment provided. Bramwell Booth's painful dilemma was that as the Army grew so did his need for funds. The great plans of *Darkest England* met with vehement opposition in influential quarters and to counter it the Army had to resort more and more to that weapon it had hitherto little needed—public relations.

All this seemed to Railton to be diversionary. He had the faith of the Old Testament Israelite who, when he woke in the morning, expected to find his breakfast waiting for him having fallen, apparently, from heaven overnight. Railton made himself something of a nuisance with his vocal disapproval of 'commercialism', by which he meant the Army's bank, mortgage schemes, trade headquarters, big brass bands, the offering of annuities and the like. He, who had caused William Booth to suffer the indignity of an all-night journey in a crowded smoking compartment, rather than spend sixpence on a new timetable, had a primitive Christian's obsession with poverty. The flood-tide of change and expansion in the Army left him behind.

His hero William Booth, at heart a preacher and prophet, was also less than enthusiastic about the increasingly complex financial and administrative aspects of the Army's development. In 1894, a critical year for Railton as we shall see, William Booth wrote to Bramwell Booth complaining not about the expenditure of sixpence for a timetable, but of twopence in stamps, when a ha'penny wrapper would have sufficed. He concluded:

'It is not wise for a money-grabbing operation to be gone through wherever I appear. General Booth ought to be seen now and then elsewhere than at Madame Tussaud's *not* asking for money!'[2]

Like Railton, he was afraid that the Army's priorities were being misplaced.

Railton was not happy about all the tactics being adopted in the United States, that beloved country where he had been the first to raise the Army flag. He seems not to have paused to consider that the conflict which beset him was part of an inherent tension in Christianity—the compromise between the ideal and the possible. In America Railton found that well-to-do Americans were lining up with the Army, even occasionally marching with it, lending their splendid homes for drawing-room meetings and wearing a Salvation Army badge as a mark of their affiliation. In Washington, meetings were held in the homes of members of the Government and attended by senators, congressmen and their wives.

This, to Railton, was a dilution of Army principles. For him the Army was a soul-saving Army and he could not see how society gatherings attended by members of the Vanderbilt family—from whom later the Army in New York was to receive a bequest in excess of 2,000,000 dollars—was germane to the soul-saving objective.[3] Time has shown that he was wrong in this judgment. As with the Army in all countries the Americans had to learn by trial and error, but their development along American lines always maintained, though sometimes indirectly, the Boothian soul-saving goal. The care of alcoholics, of unmarried mothers and other social misfits may seem on superficial examination to be 'merely' social service, but a closer look will show that the penit-ent-form, the spiritual as well as the social rehabilitation of the individ-ual, is a matter of urgent concern to American Salvationists.

During Railton's 1893 visit the Americans showed him that they knew how to fight his kind of salvation war. In that same Union Square where the Mayor had forbidden him to hold open-air meetings, a mon-ster mass rally was held and this was followed by thirteen open-air 'attacks' on sinners held simultaneously. Generally the Army's morale was good, but he found that, as in London, side issues could deflect occasional people and policies. The 1890s were a great decade for rugged get-rich-quick individuals and there were some losses of officers on this score. Railton wrote:

'Our officers in America will need to be more and more devoted to the Saviour, to be able to resist the offers that will pour upon them as the Army marches on.'

Though Americans had asked for the General—they were always asking for the 'old General'—they were happy to have Railton instead. He was the very best substitute. Delegates to the Congress came from all over America and the parade through New York astounded onlookers. Railton was somewhat carried away and summed it up as 'one of the most devil-terrifying and God-glorifying exhibitions of the power of Jesus Christ on human hearts ever displayed in this world'.

His reservations about new Salvation Army tactics he kept secret while he went back to Germany to pack. His final report was typically realistic:

'I do not pretend to brag of our achievements in Germany during those earliest years. There has nowhere yet been anything like an op-portunity for us to work as we ought to do. In spite of every difficulty God has firmly established in all parts of the country beginnings of corps, raised up a staff of German officers ready to labour more abun-dantly and endure more continuously than almost any of their comrades, and given them proportionately wider influence than any equal num-ber in any other land. These are tokens of what will yet be in all the world when we are let loose. Our existence here is everywhere a threat-ened one. Even authorities perfectly friendly require us, in the interests of order, and to avoid closure, to keep out of our halls any persons likely to be disorderly—just the persons we live for!'

In this swan song on his German command one can detect the inner stress, the toll the years had taken. There is the carping note again:

'During the eight years since our last International the Army has come to be recognized throughout the whole world as a great well-nigh irresistible force of a revolutionary character. I do not give England, America or even Australia credit for having let the Army attain such huge proportions during those years. Wherever there has been any legal opportunity—and often where there was none—it has been attempted to suppress our action. No amount of recognition of the good done by the Army lessens by half an inch the gulf between us and the part of the community which measures men by their purses or their learning, or that part of the community which does not want Christ. And whenever a traitor or a fool affords opportunity for hostile comment, the combined press of the whole Christian world is ready to announce our downfall just as seriously as ever. It is everywhere more fear than love that procures for us any attentions we receive, and "the world" knows us, thank God, today, no more than it did eight years ago.'

It is not that there was not much truth in this. There was little point in saying it and it is not characteristic of Railton. Yet with him love always triumphs in the end. He was incapable of harbouring malice or resentments. He would gladly have stayed in Germany. His final message was a *liebeslied* which Brahms might have set to music.

'Be assured that my love for the Fatherland and for every German will never be diminished even if it should be my privilege to labour for the salvation of those who have long been regarded as the foes of the Fatherland. To love all men, and to labour especially for the salvation of the worst of them, is the life-work which unites us and all our comrades throughout the world.'

In 1894 he arrived in London with about forty German officers and other German Salvationists for the Jubilee International Congress to mark William Booth's conversion in 1844. Bramwell Booth wrote a series of sketches of notable people coming for the great occasion. He put Railton first and although there is a hint of Railton's temperamental inability to be satisfied with achievements—he would complain when everyone else would be saying 'well done'—Bramwell Booth's appreciation of Railton was generous and affectionate:

'The restless, fearless, struggling spirit of advance which knows no satisfaction in what is done because of what remains to be done, and finds little comfort in a victory unless it leads the way to another, is the leading feature of the Commissioner's career ... And there are some things Commissioner Railton *does* not love! Swellosities and fine words, and Salvationists who are too big to fight a prayer meeting, and fine clothes, and excuses for making folks happy on the way to hell. These are "cursed with a curse", and Commissioner Railton curses them, too, without fear or favour.'

Railton probably did not want to leave Germany where the tide was beginning to turn in the Army's favour. His farewell from that command had not been announced and its questionable status with the Prussian authorities, and his numerous expulsions, made it in any case somewhat indeterminate. It is possible that Railton might have persuaded William Booth to let him remain had he walked circumspectly whilst in London. Instead, he created a public 'happening' in a Salvation Army meeting which was without precedent.

Marianne could only watch, filled with apprehension, as he doggedly set off on his collision course.

17

What did Railton Say?

MANY OF the great 1894 Congress meetings were held in the Regent Hall, Oxford Street, where events soon made it seem that the Founder's Lieutenant, the first Commissioner, George Scott Railton, was a fading luminary. The firmament was bright with other constellations. Marianne noticed it. She wrote:

'We used to have the meetings in the Regent Hall a good deal, and the General and all of them used to have a specially quiet room and dinner and I used to wish they would ask my husband and thereby give him a little rest. He stayed in the hot gallery of the Regent Hall having his food and translating all the time until, one very hot day, the Queen's Hall meeting came.'

Railton was cut off from William Booth's inner councils. He was out of touch with the reasons for new tactics, many of which he disliked. He did not see why the Army should make and advertise matches, 'Lights in Darkest England', even though these were manufactured to prove that the occupational hazard of 'phossy jaw' was preventable. *The War Cry* now had a huge sale and was a very lively paper, reporting great activity and advances, but giving more than a page to Salvation Army advertising: the provision of men's and women's summer underwear; Gladstone bags from 3s. 6d. each; *cartes de visite* photographs, 12 copies, 2 positions, 6s. 6d.; the offer of shares in the Salvation Army Building Association—'£100,000 already invested'—though the purpose of this invitation to invest was after Railton's own heart—the salvation of souls.

He was uncomfortable about the taint of snobbery he thought he detected. It was in part necessary publicity, public relations effort to win goodwill and bequests, one of which, from a wealthy Scot, amounted to more than £60,000. The famous Parliamentarian Henry Labouchere commended the Army in print; the King of Denmark and the Queen of the Netherlands made contribution to Army funds. Numerous members of the upper classes went 'slumming' with Salvationists. The sudden change from frowns to smiles by the aristocracy appears to have been heady wine which went to the heads of those more used to bad eggs. Railton was contemptuous: it was a patronage he would have refused. When *The War Cry* printed a list of refusals to attend the Crystal Palace Jubilee on July 3rd he was indignant. These included Rosebery the Prime Minister, Mr. H. H. Asquith, Edward Clarke, the Duke of Westminster, Lord Carrington, Arthur James Balfour, and many others among the 'top people'. The reasoning behind the publication was that though these great ones had refused to attend they had acknowledged the Army's existence!

But the straw that broke Railton's under-nourished back was the newly-launched Salvation Army Assurance Society. This addition to Salvationist operations was begun in a small way by the acquisition by transfer (and therefore without payment of the Board of Trade guarantee of £20,000) of the Charter of the Methodist and General Assurance Society. This was allowed to coast along quietly while Bramwell Booth and his advisers gained experience in what was in those days a jungle of cut-throat competition and sharp practice, not far removed from the downright fraud described by Dickens in *Martin Chuzzlewit,* half a century earlier.

Now, in 1894, as part of his Jubilee celebrations, William Booth was to launch it into the perilous sea of industrial life assurance. *The War Cry* asked for a thousand agents to begin with. Like most of Bramwell Booth's projects the Society was a success. It had a quicker growth-rate than the mighty Prudential. In due course the Salvation Army Assurance Society began to pay dividends to The Salvation Army for Salvation Army work, and for no one or nothing else. There were, and are, no directors' fees. Bramwell Booth, who was the prime mover in the business, gave the society a maxim which it still cherishes:

'Her merchandise and her hire shall be "holiness unto the Lord". Holiness unto the Lord—that is our trade mark. Anything that cannot be done in harmony with it must not, shall not be done by us and ours.'

But Railton couldn't believe that. With him as he read and heard all about the plans for the public launching of this, yet another of Bramwell Booth's brain-children, was Staff Captain Junker who had given himself to God and his private fortune to the Army. Railton who gave the coat off his back to a poor man; who felt himself a proud comrade of many officers who would not own a watch because it constituted 'worldly goods'; who had responded to the words of Jesus when He said 'Lay not up for yourselves treasures upon earth ...', saw that officers were being encouraged to 'save for a rainy day', to endow themselves against the exigencies of the future. The first Salvation Army life assurance policy was issued to a Salvation Army officer. To Railton this was a contradiction in terms since brief life is here our portion and Salvationists are always ready to die.

His revolt took place at the newly-built Queen's Hall (later to be made famous by Sir Henry Wood's Promenade Concerts and destroyed in World War II) on the afternoon of Friday, July 6th, 1894. William Booth was in charge; Bramwell was away leading a similar gathering in the Exeter Hall. Railton entered at the last moment and took his place on the platform barefooted and dressed in sackcloth—just like a friar, just like Railton! With no hint of what was to follow Booth joined in the general applause. Everyone loved Railton's eccentric gestures; all knew that he was a holy man. Dear Railton! One never knew what he would be doing next!

In his pocket, unknown to the row of Commissioners who sat alongside William Booth, and the audience that filled 'the largest hall in London', as *The War Cry* asserted, Railton carried what he called the 'infamous circular'. In many Salvation Army meetings opportunity is given for testimony and this gave Railton his opening. He held up the handbill which had been produced by Colonel Bremner, who was the first managing director of the Army's assurance society. The numerous stenographers present were so dumbfounded that not one of them recorded Railton's words. This caused Bramwell Booth considerable anguish, and numerous people high in his favour were asked what *did* Railton say. Their replies show a considerable divergence which made the Chief of Staff imagine the speech to be worse than it was. The congregation did not react adversely. After all, it was 'dear Commissioner Railton' speaking. Railton's copy of his speech has survived, and is here printed for the first time:

'I was so glad to hear our General in the holiness meeting this morning lay down the principles of self-sacrifice which he deemed necessary for successful salvation warfare. Judge then of my surprise when I found lying at my feet a dirty piece of paper. [At this point he held up the life assurance advertisement for all to see.]

'It is inviting our officers to pay twenty shillings of the Lord's money and offering to give them thirty-three farthings yearly in return—a farthing for each year of Christ's life on earth! [Some reported that he here made an unpleasant reference to Judas, but this was probably a mis-hearing.] Worst of all, this dirty piece of paper bore the signature of a staff officer [poor Colonel Bremner, who was only carrying out Bramwell Booth's instructions!], bearing the commission of our General and professing to be issued with his authority. Therefore, when I heard the General, whose commission I am proud to bear, say this morning that he still believed in the necessity of a life of self-denial and sacrifice such as enabled The Salvation Army to win its victories in the past, I was glad.'

He then placed 'the dirty piece of paper' on the floor and trampled upon it. William Booth was embarrassed and many Headquarters officers were shocked. It was an unprecedented action. Though some Salvationists agreed with Railton, official reaction was that he was 'mental', a condition brought on by overwork and worry. This explanation of any grievously untoward action had been used before. In 1892, Colonel John Lampard had jilted one of William Booth's daughters, an act of staggering courage. The whole affair became public property, as if the Duke of Clarence had jilted Princess Mary of Teck. Colonel Lucy Booth became ill, as Victorian ladies sometimes did on such occasions, and William Booth set up a small commission to report on Colonel Lampard's conduct.

The War Cry stated:

'Since that inquiry took place an opinion on the subject has been obtained from a physician who enjoys a leading reputation for the treatment of mental diseases. He states that in this particular direction, Colonel Lampard was, in his opinion, so far mentally deranged as not to be responsible for his action. In view of the grave doubt raised as to Colonel Lampard's mental accountability, the General feels that he can only suspend his further judgment on the matter, and hope that God may make plain His will. We are thankful to be able to add that Colonel Lucy is gradually recovering her strength.'[1]

The suggestion of 'mental strain' regarding Railton first appeared in a sort of round-robin to William Booth from most of the Army's leading officers. They assured the General that they did not agree with Railton, then went on:

'We all feel the importance of your taking some definite action in so grave a matter, but as we cannot but think that Commissioner Railton would never have so acted, but for the physical and mental strain from which he is evidently suffering, we would suggest that you should order the Commissioner upon a lengthened furlough, before coming to any final decision.'

Marianne, most loving of wives, rushed to help and said the wrong thing: 'He is thoroughly ashamed, and done up, and I am sure did not realize what he was saying.' But she was far wide of the mark. Railton did know, and was not ashamed, and never retracted what he said. What was wrong with Railton's protest on that catastrophic Friday afternoon was not so much what he said, which is a valid Christian argument, but how and where he said it. Railton had helped to create an Army, but he still wanted to act as if a united front, discipline and 'consultations through the proper channels' were non-existent.

William Booth did see him and the interview was a painful one. What was wanted was public apology. This Railton could not give. Railton spoke from deepest conviction, based his stand on well-founded Christian beliefs. Equally sincere Christians could hold different views about the Salvation Army Assurance Society. Christian history abounds with such contradictions. Railton knew full well that one could not have an Army in which any officer or other rank felt free to differ, and argue, and oppose authority when he felt like it. For a time after his protest, made when he was undoubtedly distraught and ill but by no means 'mental', Railton was left alone, out in the cold. His literary work came to an abrupt standstill. He was for a long time without an appointment. William Booth wrote:

'Since our interview I have hoped and waited for some definite expression of your regret for your unfortunate action on Friday afternoon but have waited in vain. In the interval I have been constantly praised on the one hand for the affection I have for you personally, reminded of the valuable service you have rendered to the Army, and warned on the other of the necessity of maintaining discipline. Of the importance of the latter there can be none who will have a higher esteem than yourself ...

'On reviewing the whole incident and your conversation on Saturday night in justification of it and bearing in mind your past history, I cannot but conclude that you really were not responsible for the extraordinary conduct referred to ... And in view of this I have decided to give you a few months rest, and I therefore desire you to go away to some quiet spot and give yourself total rest from all active salvation work and from all mental anxiety.'

In the letter just quoted William Booth intimated that he had consulted the Army's Commissioners. Railton's reply therefore was to the General and his advisers. It is too long to quote in full but here is the heart of the matter:

'Of course I most heartily appreciate the kindly feeling of the Commissioners and of all who wish to benefit my health by a few months rest, but having already mentioned to some of them the fact that I gained two pounds weight in the course of last week I really could not possibly with any sort of consistency go off resting.

'If I am told to go away from here anyhow and not to attend the meetings of the council to which we were invited I shall prove myself as capable of understanding and obeying orders as usually. But if I be told to go and rest from all active salvation work I cannot be expected to do the impossible but only to go and rest as the Chief of the Staff once "rested" in Sweden, thank God.[2] Mental anxiety I have none. He who knows my heart will lift me up again and again I feel sure.'

One of the Commissioners who had signed the 'round robin' to William Booth was Arthur Booth-Clibborn, a man of some culture and education. He had not been hindered in his career as an officer by his marriage to Catherine, William Booth's eldest daughter, better known as the *Maréchale*. He now spoke up for the isolated idealist and mentioned a factor which was the cause of much gossip and which, had the truth been more widely known, would have lessened Railton's sorrows. To William Booth, following questions about his own loyalty, Booth-Clibborn wrote:

'Hearing Mr. Hoe suddenly say "Commissioner Railton was mad", I said, "You ought not to say that of an absent Commissioner. He is desperately sincere. It is a difficult question, that of saving money, and I don't believe the General's own mind is fully made up upon the question. And in face of Christ's words 'Lay not up for yourselves treasures upon earth', it is a doubly difficult question to be positive on. I believe absolutely that Commissioner Railton acted under a very strong conviction and that his motives were pure. I believe it hurt him awfully to do it. I believe he truly loves the General."

'I gave all my money to the Army when I came in, and six years ago I sold out at a dead loss a life insurance of £1,000 rather than let it be chargeable to the Army by the interest. But I am not sure that in doing so I did the wisest thing. It is a perplexing question.

'I do not agree with Commissioner Railton's action. But I believe in his desperate sincerity and I know that he has personally no control over his wife's money. I have never expressed or felt any agreement with Railton in his action in that meeting.

'I can sign that letter with one reservation, that I cannot say anything to imply that I think the Commissioner mad.'

Marianne's money put her husband in a false position. The money was not Railton's. The old gentleman down at Torquay, though reconciled to his daughter's marriage to a Salvation Army oddity would not leave his money where Railton could get his hands on it to give to General Booth for some absurd scheme to help the poor or Christianize the Hottentots. Mr. Parkyn, therefore, created a trust out of which Marianne could take her sick daughter to Switzerland, or Italy, when the doctor so ordered and send both her sons to Oxford: shops, villas, land ripe for development to the value of £16,500, the greater part free of mortgage, and Government stocks in addition. Apart from the fact that for long periods this enabled Railton to work for the Army without any allowance at all, he gained nothing from this small fortune. He was, as we have shown, indifferent to money.

Perhaps the unkindest cut of many during Railton's long *dolorosa* at this time, came from the land where he had lived most devotedly that apostolic life of self-denial and discipline which, at William Booth's behest, he had written into *Orders and Regulations for Soldiers* and other of the Army's collection of rules. It was a letter to the General from Jakob Junker and another officer at the Berlin Headquarters:

'Our Dear General!

We feel compelled, after dear Commissioner Railton's address of Friday afternoon in the Queen's Hall, to express to you our deep regret at the utterances made by the Commissioner and to assure you that the views expressed by him are not ours.

'We can only ascribe these inappropriate remarks to a mental overstrain brought on by the constant battling against the adverse circumstances connected with the German war and the fact that the Commissioner gives so little consideration to himself, a fact which may, we fear, have more serious results, unless the Commissioner could be relieved for a time at least, from the strain of the work and by complete rest.'

We can ask why a man like Junker should feel it necessary to write in that strain about his own Territorial Commander, a man he held in high regard. Almost certainly Junker felt he had to. That was the way things were done. If anyone was in trouble with authority it was necessary, people thought, to disassociate oneself.

18

Rebel in Spain

WHAT WAS the General to do with his dissident Commissioner? Coombs, the Territorial Commander for Australia, who did not sign the Commissioners' letter to William Booth disassociating himself from Railton's action, asked that he might take the unhappy officer to Australia. But Coombs had not been as forthright in his denunciation of Railton's action as he might have been. He had dissented not from the content of Railton's protest but only from the manner of it. His request for a Railton visit was not agreed.

In the event Railton was sent to South America. There he would have no opportunity to fraternize with eminent officers while he was still unrepentant, and known to be repeating his 'heresy' that no Salvationist need insure his life, not even with the SAAS, but rather that he should lay down his life for Christ's sake. There were no eminent officers in the Argentine which was a commodious arena for martyrs —15,000 British scattered throughout the vast country who could not be reached or, in the few instances when they could, would pay little attention to The Salvation Army. That left the Argentinians who were for the most part Roman Catholic. Railton's Spanish was fluent but he knew that this would be more than a test of linguistics. The first Argentine leader appointed by William Booth in 1889 asked to be relieved of his command after 'only a few weeks'.[1] Officers sometimes lived on left-over food given to them by the catering staffs of hotels. They had been imprisoned, threatened at gunpoint and innocently involved in the inevitable revolutions.

Railton sailed in the autumn of 1894 without reconciliation with the General. The official statement was that Railton was on sick furlough. He had told William Booth he was not ill but the euphemism hid a multitude of embarrassments and was so published. This time Railton did not argue the point.

He was met at the railway station at Rosario, in Argentina, by young Captain Alfred Benwell, who had gone out to the country as a scribe, became an officer at the age of seventeen, contracted smallpox, suffered imprisonment and had his life threatened by armed thugs. He later dwelt on the visit as among the most inspiring days of his life:

'At the time of his visit I was stationed at one of the best corps, Rosario de Santa Fé. We went to the station to receive him and naturally passed through the first-class corridor coaches in which our leaders, having first-class passes granted to them by the railway company, always travelled. To our disappointment the Commissioner was not to be found. After waiting, and again searching in vain, we returned to the platform, where we found waiting for us a little man in a rough red jersey with a big yellow cross embroidered on it. This was the Commissioner. He had travelled second-class, where a good deal of smoking and gambling usually goes on during the journey; and when I asked him why he had done this since he had a first-class ticket, he replied, "The people we are after travel second-class, and I found my joy during the eight hours' journey in talking to them of the love of God".'[2]

There were open-air meetings at which Railton spoke Spanish and indoor meetings at which penitents knelt. Benwell remembered that Railton's opinion of the Spanish tongue was very high. He considered it well adapted for religious use, the 'finest known to the lips of man, stately, dignified, with unparalleled scope for eloquence'.

The worth of Railton, that which lives on in the Army, which has caused his name and reputation to grow, was shown in a visit to a prison which Benwell arranged:

'The brightest spot in the Commissioner's visit to Rosario—the second city of the Republic—was when I took him to the provincial jail. After long efforts, the Chief Justice had granted me permission to hold meetings with the prisoners. We took with us a plentiful supply of gospels, tracts and copies of *El Grito de Guerra* (the Spanish edition of *The War Cry*) for distribution. When the time arrived the warders ordered the men to the great courtyard. What a crowd! Here were sheep-stealers, horse-thieves, cut-throats, many men with blood on their hands and consciences, some of the most depraved and desperate characters to be found anywhere. Hundreds of them stood around as with cornet, guitar, and salvation songs, and afterwards with red-hot exhortations we sang and spoke of the love of God for them. Oh, how the Commissioner gloried in this meeting! And, although our time soon expired, he begged the warders to allow us to go round to the condemned cells. This was impossible. But he was permitted to speak to the inmates of the cells through the gratings. In the presence of the armed guard, therefore, the Commissioner carried on a tender and helpful talk with a condemned man, and we then fell on our knees while he prayed earnestly for the salvation of the unhappy listener within.'[3]

Properties used by The Salvation Army were invariably wretched, old shops being the most commonly used Army meeting places. At Salto, in Uruguay, Railton claimed that the small shop next to a church and the police headquarters was just right, the best of both worlds. Every meeting was crammed with attentive hearers. The authorities allowed prison visits, sometimes to men condemned to death, and the police sent ex-convicts to the Army. Church dignitaries spoke out against the Army and published broadsides libelling it. It was all helpful publicity. In the 1890s a crowd in Latin America might be an incipient revolution so police permission had to be sought before open-air meetings were held. There were always policemen listening. After Germany Railton found this supervision lenient and friendly. He came to the conclusion that the Army had a future in South America and that William Booth should expand the work. He so reported. In due course from Argentine and Uruguay the work extended to Paraguay, Bolivia, Chile and Peru. The flag was not hoisted in Brazil until 1922 and one wonders, in view of Railton's knowledge of the Germans and their language, and the large German migration to the country, whether a visit from Railton at this time might not have won an earlier victory.

He was scheduled to cross the Andes but temporarily the *Conquistador* had lost his zest for the fight. It was not sickness, though he drank dubious beverages, rather than transgress the laws of hospitality, in areas where smallpox and yellow fever were endemic. His ailment was, again, psychological. William Booth was in the United States going from coast to coast with as much whistle-stop, mayoral, press and mass meeting fervour as if he had been front-runner for the Presidency. But he sent not a line to Railton, once his right-hand man.

Railton's next sortie was an attempt on Spain. He had visited the country *en route* for Morocco as a youth and later on business for the shipping firm. On his return from the Argentine he went to Marianne at Davos, in Switzerland, where she was staying on doctor's orders because of the delicate health of her daughter. She remembered, 'He rested a little while, but he was very unhappy.' In answer to her question about the future he said: 'I don't know what I'm going to do.

They will not want me back in England. I wish they would let me open Madrid.'

He thought he could get along with Catholics in Spain as he had in South America. For a time, indeed, the Spaniards thought that George Scott Railton, with his bright red guernsey marked with a large cross, was one of them, a member of some order, doubtless a fanatic, of a sort Catholicism often produces. But it soon transpired that Railton, though in piety and charity a Franciscan, and in martial mood a Jesuit, was not a Catholic at all, and when, from a small carpenter's shop in Madrid, his headquarters, he began to distribute cheap meals to the poor, assisted by Captain Venegas, a Spanish convert from the Argentine, the authorities began to be anxious about the eccentric Englishman.

When good Spanish people were converted and social service began for the unemployed, greater suspicion was aroused, but it was the character and method of Railton himself which disarmed official hostility. Here was no Protestant ranter, no drum-thumping ignoramus. He had read the lives of the saints, could speak intelligible Spanish, was not an insular, bigoted Englishman. He spoke of Spain with respect and he knew her glorious history. According to the Army's official history of this period, 'in one meeting twenty-seven persons sought salvation and 150 entered their names as desiring to become Salvationists'.[4]

This was splendid, but what about the General and the Chief of Staff? Events had shaken Railton's morale and affected his health, but it seemed that Railton was a forgotten man. In fact, both the Booths were so busy that they were relying on all leaders to get on with the job and expect the minimum of supervision. The 40th anniversary of the Army was marked by great rejoicings at the Alexandra Palace, London. William Booth had a triumphal campaign in Scandinavia; he visited Africa, Australia, India. He successfully invaded Japan, where his Army is strongly entrenched to this day. He had councils with his staff officers. His arch opponent, Professor Thomas Huxley, died and *The War Cry,* in giving him a chilly five-line obituary, managed to infer that the fact that 'he was no friend of the Army' made his prospects in after-life extremely grim. The General was sued for libel, by a publican of all people, and attacked by the Printers' Federation for alleged irregularities in wages and conditions at his printing department. All in all he and the Chief of Staff had a hectic time and both suffered bouts of exhaustion and illness. Railton had not withdrawn his damaging remarks or promised to toe the line in the future.

Bramwell had to ensure that there would be no pockets of dis-
affection. Possible trouble-spots were France and Switzerland, where
Commissioner and Mrs. Booth-Clibborn were the territorial leaders.
The *Maréchale,* William Booth's eldest daughter, Booth-Clibborn's
wife, knew Railton well and had some sympathy with his views. Booth-
Clibborn was to become absorbed in faith-healing and resign his commission to enlist under the banner of Alexander Dowie of 'Zion City'
in the United States. But in April of 1895 the Booth-Clibborns sur-
rendered to months of pressure by headquarters. The Commissioner
wrote to William Booth:

'My very dear General,
    I enclose the letter for Railton which I have sent to K. and which
I have no doubt she will accept.
    If you wire me approval I will post it signed to Katie who is at Mar-
seilles to sign and post.
                              Eternal love,
                                   (signed) Arthur.
Marvellous meetings! A paralysed officer was healed after I laid
hands on her a few days ago.'[5]

The letter to Railton which follows, coming from a man whose
Salvationism had been suspect, with good cause, does not make pleasant
reading especially when it is remembered that he sent Railton's private
letters to Bramwell after posing as Railton's friend and inviting his
confidences.

'Dear Commissioner,
    We feel we ought to write you to say how wrong and mistaken
we were both in the letter and the spirit of things we have said or
written to you during the last eight or ten months. We have confessed
it to the dear General and the Chief, who have forgiven us. We have
seen how mistaken we were and how erroneous have been the judgments
we have formed on various matters affecting International Headquarters.
    God has renewed us in perfect love and enlightened us more than
ever upon our duties. He has called us more than ever clearly to the
mission of loving our General and C.O.S. not only with the intense
affection of relationship but with a passionate devotion of loyalty and
love and daring service. Their people are our people more than ever
absolutely and forever. As Arthur wrote the General "I am yours in
love and faith and sacrifice to the end".

We were privileged to attend some wonderful meetings of the General in England and have seen more clearly than ever how the Lord has led and is leading on our beloved leaders to right decisions and grand victory ...

As for Arthur he is conscious to a terribly painful degree (though saved from regrets) how little help he has given to the universal Salvation Army all these years, and we (both of us) are determined to rush with all our energy and capacity clear through to the end of our lives to sustain the present or any future General of the Army in his efforts for the world's salvation—filled with confidence that God will lead on our leader as in the past.

May God grant to us and to you thus fully and faithfully to carry out His purposes in this world.

Your loving comrades under the blood and fire flag.

(signed) Arthur Booth-Clibborn
Catherine Booth-Clibborn[6]

In May of 1895 Bramwell Booth wrote to Railton regarding Mrs. Railton's wish to return to England. The Swiss climate was not achieving desired results for her ailing children and the doctors now suggested Margate. Bramwell Booth was not yet ready for so close a proximity to the Railton problem. He suggested the coast of Spain for the children. This would help to anchor Railton. But Mrs. Railton knew her husband was ill and she wanted the family to be reunited.

So Bramwell Booth had to raise again the question of Railton's loyalty. The Army had become a mighty chessboard with Bramwell having the General's authority to move the major pieces as he thought best. A shuffle on a world-wide scale was in the offing and this involved members of the Booth family. In the event, the changes would involve the loss of Ballington Booth, Bramwell's younger brother, and his wife, the erudite former Miss Charlesworth. Unlike other occasional defections of leading officers this one involved a tremendous public uproar. In the United States protest meetings were held in which clergy, politicians and eminent citizens joined. It was impossible to keep it out of the papers and even the Army's press in London carried various apologia. It was all a supreme test of Bramwell's ability to withstand storms, enforce discipline, and win through, as he did, in the end. His diplomatic skill can be seen in the following crucial letter to Madrid, which some have seen as an invitation for Railton to resign. The frank admission that he had read various private Railton letters, forwarded by Booth-Clibborn without Railton's permission, was less of an enormity in Victorian times than it might appear today. This communication shows Bramwell at his best. It is typical of many that he wrote to Railton:

'Mrs. Railton has recently written to me to the effect that it has now become necessary in the interests of the children's health that she should come to live in Margate and she expresses (very properly and naturally) a strong desire that such arrangements should be made for the future as would permit of your all being together again. I have already made some inquiries with reference to Margate, and have, as you probably know, suggested to Mrs. Railton that perhaps some town on the coast of Spain might be helpful to the children, but she says that the doctors advise that if they leave Davos they ought certainly to go to Margate. Your last letters have also raised the question of the wisdom of your remaining in Spain any longer and it has therefore become necessary to consider and settle upon some other appointment for you.

'Now, I must confess, that in view of all that has happened, and especially bearing in mind our conversations before you went to Madrid, I have been very much surprised and wounded by the contents of some of your letters—recent letters to officers—which have been sent in to us. We have, as you know, all along hoped that, as the time went on, you would come to feel differently about the course you took at the Queen's Hall last July. All your past long years of unceasing toil, and our affection for you, have also constrained us to put the most hopeful construction possible upon words and actions, which in anybody else could only have led to one conclusion—and even now the General is perplexed as well as grieved beyond measure by the course you have adopted, in again calling in question our actions and decisions in letters addressed to persons in no way responsible for them.

'Especially does this apply to your letter of March 10th addressed to Clibborn, and which he handed to me when he was in England last. That letter contains some very strange allusions and suggestions (not necessary to enter into now) which seem to me to be without any sufficient grounds—it appears to be written upon an assumption, which, if admitted, would be utterly destructive to our principle of union and authority to which you have in the past as strongly as anybody living given your adherence. The General thinks therefore that it is absolutely necessary that there should be some clear and definite understanding at this moment as to what your meaning and intentions really are.

'The letter to which I refer, and which I have no doubt you will remember, seems to have been written to Clibborn upon hearing from him that he was about to visit England, and it implies very definitely your intention to attack us at any time you may find it convenient upon any matter on which you may feel that our interpretation of the principles and regulations of the Army differs from your own, and the reference in it (though a slight one) to the painful incident of the Queen's Hall, seems to show that you justify that act to yourself on the ground that we, in your opinion, have changed our minds (or methods of procedure) on certain matters, you had a right therefore to attack us, and because you chose to think us no longer consistent with ourselves you were justified in denouncing us.

'Now, my dear Railton, you know as well as I do, that if every officer were to be at liberty to put his own interpretation on the decisions of Headquarters and then refuse to carry them out, in any other sense than the one which he chose to import into them, there would be forthwith an end of all confidence, and therefore, an end of all unity, and therefore an end of all real success. It is simply impossible for either you or anybody else to work happily or successfully in the concern, unless you, or they, are able to assure the General that not only do you accept his decisions, and the arrangements and regulations he lays down, but that you accept them in the sense in which he makes them and with the interpretation he puts upon them.

'The question is, are you prepared to give these assurances, and to add to them—I think I ought to say—some sort of promise that you will not in future express any views you may have opposed to us, to others either in or outside the Army. Nobody knows better than you that the General has always been open to hear any suggestions you may have to make, and to consider any difficulties which may occur to you, or anybody else, in the carrying out of his wishes—but they must be made to him in a proper way, and not in the form of an attack, and not to officers or others, who have really no option while they remain in the Army, but to carry out their instructions.

'I have written frankly and I shall pray God to guide you. You can only have a very faint idea of the pain this business has been to me— nay, to all here who know anything about it, and I do beg of you to put an end to the wretched uncertainty about and which has been so greatly increased by the letter in question—once and for all.'[7]

But for all its statesmanlike quality the position was not quite as the letter put it. Mrs. Railton heard from Launcelot, Railton's brother, who had been distressed at what he considered to be George's perse-

cution by the Army and had been to see Bramwell Booth. Afterwards
she wrote to the Chief:

'It appears to me from Launcelot Railton's report of his interview
with you, as well as from expressions in your letter of today, that you
are now reviewing all that my husband writes through some outlook
of suspicion which gives you an incorrect idea of his feelings and motives.

'Nothing was more repeatedly said by you all to me, last summer,
than that the objection was not to Railton's expressing strong objections
with regard to certain matters, but to his doing so in public at the
Queen's Hall.

'Now that ten months have passed away during which he has by
the most constant obedience under distressing conditions proved himself to be the same Railton as ever, why should his writing freely on
these matters be so objected to? He writes in exactly the same spirit
as he used to speak in those old long business hours in the evenings at
Rookwood and Hadley when I used to sit listening and so often our
precious Mrs. Booth also, till late into the nights. If you were sometimes vexed with him then, it all came right because you believed in
his motives and trusted him.'[8]

Marianne then comes to the crunch of the matter, Railton's alleged
disloyal communications with other Army officers:

'Launcelot Railton writes that it is said my husband writes to "officers"
denouncing HQ etc. I imagine Launcelot misunderstood as George
has written to no one but the family. If he writes to Commissioner
Booth-Clibborn or Mrs. Booth-Tucker on these points, he thinks that
these letters will be considered as in the family, not as to ordinary
officers.

'But as I have gone through the copies of the last ten months' correspondence, I have felt strongly that there is not only no grounds for
suspicion against him but nothing that if read by the bulk of officers
(or soldiers either) would lead them to feel that he was other than
the old Railton—strong against anything he thinks will weaken the
Army but as loyal to HQ as ever.

'My dear Chief, I am certain you feel all the desire to bring this matter right which you express, and yet when you pray that our dear
Railton "may be himself again" I do not know whether to laugh or to
cry. It is all so infinitely sad, and yet the misunderstanding seems
so great as to be laughable.

'He *is* himself, exactly! While he is he will always have strong views on certain matters and will express them to you all, just as Railton always did.

'When you say that the unity of the Salvation Army must come before personal considerations I am puzzled. Do you mean that Railton does not feel this? If the last ten months have not proved that we care for the unity of the Army I despair that we can ever do so.

'Ten months of utter silence from the General! Letter after letter from Railton unreplied to by him! Five months utter loneliness in Madrid, with only that pioneer slumming work for which he is as unfit as he is on the other hand suited for the literary work of all opportunity for which he appears to be deprived. If he was not exactly the same true soldier as ever do you think he would have borne this, and borne it as he has done, without complaint even to me?

'You all know him too well not to be able to estimate what this has been to him.

'There is only one way to end all these fears about my husband and that is for the General to take him to his heart again. My conviction is that after one hour's heart-to-heart talk between those two, who should know each other better than almost any one else in the world, every cloud would melt away, and the General realize that he had the same old Railton and could rely upon him in the future twenty-one years as in the past.'[9]

Catherine and Emma Booth, it will be remembered, were little girls in whose home Railton lived for eleven years. They looked on him as a brother and held him in the most affectionate regard all their lives. Neither they nor he would have felt that his writing to them constituted subversive activity. There is no evidence that Railton ever engaged in anything of the sort. It would have been utterly out of character: Railton always did his fighting out in the open. In writing to members of the Booth family he was exercising his old privilege.

The reply to Bramwell Booth's ultimatum came from Barcelona where Railton was prospecting and optimistic about the future of the Army in that city. He is uncompromising. Only Railton would have dared write such a letter to Bramwell Booth knowing that William Booth, who was ill at the time, would also read it. It speaks volumes for the patience and tolerance of both that they did not use the letter as good grounds to get rid of one who was causing them great distress.

'What a relief, at last, to get yours even if I have to look upon it as the ultimatum promised by my brother, and an ultimatum to which it seems to me very doubtful whether you will consider my reply satisfactory. Clear at any rate, I trust it will be.

'It is evident that all accusations of writing to officers in a way injurious to discipline are really founded upon the letter to Commissioner Booth-Clibborn, to which you especially refer, and yet you appear to know that that letter was written at his request, with the express purpose, not of furnishing any seed of division, but material for the mission of reconciliation to which he felt called!

'Again and again I have denied and repudiated, as I do now again, any ideas of denouncing you, or denouncing any of your plans in the Queen's Hall, or anywhere else. I fully recognize the right of HQ to change plans to any extent it may desire, and the obligation of every officer to follow such changes with perfect attention, and carry them out loyally, no matter whether he thinks them wise or no. But I do not recognize anybody's right to abandon any principle of righteousness for expediency's sake, and I say that on all such questions, the meaning of HQ has been expressed not only in spirit but in print, and above all, in flesh and blood, far too often and too plainly to make any question of interpretation possible. And I may say that it is utterly impossible for anyone to follow orders diametrically opposed to each other coming professedly from the same HQ. I was astonished to find on looking into *Orders and Regulations for Soldiers,* with what completeness and detail the question of money, savings, barrack building, etc. had been gone into, so that the taking of interest out of our funds for sums lent, is not only in the most flagrant opposition to the letter and spirit of the divine law, but proves the person who even contemplates anything of the kind, as not being, as the regulation puts it, "a true soldier".

'There is a question as to whether I have done denouncing enough. Satisfied with your knowing the full depth of my abhorrence of such things, and with having no personal connection with, or responsibility for them, I have thought it enough to go straight on labouring, as I contend you and the General, and HQ generally have laboured, to raise up the "true soldier" who understands the meaning of your songs, your consecrations, your vows, and who will never I trust share in any of these abominations. If, in too much silence, I have been unfaithful to God with you, may I be pardoned as I have refrained because of my love for you and my confidence that all these wretched things would perish with the onward march of the Army and especially with the advance of that perfect devotion which you are always labour-

ing to affect. It has seemed to me *not* advisable in the general interest hitherto to express to anybody not immediately personally concerned, my views as above, so that the promise you call for is, not to
express these views to yourselves—to the members of the family, or to
officers such as Colonel Bremner who sent me, as I contend, proposals
to join in opposing all your teaching and practice on some vital question.

'To give any such pledge would be absurd, because what I have
said all along is in print, not only with my name, but yours attached,
and all my action is one endeavour to raise up the true soldiers described in the *Orders and Regulations* who understand too well the
identity of their interests with those of God and the Army to accept
any such theories as the Bank now sets up.

'On the other hand, looking to the latest English *War Cry* proposal,
or declaration, beginning "Are you aware?"—the circle of persons
to whom I may any day be forced to say in the plainest terms possible
"that is directly contrary to all you have hitherto learned, taught and
promised"—is likely so to increase, that I can see no prospect of avoiding an increase of conflict in this direction.

'Therefore, dear Chief, if there has been any uncertainty about me,
by all means let it end at once—the sooner the better. I can never do
otherwise than go straight on with the teachings and the life we have,
as I supposed, been so perfectly agreed about all these years, and if
to resent any attack on these teachings, and that life of crucifixion is
to be said to denounce or attack HQ because such attacks emanate
alas! from the same building, I cannot help it. My life is one, and by
God's grace I believe always will be.

'Knowing how you and the General are likely to be tormented by
questions as to my possible course let me say at once that I have never
contemplated, and do not contemplate in the event of exclusion from
the Army, the spending of my life in any other way than the service
of the Army. I have often rejoiced sometimes at the thought of the
freedom, especially for getting money for it, which would arise from
being outside. It is providential that yours should reach me away from
Madrid. It will I hope be possible for me to prepare the mind of
Venegas, who has not an inkling of any such possibility, that my expulsion shall not upset him. A simple statement that I have been ex-
cluded for denouncing these new financial schemes will at least prevent
misrepresentation, and the accompanying assurance that I am de-
voting myself to raising candidates and funds for the Army especially
for foreign service will, I should hope, prevent any serious shock or
discouragement.

K

'To get a home in Margate will be I fancy far cheaper now than in July, and better for the children too, and I assure you that I will spare no possible effort to lessen the damage and pain which may perhaps be inevitable in any case and I shall still hope for the happy day when all these detestable things having reached their proper and natural termination by the Army's elevation to the fulness of its own professions —there will be no longer any desire at HQ to be free from my denunciations of them.

'From here post home is one day shorter than Madrid and the journey can be done, as far as I can see, in 48 hours. Not having received the month's grant as I expected I have not one cent left. Venegas only has enough to carry him through the present week.

'For everyone's sake, I beg you, hurry up!'[10]

But should one dismiss such a man, or insist that he resign however inconvenient or potentially dangerous he might be? Much of the New Testament, the blood of martyrs, the shining holiness of countless Christians is enshrined in Railton's letter. Admittedly, it is a matter of interpretation, and in that respect Bramwell Booth was no dunce. From a valid Christian point of view his actions and patience with Railton withstand the closest scrutiny. Commissioner Carleton, who was his chief aide in the formation of the Salvation Army Assurance Society, was a man of high principle and spiritual sensitivity. Christianity is pragmatic, too. Those who write its credo or thunder its ideals from pulpits make more of it, but on-the-ground, average Christians must go out into a practical world, and find a workable formula, in which to enshrine as much as they can of Christ's teaching, for there's always more than they can grasp. It's the trying that's wonderful, and no one can say that Bramwell Booth was not a trier. It must have been exasperating for him to be accused of organizing dubious schemes for fund-raising—for despite Railton's semantics that is what Railton was doing. The holiness of Bramwell Booth's life is unquestionable.

But what could he do with Railton, his friend and guide for many years, who had the unconscious arrogance of all saints? It wasn't that Commissioners were too much for Bramwell Booth. He toppled more than one of those august personages from their pinnacles when the occasion called for it. If Railton's interpretation of Army rules was correct much of its work would have to shut down and its expansion not be possible. His abhorrence for Bramwell's 'commercial' innovations, which were to provide the Army with the sinews of war all over the world, had prevented him from examining them closely. He took his stand on theoretic grounds. If he had made it his business to find out what the newly-enlisted Army of agents in the Salvation Army Assurance Society were doing he would have found that they were not only collecting premiums, but counselling needy people, praying with them, persuading them to attend Salvation Army meetings at which some of them were converted. Their work was to a large degree social service, and still is. Often it is much more than this.

As for 'dirty pieces of paper' and the money it brought, most of it went back to policy holders, the law saw to that. The small percentage of profit kept by the Army was used to further the Army's work. But Railton could not see it this way. He maintained his own interpretation to the end.

But should the church destroy those who ask the 'impossible' of Christians? Surely it is better not to apply the torch to the faggots? Just let the 'heretic' live. Those rarefied heights of holiness that he attains make him conspicuous to his contemporaries and to those who come after. Such men there have always been. Many have greatly advanced the Church on earth. Some have fostered schism, or died prematurely and horribly. They were mad or blessed, depending on which way you look at it. But the Church is the richer for them.

During mid-summer, 1895, Railton was recalled to London and nothing more was said of a pledge that he would always be silent and accept the element of 'commercialism' inherent in some of the Army's operations. A letter from Marianne probably tipped the scales towards the exceptional degree of tolerance for the Army of those days. Mrs. Railton's letters are of high calibre; this one is highly persuasive:

'It seems to me that you all misunderstand and that you do so because of the intercourse being by letters instead of by heart-to-heart talk as in the old days to which you refer. If it were a question of his not having confidence in you I might be able to influence him, but as to these fears of his that certain matters are injuring The Salvation Army my knowledge and judgments are little and I do not expect to carry weight with him.

'I do not think you estimate fully the effects of his dwelling alone upon these fears of his, instead of being able to talk it all out with you, as in the old days.

'I implore you to let personal intercourse with you and the General take the place of letters. I do so feeling it is the only way by which this difficulty can be overcome. This I desire more fervently than I can possibly express to you.'[11]

Later Marianne expressed her gratitude for the prompt and generous response to this letter. Bramwell Booth was never one to dawdle when his mind was made up. A house was taken and furnished and by the end of June Railton was settled there with Marianne and the three children—if that word can be used of him; of course he never settled anywhere. Literary work was waiting for him and he was asked to report to IHQ as soon as possible.

Bramwell Booth had decided to keep the erring giant under his eye, providing him with an office near his own and intending to call him in for frequent consultation. He had been challenged to do something of the sort by a phrase in Railton's last letter from Spain; coming from anyone else it would have been a gross impertinence. Railton wrote it and survived:

'It seems to me clear that Spain must be efficiently represented or go to the wall amidst all the present circumstances, and that there's no hope whatever of providing the necessary impressions by letter. It can easily be arranged for somebody to see me in Paris or further north if my appearance in London is still considered so undesirable. But the more I reflect upon it the more does that appear an impossible state of things. Your long and careful letter is one great demonstration of the mountain of difficulties you encounter in procuring my re-newed recognition like any other officer. I have wished to avoid in any way making your task harder: but what can be the use when the division is so complete already that my coming can be harmful! The latest Salvation Army assurance agent, who can produce a good list of officers and soldiers induced to insure their lives, will be welcome there whilst I with all the interests of a big country in my care must keep off! And you with all your kindness do not see the accursed pass these things have already brought you to!

'I have still left you plenty of time to stop me here if a letter is on the way or it otherwise seems desirable; but failing this I will see if anything awaits me in Paris and if not will hurry to see you. The great thing is to provide immediately for the future of Madrid. I could return there perfectly well for some months if necessary.'[12]

His office at International Headquarters remained unoccupied for some time. He had a habit of collapsing as soon as he neared London.

Marianne met him at Dover and wrote that his illness was caused by 'worry and grief'. Railton wrote to Bramwell Booth:

'Dr. Miller came yesterday and endorsed the local man's opinion, with a more gloomy prognostication. Certainly he talks of getting it all away but conditional on a fortnight or more in bed and then a month with the least possible exposure for work.'

The 1920 sketch of his life put it thus:

'The Commissioner arrived in a serious condition of health, needing most careful and tender nursing. He lay ill for months from sciatica, and when he did rise from his bed, it was only to exchange it for an invalid chair. Though his sufferings were intense, the enforced inaction, no doubt, saved his overwrought brain from serious and permanent harm, and he gradually improved in the reviving air for which Margate is so famous.'[13]

But Railton's brain was never in danger. William Booth's long silence caused him pain and the impasse into which his principles had brought him worried him day and night. There was no question of his changing his principles: everyone else must change theirs. Men who live with their heads in heaven, their minds and hearts possessed with spiritual passions, are apt to be alone in this matter-of-fact world, and at forty-six years of age Railton felt himself completely isolated and abandoned.

19

Through a Glass Darkly

SLOWLY RAILTON recovered much of his physical strength and was called in to advise and assist Bramwell. For him this was good medicine. He began to write for the papers, drafted some of the appeals for money, and was asked to sit in at conferences. Overseas visits were arranged: Railton became a kind of 'Inspector-General' of the forces all over the world. But now a new burden fell on Bramwell. Railton's reports found fault with people and tactics in a way that seemed unreasonable. It was the irrepressible perfectionist at it again: Salvation Army officers were giving lectures; children were being used in performances of plays, music-items and drills. These Railton denounced as departures from the Army's direct soul-saving purpose. Some of Railton's points Bramwell heeded and sought to correct. The rest became a cross he had to bear.

During this phase of his life Railton was officially chided for his excess of zeal in acknowledging members of all churches as his brothers. That same Railton who abhorred anything 'non-Army' in meetings was himself willing to worship with men of all denominations and attend Roman Catholic services in his uniform. Though William Booth was tolerant in such matters, having said, 'I am too busy fighting God's enemies to have time to quarrel with His friends', he had to protest. Railton was offending weaker, less ecumenically minded Salvationists.

In Italy Railton fraternized with the Catholics and his policy won him some freedom to win converts. As in Spain he found it necessary not to make too much of a parade of The Salvation Army.

Though little is known of his inner thoughts on Catholicism he was tolerant of it, militant Protestant though he was, and this at a time when the shock waves of the controversies of the Oxford Movement, the re-establishment of the Catholic Hierarchy, and the pronouncement of Papal Infallibility were still reverberating over 19th century Britain.

It was reported to William Booth that Railton had been to mass, in the full panoply of a Commissioner of The Salvation Army. It was only too true. His tunic was open to display his red guernsey with a large

Lutheran embroidered cross upon it. At the door he thanked the priest whose charge to his flock had 'blessed his soul'. The priest invited the stranger into the sacristy where they knelt together and prayed for the salvation of the world. Afterwards they became friends and often wrote to each other. It was all very wonderful—but at least fifty years before its time.

It was much too much for some of the weaker brethren in the Army of that day. Later, when it was reported that Railton had wept while watching a group of young Buddhists at their prayers in Tokyo, there was further misunderstanding. Railton was not at all equivocal about his beliefs but his global vision warmed his heart towards all men of good faith. He was a citizen of the world. But the majority of Salvationists had not Railton's opportunities to acquire catholicity. Bramwell Booth tactfully passed on William Booth's requests that Railton refrain from giving distress to those who could not understand. One can imagine William Booth grumbling: as we are too busy to quarrel with our friends Railton should be too busy to hear mass, or weep with Buddhists.

At least one Italian Salvationist understood Railton. Captain Virginio Paglieri, who accompanied Railton on an Italian campaign in 1897, wrote:

'The Commissioner held a series of meetings in the Waldensian Valleys, then in Cuneo, Turin, Florence and Leghorn. He passed through the country as a life-giving flame ... He was helped in his study of the Italian language by his knowledge of French and Spanish, but during the eight or ten weeks of his stay he became able to express himself with ease, and to hold conversations with the people in an astonishing manner.

'I watched his work, first among those who were largely Protestant, and then among the Catholics. Never did I meet any soldier of the Cross who understood so perfectly how to adapt himself to such opposite conceptions of a religious life. One almost wondered whether he were the same person. Not only his ideals, his language, the illustrations he used, were entirely different, but his very life in all its manifestations seemed to undergo a radical transformation. Yet there was nothing forced. All appeared as natural as though, by virtue of a law similar to that which controls the colouring of birds and animals in Arctic lands, he were irresistibly affected by his environment.

'Though I had myself been a Catholic, and then influenced at one time of my life by strict Protestant principles, I could not understand a course of action as enlightened as his ...

'Looking back I see that the Commissioner was inspired by the missionary spirit in a far wider sense than is generally understood. He was a missionary—not for a province, a land, or a people—he was a missionary for the world. All men and all peoples could have found in him a champion of their race. The salvation of souls was his passion. For this reason it was that his religious anti-formalism went to such extremes that he tolerated and even shared all forms of worship in order to reach his aim—the salvation of the individual soul. Such largeness of outlook and breath of spiritual greatness lifts him, in my judgment, far above ordinary men. Railton was one by himself!'[1]

This comradeship with all mankind showed itself when Railton had to deal with troubled or delinquent officers on Bramwell's behalf. Railton's solitary missions were often secret. Bramwell Booth on occasions asked him to journey in mufti; his uniform would attract attention. In many trouble spots in Europe and even farther afield Railton became Bramwell Booth's 'secret agent'.

His long absences disrupted his family life. Marianne never ceased trying to understand the apostolic fervour that drove him on, as restless as Wesley. But the children found that in absences of six months or more his image faded. The boys began to blame The Salvation Army for the loss of their father's company. His daughter, Esther, who once underwent a serious operation during her father's absence abroad not unnaturally began to dislike the movement that deprived her of her father.

Of course he wrote to them—many of his letters survive—but always it is plain that for the time being his heart is where he is. In France he wrote thus:

'But I confess that I have only a quarter-eye for scenery anywhere, and, above all, in this country where I can only see thirty-six millions of the noblest men and women perishing almost without as much as a look of pity from anybody outside their own frontier. Has France committed the unpardonable sin against mankind, because a hundred years ago it cast aside, with supreme ability, the pretence to religion which so many nations still tolerate where they know that religion itself no longer exists? Why have so many of us elsewhere come to look upon France as though it were impossible for Jesus ever to reign there?'

'The French,' he said, 'are as indifferent to religion as the English, but at least they will listen or walk away without violence: they do not spit or throw bricks. They can even be got to pay for the privilege of hearing us, and would come by the millions if the Army would allow that bad republican habit of "contradiction and discussion".' Down at Die, near the Alps, he took part in meetings twice packed with conscripts of the French army, some of whom knelt at the penitentform while one, whose 'pay was less than a penny a day', paid a shilling for a Bible. Most of the towns down there, said Railton 'were divided into perfectly hostile halves, as in some towns in the North of Ireland'. Railton being Railton however: 'We were received by the Catholics, as a rule, with kindness and I was glad to hear an officer say that one visit to a Catholic church had ensured a full audience where up to that time there had been only a contemptuous enemy.'

Railton found that the French peasants lived on a diet as spartan as his own. In winter, for the poorest Salvationists, there was black coffee and bread, with occasionally a little sheep's milk. On this a few faithful soldiers of *Armée du Salut* would march for miles, hold open-air services in deep snow 'though hemmed in on every side by religious ice'. A girl Lieutenant, 'being suddenly swept away by fever', when asked for a last message replied, 'Tell them I am hidden in the heart of God.'

Now in charge of France were Commissioner and Mrs. Booth-Hellberg—Mrs. Booth-Hellberg being that daughter of William Booth who had survived the broken romance some years before. Indication of the closeness of Railton's relationships with William Booth's temperamental and gifted children is the fact that Lucy now asked Railton to intercede for her with Catherine, the formidable elder sister, Mrs. Commissioner Booth-Clibborn, who with her husband had farewelled from France for the command of The Netherlands and Belgium. The anxious Lucy wrote:

'I am sad about the *Maréchale*. I wrote a long letter the other day, in fact a month ago, but I have had no reply and I cannot bear to feel there is a cloud between our two sister hearts. Can't you help me? Can't you explain our position and make her believe there is no personal feeling against her? Do try every way, Commissioner. Keep the place we have gained in your heart. Won't you? Come and help us again bye and bye.

'I leave for Paris on the 26th and we start in April a six-week campaign in Paris. I wish you could look in on us. You have heard of our victory in obtaining a hall next door to Le Moulin Rouge! Is it not splendid!'

Railton's correspondence with Amsterdam was to bring down upon him William Booth's displeasure. He did not like interference from anyone in family matters.

Railton's objections to lectures in Salvation Army meetings were so persistent that they wore down Bramwell Booth, and regulation was issued against them. However, this proved to be of little value for people just gave 'talks' on announced subjects, a means, it was thought, of attracting more hearers. The regulation was not sustained. Railton was asked by an unwitting secretary of William Booth's 'to provide suggestions for material for the Founder's lecture in Berlin'. This was another battle Railton lost; it is doubtful if he should have fought it though his motive was good. Lectures meant a chairman, who might talk for a long time and, possibly, be a bore. It also imposed a formality on the occasion which is uncharacteristic of Salvationist proceedings. Worst of all it used up time so that there was little left for a prayer meeting and the quest for converts. In Railton's opinion every Salvation Army gathering should end with a prayer meeting.

Unexpectedly some of the most rigorous opposition to the Army had been encountered in that peaceful citadel of religious liberty, Switzerland. The Swiss saw the error of their ways and realized that General Booth had defeated them. Railton attended the first public meeting in Geneva at which the speaker was William Booth. The General had asked for the famed Hall of the Reformation which one would have thought as suitable for him as he for it. But he was told that it could not be let to him unless he would doff his uniform. This would probably have meant the old man appearing naked, for it is unlikely that he possessed mufti. In any case, he would have been as willing to cut off his right arm as to accede to such a request.

But William Booth's meeting, in St. Peter's Casino, was crowded; he had a favourable press, and the Chief of Police of the Canton told Railton that he might consider 'all exceptional laws against the Army as being dead'. At Neuchâtel the populace were not aware of this new liberal policy. Stones were thrown through the windows of the National Temple where William Booth was to preach. Various influential ladies and gentlemen rushed for the doors in fear for their safety. Above the noise of breaking glass and the shouts of the mob outside Railton heard William Booth bellow:

'If a few stones can make you so uncomfortable now, what will you feel when you hear the archangel's trumpet calling you before the bar of God?'[2]

Afterwards, when the timorous had calmed down and the police had dispersed the stone-throwers, William Booth was allowed to speak and the people said there had not been such preaching there for centuries. One of the stones which had cruel edges Railton kept as a memento and it was used by the family as a paperweight.

Meanwhile Railton saw his children occasionally and wrote to them often. He learned that twelve-year-old David Railton attended Mrs. Bramwell Booth's Christmas party for the children of staff officers. 'I liked the General best,' he said, 'and wasn't it terrific? He told us, the General I mean, that the Chief of Staff, Bramwell, when he was a boy, never told him a lie!'

David remembered gratefully that his father had a caution and reserve about religion. 'He would never rub it in,' he said. But sadly the son remembered that his father 'never played games in his life'. David and Nat were enthusiasts. Later they both came to realize that there was a toughness in this prayerful man that made their rugby heroes milk-sops by comparison. 'His kind of religion,' wrote David, 'is a thing you have to be frightfully hardy for. You cannot be soft; you have to be a man for his job.'

Gentle with everyone, he could never be the heavy-handed tyranical parent his times required him to be. He walked six miles with David talking about the prospects of a university. Oxford, to which his sons aspired, though reformed since 'the bad old days', was still a bastion of clericalism. He did not want his boys to be theological pundits, or have them influenced by the modernism of Benjamin Jowett and of the notorious *Essays and Reviews*. But Railton lost, as must all men of prayer sometimes. It is, perhaps, God's protection against undue pride.

In the long term, all was well. The time came when Railton visited a new ordinand of the Church of England, the Reverend David Railton, at two o'clock in the morning, at Liverpool, having just arrived home from a campaign abroad. His 'prodigal son', though he had left the fold of Salvationism, was beginning his Anglican ministry in the Liverpool slums.

David, as a Anglican minister, not unnaturally regretted his father's early-Victorian evangelicalism, his insistence on Salvation Army songs and music only in the home, his fear of 'the world'. He thought that Railton's uniform, his inability to relax, his insistence on 'full Salvation Army guard' at all times, cut him off from educated men who never appreciated his worth. 'Because he was always in full uniform, and always in the full war spirit, he would not give other men time to express their side of things.'

There was a scholarly clergyman nearby whom David wanted his father to meet. He knew that the men had much in common, culturally, but he asked his father not to go in uniform. Otherwise his father would 'preach' at the parson and there would be no chance of accord between them. But Railton rarely had time to do this and the boy was grieved, as he was about so much on the very straight and narrow way his father trod. He took his father to task concerning his assumption, in David's opinion the general Salvationist assumption, that if a man did not talk religion he was not religious. 'My father would say, "He is not very spiritual", just because the man was not on fire outside,' is how David put it.

Nathaniel and David tried to convince their father that the Church of England had reformed itself. 'We agreed,' wrote David, 'that when the Army began everything was dead, but look now. If a man wants "a free and easy" he can have it with us.' But Railton doubted the judgment of his sons and from his very occasional periods in England he could hardly learn much about the situation himself. David loved his father and put him on a pedestal as a saint, but it is impossible to deny the truth of his charge, 'Like all zealots he found it hard to admit he was wrong.'

Of course the boys knew that he had differences of opinion with the General and the Chief of Staff of the Army, and with the recklessness and cruelty of the young they sometimes used this as a weapon in argument with their father. 'But,' wrote David, 'he was so loyal to the Army that when we began to probe he would refuse to be drawn and fall into silence. One of us would say, "Ah, you're on the right track now! Answer, Father, answer!" But he never let the Army down.'

The boys did not have things all their way. The first time David received permission to go to an Anglican service was to hear Archbishop Frederick Temple. They pressed their father to go with them but this his crowded Salvation Army programme did not allow. When he arrived back at Margate he asked the boys, 'How did the Archbishop do? What did he say?' But boys are not good hearers of sermons and they could not remember a word of the great man's discourse.

'The only thing we could remember,' David admitted, 'was that he had upset his glass of water. Father roared with laughter at this. "Why, any Salvation Army lassie could do better than that!" he said.'

Of course the children found contradictions in their father's make-up. Esther, his daughter, claims that he was an Imperialist in the political, Lord Rosebery, sense. This cannot be, but he was certainly not 'a Little Englander'. It is a paradox that The Salvation Army's foremost ambassador of peace never defined his position as regards war. He seems not to have considered the Quaker viewpoint, a deprivation created perhaps by his utter dedication to The Salvation Army. Pacifism as such was not much heard of before 1914, and Railton died in 1913. He thought that the Great War, which he foresaw, would be short, and he regarded the Kaiser as a man of peace. But one cannot know Christ as Railton knew Him and understand the kingdoms of this world. Railton was a child politically. The completely non party-political role of The Salvation Army, which he helped to create, inhibited expression of views on peace and war, and Salvationist detachment can create political naïvety in some. But it is more than doubtful whether a follower of that super-Imperialist Joseph Chamberlain would have been *persona grata* with the Boers during their war, or given travel facilities as Railton was in Russia, China, Japan, Germany and many other lands.

For a man who was born in the first half of the 19th century, though only just, and whose philosophy of religion was more akin to that of the austere evangelicalism of the 1830s, Railton was certainly not typical. David, who learned of the rigid Sabbatarians—Pusey, Faber, Wilberforce and the rest—chided his father on the enormous amount of Sunday travelling he did. He would journey by train here, there and everywhere on the Sabbath. David even came to the conclusion that his very out-of-the-ordinary father had opted for the Continental Sunday.

And while he sought to save the Swiss, the French, the Germans his children lost him. To some extent even his beloved Marianne became a stranger. All of them loved him: they knew he was genuine; but they could not keep abreast on the narrow road he trod. David hints at this separation:

'Nat and I once had a snowball fight with him in Switzerland. He went up the mountain with tremendous easy strides. For a moment, I thought, he is not a Salvationist, and there at the top the snow was deep and he vanquished us. Then he sat down and we were together. But we would not see him like that again for years.'[3]

It is unlikely that they ever saw him again 'like that'. Most of the time, in that admixture of heaven and earth which made up Railton's life, his own only saw him 'through a glass darkly'.

20

'The Greatest Religious Show on Earth'

RAILTON'S FIRST distant expedition as Travelling Commissioner was to the West Indies, in 1899. He was given a public farewell at the 70th birthday celebrations of William Booth, held at the Exeter Hall, where he paid tribute to the old man, who was away on an Australasian campaign. Bramwell Booth announced Railton's assignment but there was no personal word for Railton from the General. William Booth had other problems on his mind. In Australia he was upholding his son Bramwell, the Chief of Staff, at the risk of losing Herbert, another son, who was the Australian Commander. He did not interfere when the clash between the two brothers caused Herbert to withdraw from the Army.

The General had good reasons for insisting on close formation of the Army ranks. Another son, Ballington, and his wife had seceded from the Army in the United States to form The Volunteers of America. Yet the Army was expanding rapidly. Administrative burdens lay heavily on Bramwell, and William Booth made sure that he received all possible support. The General's sorrows at this time, including very poor health, made him consider that the time might not be far off when the Last Post would be sounded over his remains. He was ever lonely without his beloved Catherine; so wretched through indigestion, sea-sickness, the effects of hot climate and exhaustion, that to 'lay down his sword' seemed to him sometimes the promise of a happy release. This was why he sent no olive branch to the rebel Railton, who sailed alone to the West Indies, steerage, and carrying one small bag.

Railton's campaign there received scant attention. If a holy man may sulk, then Railton was sulking. There was some sort of ban on his writings yet there was much for him to frown on in those copies of *The War Cry* that reached him in Guiana, Barbados and Jamaica, weeks after publication. In further celebration of the General's 70th birthday, and 'the close of the century', a great exhibition was being staged by the Army at the Royal Agricultural Hall, Islington. It was a phase in Army development which led to another serious collision with authority by Railton.

The years of coolness or hostility, actual persecution and misunderstanding suffered by Salvationists had given way to official approval and public acceptance. The perils of mob-violence were exchanged for the snares of adulation and flattery. While Railton was discovering dire poverty in the West Indies, where emaciated workers were getting 6d. a day if they were lucky, the Lord Mayor gave a dinner for the Army at Mansion House, for which the guest list read like a page from Debrett.

The socialite, Margot Tennant, who became the wife of Britain's wartime Prime Minister, H. H. Asquith, undertook slum visitation after a chat and a prayer with William Booth in a railway compartment.

'Swells', Railton termed this upper strata of the population, though his disapproving attitude was not conditioned by political considerations. His objection was always one and the same: the Army had more urgent tasks before it than the cultivation of 'the idle rich'. He did not understand the reasons for the public relations exercises, the 'lion hunting' of Bramwell Booth and his advisers. They had to have public interest before they could raise urgently needed funds. Yet they probably overdid the operation. The Army in Britain has never repeated on such a scale the cultivation of 'the notabilities of the Literary, Religious and Scientific and Political world' as the 1899 Exhibition publicity put it, or been quite as avid for press approval.

William Booth, who arrived home from Australia in time to conduct evangelistic campaigns in halls adjacent to the Royal Agricultural Hall, never regarded exhibitions and other public relations forays as more than unavoidable adjuncts to the main task. It is reasonable to speculate that he was taken aback by the scope of his 70th birthday celebrations.

The War Cry headlined the Exhibition, THE GREATEST RELIGIOUS SHOW ON EARTH, a claim worthy of the yet unborn Hollywood film colony. The *Daily Chronicle* conceded that it was 'A WONDERFUL SHOW' and one might have looked for the hand of Bertram Mills, the great showman behind it; he had been a Salvation Army bandsman at Marylebone. However, this time he was guiltless. There was the Bird Fanciers' Paradise, 2,000 specimens, from the peacock to the humming bird. Railton might well have asked what *they* had to do with saving souls. In fact they advertised the Hadleigh Farm Colony where 'down-and-outs' were being rehabilitated. Queen Victoria bought some of the poultry and Cecil Rhodes spent £150 on prize birds to improve the strain at his cottage at Cape Town, though, alas, as he was soon to be beseiged at Kimberley, he probably had no opportunity to assess the result of his investment.

Railton, who might well be termed 'the father of Salvation Army journalism', had a shock when he gazed at a picture of some of Mr. Rhodes's hens in transit at Waterloo Station, and pictured boldly in *The War Cry,* that paper dedicated to the glory of God and the salvation of mankind. Side-shows, and other attractions at the Exhibition, he read, included the Converted Rat Eater, the Fantastic Cinematograph, the Saved Zulus' Kraal, Joe the Turk's umbrella from America and Miss Florence Worth, the converted actress. Employees of the Army's 'Lights in Darkest England' Match Factory, whence phossy jaw and sweated labour had been banished, were present in force, as well as the information that the Duchess of Sunderland and other notable ladies allowed only Salvation Army matches to be used within their mansions. It was suggested that Salvation Army pigs 'behaved themselves with remarkable sagacity' and that 'Noble Authors, Sceptics, and Men of Renown have expressed their Unadulterated Appreciation'.

The national newspapers were enthusiastic even if at a loss for the right phrase in this unfamiliar territory. *The Daily Telegraph,* for example, as quoted by *The War Cry* reported that 'Mr. Bramwell Booth has organized an elaborate programme of entertainments, musical and knee-drill concerts, for the fortnight the exhibition will be open'. If Salvationists could understand this at all it was a hideous mix-up of the sacred and profane, and just what Railton had been campaigning against for ten years past.

But the austere *Times,* which had been less than friendly to the Army in former days, and had provided Huxley and others with their platform to attack William Booth, gave a fair and friendly report, mentioning 'the serious purposes underlying the whole, which finds expression in services conducted by General Booth and his officers'. *The Manchester Guardian* introduced a mildly sour note when it complained that it was hardly necessary in these days to state that the Army's bands were playing all round the world in city, town and hamlet. By this time thousands of ardent Salvation Army bandsmen were rousing hard-working Victorians from their Sunday morning lie-in.

Any who might see sour grapes in Railton's disapproval of all this, and quote his earlier commendation of sensationalism in religion, should remember that Railton approved of almost anything 'for the gospel's sake'. It was 'social nonsense', and 'commercial sidelines' which

L

he regarded as wasteful and harmful diversionary tactics. He cannot have been pleased to read, just at this time while he was in the West Indies, that the Army in America had itself launched an Assurance Society with fifty agents as a beginning. He was glad that this venture did not long survive.

In British Guiana, Barbados and Jamaica, Railton had every opportunity to get his priorities right—soul-saving meetings out-doors and in, crowds of hymn-singing islanders, so knowledgeable of the Bible that the familiarity became a barrier. There were prayers and hymn-singing hour after hour. This needed to be controlled for 'emotionalist revivalism' was not wanted, said people on the spot. Railton could maintain reasonable calm. The Army was newly-established in Barbados but he found three centres thriving with penitents kneeling in open-air meetings. The islands were in the economic doldrums. Newly-won converts soon became true soldiers. 'No reports will ever tell a hundredth part of the ministrations of these comrades to the destitute,' Railton wrote. This was the real Army mission; much more in line than building 'Japanese chop-shops' and 'Eskimo igloos' at that time-consuming 'Greatest Show on Earth' from which he had been banished.

In Jamaica the work was recovering from a serious reverse arising out of an article published in London, in *All the World*.[1] This reflected on the islanders' morals, blithely listing their illegitimacy rate of 75%, their addiction to 'liquid damnation' rum, which was absurdly cheap, particularly because there was difficulty in selling the island's sugar crop. But the worst curse of all, said the non-smoking Salvation Army writer, was 'the curse of tobacco'. Cigars could be bought for fifteen shillings per thousand and eight-year-old boys smoked them in the streets. 'Twist', ropes of wild tobacco, were 3d. a yard.

Though Disraeli had not protested when Railton attacked him in *The Christian Mission Magazine* for adjourning the House of Commons on Derby Day, or the Prince of Wales indicated any disapproval when *The War Cry* censured his gambling proclivities, the Jamaicans reacted violently against this slur on their morals. They did not read *All the World*—most of them could not read at all—but a local citizen had the article summarized in the Jamaican *Evening Express* and gossip did the rest. The army citadel was besieged, the officer under whose name the offending article had appeared being inside, with his wife and five small children. One of the children was injured and the youngest died, though that was coincidental. Police reinforcements were needed to restore order and the unfortunate offending officer was recalled to London. It was a reverse from which the Army did not fully recover until a decade or more had passed. For four years, indeed, operations ceased entirely.

Railton's visit hastened the process of recovery. The brass band which went down to welcome him to Kingston was not allowed to play at the wharf, the reason being that it might confuse the crew bringing the vessel to land. It was not a very tuneful band. A church was packed that same night and Railton stood for two hours in the open-air service at the Market on the following Saturday. Jamaicans knelt in the dust to confess their sins.

There were sixty corps on the island but some consisted of only a few Salvationists. Two lassie officers would be sent to an area to 'dig themselves in'. They would have no home, no money, no food, no certain prospects of success. If they could find some sort of hut, with backless benches, lit with paraffin, and a cheap lodging for themselves they would then drum up a congregation. Hardly any of the islanders had a clock or watch so that it was no use announcing the time of a meeting. 'Drumming' must be taken literally. If the girl officers attracted a congregation they made a collection, and, in time, they would receive gifts in kind. Their needs were minimal: there was no question of a regular salary of a stipulated amount. If they won their battle they might eat; if they lost they might go hungry. That was the Army way. Railton approved of it and lived by it.

Railton found the drums trying to his nerves, like 'a continuous thump-thump from a steam-hammer mingled with the passing of a long luggage train'. Yet such efforts had already won a large force which trekked to Kingston from the outlying parts of the island for a congress led by Railton. The West Indian officers needed no other provision for a week's stay than benches on which to sleep and the promise of tea and bread. Some had marched for nearly a week from their outlying commands.

It was all very wonderful—the real Army: persecuted, too poor to buy flags, wearing a motley collection of uniform after the style of Garibaldi and his Thousand. It gave Railton nostalgic memories of the force raised up in the pioneer Christian Mission days.

His exile in the West Indies ended with a second visit to British Guiana. There a large crowd gathered to hear him in the open air. An officer from Jamaica who accompanied him wrote:

'When he came out to Demerara we had had no rain for about six months, and we had everything fixed for a great demonstration. We prayed that God would bring the spiritual as well as the natural rain. He asked the Lord to send it. There were about five thousand people in the open air round the trees, and we stood on a large lorry, and while we were having our meeting the long-desired rain came down in torrents. We had to go and seek shelter under the van.'[2]

But a more deadly rain was soon to fall in South Africa, a rain of lethal bullets from the guns of Boer sharp-shooters.

21

'A Great Worry to Me'

RAILTON HAD hardly arrived home at Margate before Bramwell Booth asked him to leave for South Africa. He sailed on New Year's Eve 1899. His task was to negotiate with General Buller, Lord Roberts, Sir Alfred Milner and other military and political figures to win facilities for the opening of Salvation Army red shield work among the troops, not only in camps and bases but up with the front lines. The Boer War was in some ways the last of the 'gentleman's wars', and Railton was also expected to get over to the other side to seek freedom to establish red shield work among the Boers.

Railton's mission was largely successful, but he met with many frustrations. Neither the military nor the politicians wanted civilian interlopers. It took months of patient toil before The Salvation Army won its foothold. In addition to Railton's hard work, success came largely through the determination of Staff-Captain Mary Murray, a remarkable officer sent out by Bramwell Booth. The daughter of Sir John Murray, KCB, she was used to arguing with eminent military men. Her father was one. There was great need for Salvationist effort in hospitals, rest camps and occupied towns. Despite Foster's Education Act many British soldiers could not write a letter and Salvation Army lassies wrote thousands of epistles to wives and sweethearts in the course of the war. Salvationists were among the besieged at Mafeking and Kimberley and about a third of the Army's corps in the war-stricken areas of the Cape Colony had to close. Some Army halls had been commandeered by the military and Salvation Army officers in the Transvaal had been 'requisitioned' by the Boers, as *All the World* put it. All able-bodied men who could ride and shoot in the Transvaal or the Free State were called up.

William Booth had issued an eve-of-war manifesto in which he repeated that The Salvation Army was the friend of all and would seek to serve the men, women and children on both sides. Railton was to find that this was easier said than done. He had some sympathy with the Boers: he could never be unthinkingly partisan. 'Oom Paul' Kruger, the President, was a great man for the Bible, which he quoted at the Governor General in Cape Town, much to that worthy's indignation. Sir Alfred Milner, the great Proconsul, had no time for such irrelevancies. Commissioner George A. Kilbey, the Salvation Army leader in South Africa, saw the war as a clear-cut Britain-in-the-right affair, which was not Railton's view of it. They had differing views on tactics. Kilbey did not share Railton's wish to devote men and resources to work among Africans.

Soon after General French relieved Kimberley, Railton was given a pass from Cape Town to visit the town, where a rescue home for young women was in charge of Mrs. Captain Cass, the widow of an officer killed in the Mashona rising (a street in Salisbury, Rhodesia, is named after him). The Corps at Kimberley had continued to hold meetings all through the siege. During bombardments Ensign Kiddle, the officer-in-charge, had conducted services at the mines to which the people fled for safety. A Salvationist was killed on the hall roof when a shell from a Boer 'Long Tom' gun struck the building.

In the sense it would be known in the Great War, or had been known in the Crimea, there was no front. During 'Black Week', when many guns and men had been lost to the British, the Boers inflicted terrible casualties by their ability to appear as from nowhere and then vanish. At Dundee, where The Salvation Army had a soldiers' home, the Boers appeared suddenly in the mist. The British General in command was killed with many other officers and men. Women and children spectators cheered whichever side they favoured.

A Colonel Martin, with Lord Roberts, French, Ian Hamilton, Kitchener and others whom Railton approached without success, wanted no civilians cluttering up the veld:

'I regret that I am unable to see my way to granting you a pass. I above all can quite appreciate your feeling of being here when a man's work is at the front. But I should say that in any case the bulk of your work would be with the sick, of whom the majority are here.'

Yet the military would have done well to listen when Railton suggested additional help at the front line with medical services and troop welfare. Nearly two-thirds of British losses in the war were due to disease. One correspondent wrote that this was due to 'criminal neglect of the most simple laws of sanitation'.

Many of the dead had drunk water from rivers into which slain cattle and the bodies of their comrades had fallen. There was a plague of flies; dysentery and typhoid were endemic.

Salvationists set up their soldiers' homes in or near to camps; they visited the hospitals, conducted meetings among the men, some of whom were Salvationists, others who became Salvationists through their ministrations. They learned that a Salvation Army officer called up by the Boers had been killed at the Modder River, where four Salvationists in the Black Watch had also been killed.

Salvationists were fighting Salvationists, the first time this had happened. William Booth wrote to Salvationists in *The War Cry*:

'I caution you against being carried away by those passions that are, I am sorry to say, being inspired by the war.

'Don't suppose that you are under any obligation to have an opinion as to the righteousness or otherwise of the war. It is doubtful whether you possess the necessary knowledge ... to be able to do so.

'Whatever views you may entertain on the matter you must never forget that war is, by the consent of all good people who have any knowledge of it, a horrible calamity.

'Remember that the success of British arms, however desirable it may appear to you, must and will involve great suffering, wounds and death on the side of the Boers, because it is "the loser that pays". Even if you have a feeling that these people are in any sense in the wrong, or are your enemies, in this matter you are bound to love them, to pray for them, and do your utmost to promote their well-being.'[1]

Booth's words gladdened Railton's heart. It was in that spirit that he toiled in Africa, often with small success, pained by long silences from home and anxious about the progress of The Salvation Army. His heart was torn by waste of war; the whole land was ravaged by it. For Britain 450,000 men were needed, of whom 22,000 died. The Boer death toll was 24,000 of whom a large number were women and children who died of sickness. The Chancellor of the Exchequer in London said the war would cost £10,000,000. In fact, it cost more than £200,000,000. In the land of gold and diamonds the finances of The Salvation Army collapsed and Bramwell Booth had to send frequent grants to shore up the national work as well as find men, women, material and money for the red shield services.

Funds were not easily come by though Rudyard Kipling helped with his *Absent-Minded Beggar* (to Sir Arthur Sullivan's music):

> ... Will you kindly drop a shilling in my
> little tambourine
> For a gentleman in khaki ordered South?

Everyone sang it and many paid. Tons of 'comforts' and numerous volunteer relief agencies and workers arrived in South Africa, some from Canada, Australia, New Zealand and even the United States. Some of the money came to The Salvation Army and Bramwell Booth used it well. When the war was over a Salvationist could look both Boer and Briton in the face and not be ashamed.

But this second South African journey had seriously adverse results for Railton. He wanted to paint the map not red, but yellow, red and blue, the colours of the Salvation Army flag. If Britain was to 'rule the waves', and the world, it must be government by proxy, for God. One of his favourite hymns was Frederick Faber's 'Hark, hark, my soul'. Railton adapted it for use in The Salvation Army with a chorus which went:

> Salvation Army, Army of God,
> Onward to conquer the world with
> Fire and Blood.

The Fire was the Holy Ghost, as at Pentecost, and the Blood was of Christ, slain at Calvary. No need then, for Boer to slay Briton, Briton to slay Boer, the blood of both to stain the veld red in a senseless conflict which, as time would show, would settle nothing. Christ had died for all men; all men were the children of God; Boer, Briton, Kaffir, Zulu, Cape coloured, and the Chinese coolies, whose indentured labour in the Rand mines, in terrible conditions, was soon to blow up into a scandal which would gravely harm Milner's reputation.

Railton was still out of favour in London, unrepentant, complaining to the Booths who were bearing a well-nigh intolerable load, striving to find officer replacements, raising funds—about £20,000 for famine relief in India—leading meetings, conferences and congresses at home and abroad. In newly-opened Japan there were riots and assaults upon Salvationists when the Japanese *War Cry* attacked those who organized prostitution, and advised the girls of their rights under Japanese law.

Yet amid all this Railton wrote to William Booth:

'I am trying to get Kilbey to veto any of the displays and entertainments with children as actors or participants which have here so largely reduced you to a cheap music-hall affair. All the appliances for the whole thing are pushed by Trade Headquarters, and yet I question whether there ever goes up to heaven a more heartfelt "God bless the General" than from a crowd of parents who have seen with tear-bejewelled eyes the performance of "those little darlings" who for weeks previously have been drilling Sunday and weekday for "the show". You do not hear people say "my children like to go to the Army Sunday-school", but, "they like to go to your drills"!

'Why am I to be thought sour-spirited because no statistics as to the number of thousands who appreciate these shows lessens my perception of the fact that your first great purpose as to them is being utterly frustrated? Here, and in every other instance, it is no question of a "want of perfection" but of a systematic destruction of the lines and theory and practice which you have not only laid down in print in *Orders and Regulations* and *Darkest England,* but keep reiterating every month in the most positive ways ...

'The Commissioner simply asks me where I am going to find the white man who will give himself up to the natives, to be actually amongst them in the way I consider indispensable. I believe we can get hundreds of such men and women out of Scandinavia and plenty of support for them too.'

Bramwell replied to Railton's broadside:

'Your letter of August 6th strikes me as being about the most feeble thing that ever came from your pen ...

'If we are going to say that the principle of rewards is to be eliminated from human affairs we shall have to consider the abandonment of punishment. There is no more inconsistency in offering a book to a child as a reward for punctuality, good conduct, attendance at the meetings of The Salvation Army, and persevering in keeping its commands, than there is in offering a crown of glory to those who are faithful to the end! Both are an appeal to self-interest—if you like to call it such.

'I abominate, as much as you do, the idea of any efforts which do not aim at the salvation and holiness of old and young. But it is no use supposing that everybody is going to look at everything from your point of view—or from mine. What is the meaning of being all things to all men, if I may by any means save some? He evidently gives up the idea of saving the lot: but he is resolved to do his best for all if by any means he may save a few.

'However, Kilbey writes in better spirits. In the name of all that is sacred I prohibit you from saying anything to him that is likely to upset his confidence in what we have settled. So far I do not think you have done him any harm—but do be careful! Remember that you will come away and leave him there.

'Now as to what you are to do. We are disposed to your staying on a little longer. The British authorities seem to think that the thing is coming to an end in the Transvaal: and if so we should like you to be in Johannesburg before you leave, as you will probably see things in a different way from anybody else. I have a great notion that for some time to come these places will be satan's seat, and we ought to do something.

'As to the money we are quite prepared, as I told you before you left, to help Kilbey in the inevitable. It was no great effort to us to send that £500 as soon as we had seen his careful statements.

'The last I heard of Mrs. R. and Esther was decidedly good. The ms. you have sent is very good. Although we have to shorten it a little, I want you to go on and finish it. You do not say anything about your health.

'Dowdle is gone! The General is not very well. He will work at such a pace. Don't exaggerate passing difficulties. Our great problem is to keep Jesus Christ to the front, that is to the mass. Our one hope is attack—and there <u>are many</u> forms of it.

'I love you, but you are a great worry to me at times!

Your affectionate,
W.B.B.'

Dowdle was the first Army Commissioner to be 'promoted to Glory' as Salvationists say. A romantic figure, converted railway guard and violinist, he was nine years Railton's senior. As Secretary to the Mission it had been Railton's task to guide him through his novitiate as a missioner. Dowdle was one of the great-hearts. A foundation soldier of The Salvation Army, devout, devoted to the Booths, uncritical of the tactics developed by the Army. He could not be any 'rebel's' friend; yet Railton loved him and his passing was severance of a link with pioneer days.

With most people in Britain, Bramwell Booth believed that the war would soon be all over and during 1900 *The War Cry* more than once gave expression to this view. Lord Roberts left Africa in 1900 for a hero's welcome, the Garter and an earldom. He thought that only mopping-up operations remained. Kitchener found that 'the new war' was to be worse than the first: guerilla war which lasted until May 1902.

Before leaving South Africa for Mombasa, in East Africa, Railton went to Mafeking, whence most civilians had been ejected by Lieut-Colonel Baden-Powell just as the Boers arrived from the north. As Salvation Army officers do not regard themselves as civilians, the two in charge at that northern town were very indignant at being forced to leave. Perhaps it was for the best. The hall and quarters were damaged by the bombardment and the people suffered many privations.

Railton stayed a few days in the relieved town. He led a meeting crowded with railway men and soldiers, so many that some had to sit on the floor. One soldier, who had been 'mafficking', kicked a hole through the drum. But doubtless it was all good clean fun. The Commandant ordered the band not to play after dark because the music interfered with the work of the sentries, still in the trenches at nights. No one could object to that. Two lassie officers, given passes to return, showed courage worthy of a Slessor or Nightingale. The town was full of troops, some of them drinking too much; there were no windows left in their quarters which had been damaged by shellfire. Indeed, some wit had fixed a notice to the door, 'Open gently, or the house will fall down.' It was infested with nocturnal ants. The girls were shocked to find them all over the bed in their thousands. For a fire, to make themselves morning tea, after a sleepless night, they burned one of the boxes in their luggage. Railton was sure that the future of the Army was safe in the hands of such lassies as Captain Quarterman and Lieutenant Cullinan.

One of the last letters Railton wrote to the General from Africa was inspired by such devotion, and he was optimistic about the future elsewhere:

'My realization of the choice character of the people who carry on this work, and their splendid self-denial, intensifies the violence of my detestation of the methods which produce so devilish a result as I consider it to be.

'It is no question of "want of perfection" but of systematized destruction of all you have fought to accomplish accompanied by the perpetual "better than ever" chorus!

'You allow yourself, dear General, to be tormented by the spectre of a sour-spirited correspondent, incapable of looking favourably on what is not done just as he would desire, or under his own wing. That correspondent does not exist. In spite of everything, my days, so far as they are passed in the war, are happy ones. Trained as I have so long been to an almost solitary life, it is less and less unpleasant, and having no resource but patiently to wait for the opportunity of useful service that is bound to come ...

> I can subscribe myself still,
> Your happy Lieutenant,
> Railton.'

In December he arrived home, having sailed from Mombasa on the German s.s. *Kaiser* and having finished his journey overland from Naples. He had been away nearly a year, and made straightway for home. A letter from William Booth followed him:

> 'My dear Railton,
> I half expected to see you yesterday, but could quite understand your eagerness to get to Margate ... I am at Ramsgate on Saturday and Sunday, all being well, where I shall hope to see you if there is nothing in the way of your coming ...
> 'I hope the effort made on behalf of Esther is turning out well. Give my love to Mrs. Railton and family, and believe me,
> Your affectionate General,
> William Booth.'

Here the grand old man was going more than half-way towards reconciliation with Railton, who did support him during the following week-end at Ramsgate, speaking about Africa in the meetings to an immense audience. In 1900 everyone wanted to hear about South Africa. People noted that, unusual though it was, Railton looked well and was browned by the African sun.

22

With Arrogance and Folly

ONE OF Railton's first tasks after his arrival in England was to complete *Our War in South Africa*. Bramwell Booth had a well-developed nose for publicity and was aware of world interest in the war. The Boer capital, Pretoria, had been taken and President Kruger was an exile in Europe, hoping to interest the Dutch, the Germans, and other Continental powers in the Boer cause. He had said before he sailed, 'The real struggle has begun' and, in truth, Kitchener found the Boer without a city, a fugitive on the veld, was more formidable than before.

Sir Henry Campbell-Bannerman, the Liberal leader in Britain, condemned 'the methods of barbarism' which Kitchener used, such as the burning of farms—the American General Sherman's 'scorched-earth policy' made necessary, Kitchener said, by the ease with which Boer commandos reoccupied the farms or were nourished by them. To house the women and children rendered homeless by his policy Kitchener created what have since been called 'concentration camps'. Events made the ill-omened words appropriate. The British Army could not cope with a problem of such magnitude. Sanitation, food-supplies, accommodation and medical supervision were all inadequate. Epidemics killed many women and children. The resultant scandal gravely harmed the Government and brought condemnation from observer nations.

One watcher, who was not heard or considered during all this, was the African. There was a 'gentleman's agreement' that neither Boer nor Briton should involve him in the war. In the few instances where this dispensation was not observed the benighted African was singled out for exceptionally ferocious treatment as if he, and not his masters, had been the offender.

Railton prayed with the Africans, walked with them, rode with them in their railway carriages. There was little or no colour-bar as such, among the Victorians. When Milner talked of race supremacy, as he often did, he was talking of the British and their Empire: it was a supremacy of technology and culture. To a Boer supremacy was the right of those who read the Bible, believed in the Bible, and lived according to it. That of course, was a matter of interpretation but the Boer was sure he understood it well. The conglomeration of whites, the more or less Godless Uitlanders from many lands, who flocked to the gold and diamond mines, who were drunken and dissippated, who clamoured for the vote at Johannesburg and made war inevitable, were to President Kruger's way of thinking worse than the black Africans.

Historians have said that the Great Trek, Boer intransigence, and the war itself, were in part caused by a more tolerant attitude towards the African shown by white immigrants, especially the British. But Railton did not see this greater tolerance. He wrote sadly, after visiting the Zulu kraals, and watching the dispossessed Zulu in the towns:

'They are still at liberty to marry as many wives as they can get, and the getting of wives used to depend upon the payment to the bride's family of so many cattle. Since rinderpest has made the cattle scarce, a money equivalent has to be produced; and in order to get the cattle, or the money, the young man will come into some town and engage in employment in which he can quickly earn money. The wages paid are often scandalously small; but the Zulu can live so cheaply that he manages in a few months to save up the amount he came to earn. Then he returns to his kraal or village entirely unchanged for the better, and generally a little for the worse.'

He went on to tell of their enforced and ludicrous 'European dress' a 'pretty sort of red knickerbocker suit made of print, with red facings'. Or the Zulu got hold of a pair of ragged trousers and a discarded red tunic, khaki now being worn by the regular army. He may pull a sort of rickshaw, in Durban or elsewhere, and Railton described what may happen:

'Of late years there has been introduced a new industry, by the adoption in South Africa of the Japanese jinrikisha—a sort of low gig or big perambulator with a folding cover which, when up, makes the vehicle something like a Hansom cab. A Zulu takes the place of the horse between the shafts, and so well is the riding-weight balanced, that the man has sometimes difficulty to keep the shafts down ... When the road is uphill it may be anything but a joke to the Zulu, and yet the whites will in such cases often beat or kick them savagely if they slacken their pace at all. Remember that all South African society has been so pervaded with the cruel sort of feeling towards anybody not white, that few people are even struck by the appearance of any ill-treatment of them. Ladies, who are considered models of all that is Christian and gentle, will treat a Zulu servant as they would never think of treating a lap-dog.'

Railton visited Zulus who were maimed in the war, dying of tuberculosis, resentful of the British, sick from hunger, bored by lack of fighting, wary of the white man's God, suspicious of The Salvation Army and filled with nostalgic longing for the old witchdoctors.

The Salvationists were not alone, of course, in attempting to Christianize the Zulus but Railton saw the Army accepting this formidable challenge and making notable advances. Those who, in the old days, would have been warriors exempt from manual labour could be seen making bricks and building Salvation Army halls, setting up water tanks, fixing the corrugated iron roofs. The Army gave simple lessons in the three 'Rs' for which adults and children would walk ten miles or more. Major J. Allister Smith,[1] who became a Commissioner, is said to have introduced the plough to the Zulus and his wife was one of the first to teach their women needlework. Some converts became Salvation Army officers and one, Major Mbambo Matunjwa, was awarded the Army's highest distinction, the Order of the Founder.

Non-Zulu Africans, of various tribes, were somewhat contemptuously referred to as 'kaffirs' by the whites although the African disliked the term which was used by the Arabs as referring to all non-Mohammedans. Railton worked among this group in Cape Colony and Natal, and took a pessimistic view of them. 'We are largely ministering to a thoroughly drunken and despairing people.' Yet, about East London, King Williamstown and Cape Town kaffirs were won to the Army. Railton went with local Salvationists to a beer sit-in as it might be called today. The brewing and selling of the beverage was prohibited by law but the Army officers visiting the locations could usually smell out when such communal drinking was taking place. If the men were drunk the Army might be allowed in; a meeting would be held and sometimes a drunken African would 'seek salvation'. He might hardly know what he was doing but that was of less importance than the fact that the officers got his name and would visit him when he was sober. Many converts were won in this way.

Railton concluded *Our War in South Africa* with a scorching indictment of those who exploited the African, making a plea for humane treatment and understanding that was decades before its time:

'The natives, after their hard toil in the mines, simply squat or lie down on the floor of these rooms, or of the square, which is practically their prison for the six months of their contract time.

'In either case, the plan adopted is to let the native, whilst working for his "Christian" employers, live exactly as if he were away in his heathen village; but without anything like so good a home as he has there. No wonder that the general effect upon them is to lower rather than to raise them. Drink is their only comfort ... If any company or town were to try and help the people of a location to get better homes they would succeed rapidly, because these natives are eager to imitate everything European. But then, if so helped, they would very quickly be able to do all the work that white workmen now do; and, as scarcely any white people wish for this result, the natives are left, so to speak, in the mud.'

African locations then were often insanitary and contagious death traps, 'the excuse made for banishing the African half-a-mile or more from the town'. Railton none the less believed that white officers would be found to live on these locations with the Africans. About this he had one of his numerous differences of opinions with Commissioner Kilbey who believed that Railton's idea was impracticable and that white officers willing to throw in their lot with the African to that extent would never be found. Yet Railton wrote, and Bramwell Booth approved his words for publication:

'Consistently with all the rest of their system, the people in the towns generally object to any white people going to live in locations for the good of the people's souls. But the Army, having succeeded in some cases, will, no doubt, eventually succeed everywhere in overcoming this obstruction, as fast as it can raise officers willing to go and live amongst the people.'

Railton's identification of himself with the African, in the closing pages of his book, and his appeal to officers to give themselves to the African continent is un-Victorian. The old-style paternal, patronizing note is absent. It is a testament of a citizen of the world, a 'prince among internationalists' indeed,[2] as Commissioner Catherine Bramwell-Booth described him in her life of her father. Railton's own conception of what The Salvation Army must do for the African is enshrined in his book.

At Tramelan, in Switzerland, in 1901, he wrote his epilogue:

'Should the Dutch and English be blended into one community, very large numbers of the former who have hitherto been too far from us, may become our soldiers and officers. Even should the two races hold apart, the Army may be developed, as in Switzerland and Finland, with Dutch and English corps stirring each other up to holy rivalry, to the glory of God and the help of millions of people.

'But the great question of the Army's future must needs to be connected with that of the native races, about which it is even harder to predict anything. As already pointed out, the treatment of the black and coloured races has hitherto been almost equally bad, whatever the nationality of their white masters.'

Then came a postscript, at which Bramwell Booth must have looked closely:

'I have been sadly disappointed as to the effect of the war, in England and in Europe. I had hoped that it would promote a real interest in the peoples of that vast country where, for another year since I left it, war has been continued in one way or another. But the treatment of the whole matter by the Christian and unchristian Press of the world has been the most lamentable demonstration of white ignorance, arrogance and folly that could have been possible.

'Amidst all the tons of paper occupied by denunciations of English or Boers, of war, or of individuals supposed to be specially responsible for this or that act of war, how many square inches of paper have been used anywhere to plead the interest of the peoples of Africa?'

23

'St. George' in France

THE FIRST years of the new century were difficult for Bramwell Booth. The death of the Queen coincided with economic slump, social distress and industrial unrest in Britain. This constituted a challenge to The Salvation Army, whose General, in his book *In Darkest England and the Way Out,* had written brave words about a better land.

The new king's entente cordiale with France exacerbated German suspicions of Britain and created international tensions which added to Bramwell's burdens. The war dragged on in South Africa and the London *Express* charged that W. T. Stead's attacks on Kitchener's management, *Revelations of a British Staff Officer,* were based on confidential reports sent to Bramwell Booth by Salvation Army officers. These were working with both Boer and Briton but the charge was none the less absurd. Bramwell Booth loathed war and it would have fared ill with any Salvation Army officer who had used his position to retail military gossip.

Cholera joined famine in India and numbers of officers lost their lives. There was plague in Hong Kong, and Mont Pêlé erupted on Martinique in one of the greatest natural catastrophes known to man. But worse was a series of breakdowns of officers who could not keep up the killing pace demanded of them by the onward march of the Army.

Toward the end of 1901 Railton was sent to take charge of France, where Booth-Hellberg, a devout, hardworking commander had broken down. The invaluable Commissioners Elijah Cadman and George A. Pollard became ill, as did key men Colonels John Lawley and David C. Lamb, the latter, noted for imperturbability, of a 'nervous ailment'. This, as yet, obscure malady was to show itself again and again as the stress and strain of the war told on leading officers. *The War Cry* of the first decade of the century carried alarmingly long lists of officers 'promoted to Glory' and many paragraphs concerning sick officers. Like Kruger's war, Bramwell Booth's war was costly. Yet he seemed to have the strength of ten, working morning and night and every day. The old General was sombre, and moody, tending for the while to feel his years, very concerned with his bodily ailments. Bramwell was the soul of optimism, finding time to write a number of cheerful little books for young people, conducting the first series of what are now regular and valuable Salvation Army institutions—young people's councils. He also founded the corps cadet brigades and gave youth its place in the Army, greatly improving the Movement's long-term prospects.

Before he went to France Railton completed one of his most significant books, *Commissioner Dowdle, The Saved Railway Guard*. He must have felt a pang when he wrote of the departed warrior: 'To the General it was always a great pleasure to have the Commissioner with him in his meetings and especially was this the case when unusual difficulties of any kind arose ... This fellowship between the two was without any exact parallel.'[1]

Railton was not capable of such complete subordination. Plain John Dowdle was content to let his General do the thinking: he, Dowdle, would help with the praying. It was Railton's misfortune that he felt himself to be the custodian of that strict evangelical tradition handed down by Catherine Booth: he had a mind of his own. In such a role it was inevitable that he should sometimes be an inconvenient friend.

Railton went to France as a trouble-shooter. Booth-Hellberg's breakdown had been aggravated by a small-scale mutiny. Some officers and soldiers were lost and some interference came from Amsterdam, where Booth-Clibborn and the *Maréchale* were the territorial leaders. Lucy, it will be remembered, was the child who had passed on to Railton her smallpox virus. She now wrote from Paris:

'Dear Commissioner,

I am so pleased to know the General has appointed you to France. We had a council here yesterday to honour our going and your coming and they were all so pleased it was you. They feel already they love you and that you love them and understand their great difficulties. I feel so too. The Commissioner spoke of you with the truest love and esteem and I told them how good you were to me when I was a little girl and how some things you said and did then left their mark upon my heart for all my afterlife. May God bless you, dear Commissioner, in your new task and give you all the faith and courage this country demands.

'Yes, believing still for victory in dear France—

Lucy Booth-Hellberg.'

William Booth wrote to Railton in terms that suggested some rapprochement between his first Lieutenant and himself:

'I am sorry to hear that you have been unable as yet to report things all settled your way.

'You must, dear Railton, go softly or we shall have such troubles as will effectually prevent the blessed results we are both hoping for in Paris.

'I am sorry under the circumstances you wrote so peremptorily to Amsterdam, though it is quite true that such a letter to people in a right state of mind would be the proper thing and bring a straightforward answer.

'But then you know where we are. We don't want the thing to boil over just now—indeed I don't want it to boil over at all.

'It's again on the cards that I go to the States and if we can get the campaign over "in peace" it is most desirable! So if you don't get an answer to your liking leave the thing alone. *Let it slumber!*

'Now with regard to Paris you must keep in peace and make other folk do the same. You can so shape things that the entire scare will soon be forgotten.

'Perhaps the two officers who wrote those formidable letters may be beyond your power to pacify. If so, very well. But we must have no further losses if we can prevent it.

'You know that you went to Paris with the full understanding that the present social efforts should be maintained or not interfered with unless on my *full consent. I shall hold you to that. You will not fail me. I am full of confidence that you will not.*

'If things are not exactly to your idea of perfection—don't whisper your discontent. You have people hanging round you who will with or without intention twist what you say to unpleasant account.

'Don't commit yourself to any one individual. Take up an independent position. Represent me.

'Go softly; the world wasn't made in a day. Beware of sensational people. The Army leans in that direction. Have a care of the tendency. Have faith in God, in the Army, in the General and in your comrades. Remember that it is a great deal easier to make holes in people's hearts and confidence than it is to heal them.

'Relying on your understanding what I wish and your determination to carry it through to the best of your ability—indeed whether or no.'

One man who soon learned the practical details of a Railtonian oversight was his Chief Secretary, Albin Peyron, who found that when he accompanied his chief he had to travel third-class on the railways and suffer make-shift meals, or no meals at all, with due stoicism. His wife remembered Railton:

'Few officers did as much for France ... The French are not so much impressed by great things; they see these to perfection in the Catholic Church. They look at the man. What impresses them is the individual, pure and holy, with the light of God shining from his eyes. Some say that the French are light—that from some aspects they are not a deep-thinking nation. But in religion they ask for the deepest depths of seriousness, even for the tragedy. The Commissioner was always simple and reverent, and there was never any empty show or "tomfoolery" about him. I have known him ever since 1886. He has been of great help to me personally ... I consider that he did more to revive the spirit of prayer, during his stay in France, than anyone else.'[2]

In *Une Victorieuse Blanche Peyron,* by Raoul Gout, we are told that Railton was in Switzerland, in Chaux-de-Fonds, when he received the message that he was appointed the Commissioner for France. Gout quotes Railton:

'That night I went on a round in the cafes with the *Cri de Guerre.* A man poured a large glass of liqueur on my clothes. For the first time in my life I made a close contact with that liquid; I took it as a baptism for my work in France.'

Then he quotes Blanche Peyron:

'He was like John the Baptist, his hair shaping a crown round his head, bald at the top; his forehead high; beard gray; black sparkling eyes under thick eyebrows. His tunic open showing a coarse red jersey with an enormous yellow cross—madman of divine love, like the Little Poor Man of Assisi. "These enormous headquarters of the Army, I detest them," he said. Of money he spoke with contempt: "Winning souls is my salary."

'Railton was no friend of the social work: "All this 'social' does not save." He kept repeating: "France is on the brink of a precipice. Neither soup nor coffee are sufficient to save her." To him the work of popular evangelization was much more important than all the social activities, and on this point he is in full accord with William Booth, who has said: "You don't cleanse a man by washing his shirt". A town crier for the King of kings, Railton understood the war only as aggressive, rapid and victorious preaching in the street. "The gospel needs to be shouted out in the streets with the energy and obstinacy of tradesmen and hawkers, and they who oppose us."

'Born to discover, and to play the role of an awakener, Railton was no governor or administrator. He could say with Joubert; "I am good at sowing, but not at building and establishing." Being unpredictable he constantly alarmed his co-workers with unexpected ideas.'

The work of The Salvation Army showed new life as Railton led revival campaigns in towns and villages. Halls filled without difficulty. Bands were formed and established. Soldiers and recruits were sworn in. The cadres of corps cadets became 'nurseries' for candidates and brought into the Army 'elements above the average of intelligence, ability and spiritual life'. Railton's influence was not confined to the Army; here and there the churches too experienced a time of expansion.

Though Blanche Peyron was not in agreement with Railton on several points about conducting the war, she saw in this 'St. George'—her private name for him—a tremendous force against the power of formalism and spiritual death. Railton 'created an atmosphere of savage bravery'. He promised his officers blows and blame, all the disgrace and privation, but at the same time communicated to them a pride in the disgrace and privation. He stirred up the spirit of sacrifice. He 'possessed the virtue of poverty which is the sister and constant companion of apostolic power'. In fact, the force of The Salvation Army is 'not its military discipline, nor its organization or its social service, not the absolute character of its doctrine, not the abilities of its superior officers, not the eloquence of its apologists, nor the skill of its advertising—it is a joyful acceptance of a life in poverty, giving all to the benefit of the lost'. It was from 'St. George' that Blanche Peyron learned this lesson.

Despite his General's misgivings Railton weathered the storm in France. He heeded the warning not to hinder the social work. In its austere evangelicalism Salvationism in France still bears Railton's impress. He was never much of a man for the office and as the Territorial Commander he visited the cafes and back streets:

'I had a splendid Saturday afternoon in the cafes with the *En Avant*. The card-players stopped playing, and all listened with Breton reverence whilst we sang. With that and Sunday afternoon at the lowest cafe we raised the congregation in the hall considerably.'

He went to help striking coal miners at St. Etienne and was asked savagely, why God, if there were a God, allowed the potato crop to fail at a time of such great distress. It was the sort of question he could answer. The *concierge* heard him singing in his bath, a habit he had. She was so attracted by the liveliness of one of the songs that she asked him could she have the words. Not only so but he taught her to sing them and the woman joined his *Salutistes*. He went with a party of about twelve to the French Grand Prix, run on a Sunday as always. He announced that *En Avant* would carry a valuable tip for the race. It might have saved a lot of money for any gamblers who heeded it: *'Whenever you are tempted to gamble, hurry, and put twenty kilo-metres between you and the races.'*

They sold many hundreds of their papers and the gambling fratern-ity were not pleased. But in the main the crowd, estimated at 100,000, was friendly. The worst that happened was that a drunk, in immacu-late clothes, with top hat and cane, went before their march singing:

> The Salvation Army,
> To Charenton-ton-ton.

Charenton was the largest lunatic asylum in Paris.

But within a year the Army papers in London announced that Rail-ton was again extremely ill, and he came home to Margate for rest and treatment. Bramwell wrote to him:

'My dear Railton,

I feel very concerned about your health. I hear from Paris a really grave report of your weakness. What I am afraid of is another break-down such as you had years ago. You know what a long affair it was.

'Now we have a scheme for France, but before we make any move I want your view and the sooner therefore I see you the better, on that ground. I shall wait to hear how you are. I agree entirely with you that the soonest possible is the proper time to settle the future.

'As to yourself—I take it that just you must pick up a bit. But I do feel that if in the Providence of God it should be practicable, and agreeable to you, or at least not disagreeable, to be near IHQ for a time it would be a help and strength to me. I do not attach great importance to your fear of the bureaucratic zone. It is more in appearance than in reality, I assure you . . .

'The news from the States is still very contradictory. But it is not very new. Dowie is still silent. Herbert won't touch him. Catherine and Clibborn are evidently held very lightly and the Restoral affair hangs fire. Dowie is now saying that the great smash prior to the Millenium period is at hand and out of it is to arise some kind of a preparatory theocracy of which he is to be head! He is buying land for Zion at Jerusalem! Meantime he says he will never publish any accounts!

'The people in W. Africa have sent home a man to be trained—a likely fellow. They will send more if we wish—at their own expense.

'The Boer Generals said we were the only people who had done anything for the spiritual concern of their armies. They spoke most warmly. If we had men there is great chance in the Transvaal.

'Love to Mrs. R. and the children. I hope Esther keeps better.

Affectionately,

W.B.B.'

It was at this time, October 1902, that the old General in a seventy-minute speech at the Exeter Hall, in the Strand, made his oft-quoted remark about his children. He was soon to leave for the States where the rebel sextette—Herbert, Ballington, their wives and his daughter Catherine with her husband, the former Commissioner Booth-Clibborn, were causing anxiety for the future of the Army. Said the seventy-three-year-old parent:

'The Salvation Army does not belong to the Booth family. It belongs to The Salvation Army. So long as the Booth family are good Salvationists, and worthy of commands, they shall have them, but only if they are. I am not the General of the family. I am the General of The Salvation Army.'[3]

Each sentence was halted by prolonged and intense applause, highly significant in the Salvationist climate of that time. Railton was not present but he would have read the *War Cry* report with interest. Herbert Booth, particularly, had given people the impression that he did regard the Army as a Booth family concern. Apart from this none of the Booths had ever given cause for fear that they were not good Salvationists except, Railton might have said, Ballington and his wife, when love of the United States compelled them to put American domicile before obedience to farewell orders. Having suffered similarly in

America, and numerous other commands, and having always obeyed even though with a little argument, Railton was yet again confirmed in his love and respect for William Booth who thus proclaimed and maintained, at such cost to himself, this basic tenet of Salvationism.

Soon afterwards Railton's farewell from France was announced. He had been home to Margate but returned in November, partially recovered, to make preliminary arrangements for Bramwell Booth's temporary solution for the administration and manpower problems on the Continent: France, Italy and Belgium 'belonging as they do to the Latin race' and 'having close relationship to each other by other affinities' were joined in one command under a new Commissioner, Ulysse Cosandey. Railton had been consulted on this whilst in England but it seems that he had his doubts. Bramwell Booth wrote:

'I was very sorry to hear from Kitching this morning that before you left London last night, you had spoken to him with such a measure of anxiety about the combination of the three countries after all. Now this is hardly fair. You and I discussed it *ad nauseum*; we agreed it was not a perfect arrangement, but that having regard to all the circumstances of the hour, it was *the best we could do*. We told Cosandey; we told Peyron; the General confirmed the arrangement by cable, and it has to go forward. Now you must not let your anxiety, which I fully sympathize with (and, indeed, which I to a certain measure share), lead you to take a depressing view of the situation, or to let a word escape you to any mortal man over there! What I am most anxious about at this moment is that you should put a smiling face on to the new arrangement, especially as regards Cosandey.

'He will have enough to do without having the impression in the mind of the smallest Lieutenant that you have any misgivings about him. It seems to me pre-eminently a case in which we must "hope all things", and I rely upon you to help me through on this line.'

But Railton's misgivings were justified. Railton, who knew his Continent better perhaps than anyone at Headquarters at that time, felt that though Latins may have something in common they also had wide divergencies. In the event Bramwell Booth's attempt was not a success.

Discreetly Railton came away silently for a brief period of civilized home life. France was his last territorial command. Marianne, David, Nathaniel and Esther rejoiced at the prodigal's return. In his last letter to Marianne from Paris, he wrote:

'They considered that they owed my presence in France to you, and that you, left alone with the children—one of them sick, and even seemingly dying at times—had made a sacrifice for France's sake which they would never forget.

'There really was no gammon about it. We had had a very warm, jolly meeting, and it really helped me to receive in a far heartier way than ever before the tender inquiries for Esther and you all which have always been rained upon me wherever I go.'

24

Alone at the 'White Man's Grave'

AS RAILTON was now working at Headquarters Bramwell Booth insisted that he should have reasonable accommodation on those weekdays when he was not able to get home to Margate. He wrote for the Army papers, attended conferences and represented the General at the installation of leading officers sometimes abroad. There the Salvationism was sometimes extremely austere:

'In Brussels I saw, I reckon, the champion mother of the Army. Think of a shelter Ensign's wife with a baby down with bronchitis, and four other children, when all the place is being pulled down and rebuilt around her. The children were in perfect order and the little sufferer getting better. These are by far the poorest officers in the Army, I should think, and yet so bright and earnest.'

In Holland the Commissioner took 'a very big drum' and banged it all over Groningen, writing confidently to Marianne: 'We shall have a buster tonight when we are all united in the warmer corps of the two.'

He had been billed as 'the great man of God' but,

'Alas: for the great man of God. He cannot get in more folk than the little congregations they usually have. Last night it was only thirty, but I had a good time and led one woman, with a baby in her arms, to the Penitent-form.'

He informed Marianne that on twenty-two shillings a week the ironworkers had children better dressed than 'the average of your sons'. By contrast William Booth's campaign in the United States, about which he had felt so much apprehension, had begun with a tumultuous welcome, and increasing fervour from coast to coast and back again. He lunched with President Roosevelt at the White House and opened Congress in prayer. That same year Emma his daughter, known as the Consul, and wife of Booth-Tucker in charge of the work in the United States, lost her life in a railroad accident in Iowa. The old man bent under the blow.

The Army had been invited to open work in West Africa, in 1902. A James Napier had appointed himself captain and meetings had been held in Sierra Leone. As invitations persisted Bramwell Booth asked Railton to go prospecting. Before he went Bramwell tried to convert Railton to vegetarianism in the interest of his own health, and asked him to look closely into the problem of West Coast diet. *The War Cry* of this period informed its readers that leprosy was probably caused by a diet of dried fish and that cancer was hereditary and highly contagious.

But Railton, who ate little enough at best, was not joining the Booths on a meatless diet. As always, when principles did not conflict with loyalty to the Army, he stuck to his guns—and meat. Bramwell wrote:

'What you say about the West African negroes may be perfectly true; but it is notorious that they seldom reach any old age. In fact, an old negro is almost unknown in those regions until you get right inland, and there, vide Stanley, they are mostly vegetarian, and although they occasionally go in for a bit of leg of man when they cannot get leg of mutton, it is so exceptional and occasional that it has very little effect. But then I was not speaking of the native, I was rather speaking of the white man, was I not? I am certain he can't live in the West Coast of Africa and eat flesh, and I believe it is simply this that has killed off Guinness's people on the Congo, because you will remember they are all teetotallers, and yet they all die and nearly all die of fever. Still, I am bound to say that when you come to Moses you have me at a distinct advantage, although of one thing I am dead sure, they would never have got through that 40 years in the wilderness if they had had flesh food. You will, I have no doubt, allow that the manna was a fruitarian type.'

Railton survived, but only just. His mission was to find where, in that vast disease-ridden area, the flag should first be raised. Labour and life was short on the West Coast.

'The landing question is a serious one, even physically. It is amusing to hear Europeans criticizing the slowness of the negro when after many years of occupancy they have never built a pier or wharf at most of the oldest ports.'

As he was being rowed ashore to the Gold Coast a 'fellow passenger kindly assured me that eight people had been drowned here last week'. In the villages the Africans clapped their hands in the open-air meetings and he taught them to sing 'We will all be soldiers in the Army of the Lord'. Europeans told him that the negroes would not work. Railton doubted this. He saw sweat pouring down their broad backs while they toiled, singing awhile 'Carry a mountain, yes, we will'. At least, that is what a linguist told Railton they were singing. His own flair had not yet caught up with the tongues of the West Coast— 'thirteen languages in the German colony of Cameroon'. He wrote: 'I firmly believe that The Salvation Army will yet remove the mountain of the white man's prejudice against all who are not white, and make him see what the African can do and be when he has that fulness of liberty, equality and brotherhood which God can give.'[1] But this was Railton the visionary, the prophet.

He was soon reminded of the harsh and present realities. At Accra, on the Gold Coast, he was staying at a native hotel, alone as always. He slept on the floor. His colleague, little Elijah Cadman, who travelled the world for the General at this time, always took 'a man Friday' with him, and sometimes additional staff. Though no Salvationist travelled in luxury, the General, and sometimes others, often journeyed as guests of shipping line or railroad company. Travel in the very cheapest and roughest style was one of Railton's specialities. It could have been inverted snobbery. His eccentric style was expected of him, written up in *The War Cry* and talked about among officers. Did he feel that he must live up to his reputation? The evidence is that he regarded himself as an apostle of Jesus who must leave all, carry no purse, and have faith that his needs would be supplied.

By staying at a native hotel in Accra, Railton cut himself off from the European strata. It is no wonder that when he became seriously ill he was left alone to die. No doctor was called. There were no Salvationists in the area. He owed his life to two African women Methodists who called by chance to see him. He had previously attended a service led by their Methodist pastor. They were told by the African proprietor that the white man was dying. This was no uncommon event—the fever-ridden coast was known at that time as 'the white man's grave'.

The African women hurried to tell their minister. The missionary

sent for a doctor and went himself with a servant who carried a bedstead and clean bedding. Then in succession, the minister, the African,
and the women watched over Railton while he went to the brink of
that dark, deep river he had glimpsed before and which, it seemed,
he had an unuttered wish to cross. But his time was not yet. He was
nursed back to life and wrote to Marianne:

'My darling,
Here I am fairly stuck with a tip-top doctor, and the Wesleyan
minister, who means to watch by me tonight. You need have no concern when you get this for I have told the landlord how to cable if I
finish.

'It may be, however, that I am not able to take the steamer which
will bring this on Thursday; and if so, you will know that I am following as quickly as I can. I do not think this is fever but only a compli-
cation of one of my bad attacks of lowness of the heart; so keep believing, and if I can I shall be in Plymouth December 20th. But I
still hope God will make me quite better to finish my programme, including the Canaries. I shall, of course, send you a cable before this
gets in, to put you at your ease.

'God be with you all, darlings. He will in any case; but I think
you will find me turning up in first-class condition.'

But, just in case, his last will and testament arrived in London, with
all possible contingencies provided for. His executor was Brigadier
Theodore Kitching, of a Quaker family, a man after Railton's own
heart who became a Commissioner and who was the father of the
seventh General of the Army, Wilfred Kitching. But Railton was one
of those hardy warriors sung about in World War I: 'Old soldiers
never die.' Though he was carried aboard ship at Accra more dead
than alive, he was much better when Kitching met him at Plymouth
in December 1903. The ship's doctor could not say what was the
matter with him—Railton usually had this problem with doctors.
But he was able to smile wanly and listen to the news of the forthcoming great 1904 International Congress.

It is tempting to look for something other than coincidence in what
happened next: another great International Congress, these ten-
yearly celebrations of Army progress, all of them disastrous for Railton.
After a decade had allowed wounds to heal, and a degree of amiable
understanding to develop between the Booths and Railton, would
1904 be another ill-starred year? Whatever his thoughts, and his wish

to arrive home in 'a first-class condition', he had a further collapse: pneumonia set in and for many weeks he hung between life and death. He was not seen in public until June, 1904, at the great Congress. It required four long months for Marianne to nurse him back to health. Then during the Congress he had his final, critical confrontation with the General. Perhaps, because Marianne and the boys were involved, it was more serious than any before.

25

Mother and Sons

THERE WAS misunderstanding at Headquarters as to Railton's finances, for Victorians assumed that a woman's money became her husband's on marriage, as usually it did. The Rev. Mr. Parkyn had overcome this by making a ministerial colleague, the Rev. John Bradford, the sole trustee of Marianne's estate, with full power to ensure that the income should provide for her welfare and the upbringing and the education of her children. The Salvation Army was in no way to benefit, and Railton never wanted treasure on earth.

During the first decade of the 20th century about a third of the population of Britain lacked the bare necessities of life. There was no unemployment insurance, no old-age or widows pensions, no free medical service. The pawnshop and the hated poor relief stood between the unemployed and starvation. This confirmed William Booth in his change of tactics for The Salvation Army—which Railton opposed— the development of social schemes as adjuncts to evangelical work. It also created problems for Marianne. Her chief assets were house properties in Leytonstone, North London. This was a respectable district but unemployment among artisans was rising, rents were falling, there were many houses to let. Moreover her trustee, as a law suit was to show, mismanaged the estate. Marianne's income fell from about £600 a year to £300—'if Mr. Bradford pays up'. This was by no means a certainty.

In the early days of the Army some officers did not draw a regular allowance and many did not draw up to the permitted amount; they lived in great part 'off the country' or they had private means. This seems to have been encouraged in early days until it was used against William Booth by malcontents who charged him with starving them. Railton regarded the drawing of a regular weekly or monthly allowance as a routine matter beneath the consideration of one who had written the biographies of George Fox, John Wesley, Gideon Ouseley, and Jakob Junker of Berlin.

In later years this led to some bitterness and misunderstanding among Railton's children, and in view of the next painful brush Railton had with the General it is necessary for us to be less casual than Railton with regard to his finances. At Margate he was living in a furnished house supplied by the Army, as is usual with its officers in Britain. In 1902 Bramwell Booth had offered him up to £3 10s. 0d. a week in addition; at that time this sum was the full scale for a Commissioner, but Railton refused the full amount. Marianne reared the children and had them educated at her own expense. Railton was often away for long periods and had little or no awareness of the hard facts of economic life. The Army paid for his third-class or steerage tickets and provided him with the frugal fare he ate. He received less than most of his rank, but because he wanted it that way. He may have had qualms because Marianne had been compelled to withdraw from the active Salvationist life of a Commissioner's wife and because she had money of her own.

For the ten years up to 1905, according to Marianne, Railton had about £125 a year from the Army. While in Germany 'only house rent, that very small, no salary. For six years before that £100 a year, and rent. For the eleven years before our marriage sometimes a little salary, sometimes only food and clothing.'

It should be added that during the Christian Mission days and the very first years of the Army, Railton's rewards in earthly terms were no better or worse than that of the Booths or other workers. For the last eight years, until his death, he received £150 a year and a furnished house. Railton preferred life the hard way.

William Booth set a good example in Salvationist labours in the summer of 1904, as part of the build-up for the great Congress. He was received by King Edward VII at Buckingham Palace and later by Queen Alexandra. He traversed the country with five motor cars, daring contraptions supplied by a hire firm and driven by 'navigators'. Asked if he enjoyed it, the dyspeptic old man replied, 'Enjoy it? Four meetings a day and flying at this rate through space?' The car was doing about twenty-five miles an hour, at speed, but vibrated so violently that it felt like a hundred. Scott Montague, M.P. wrote in *The Car*: 'This somewhat upsets the idea, which even now exists in a few unenlightened corners of the land, that the automobile is an invention of the evil one.' Harold Begbie accompanied and the *Express* sent two reporters. *The Freethinker* commented acidly, 'Go by car with General Booth, souls saved while you wait.' But in fact many souls were saved and for that end-product William Booth, tortured digestion notwithstanding, would have been willing to try an Apollo rocket. But Com-

N

missioner Pollard, the organizing genius behind the Congress, had another nervous breakdown.

Meanwhile Railton had again journeyed to Finland where there had been constitutional problems, some attempt on Moore's United States pattern, to make the Army completely nationalistic and autonomous. For such a difficult assignment Railton was just the man. The arguments of the rebels dissolved before the power of prayer and holiness embodied in complete self-renunciation. There was a minimum of loss and Finland is a proud Salvation Army battlefield to this day.

During this 1904 visit Railton noticed the increased 'Russianization' of the country, large numbers of Russian troops and officials in Helsingfors, the capital. Not long before the Russian Governor of the little subject land had been assassinated and the hand of the Czar lay heavy on the people.

Railton had visited St. Petersburg en route, and knew something of the terrors past and pending in Russia. On the Nevski Prospekt, where the anti-Russia-Japanese War riots had broken out, and where troops had opened fire with large loss of life, Railton visualized the soldiers of The Salvation Army marching down the wide straight avenue claiming Russia for God. He made application for the Army to be admitted.

The Army would go, and have its victories, and Railton's vision and faith helped to open the way. But for the time being the Russian Baltic Fleet, on its way to the Far East and the defence of Port Arthur, took fright in the dark in the North Sea and attacked a Hull fishing fleet. Some British seamen lost their lives. Using the words, 'Russian Outrage', on the front page, *The War Cry* reported that the skipper and mate of the trawler *Orane* had their heads blown off their shoulders. This was true enough but hardly likely to forward Railton's efforts with the Russian Ministry of the Interior, which read *The War Cry* as does its equivalent to this day.

Meanwhile, in intervals between visits to six Continental countries, including Germany, Railton fell into another dispute with the General. To understand it one needs to know more of Railton's private life, what little he had, and the strong Salvationist loyalties which the families of every leading officer were expected to demonstrate.

The Booths set a high standard in this. All William Booth's children became officers and he was inclined to assume that, in respect to his Commissioners and Colonels at least, a similar *esprit de corps* would prevail. Usually it did and much of Railton's sorrow arose because his family was a notable exception. In the year that Bramwell Booth's eldest daughter, Catherine, entered training and celebrated her 21st birthday by giving tea to 500 cadets at the Clapton Training Garrison, Railton's eldest son, David, that same lad who had spoken dutiful Salvationist words at the General's Christmas party, went up to Keble College, Oxford. Catherine was the first of a contingent of Booth children who would become officers: Miriam, Mary, Bernard, Olive, Dora and Wycliffe.

This was the way all sons and daughters of the regiment should go. But by 1904 there were signs that the passing of Victorian filial authority, the austerity of Salvation Army life, and the disposition of some children to resent real or imaginary injustices suffered by their parents on Salvation Army service, were creating a new situation.

At staff councils following the Congress, strictly private, William Booth felt himself obliged to denounce what he considered to be disloyalty to the Army, and Railton, who had been abroad for some weeks, jumped to the conclusion that the General's remarks were aimed at himself.

He wrote to Lieut.-Colonel Theo. Kitching, secretary to Bramwell Booth:

'Sure of the personal sympathy of yourself and Mrs. Kitching in any matter affecting me and mine, and trusting also to your diplomatic skill in an emergency, I enclosed yesterday a note to the Chief, whom I am very sorry to trouble just now, and I tell you the whole story which I do not want to keep from anyone who ought to know it; Commissioner Howard for example.

'How perfectly my whole heart went with the General when at the Commissioner's council he was denouncing, with a bitterness that rather surprised me, the monstrosity of having anybody's sons helped out of the Army's funds if they were aiming at "a worldly career". Little did I imagine that it all applied to my own family; I only learnt after my own people had got to York that David had passed some examination which opened his way to Oxford and that he wanted to go there, on the plea that he could never hope to earn his living otherwise than in some quite tutorial position, and that without a degree he could not hope for any permanently valuable berth of the kind.

'I immediately replied both to him and his mother:

"You seem to have no conception of the terrible position I am being driven into. Not only is my family life to be made a mere memory, and a very bitter one, but I am to be set before the whole

world either as one of the meanest of swindlers or the most unreasonable of bigots, or both. And then you say (in effect) 'Be com-
forted for it cannot begin for two months yet.'

"It is strange that you do not see the position in which it threatens
to place you also, for what could any person, even in *the* church,
say as to the mother who during her husband's absence on missionary work manages so as to ensure an utter separation in heart
and life between him and his children and keeps him in the dark
about it all up to the last possible moment?

"To go on occupying an Army house or drawing a Salvation
Army family salary under the circumstances seems to me almost
unendurable, though to flinch, or to disappear and give colour to
the idea that I must have known all along, seems just a little worse.

"What you say of D's condition (so set on it that to oppose him
might cause insanity) goes to show how mercilessly and forever I
have probably been severed from him for life in any case. And all
for a fancy that may prove no more substantial than the one about
the organ (the great excuse made to me for getting him away to
Macclesfield where he was turned, as I believe, Oxfordwards)." '

But David's fees were met out of the Parkyn Estate, and it is most
unlikely that William Booth was 'throwing stones' at Railton in his
meeting for leading officers. The General was well aware that times
were changing and David was certainly not the first son of a Commissioner to opt for a different path from his father's. The percentage
of officers' children becoming officers would decline further with the
years.

William Booth never needed to 'throw stones' from the pulpit; to
hit at individuals in that way was an offence which was frowned on.
His experience with his own had lately shown him how unpredictable
children can be and he knew his Army was a volunteer one, despite
his famous claim to the contrary. He had never called for a Salvationist conscription act.

Railton's letter to Marianne seems to imply that she should have
coerced her son into the Army. Even had she been able to do it, the
Army would not have wished it so. David had come to feel that the
Army had separated his father and mother and subjected both to
a degree of rigour that was unreasonable. The educational system of
late Victorian England was class-conscious. The Rev. Mr. Parkyn's
money had made David Railton a public school type. In the climate
of that time what followed was almost inevitable.

But neither mother nor son sought to deceive Railton; they merely wished to shield him from pain. Yet Railton was so distressed, as his letter to Lieut.-Colonel Kitching shows, that he lost his habitual reasonableness.

Nathaniel Gerard, Railton's second son, a chaplain in World War I, wrote to his mother from the Duchess of Westminster's hospital at Le Touquet in France, in 1917:

'You say I never knew Daddy at his best—perhaps not at his freshest physically—but all life tends that way. With you there was the joy of a heavenly union of God's own making. Two lives with only one object —the service and will of God. Love at its highest and best because so entirely natural and unselfish.

'The children were a problem. Nothing but a bit out of your life could have saved mine and so you gave it, willingly, never counting the cost. Then the great decision: Daddy or children? None but true and perfect lovers will ever know what that cost you both. I hardly know which I pity most.

'Of course The Salvation Army was a great help to you in that way. You could throw off all swank, all pride, all attempt at being anything but a woman toiling for mere existence and the life of her family. But what it must have cost you God only knows: all the comforts of clean hands and soft raiment gone at one blow. You cooked, scrubbed, mangled, just like the roughest of the daughters of toil.

'And all the time you must have longed for your lover across many a sea. When he did come back he always saw the joy of his life as he first knew her. His children he loved; they interested him as commodities for the future well-being of men. It was easier for dear Daddy. It always is for a man. He had his job and it absolutely consumed him. Yet for one so absolutely strong, for one who never cared two hoots about any other woman, the separation must have been intensely agonizing. So often entirely alone, shunned by those who owed him everything, and before whom—thank God—he never, never bowed. So often worn out, depressed, cold, unfed, how he must have hungered for you. How he must have been inclined to regret the intervention of children at all.

'One of the most saintly traits in that great character I think was this fact: that as we grew older, and more uppish and narrow, and intolerant, and unmannerly in expressing our views about his life's work, he never once summoned that just, scornful, bitter invective against us who were the one obstacle between him and the one he loved best in all the world.'

Fifteen years before, when Nat had first knelt at the Salvation Army penitent-form, his father had written from Paris:

'It pleases me all the more that you should have gone to the form in the presence of so many witnesses, without its being understood fully by them. God, who saw that you were so determined to show yourself fully His in the presence of your friends and all, will give you the help you may need at any time to fulfil your vow ... I am glad that you look at things carefully; but I fear you do not read *The War Cry* enough to see much of the good side.

'Nobody detests *War Cry* flattery more than I do, especially as it has so penetrated everywhere that I have to struggle against it here. If you look at our present *En Avant* you will see a portrait of me, and the descriptions of our doings are far worse than the English, considering how small we are. But then there is a lot of real faith and affection about it and, after all, there is no place to compare with Hadleigh in England (as you will feel when you have been there) and there is nobody like the Chief; not a man so highly placed in the country who speaks out so simply and boldly to all sorts what you and I believe—and who is influencing so many young folks to give up their whole lives to God.'

Nat was plagued with poor health, and lack of confidence in himself, which made his school life a torture. In 1903 Railton wrote to him from Accra:

'I do hope that the examination bogey is all gone forever, and that you will soon see a practical way to turn to account the valuable abilities you certainly have got.

'Think of it—I have two man sons. It cannot be that God, having let such a couple live from the day of that little photo I love to see on the wall, should not give them courage enough and revelation enough to cast under their feet all regard for the past that could hinder their usefulness in the present ... I hope you will both read Commissioner Oliphant's *Life of Savonarola* for it is so far better than I had hoped he would be able to write of a Catholic monk. It shows what tremendous men God makes for Himself.

God bless and guide you, dear boy.'

The religious development of his children proved to be a nightmare to Railton. He knew that none of the Booths had attended universities, but had become young soldiers in the stimulating atmosphere of an ardent Salvationist home, wearing uniform and badges, becoming corps cadets, learning to be musicians and public speakers while in their teens.

This was Railton's ideal. Just as others nominate their unborn sons for Eton so he had chosen officership for David and Nat before they were born. But Marianne had other ideas. She was with the children when Railton was away. She knew her own agonized expressions and repressions. She knew that David disliked the Army 'because of what it did to my mother and father'. That his father did it to himself, in God's name, could not lessen David's resentment because the boy did not understand.

Marianne liked to think that the problems of her precious trio arose simply because they were highly strung and physically delicate. But Salvationism, which Railton wanted from them, is not dependent on nerves and navvy-like physique. The suspicion among Salvationists was that Marianne molly-coddled her fledglings, that her money made them snobs. Railton's long absences from home disqualified him as an influence. Marianne would have been less than human if she had not shown signs of strain and grief because of her prolonged grass-widowhood. True, she had married a Christian nomad—to be 'his continual partner in the war'—but no other Salvation Army officer carried that hard rule to the lengths that Railton did.

His bias against formal education is the one of Railton's prejudices most hard to explain. Dr. Pritchard, the present Head of Woodhouse Grove, Railton's old school, points out that in the 1860s, when Railton was at school, there was strong resentment among nonconformists because of their exclusion from Oxford or Cambridge.

But to Railton the crux of the matter was the social and religious effect of higher education. It made men 'gentlemen' but not good Salvationists. Even today, when the universities are open to all classes, when Oxbridge can be conquered by the children of working-class parents, it is still argued that higher education tends to diminish the numbers of candidates for religious vocation. Sir William Armstrong, present Head of the Civil Service, himself the son of Salvation Army officers, who won a scholarship to Oxford, has argued that the process of social change which follows the higher education of a working-class boy results in that boy moving into the middle class where he is sometimes lost to the religious persuasion of his parents. This was true in the past, though perhaps not so frequent in English life today. In Railton's time class-consciousness was even more pronounced and he feared the effects of higher education on his sons. He wrote:

'Certain I am that the entire programme of English schools, based upon the demands of universities, is as foolish as it can well be. I learned all that was of real value in spite of, rather than thanks to, the excellent school to which I was sent.

'To fool away one's best hours and powers in pretending to learn something of languages no longer spoken even among scholarly men, and to aim at passing examinations that make demands rather on the memory than on any other faculty, is the pathway into which I fear to this day English lads who go beyond the elementary schools are led. What insanity it all is, as contrasted with the systems I find adopted on the Continent, and which, whatever their defects, produce lads capable of the most rapid practical use of several European languages, or of striking into any course of technical or scientific learning that will fit them for whatsoever calling they may be destined.

'I cannot doubt that it was God who guided me so as to fit me best with what he had planned. To this day I am content to know nothing of the names of those wonderful rivers 'on' which geography informs us that most of the country towns are found, provided I know what railways will get me to them. I am content for any child to surpass me in accuracy as to the dates when some useless king began and ended his reign if I can only feel sure I know who have and have not done much for England and why they helped or hindered it.'

This was for readers inside The Salvation Army and hardly squares with the idea of a world-traveller, tolerant, multi-lingual and well read. But in his day The Salvation Army did not regard education beyond the elementary stage as a number one priority.

From Japan, in 1906, Railton wrote to Nat still ill and baulked by exams:

'If you get chances to see a lot of Switzerland and Germany, and learn to speak the two languages well enough, especially German, it can place you far above nearly all the Oxford lot for getting on in this century. So be glad, and do not let anything worry you—you might so easily glide into some scheme of usefulness along with Mama there, or in Germany better still, that I would not dare to press your going elsewhere.

'And yet, of course, I need not tell you how much more natural it would be for you all to come and help me. There can be no doubt I can get hold of lots of the students here and you could be a helper to me in all sorts of ways, no matter how little or how much you were able to do. They are now having ten-day contests of wrestlers and ju-jitsu champions.

'This country has now got so linked up with China, without the Western "powers" realizing it, that they too will in a few years be able to boss and laugh at all the world, if no hindrance arises. Nobody can measure our future influence, therefore, if we get hold of these grand young men of today. And you can help, if you care to.'

But Nat persevered and went back to Oxford, where he did get a degree. He was Archdeacon of Lindsey when he died, aged 62. As he grew older and stronger he became more aggressive, less reluctant to question his father's ideas. After one argumentative letter Railton replied:

'Your letter shows "a chip of the old block" as to writing, anyhow, who may yet be able to plead many a cause with his tongue to greater effect.

'But my dear boy, you let out the whole thing in that one word, "gentlemen" forsooth, because by one means or another they have got up, and have reasonable hope to keep up, above the toiling millions of their various lands, and thus there comes in the enormous superiority of Eastern, and to some extent, even of American culture, where every effort is made that *everyone* may be in a more real sense, a gentleman or gentlewoman.

' "The" Church, with the help of all its stolen buildings and revenues and positions, cultivates that hateful "gentleman" style, even towards the noblest dissenters. The air of the condescending curate always seems to me much more offensive than the vilest abuse of the low-class publican.

'I reckon to be a constant associate of the real gentlefolk, men and women who have the character to be gentle and loving to everybody, and no matter what race. For that reason they can never join in any dissenting railing against "the" Church, any more than in the latter's attack upon all the rest, and rough though they may be in both manner and speech often, my ladies and gentlemen do strive to devote themselves night and day to the real benefit of the very people who are least likely to appreciate or reward them for it down here.

'To think that I should be hunting men for such immense commands as our Far East offer, yet my son is looking towards a life amongst these Church dwarfs!'

Sometimes, quite out of character, Railton boasted. He did it to boost the Army in the eyes of his hypercritical sons:

'The fun of it is that our "ignorant" men are rising above the level of university men everywhere. Your Archbishop wired for me on Friday, received me (his wife too) just as if I had been one of the family, lunched me and undertook to put to the King my ideas as to how the Royal Family might at this time help Turkey and other countries. I could not but wonder how many poor rectors might long for such a reception in vain. And remember that each fresh step we take in any part of the world is helping to open our road more and more everywhere. Our Colonel Wright has been having a similar welcome from President Diaz, of Mexico, a far more influential man than most kings.

'Now I defy anybody to find any reason for all this other than that we have put, and kept, God first, and made a road for everybody to climb, simply by His power, ignoring all the qualifications the world and its churches still reckon indispensable.

'So far from dear mother's looking "worn and worried", I'm more struck daily with the impossibility of believing she is in her 60th year. That we should have none of our children with us in the fight is the only shadow I can see on the picture. Amid all officers on the platform last night at Ramsgate—mostly young—she looked, I thought, one of the youngest and spoke with a freshness and power likely to surprise anybody who had never before heard her. Yet there is not a church in the country that would give her any such opportunity.'

During his oft-interrupted studies, long absences from school, young Nat visited the Army corps at Margate and picked up gossip which he retailed to his father. Railton replied:

'Always wait till you hear the other side of a thing before you accept any theory that condemns 101. Always think "IHQ means my father", for who can tell what I have and have not some time advised? This girl's story may be perfectly correct, and she may have shown herself a splendid woman of God, such as we have thousands of. But she may not have been such a princess as a commanding officer as to make it seem best to let her be that again, at once. Besides there is always the thought of others no less deserving who may have to go down a peg on readmission rather than let it be thought that desertion is nothing. If she is capable of being a commanding officer she will be made one again very soon, you may be sure.'

Nat asked his father for advice on gambling:

'You ask me about betting. Betting is universally recognized as a bad and ruinous thing, though none of the silly Governments care to suppress it and the bookmakers as they ought to do. Betting is money promised for no real equivalent. A bet won means necessarily a bet lost; that is 'A' takes money from 'B' not for anything supplied to 'B' but only because a bet has been made. Then this money, not honestly earned, is generally taken away from some worthy object ...

'Betting is, I fear, more widely and radically destructive than drink itself, and renders all who mix it more and more callous to the losses and sufferings of others. May God spare and strengthen my dear boys to earn an honest living by honest work.'

Both David and Nat lauded school games. With Mrs. Catherine Booth, perhaps because of that beloved lady, Railton was the complete reactionary on the subject. From South Africa, shortly after 'Black Week', when British marksmanship, tactics, training, mobility and quality of leadership showed up so badly against the Boers, Railton wrote to his sons: 'What a difference it would have made in this war if all those swell English boys had taken as much trouble to be of use as they did to learn football and cricket!' Railton certainly did not agree with Wellington that Waterloo was won on the playing fields of Eton.

During the great Welsh, Evan Roberts revival of 1904, which swept through the coal-mining valleys, thousands of Welsh miners and their families were converted in the chapels which, for two decades or more afterwards resounded with song and fervent Bible oratory. The Salvation Army was involved and Railton was sent to fan the flames. He had campaigned in Wales in Christian Mission days. He wrote to Nat from Swansea:

'I am glad David let me see a little of his thoughts, though they are more of regret for leaving me than of any return my way.

'I have found a happy alternative to any mixture with that "swell gang". You can get as much education as ever you like in Wales from the lowest up—in the most bracing air and always in association with quiet, humble, decent chaps who aim only at making the best of life as they understand it. Nobody would dare to sneer at David for associating with me or the Army if he were in gown and mortarboard at the university in Cardiff. This is such a splendid country for health and opportunity to influence the young people for God. One of the great glories of Evan Roberts is that he cut and left the "studying for the ministry" to be a blood and fire minister.'

With the unwitting cruelty of the young, David and Nat retailed to him adverse gossip and press comment on the Army. They were convinced that the Army's press gave less than equal coverage to their father's Salvationist activities. But Railton never encouraged any anti-Army sentiments in his family. The following note to Nat was from Wigton, Cumberland—the scene of Railton's boyhood conversion:

'We must have a good talk as to the Booths when I see you all next. *The Christian* statement is as unjustifiable as many others it has made. How many worse reproaches could be made against me who, knowing them all so well, never mention anybody's name in *Heathen England,* or in my latest book, the *Life of Commissioner Dowdle.* And all for the same reason for which the General may very reasonably omit to make any mention of me. I always think, "I can write any amount once they are safe in heaven. But before then, how do I know if they will not go off and leave the Army."'

A letter to David takes up the same theme:

'All your feelings should be against *The Christian,* which all these years has seldom given us a good report without putting in some nasty little bit like that to take off the good effect. The remark I cannot but think was due to Harding, the ex-officer, and any attempt to lessen the sale of the book (the life of Commissioner Dowdle) could only be likely to lessen and not to add to my influence in the world. Never let anything any Christian paper or ex-officer says worry you.'

From Paris, late at night, with a revolt on his hands, he writes happily:

'Langford has gone to bed and I am waiting still for the last visitor —dear old Major Peyron, who travelled all last night, third class, to come to my aid, and who will be very weary by the time he gets here to sleep, having spent all the evening trying to talk some rebels into shape.

'But they will go with the Clibborns, I fear, and all be in opposition to me yet. And I do want to have the real prayer and sympathy of my own family behind me.

'Do not let anything you see or hear in Margate make you forget that God raised up our Army so that He is able to remake it whenever (as here) it needs remaking.'

When David had to represent him at the funeral of a relative Railton wrote from China in what proved to be an accurate forecast as to his own 'promotion to Glory'.

'The whole thing could not but remind me of the great probability of my having just such a finish at any time, and though I hope it may please God to summon me when at home with darling Mother, yet I cannot but see how much greater the advantage of such an end would be if at sea, or in some tropical land where you get popped out of sight with so much less trouble and expense.'

A letter that shows Railton far below his best is one to David when the boy was accepted for Keble College. It shows some of the anxiety that was tearing at the father's heart though what he feared did not happen, perhaps because of his prayers and faith:

'I am not sorry that you have given me no address so that I cannot write you direct and that I can say I do not know it. I am also glad to think I can say to anyone that your home is still at Margate, though if pressed I should have to admit that you spent part of the year studying at Oxford. You cannot imagine the horrible feeling of talking with comrades everywhere about their children and hoping to keep off any query as to mine.

'And yet I am writing because you do and I would not fail to encourage any desire or effort by you to be different from others— really to pray, to please God, and lead others to do so.

'You surely hear something of this wonderful Evan Roberts who has broken loose from Wesleyan studies and by whom God is stirring all his own country. It would sound all the better if it should be said that "David Railton was at Oxford when God aroused him and he turned with natural loathing from the heathen books which that great Christian university had put into his hands and threw all his energies into the salvation of his country" ...

'I saw lately that the old sillies at the top are enough stirred by the rapid ruin of their country to think of putting German in the place of Greek, which would give you no doubt a chance of not only easy distinction but of getting into the ranks of the practical folk who may help to rescue the country from impending eclipse by practical nations. But I think again, "If they go in for German what will they get people to read and study? Certainly not any practical books of any use but the infidel ones or the old silly poets and play writers of 100 years ago." Even that, however, could not be worse than setting up people over all their fellows because they have learnt how best to translate the filthy thoughts of Roman and Greek heathen who helped beautifully towards the extinction of their own countries.'

This consideration of Railton's relationship with his sons can end as it began with a letter from France, this time from David Railton. He writes to his brother concerning a request made by Eileen Douglas who had begun a biography of his dead father:

'I wonder if they are really writing the life of Father. They want Mother to give my private letters. If she does not they will say with some truth, "We could not see the General's letters to Railton, so of course we were unable to write a complete 'Life'."

'In the days to come, if I am spared, I would write a few true sketches of Father: My Father's religion was very matter-of-fact, and simple. At 12 noon he would kneel down—on the Cliffs—before the world, and pray enthusiastically. He would rise up refreshed and as a man out to win the world for God.

'I would rise up blushing, prepared to let the world go to the Devil sooner than do that again. He was a man. He would positively rage at the notion of the slow pious-voiced "saved" individual who so often posed as the elect of the Lord. His wrath was just as fierce if he heard of the General or some other staff personage making a fuss about where he slept and what food he ate. Such men were as much anathema to his soul as a new theology to an orthodox prelate ...

'Daily, Father becomes a great hero to me. He must really have loved our Lord. He never whined in his letters about the misery of being away from home. Nor did he curse the deity in the way of the French or German people. To me the thought of his many long separations from his own wife and children is just one long terror.'

26

Agreement to Differ

THE YEAR of the 1904 Congress was a series of triumphs for the General and the Army but it was the nadir of George Scott Railton's career. When the first rumblings of the storm were heard he was ill and quiescent down at Margate. He had sent in his report on the African West Coast to Bramwell, who had agreed that the Army must at least appoint a man to Lagos and another to Freetown. 'Who it is to be I can only ask God to make known.' Some parts of Railton's report he did not care for, a not unusual reaction: 'I wish some things you say could have been said otherwise.'

During March Railton was able to visit London to see the General. The Chief was also present. Both men were anxious about their beloved, though difficult, Commissioner. London would soon be visited by Salvationists from the far corners of the earth for 'the most important series of councils and public meetings ever conducted in our history', as William Booth declared. There must be no more mutinous Railtonian gestures. The Booths knew how highly Railton was regarded by Salvationists, who were aware of the simplicity and holiness of his life, his self-sacrifice and intensity of faith. Neither William nor Bramwell Booth was accustomed to leading officers who continued in vigorous and fundamentally differing views from their own. The occasional rebel either came into line—often the Booths came some way to meet him—or he withdrew from the Army. It was important to them that saintly, beloved Railton should keep in step, setting a good example to the rank and file. Hence Railton's summons to London. But the interview was disastrous. Railton would not yield. Bramwell wrote afterwards:

'My dear Railton,

I fear you can form a poor idea of our disappointment in the outcome of the interviews on Friday last.

'Kitching told me yesterday that you seem to think we were entertaining some personally unkind feelings. Now this is a mistake, and would be unjust. Our affection for you is as great as ever. It is a bitter disappointment that we seem unable to use you.

'I propose to have a talk with Mrs. Railton and am asking her to come up and will then write you again.

'Meantime, rest. I thought you looked flabby.

Affectionately ... '

Of course Marianne was distressed about Railton's unhappy relationship with the General and the Chief. She had been writing to Launcelot, the Wesleyan minister, who had introduced Railton to William Booth and who considered that he was responsible for Railton throwing in his lot with the Army. Quite unintentionally her letters sparked off another crisis. Marianne's letters were such a tale of woe that Launcelot decided to write to the General. His effort was about as helpful as the anarchist's bomb which, at this time, blew up one of the Russian Grand Dukes in Moscow. After Launcelot's letter had been despatched he sent a copy with an explanation to Marianne:

'I was having my siesta on Friday afternoon when an urgent message roused me. I was to get up and write to the General. What about? And knowing the voice that spoke I straightway obliged.'

The letter to William Booth contained the following phrases:

'George has had a narrow shave. But though very weak seems to be slowly recovering. I hope he will be spared for many more heavy fights. Is it not time that the results of the slight departure, from your point of view, from his unswerving loyalty, committed when he was under great strain, should be dismissed, and that he was restored to his old status? He acted from the purest motives. You know very well that his name stands in the Army and outside for the fullest devotion to the highest ideals of life and service. The coming of the Congress seems a fitting opportunity for burying the past.'

William Booth took a poor view of this intervention from outside the Army and he reacted with such anger that Launcelot feared he might dismiss his brother. He therefore wrote to the leader of the Welcome Mission at Portsmouth. Its Director, Thomas Hogben, suggested to Railton that 'big things' were tottering because 'they had

o

grieved the spirit'. By this he meant the Army. The Portsmouth Mission 'was increasingly successful', he added. He invited Railton to communicate with him but there is no evidence that he did. Railton never contemplated resigning and for all William Booth's anger he never intended dispensing with Railton's services.

But William and Bramwell Booth were in no mood for time-consuming parleys with their saintly Commissioner. Great schemes were afoot for the realization of important *Darkest England* projects. The wealthy and influential Lord Rosebery, imperialist and Prime Minister, came forward as a supporter of the General's land settlement schemes. Mr. George Herring advanced £100,000 for the financing of a pilot project on which unemployed men should have housing, tools and training as smallholders. Rider Haggard, who had been to the United States to study American ventures in this field, published a Blue Book advocating British land colonization. William Booth addressed parliamentarians on the subject.

But Rider Haggard had to disclaim publicly any intention on the Army's part to seek to 'indoctrinate' the unemployed, to use public land and money as a means of bringing religious pressure on needy men and their families. The national press mentioned this aspect of the proposals. *The Freethinker* was critical and the trade unions suspicious. So the Army disclaimed any intention to use social relief to gain conversions. The Christian diehards then said, as Railton had always contended, that this made the scheme 'merely humanitarianism'. Worthy though it might be he was quite sure it was not the Army's objective. William Booth's purpose, as Railton had written it into the Army's constitution, rules, doctrines and literature, was to 'Go for souls ...' If there was any chance that the General was being sidetracked from this great mission, then it was Railton's intention to save William Booth from himself.

But the General was in no danger on this score. The great pragmatist was adept at facing new situations: he intended to have the best of both worlds. With patience wearing thin, the grand old man wrote to Bramwell:

'I can think of nothing fresh to say. If Railton withdraws the letter he wrote and is willing to work in harmony, and confine his criticisms to us, and take his appointment, whatever it may be, and do the best he can with it, I am willing enough to let the past be the past. But he must not say that I or The Salvation Army have changed, except in the sense of evolution.

'I suppose he would have objected to Jesus Christ feeding the people in the wilderness without having a Penitent-form!

'Stand firm. Make the Railtons feel that we will have The Salvation Army our way!'

Both the Booths believed that there was an indirect as well as direct way to 'save souls'. Men on British smallholdings, like patients in Indian hospitals—protected by law against over-zealous religious pressure from Salvationists—were allowed to respond voluntarily. The Army knew that 'brain-washing' could be a self-defeating process. But put good men and women among these unconverted unemployed, sick, alcoholics, leprosy patients: the good life is the best sermon. No one can object to that kind of pressure.

Yet the sick man, in a cul-de-sac down at Margate, suffered feelings of frustration and irritation. There was, he thought, too much adulation of Salvationists; little or no self-criticism by Salvationists. The bricks had become bouquets. In Railton's opinion the Army was being knocked off balance.

There were other reasons for Railton's fear that the Army might be losing its first love. In a bold gesture the Americans chartered the Cunard liner *Carpathia* to bring their party to the Congress. The ship had accommodation for 1,000, but Bramwell Booth limited the party to 400. Railton saw this as extravagance. A painful barb was a *War Cry* announcement that every purchaser of the paper could be covered by an Accident Insurance Company policy. This sales promotion stunt, as chimerical as a similar scheme which resulted in a costly circulation war among national newspapers twenty-five years later, took up precious space. There were also two pages of advertising. The Salvation Army Assurance Society announced that it had over 1,500 agents and 400 officers, though as we have noted Bramwell Booth could hardly find two men for Freetown or Lagos where 'do-it-yourself' Salvationists were waiting for leaders.

As the first spring-time visitors risked the wind and showers on the promenade at Margate, Railton sunk further into despondency. After one stormy interview with William Booth he chose to believe that he had been dismissed. Marianne went up to see William Booth again and telegraphed, 'Chief certain you totally misunderstand General. Am to see General...' A subsequent note from Railton to William Booth indicates either a modification of the General's ultimatum or of a misunderstanding on Railton's part:

'My dear General,

I am pleased to gather from your remarks to Mrs. Railton that in telling me, last Friday, that as I could not make myself think otherwise than I do, there was no other possibility than for me to take a separate path from yours, you did not mean to take that as a final decision on the spot, but only in case I could not agree to act in accordance with your wishes. The great necessity seems to be for me in some way to contrive either not to express what I think or to find ways and means of doing so otherwise than heretofore.'

Railton must keep his idealistic principles to himself and not try to persuade those weaker Salvationists of the need for Railtonian perfection.

In the meanwhile Launcelot, meaning well, made matters worse. He wrote to his old friend the General. Some indication of the tone of his letters can be gathered from later correspondence with his brother:

'Dear George,   March 26th, 1904

My first missive was like the first gun across the bows of the great ironclad calling on him to pull up—he only slackened speed a little, and took the little lady up the side of the ship, and with his Chief spent a long while chatting over nothings. This second shot will be what they call a "bolt from the blue", and may possibly give him pause. We shall see what comes. If nothing, then there are a good many more shots in the locker. I am not short of ammunition, and it gives me much pleasure to use it. My soul has been wonderfully blessed thus far during the attack.'

He was enjoying the battle: Railton was not. Launcelot's next letter (April 2nd) gives not only the General's terse reply but part of Railton's protest:

'You have not returned the General's letter to me: please send it next time you write. I am really surprised that you should make use of the copy of my letter (sent to you in confidence). This only shows how completely you have come under the infatuation which possesses the Army generally with reference to the General ...

'You say that to such a letter as I wrote, "no sensible man is likely to reply at all". Well, perhaps the General is not a sensible man. I have doubted his sense many times when I have seen the ridiculous homage paid to him by his regimentals. No man quite sane would demand or accept such obsequious attentions.

'And this is what the Great Man says, "Dear Mr. Railton, I have received today on my return from Glasgow your astonishing letter of the 26th. I have neither entertained nor expressed either to you or to anyone else any such intentions with regard to your brother, as you attribute to me.

Yours faithfully...'

But Launcelot went from one well-meaning blunder to the next:

'They must restore your name to its old place. Third it is. It ought now to be first, but to save their face I will not insist upon anything but what you had before.

'The past must be written off. They must treat you in finance and every other way, as the other "hierarchs". You must be a party to the policy of the Army for the future as you were of old. This is the irreducible minimum, and the alterations must be made before the Congress and appear on all the programmes. I intend to leave no stone unturned to secure this, expense or no expense to them, or to me, they must make the matter right by the Congress. The General is too weak for his place. The Commissioners round him command the situation. The Chief, as well as the General, is helpless.'

This is a complete misunderstanding of the situation. William Booth was never other than master of the situation. He left much authority to Bramwell because he wished it so but when he wished to intervene no one said him nay. The picture of Bramwell is ludicrous. He was a veritable dynamo and, except where the General wished otherwise, completely in command.

Inclined by nature to be one of God's angry men William Booth displayed patience, love and wisdom towards Railton. He wrote to Bramwell:

'I have been thinking very much about Railton and feel that we are not making the best of this opportunity. Perhaps it would have been best to let him see Launcelot's letter—and have asked him what answer ought to be made to it. Launcelot ought to be answered and we ought to make George feel that although we love him, and all that, it depends upon himself and his putting himself in accord with our wishes.'

Bramwell then sought to arrange another interview. At first Railton shied away. He seems to have fallen into unwonted, unsoldierly self-pity. He wrote to Bramwell:

'This proposed joint interview is not likely to serve any good purpose. Mrs. Railton tells me that the General was very much annoyed at my silence when I was last at Hadley and thought even that I was hardly listening to him; yet I have said and written all I have to say or write on the subject.

'Of course I shall greatly regret it should you say that by not coming at this time I have prevented the General from making with us the arrangement that you desired: but really in my present condition I can see no such prospect, all the more because of some letters which I find my brother has written to him. If the contents, as described to me, have surprised and annoyed the General as much as they have me, they have not improved the prospect of any interview at present.'

Marianne's tactful postscript may have saved the situation:

'My dear Chief,

George seems so poorly as a result of these cold winds that I have rather opposed a journey for him. But I should like to repeat all that I said to you and the General as to his being as absolutely willing as ever to go anywhere and do anything he can for the Army—and as precisely the same as ever in affection to you all.

(Nothing that his brother may have written has been inspired or approved by him.)

Yours affectionately . . .'

His health improved, Railton made the journey and its result can be deduced from William Booth's note of April 11th. William Booth and Railton agreed to differ:

'My dear Railton,

I accept what you say in the sense in which, I believe, both you and Mrs. Railton mean it. I will dismiss from my mind your brother's letters, at any rate so far as they affect you, and I understand you to accept my view of our interview at Hadley Wood at which, as I said to you on Friday, there was nothing approaching dismissal in my mind, and where the objection named by me was not to your thinking in some things differently from me, no matter how greatly I might deplore it, but in your expressing to other people different views, and in your seeming so slow, if not unwilling to rejoice in what is being done because you see some things in which you cannot heartily agree.

'You know, no one better, what I am struggling after. The fact that we only progress towards the goal by slow and painful steps and in spite of dogged and desperate resistance from the world, the flesh and the devil, ought not, and must not, make you over-critical or censorious.

'However, if bygones can be bygones so far as any unpleasant memories are concerned I shall rejoice most heartily. I hope you will soon be better and again able to take serious work.

'This is the first letter I write in my new, that is my 76th year, and I send in it my love to yourself and Mrs. Railton. I leave for Scandinavia and Germany tonight. It will be rather a heavy pull. Pray for me.

Your affectionate General ...

'Will you thank Esther for her nice present made by her own fingers. Just in. I must write her my wishes for her future. God bless her.'

This hitherto unrevealed episode of Salvationist history is necessary to a balanced understanding of Railton's place in the Army, and a correct assessment of the calibre of leadership shown by William and Bramwell Booth. It is fair to add, on Launcelot's behalf, that he was unintentionally misled by his brother. A final extract from Railton's correspondence shows this:

'Dear George,   April 14, 1904

Now that the brave old seventy-five tonner has gone out of range for a little while, I have time and opportunity to give a little attention to you. But before commencing that useful and needful operation let me copy the last "despatch" received from HQ dated April 9:

"Dear Mr. Railton, your letter from Newport with its peculiar mixture of compliments, and threats, is a still greater surprise to me than the one that preceded it.

"Your brother tells me that he has no sympathy whatever with your views, in which case, it does not seem necessary for me to make any reply to them. I am quite sure that you will sooner or later come to see that you have been totally mistaken in the strange course you have thought proper to take in the matter, and very much regret it.

Yours faithfully . . . '

'I wonder what view the writer of the above would think of you if he had a sight of the letters you wrote to me in the first stage of this episode. And I wonder what any unprejudiced Christian man would say of a younger brother who, having written to his elder brother for advice when he expected to be turned adrift on a small pension, his own health being broken, and hopes of recovery very slight, now rounds on that elder brother, and disowns him in favour of a man who, having sucked the younger brother dry, meant to throw him in the gutter? Ordinarily such an action on the part of the younger brother would be denounced as both unnatural, and un-Christian.

'I did not expect you to approve the words of invective God made me write—your closer relationship with the General would make that style of thing inadmissible—but I cannot see why you knuckled in at all.'

But Railton had not intended Launcelot to join in the fray against the General and the Chief: he was quite capable of taking care of himself. As he had agreed not to circulate his views among officers in general, he would have been less than human if he had not wished to take his older brother into his confidence. However, Launcelot jumped to a number of wrong conclusions. The basic difference of opinion between Railton and the Booths is a subject about which the Church has argued for nearly 2,000 years and will continue doing so for a long time yet. It must remain an open question as to who is right.

27

Bugs and Babies in China

THE CHARISMA about the old General grew enormously. His motor-cades throughout Britain brought out the believer and doubters, drunken and sober, young and old. As he approached his eightieth birthday his eyes gave him trouble. An operation for cataracts was reported in the world's press as if he had been the Czar or the Kaiser. King Edward sent a personal letter of good wishes and a hundred guineas for the Self-Denial Fund. But though the old man rivalled Railton as a world campaigner their paths hardly ever crossed. The old relationship could never be restored.

It is possible that some of Railton's many journeys to distant outposts after 1904 were for the purpose of getting him out of the way. He was argumentative and uncompromising. Commissioner Cadman often travelled with the General. Railton did not. William Booth suffered from headaches, sea-sickness, indigestion, bouts of irritability. And no wonder. His conferences, lectures, meetings, journeying from pillar to post were enough to exhaust a thirty-year-old, let alone a bereft man, in poor health, near to eighty.

Commissioner T. Henry Howard, the Foreign Secretary, often travelled with the General. He was to be the new second-in-command in the Army when the Founder passed on. He had charm of manner, business efficiency, and a great capacity for hard, routine work—though he had not been in at the very beginning as had Railton. Whether William Booth asked for, or wished Railton to be kept outside his entourage is not certain. Perhaps not. He was usually content to leave such matters to Bramwell, who would not want the General to be subjected to harassment of any kind during his long voyages and campaigns.

Railton's voyages were not luxury tours as he makes clear in a letter to Marianne written during his 1904–1905 first visit to Japan:

'This voyage, since Suez, has been the worst I ever made. I cannot be of any use till the heat is over. I must be enormously older than even two years ago ... Of course steamer nights are never good, especially if you are just at the steerage and with so very much additional heat from the engines. But I have never had such a succession of bad nights.'

At Colombo Railton was able to get on a German ship on a cheap second-class ticket, unwonted luxury. They also had a few days at Singapore. He wrote to Marianne again:

'For the first time in my life I have a solitary cabin on the floor below the saloon with electric light, of course, and an electric fan all to myself and a ventilator from deck too! It is the quietest company I was ever in though there are some children, some Chinese, and Cingalese. The most, however, are Germans of the jolly drinking sort. There are four bad girls, Japanese, as well as a number of Japanese gentlemen; but here I sit with the smoke-room to myself all the morning. They are all apparently feeling the heat more than I do—jersey, coat and all, so they keep their seats on deck, and I write as much as I like here.

'I am writing hard at my new book *These Forty Years* which will be my view of The Salvation Army for the Japanese. But I am full of the idea of making the most of my chance in Japan and China, through the press, and I am eager to know what IHQ are feeling as they read my view of the Rider Haggard Blue Book![1]

'I found there were 400 or 500 Japanese prostitutes in Singapore and their "Protector", who is also the "Protector" of the Chinese, seemed to me one of the worse specimens of the British official who "could not see his way" to do anything. The Japanese Consul was very different, though he said he had to be cautious because they would sometimes complain of one house only to get into another, or parents would try to get away a daughter they had sold to one house, hoping to sell her again in Japan! He was all I expect to find in a Japanese.

'Those on board are, however, like almost all the rest, too swell to speak to me! I enjoy the quiet and solitude and the tribute in our "not belonging that class".'

But when he arrived at Tokyo, even though his health was good his spirits were at zero. One problem was that for all the esteem with which he was held—and Colonel Henry Bullard, the man in charge in Japan, thought highly of Railton—he had no authority. That was in the firm control of the Foreign Secretary in London who was under the eagle-eye of Bramwell Booth. Railton was a Salvationist Don Quixote, but without a Pancho, or even a mule. He went from the British

Ambassador to the Japanese War Department, all without reference to London or to Colonel Bullard. He reconnoitered in China and Korea. The man at the British Embassy in Tokyo with dark, diplomatic cunning, wanted to know what the Japanese were doing in Korea. The Japanese War Department was puzzled as to why an Englishman wanted to visit Russian prisoners-of-war, and they feared the worst. But he got his passes, permanent ones to six 'Prisoners' Asylums'. These were all made out in Japanese and tortured English, to 'General G. S. Railton'. Railton brushed up his smattering of Russian.

He wished to pray with the Russians, take literature to them, and perhaps arrange for their letters to be expedited. Many of the naval officers of Admiral Rodjestvensky's ill-fated fleet, which had attacked the North Sea fishing vessels and later been destroyed by the Japanese fleet, understood German and heard Railton gladly. He obstinately took third-class on boats to Hong Kong and Korea. It was a matter of conscience. As this class was for 'coolies only' Railton put a Chinese shirt over his tunic, outside his trousers, and passed muster. He picked up bugs from his wretched sleeping environment and wrote of one voyage:

'I never before travelled with so many mothers and babies of the poorest appearance; our deck is almost covered with them. And babies' cries are as plentiful as if one were in a maternity hospital. But all that is only an appeal to any true Salvationist who cannot but wish to see and to know life among the poorest.'[2]

Bugs and babies and all were a ready price to pay for the salvation of the poor. The great Japanese Salvationist, Gunpei Yamamuro, who became a Commissioner and wrote *The Common People's Gospel,* which sold more than half a million copies, found Railton a man after his own heart:

'He was the first Commissioner to visit us. He came to us the first time during the war between Japan and Russia. He visited various corps and took part in small meetings, not as the great Commissioner, but just as a simple soldier of The Salvation Army. He delighted to attend open-air meetings, and at Kobe addressed himself in the open-air to a number of foreigners of mixed nationalities, speaking alternately in English, French and German. He set to work at once to learn the language, and soon learned to sing "Jesus saves me now" in Japanese, often singing at the street corner to the people.

'He taught us many lessons that we shall never forget, among them the spirit of true simplicity and meekness. He also gave us a wonderful example of love for souls. I remember he visited Yokohama prison, and there found a man who had been a spy. He talked with him in the cell and urged him to seek Christ.'[3]

This prison convert is probably the only one-time spy ever to become a Salvation Army officer.

Opposite the university Railton opened a hostel for students about which he wrote to his daughter Esther:

'I should like you to see my little home here, though it is by no means the place that I should invite you to. Of course, I sit on the floor and eat in the Japanese style; our beds are laid on the matting at night, and all stowed away in the morning, but we have some chairs so as to make foreigners like you comfy when they come! We prefer the Japanese fashion, sitting on our legs on the nice thick mats; and I assure you it is all delightful, especially when we feel that we three are going to arouse a whole city with our *War Crys*.'[4]

An English visitor wrote of this venture:

'He had a very nice thing going among the students in one of their own public halls. A lot of these young fellows accepted Christianity. They were only babies, but they lived up to what they knew, and Commissioner Railton gave them every opportunity of testifying. His faith for everybody was charming. He could see in every Japanese a future missionary, though nobody else could.'[5]

Against the wishes of Headquarters in London, Railton went alone into China where he attacked the white-slave traffic, among other evils he disapproved of. This, in a country where not long before, the Boxers had slain the missionaries, was a typical Railtonian suicide mission. The Salvationist 'Foreign Office' was highly displeased. The proper forms had not been observed; permission had not been given. But Railton would not learn. He cabled London—'Have opened China with rescue home'. For this he had the assistance of Major Matilda Hatcher, a Salvation Army officer from Japan. She lived for a short time among the girls and women of Tientsin gathering information which Railton placed before the authorities. He wrote to Marianne:

'I get the exhilaration I do because I am like a naughty boy out of bounds. Not only my little wife says "Don't go there", but no sooner do I get a good prospect in China than headquarters cables to know when I am going back to Japan. And instead of any reply I turn off to the interior and then down here! But do not be afraid: you'll see I shall be all right. Oh, if I could see my wife and family landing on the Bund to help me rouse up China!'[6]

Railton passed through China, unharmed, treated with kindness, fed and housed as he went. He had a Chinese cap, with a prominent red tassel, and the words 'Salvation Army' inscribed on it in Chinese characters. With his red guernsey and soldier's tunic he must have looked impressive—perhaps something like a Chinese war lord. In Manchuria, in winter, sleeping on wooden floors he appreciated the huge sheepskin coat given him by a Japanese business man. He wrote home:

'There are no bed clothes. Everyone carries their own. But for my sheepskin I should have slept on bare boards. As it is I have spent the past three days in my clothes. But the stories of Chinese dirt are, as usual, misrepresentations. They are very particular to wash their faces each morning and after every meal. They spit a good deal but I get used to it. After all, it is only the old English fashion.'[7]

He was photographed in his splendid coat, the most impressive depiction of Railton that survives. But, alas, that was in Japan; when he arrived home, having journeyed in the coat across Russia, on the trans-Siberian railway, Railton's coat had vanished. He had given it to a man poorer than he. Railton could not have looked forward to wearing his splendid coat in Britain where it would have looked opulent. He would not wear the frock-tail coats which were in those days part of the imposing uniform of senior Salvation Army officers. When new uniform arrived, of frock-tail length, Railton simply cut off the 'tails', and sallied forth in the shortened uniform of his own design.[8]

By the time William Booth was ready to visit Japan in 1907 Railton was a Far Eastern expert, and Colonel John Lawley, who went before William Booth to smooth the way for his campaigns, was acutely apprehensive. Lawley remembered Berlin: the old time-table, the unworldly forgetting of meal-times, reservations, privacy. Railton had decided that William Booth must go to China and was planning accordingly. For various strong reasons this was not convenient but Railton pressed hard for it.

Lawley told Railton that the General could not go to China. 'Why not?' asked Railton. Need Generals visit only established battlefields? What about reconnaissance of new areas? Where was the old fighting spirit? The stand-like-the-brave attitude? If General 'Chinese' Gordon could walk unscathed through the Chinese rebels, carrying but a cane, protected against all bullets by 'white devil's magic', was the heroic General Booth to be put off merely by stormy waters, poor trains, rough voyages?

Lawley was not well-read in history but he knew his William Booth. More to the point, he knew his Bramwell Booth. Lawley hardly dared to think of what might happen to him if he hazarded the old General's precious and fragile frame on the China seas, and rivers, and amid that unpredictable people. It was not that William Booth would not have been ready. But Lawley knew that the Chief in London would not approve of it and the Chief knew best. One must stick to the brief. Everything must be as planned.

'Lawley, you're a backslider,' Railton said, and lamented the emphasis in civic receptions, press conferences and Salvationists demonstrations. 'We must go for souls,' he told Bullard and Lawley, which was both unkind and unnecessary. Neither of the men needed to be told what was the Army's over-all strategy. But Railton did not appreciate the need for public relations or the tight London control of the General's programme. With the General's party was Lieut.-Colonel Edward J. Higgins, Under-Secretary in the Army's Foreign Office. Higgins was an up-and-coming officer, who would be the Army's third General. Part of his duty was to send regular reports to his superior, Commissioner Howard, the Foreign Secretary. But he also wrote to Bramwell Booth:

'The General is rather tired tonight and seems to be suffering from headaches. There is no doubt the past few days has been a heavy tax upon him physically and nervously he is overdone, but he has wonderful recuperative power and I believe he will be ready for the Emperor in the morning.

'*Commissioner Railton is not helping matters*. I have been compelled to take a rather strong line today and he is, I can tell, very upset, but there is no other course open. He is so contradictory, goes back upon his own statements again and again, and changes front every day; but I won't bother you with it now.'

There was nothing William Booth would have loved more than

one long-continued soul-saving campaign in China and Japan. But he had to see the Japanese Emperor, and talk to the newspapers—the future of the Army in Japan would be influenced by his so doing. It was good to let Japanese young people demonstrate in youth rallies, and to have the support of members of the Japanese Government on the platform while William Booth lectured on the Army's world-wide operations.

William Booth knew that Railton opposed lectures as he opposed much else. He respected his views. He said:

'Railton says I should not lecture for an hour but let the charlady and the servant-girl speak instead. Well, I am free and will not do it and Railton is free and can do it.'[9]

What could be fairer? But the old Railton nostalgia was at work. The dear old Christian Mission had one great aim, to enlist and drill converts and send them forth. But now public relations had a high priority. The Emperor expected to be asked to receive William Booth, so did President Theodore Roosevelt, the Kings of Denmark and Sweden and many others in high places. The old man was larger than life. He had to talk to reporters and go through the weary protocol of civic luncheons, Mansion House receptions. He must acknowledge the existence of the middle and upper classes. They were the only people who could give him the sinews of war for his Army.

The General saw Japan and conquered; then he departed leaving Railton in the Orient. During this phase of his life he visited Java, as Indonesia was then termed, the Philippines and the Malay Straits. Where the Army had not 'opened fire' he pushed plans for it to do so. Where the work existed he strengthened it by his presence, prayers and faith. But Railton could not be expected to do things 'through the proper channels' as witness the cable which shocked HQ in which he intimated that he had commenced Army operations in China. He believed China was ready for The Salvation Army. But Bramwell Booth had to obtain official permission and find the money, the men and the women. All over the world there were appeals for the Army to begin operations. Bramwell Booth preferred to make adequate preparations before launching his attacks. The Army flag was unfurled in Peking in 1916.

28

The Scout of
The Salvation Army

WHEN LAWLEY left Japan he had written in his journal, 'Railton takes no thought for the morrow and not enough for today.' He was prematurely worn out. His brother, Launcelot, who had been as a father to him as a boy, and who had crossed swords with William Booth on his behalf, had just died of a heart attack. Railton wrote to Marianne from China:

'I am feeling very low, and am sending for a doctor. I could not be more nearly at home than with these friends, who will do all any one can do. An attack like my old ones has left me very low, and in this heat and under orders for the Philippines I cannot but see it is an awkward crisis. If it is a finish it will be as like Launcelot's as possible, but for my darling's sake perhaps I wish it to be at home instead.'

But later, the doctor examined his heart and pronounced it quite sound though he was against him going to the Philippines. However, Railton did go. He also journeyed to Siam, where he was bitten by mosquitoes during sleepless nights. Here he met a young man candidate and kindred spirit, who said, 'I must become a Salvation Army officer. Otherwise I might make money and that might lead to misfortune.' Who but Salvationists could produce such thoughts nowadays, asked Railton. He paid his second visit to Java and found the number of officers increased from twenty-two to fifty-two. Many of the Europeans had learned the language, the sale of *The War Cry* and village work had greatly expanded. A beginning had been made in the treatment of endemic eye disease, under Salvation Army officer Doctor Vilhelm A. Wille, who became a notable eye-specialist. Work among 12,000 leprosy patients had also begun and both branches of endeavour in Army clinics and hospitals continues in Indonesia to this day.

He went home briefly before resuming his wanderings. He told his daughter Esther wonderful tales about Siamese princes, Chinese camels, and lunches with the British Ambassador in Peking. He sang to her in Japanese, Malay and Chinese and showed his many passes, splendid letters of introduction and oriental maps. Of course, she saw his marvellous Chinese hat which to the discomfiture of the family he sometimes wore about Margate. Esther found that there were some compensations for having a father one saw so rarely. The feeling of resentment against the Booths was growing in her, 'for taking Papa away from us', as she put it.

This was unjust but understandable. It has been felt in other armies, by other sons and daughters of the regiments. Esther Railton was not alone in The Salvation Army in feeling as she did. Yet Railton, like every Army soldier, was a volunteer. He did not journey for the Booths, but for God. As the girl grew up his letters to her ranged over a wider field. He tells her of the Mormons, whom he met in Canada. They had been 'missionizing Europe'. Their converts were 'mainly decent Scandinavian families. If their polygamy is really ended they may become a harmless enough people.'

There were many cheerful, informative letters from what soon came to be known as the War Zone: France, Germany, Russia, Turkey and the Balkans. The brew was simmering in the cauldrons of Cabinet rooms, royal palaces, embassies, country house-parties and small hovels, down dark alleys, where nihilists and misguided patriots studied the fine art of bomb-throwing. Railton was optimistic about the opening of Army work in Russia and Turkey. Politically he was an innocent. He thought of men as being as selfless and charitable as himself. While Asquith in London, President 'Teddy' Roosevelt, in Washington, the Kaiser in Berlin, and politicians and defence chiefs in other capitals were forming their array for the holocaust to come, Railton wrote:

'No organization has destroyed in the minds of so many the old idea of strangers being "foreigners" as our Army. So entirely are multitudes of our officers and soldiers accustomed to the sense of brotherhood and sisterhood with comrades of other lands and races that we hesitate often about the use of the word "foreign". The true Salvationist feels at home wherever he may be sent.'[1]

He could write this though Japan had just fought her war with Russia, and America with Cuba. The Kaiser was sending alarmist telegrams; Russia and Austria and a group of belligerent little countries in the Balkans were poised to take each other by the throat. Even of citizens of the United States, whence a bevy of rich and beautiful brides arrived to wed English dukes and lesser nobility, it was considered appropriate for the English to use the word 'foreigner'. The liberal-minded Conservative, Balfour, had encountered Foreign Office resistance when he wished to drop it from official papers during his term as Prime Minister.[2]

Shortly after Railton's article appeared The Salvation Army expunged the word 'foreigner' from its terminology, as mentioned earlier, but Railton found it had deep roots elsewhere. When he tried to enter Russia again, in 1908, he found something interposing: the prototype of the iron curtain; but while he waited for the slow Russian bureaucratic machine to grant him a visa he did not waste his time or repine. In Odessa he spent one Saturday evening visiting a number of the City's eighty-three Jewish synagogues. How this could help is not clear, but it did demonstrate Railton's catholicity. He had to keep his Army hat on, of course, and submit to being kissed a number of times by various elders. He knew the truth of Cowper's words:

> To me remains no place nor time,
> My country is in every clime;
> I can be calm and free from care
> On any shore, since God is there.

Stolypin, the Russian Prime Minister had told W. T. Stead that he saw no political reason why The Salvation Army should not be allowed to operate in Russia. 'It might at any rate interest the people,' he said. Stead had been told by a Russian painter who had attended the meetings, in the Regent Hall, London, that 'if such a bright, brotherly, social religion were to enter Russia it would spread like a prairie fire'.

But the Orthodox Church in Russia was not well-disposed towards dissenting groups. The Baptists were already trouble enough and it was not hard to make the Czar and his advisers regard religious sects as fermenters of radical thought. Indeed, they had been in Britain. Open-air meetings were forbidden in Russia; marches and processions sometimes acted as a match to a powder-train. When, in 1905, a well-meaning priest led a march of unarmed peasants towards the Czar's palace in St. Petersburg, troops opened fire and Cossacks charged, slaying hundreds. The day has gone down in history as 'bloody Sunday'.

When Railton did get into Russia for his 1908 visit he met 'more titled people than in all my previous life' and used his not inconsiderable skill attempting to remove official objections to The Salvation Army. He led crowded meetings in St. Petersburg and was confirmed in his belief that when the Army established itself in Russia it would be from Finland, which indeed proved to be the case, in 1913. Though Railton wrote to the Czar Nicholas—he was never backward in approaching the highest authority—he received polite official replies but he did not get into the Imperial Palace.

But a truly great and holy Russian was at this time in the throes of inner-conflict startlingly similar to Railton's. One can believe that had Leo Tolstoy known of Railton's life and faith, and presence in Russia, he would have wished to meet him. Tolstoy was plagued by so many bores that the Salvationist might have been an agreeable change. Born of good family, Tolstoy had freed his serfs and shown such sympathy for the poor that he became an object of suspicion by the police and was intermittently kept under surveillance. His austere interpretation of religion caused him to be at odds with his wife— who like Marianne, found him a feckless husband. His children considered whether they should have him put into custody in a mental asylum. A profound mystic, Tolstoy gave away parts of his estates and the copyright of books which included the world's greatest pacifist thesis, *War and Peace,* and the compassionate study of a prostitute, *Anna Karenina,* a story so great that it can be compared only with the Bible narrative of Jesus and the Magdalene.[3] At the end, two years after Railton's visit to Russia, Tolstoy, a homeless wanderer, died at a railway station—as Railton did. Tolstoy found it hard to find a kindred spirit. Railton might have been one.

William Booth, who visited St. Petersburg in 1909, did not meet the Czar either. He was permitted to sit in on the proceedings of the Duma, as he had done in the Senate at Washington, but not to pray aloud. It can be taken for granted that he prayed silently for the strife-ridden country and its ruler, an autocrat like himself, but one who was obstinately fixed on a collision course with his people. Nicholas would have been well advised to talk to the General. He might have learned something of Booth's understanding of poverty and compassion for the poor, at which the Czar was so inept.

Turkey, so long the 'sick man of Europe' had, by her cruelties, caused Mr. Gladstone to come out of retirement and consign Prime Minister Disraeli into Opposition and the House of Lords. Now, as Railton visited the country in 1908, the Young Turks secured the support of the army and made demands on the Sultan which astonishingly he granted, after he and his forbears had refused for centuries past. Thereupon Bulgaria declared her complete independence and

Austria annexed Bosnia. Germany watched over all, as the Kaiser said, 'in shining armour'.

None of this mattered to the Booths or Railton except that the liberalization, which seemed to be on, made things more hopeful for the Army to expand in the Balkans. Railton spoke at various public meetings in Constantinople and was photographed reading *The War Cry* to Young Turks, some of whom looked well on in years. How much they understood is not known but Railton had an astonishing flair for making himself intelligible in any language. Frederick Moore wrote of Railton in the London *Daily Chronicle* as 'The Scout of The Salvation Army', and went on:

'When a priest of the Koran listens to the preaching of a Salvation Army man a state of humility has indeed come over Turkey ... The Armenians—men on one side, women on the other—filled the meeting room, with the exception of half-a-dozen benches left at the front for the Turks. They had sung several hymns before the prayers in the mosque ended, and the Turks came over the road. In all there were about thirty, and they appeared but little out of place, though it was a new experience for many to be in a room where men and women associated. There was a green-cloaked Mullah, with a green cloth round his red fez; another with a brown cloak and white turban; two or three Softas, or religious scholars, also cloaked; several officers of the Army, intelligent-looking young men; one policeman, a veritable fanatic in appearance, with beady eyes and a terrible hook of a nose; of the others dressed mostly "*a la franca*", one or two more white fezzes, a feature of the boycott against Austria, whence the red fezzes come.'

He went on to describe Railton:

'He stood in his military uniform the Turkey-red shirt conspicuous, at one side of the reading-desk, where-on lay the Bible, and an Armenian, a portly, dark man in a frock coat, stood on the other side, translating the sermon, sentence by sentence, into Turkish—which is understood of Armenians as well as Turks. I do not remember the text, but it might well have been that of the new regime, "Love one another".'

A young Turk thanked Railton:

'As everyone is attached to his faith and beliefs, we could not thank too much the honourable person, who, at the cost of a thousand troubles, has come from England to remind us of this holy duty ... England ensures material tranquility to all creatures living under man's name; and not content with that, she organizes the great Salvation Army and sends the chiefs of that Army to the ends of the universe to work for the eternal salvation of humanity.'

At the end of the meeting:

'The long-cloaked Muezzin stooped to kiss the hand of the Salvation Army man, a sign of respect which a Christian rarely receives ... We understand that the Commissioner has discussed with some Young Turks the project of taking over one of the old battleships that lies perpetually moored in the Golden Horn, in order that they may have of it an Elevator, lifter of humanity.'

But the Railtonian ideal of love could not survive the wars of 1911–12 in which Italy and the Balkan League attacked Turkey, though during the Balkan War and its terrible aftermath The Salvation Army contributed ambulance teams and relief work, partly in Constantinople. This was to be the fate of many of Railton's missions now, forlorn hopes and lost causes. William Booth, in hardly legible handwriting, for his eyes were giving serious trouble, wrote to Bramwell in January 1908:

'AUSTRIA. I don't like beating a retreat. If Railton is going that way could he not visit the place and investigate?
RAILTON. *I ought to see him.* I must see him. There must be some way of linking him up *closer* and using him to better advantage.'

There were the elements of inevitable tragedy here. William Booth's Army was a mighty Army now. There were methods of control, standardization of procedure, even as there is in all armies, a certain professionalism. The International Secretary was responsible to Bramwell Booth for the organization of overseas visits of the sort that engaged Railton for the last years of his life.

Railton would not keep the rules in the little matters, and some men at desks at International Headquarters tended to overlook the fact that he always went 'straight down the line' in big matters—this man who had done more than most to make The Salvation Army.

Howard was a devout, erudite, courteous, precise man. He taught, with some theological expertise, the Methodist concept of holiness. With Mrs. Booth, Railton was chiefly responsible for weaving this strand of the Christian faith into the pattern of the Army life and service. But Howard was close to Bramwell Booth and, in due course appointed as Chief of the Staff, second in command of the Army. Not a line from Howard can be found in the Railton papers, though Railton wrote to Howard:

'What on earth can be the reason that you great people do not want to see me or write me a line, or apparently to have me anywhere on the foreign field more than can be avoided? Of course the silence of *The War Cry,* after reporting me gone from here, I can heartily laugh at. But one would have imagined you glad to have a Commissioner eager to help these little things from dying out ...

'Why not go in for utilizing my sixty-second year to best advantage? Perhaps you say, "It is between the two offices you get adrift." True I am in touch with the Chief, but let this prove to you, at any rate, that I have never had any wish to ignore you too, if it were only possible to get at you.'

But it was not as simple as that. Howard's position put him in day-by-day proximity to Bramwell Booth. Railton, because of his private crusade to stop the Army going the way the Chief of the Staff wanted it to go, was not *persona grata*. Bramwell Booth was too busy, and often not in the mood for arguments—even restrained, enlightened and civilized Railtonian arguments. There was a more complex psychological reason why Railton's face was not seen as often cheek by jowl with Bramwell Booth. The Chief of the Staff thought highly of Railton, and he knew that his father loved him. Railton's unhappiness, and the sight of his amiable but serious face set on raising objections to the latest of the Army's schemes, disturbed Bramwell.

The Editorial Department discovered that Railton wrote articles that were unpublished because of their critical tone, uncompromising frankness, their opposition to policies approved by the General and the Chief. The Overseas Department knew that he went where he would, often disappearing into Asia or remote parts of Europe so they did not know whether he was martyred or jailed, dead or alive. He founded a student's hostel in Japan on a budget of seven shillings a week, without official permission. It was not the done thing. The music people were aware that he had policy reservations about big bands for he was against anything which was not a direct assault on sin and Satan, in his opinion the Army's only reason for existence.

Meanwhile Bramwell's firm hand was guiding the Army through transitional years, from the plain evangelical mission to the immense diversification and international flexibility of the present-style Salvation Army. It is hard to see how it could have survived in any worthwhile form without these developments. A considerable degree of professional ability is demanded before Salvation Army missionaries are admitted to Central Africa, India or South America. Those countries will admit Salvationists with Bibles, but they also need textbooks, diagnostic equipment, and college degrees or diplomas. Much of the effort is indirect, a tactical approach of which Railton disapproved.

In the United States, Australia and New Zealand, Scandinavia and the continent of Europe large sums of public money are expended by the Army in social services that begin with the new babe of the unwed mother and go through the full range of human need to the homeless aged. Little of this work would be possible without 'the diversionary activities' that Railton condemned. But William and Bramwell Booth were as much lovers of souls as Railton. But how do you save an alcoholic, a drug addict, a homosexual? His human condition will have to be professionally treated before he can be saved, with a fighting chance of holding on to his salvation when the devil's thunderbolts are hurled at him. William Booth is said to have remarked, 'It is no use preaching salvation to a man with cold feet or an empty stomach.' Railton always acted as though William Booth meant 'Go *straight* for souls'. What he said was '*Go* for souls and go for the worst.' He did not rule out a roundabout way.

Administratively, the Army as it is today is largely the creation of Bramwell Booth. But Railton, whom many have called saint—though this is not a Salvation Army 'rank'—had his victories too. It was not in vain that he left wife and children, friends and home—and sometimes happiness—for Christ's sake.

Privately he wrote, 'They're making the Army into a circus', and in the first flush of popularity, with its great exhibitions, Crystal Palace rallies, poor man's bank and poor man's lawyer, hotels, even a restaurant which he found in France and which shocked him greatly, there did seem to be a danger of the Army's becoming something quite different from what God intended it to be. Young William Beveridge, soon to be Director of the London School of Economics, was studying the Army employment exchanges and other social activities. Lloyd

George, the Chancellor of the Exchequer, was becoming an enthusiastic social worker, 'soaking the rich' to get his money, much to the disgust of the House of Lords. Railton was afraid that the salvation war would become an appendage of the embryo welfare state.

He cared as little for Beveridge's approach in the Edwardian age as he had for Arnold's in the Victorian. He agitated, preached, wrote, fought the good fight as he saw it. Some officers, assuming quite wrongly that Bramwell Booth expected it of them, avoided Railton and withdrew their friendship. But in the Army generally, among the rank and file where none of this was known, Railton became a legend. If his articles in *The War Cry* were not printed, his life told a larger story. In his continuing emphasis on the Army's first purpose he did much to preserve a balance between the necessary, but merely expedient Army of the Helping Hand, and the greater, far more difficult goal— *How to Reach the Masses with the Gospel.*

29

The Cavalry of the Skies

THE LAST years of Railton's life were anti-climax. Though he was regarded with affection by the General and Bramwell Booth, he was not in the mainstream of Army activities. His eccentric views made him an outsider. When at home he journeyed up from Margate to International Headquarters to find that his office was a void. 'They come in to use the telephone; that is how I get the news,' he told Marianne.

Various people sent him to Coventry for he was at odds with the Chief of the Staff. Yet Bramwell often sought a reconciliation with Railton. He was well aware of his wide influence and his major contributions to the development of the Army. But Railton would not be reconciled, except on terms which would have meant a diminution of the Army's activities in ways which would inhibit its international flexibility and possibly paralyse it.

Railton agreed with Paul, in the New Testament, that the love of money is the root of evil. It hurt him to see the Army set aside officers whose task it was to raise funds. They should be seeking souls. But this idealism was a luxury Bramwell Booth could not afford. William Booth asked for an initial £100,000 and £30,000 a year endowment for his 'Darkest England' Scheme and got it. But had not the officers under Bramwell's direction given the problem much of their time this money would not have been forthcoming. William Booth, though unskilled in fund-raising, none the less saw its necessity and appreciated Bramwell's skill in that field. After reading parts of Railton's latest annual report, the General wrote:

'My dear Railton,   Amsterdam, February 22nd, 1910.
    ... The Chief writes me that he is pleased with those parts of the report which you have already sent him, and that he thinks the book taken altogether, likely to prove useful ... It is no use depreciating the press. Instead of belittling it we must take hold of it and use it. I had the owner and editor of the *Handelsblad*, the most influential paper in this country, on my platform on Sunday afternoon, speaking

eloquently and enthusiastically of the Army and the General, and saying that all the influence that religion had on him dated back to the
addresses he heard from Mrs. General Booth in London forty years
ago. We must capture the press and make it go our way, and you must
help us to do this.

'I am not bright in health, but still keeping on my feet. I am troubled
now with a sort of vertigo, and overflow of blood to the brain. I thought
that I had too little blood, but the doctors appear to be of the opinion
that I have too much, and they all swear that I must be careful or I
shall go off in a hurry and leave you to take care of yourselves, which
at present I don't think you are capable of doing, even with the Chief,
yourself, Kitching and others, whom I appreciate very much, included.

Your affectionate General . . .'

Though Blériot had flown across the Channel in 1909, augury of the
day when travelling Salvationists would have wings, most of Railton's
journeyings were by slow boat and chilly trains. The young man who
had boarded a horse-drawn tram on the first stage of his expedition
to America, in 1880, had certainly been around; something like
300,000 miles as a Salvationist wanderer.

Travelling steerage to the United States in 1912, in a Red Star
liner, which was carrying our 'brothers and sisters of South Germany,
Poland, Austria-Hungary and Bosnia, who are looked upon as dangerous
and undesirable by many',[1] he noted that 'at dinner only two of sixteen
men at the table wore their jackets. But that only opened up my
way to sit, as I love to do, in my jersey, whose cross made me the more
at home among my Catholic room-mates.' There was a piano in the
music-room at which a Dutch girl helped Railton to sing 'The Lord's
my Shepherd'. On the outward voyage there was no insect life in
the berths which Railton found 'astounding' but thought that the
reason was probably the Red Star policy of throwing overboard all
steerage straw mattresses and pillows at the end of each round trip.
This meant, however, that when you travelled back from New York,
as Railton did sometimes, you had the old used straw pillows and
worse. But Railton always 'slept well and asked no questions likely to
make me uneasy'.[2]

He thought the behaviour of the so-called 'brutish multitude' in
steerage better than the 'boulevard spirits on both decks' up above.
Down below all unmarried women must go to their quarters by nine,
and the married folk by ten. Railton was no forerunner of Dr. Kinsey

but his opinion was that 'among the better-class passengers there are those who look for their chief diversion in the long weary days to excess of drinking, gambling, or flirtation (to give it its mildest name),[3] He was asked how he could tolerate the crowded communal berths below deck, the drinking, swearing, sickness, squalling of babies, with neither sheets nor blankets for his mattress. How could he put up with anarchists as bed-fellows, men who complained of being 'treated like dogs', who would lie sleepless only to think of those on the decks above 'treated to every luxury'? To these Railton made answer:

'The Salvation Army is the twentieth-century adaptation of the 'Little Brothers of the Poor' who, in the days of St. Francis of Assisi, proved their brotherhood to the Master by their ceaseless toil for the needy.'[4]

In places as public as railway stations, he knelt to pray and read his Bible. Usually he was afforded reverent silence. He spoke to many of God and prayer and faith. Some of the emigrants remembered for a long time the last words they heard before they stepped ashore in 'the land of the free'. George Scott Railton was not a man one readily forgot.

All the time, in the precious intervals aboard ship and on trains, in lulls in the salvation war Railton wrote and wrote, often with his knee as a desk, in the spidery neat hand that was the despair of compositors. His major opus was *General Booth,* published by Hodder and Stoughton, in 1913. This might have been a great work; instead it was a great opportunity lost. On the stocks for rather more than three years, because after Bramwell Booth's fastidious eye had scanned it the revisions were numerous and drastic. Almost certainly it is not the book Railton wanted to write, that he could have written, and should have written.

The book contained nothing of the 'General and Lieutenant' relationship which transformed the Mission into an Army and which only Railton or William Booth could have written. The eleven years' life in the Booth's home is omitted. The pioneers are mentioned only in passing and then not by name. Railton's expedition to the United States is an astonishing gap. The flat, unbalanced record of William Booth's career is the work of a tired man, or one who wrote to order. It is certainly not the life Railton would have written at his best. His William Booth would have been more human, capable of making mistakes, yet warmer and greater than in this record. As can be inferred from

Bramwell Booth's preface, this biography had its marked limitations, and it was an open secret that Harold Begbie had agreed to do an official two-volume biography which the war delayed until 1920, when Macmillan published it.

Grown familiar with disfavour, Railton soldiered on, his body largely worn out, his spirit as indomitable as ever. He wrote home to Marianne:

'The Lord has again seemed this week both to encourage me a little and to desert me a lot. If He does not choose to do any more by me, why should I care? I have been His Samuel of today as best I can.'

A doctor had assured him, not long before, 'Your heart is all right'. Yet in 1912, in the United States and Canada, as he subjected himself to snowstorms, cold trains, marches through blizzards and half-frozen open-air meetings Railton felt this was not so. He wrote to Marianne again:

'I must be ill or rapidly ageing. But then I go out into the brilliant sunshine and trot along over the snow and ice, trying to pray away my feelings.'

In Canada they billed him to lecture. It was not in him to be churlish so he tried, but people noticed that after starting off formally he was soon away on a Railtonian plea, either for his Christian audience to be holy or for his un-Christian audience to become converted—this took in the civic leaders, mayors and parliamentarians who doubtless needed the exhortation as much as any. It was not in Railton to compromise. He was, in this respect, a formidable man to have around. All who came in contact with him, family, friends and strangers, either had to adjust to him or 'watch from afar'. This is why, for much of his life, Railton was essentially a lonely man.

In the United States, where the method of Salvationist endeavour was so widely opposed to Railton's idealistic view, and where lectures were popular, there is no record of Railton's being asked to join the lecturers. Indeed, it is a paradox that ought to have given Railton food for thought, and perhaps did, that the country where he had led the official invasion forces, which had developed a highly professional business, Railton's approach and utilitarian method of achieving religious aims, could also respond to his piety and appeal for apostolic simplicity. In Commissioner Samuel Logan Brengle, of Boston, Massachusetts, a prophet of holiness rose up who, unbelievably, synthesized second-hand clothes shops and public relations campaigns on behalf of the poor and needy with the truly holy life.

On a birthday Railton had written:

'Far from expecting to live out much of my second half-century I know that at any moment I may pass into the Heavenly Fatherland. Today's great news to me has been that of Major Elmslie's glorious rush up the railway station to heaven.[5] I wish for no better ending to my warfare ... Whatever kind of end it may be I should like there to be no possibility of doubt that up to the last minutes I belonged to The Salvation Army.'

For his last journey to Le Locle, in Switzerland, where he was to assist his friends, the Peyrons, in an evangelistic campaign, he wore a new suit of uniform, a rare event. On one of his last Sundays at home he had taught the children of the Sunday-school at Margate to sing choruses on the sands for admiring holiday-makers. They must have seemed amazingly accomplished children for 'they sang in twelve languages'. When he arrived home after the seven o'clock kneedrill (prayer meeting), gifts lay beside his breakfast plate, for it was his sixty-fourth birthday. He liked particularly a pair of flexible slippers. 'I can slip these into my pocket as I travel,' he said. So he did but he did not get much chance to wear them. He was ready for shoes of another sort:

I got shoes,
You got shoes,
All God's chillun got shoes;
When I get to 'eaven,
Gonna put on my shoes,
And wear 'em all over God's 'eaven ...

Though the writers of the Gospels, and a long line of dialecticians since, have put a premium on Christian poverty, those who practise it find it a heavy cross. Railton had to change trains at Cologne on his way back to Amsterdam from Switzerland. The third-class compartments did not go through and Railton was travelling third because there was not a fourth. It would be a long wait, he was very tired and carried his own bag as usual, for he was obstinately without the ADC or secretary Bramwell Booth would have been happy to provide for him.

But his wait would be in Germany, the country he loved, next to England, most of all. So in the dark he walked and inquired and found the quarters of the Salvation Army officers where, happily, one was a soldier he had sworn in when he was Territorial Commander for Germany twenty-one years before.

Railton was welcomed as an Elisha to the school of the prophets. They talked of old times and they forgot their astonishment at this Englishman who did not share the general English anti-German feeling —heartily reciprocated—less than one year before the shots were fired at Sarajevo. He could speak their language too, unlike most of his countrymen, lazily mono-lingual, though they ruled half the earth.

Before they broke up Railton knelt to pray, something he did as naturally as he breathed. They sang an emotional, rather plaintive refrain, one Salvationists still sing. In English it goes:

> Walk with me,
> All the way from earth to heaven,
> Blessèd Master, walk with me.

Railton did not have far to walk. He would not let them go out with him. Time was short and he hurried. Retrieving his bag from the cloakroom he rushed up the stairs to the train—in his condition this was suicidal. The train was waiting. He jumped in. Sat down. Leaned back. And that was the end. It was the 19th of July, 1913.

It would be sacrilege to say that Railton had died. In his own phrase he had been 'promoted from the infantry of the earth to the cavalry of the skies'. Thus he had put it in 1876 when he thought that small-pox had marked him for her own. In his bag was his little Chinese hat, which had embarrassed his son David in Margate, but which Continentals liked immensely when he wore it and told them of their Salvationist comrades in Japan and other parts of the Far East. Because of Railton's pleas some of them would give their lives for Christ in China where the Salvationist battle was not yet joined.

In his pocket was found a strange, but highly useful document, carefully written out in English, German, and French in Railton's own hand. It was headed, 'For any authority finding me dead or unconscious.'

To the Police.   G. S. Railton, for years, since 1898, suffered
                                                    from heart weakness.

Address: 101, Queen Victoria Street,

London. E.C.

If found anywhere dead or unconscious, please

If dead. Bury on the spot as quickly and cheaply as possible, reporting—as above.

If any church close by will bury, good.

If not, do not trouble. But report.

If found unconscious. Get into any hospital. I do not want to burden
anyone.

You can rely on The Salvation Army to pay any really needed
costs, as of a poor man—no flowers.

101 will report to my dear wife and family; but I do not want any
of them to have the cost and misery of coming to bury or nurse me.
My love to everybody. Amen. I am going to heaven. Meet me there.

It was a time when Salvation Army funerals were one of the sights
of London, with big bands, tremendous marches, bright uniforms,
happy tunes and flags a-flying—something like the Lord Mayor's Show.
But it is always genuine, as Railton claimed, no occasion for mourn-
ing, but rather the promotion of a soldier. Though family and friends
try to see it this way they cannot always succeed and there was grief
at Railton's farewell. The idiosyncratic rebel was loved the world
over. Telegrams poured in and tales were told. Bramwell Booth led a
magnificent series of obsequies from the Congress Hall, Clapton, to
Abney Park Cemetery, where Railton's remains were put beside those
of William Booth, then memorial services in the Westminster Central
Hall. There the International Staff Band played Handel's *Dead March,*
and they sang four of Railton's songs. A galaxy of the Army's leading
officers present came from Germany, Switzerland, Scandinavia, France
and Belgium, Holland, Canada and South America.

There was so much to say that five long memorial services could
not contain it. It was related that two young officers, who slept longer
than he, found him happily polishing their shoes when they came down
to breakfast on Sunday morning. One recalled that in April 1906 Captain Bertram Hayes, of the White Star liner *Majestic,* was asked by
Mr. George S. Railton, one of his less affluent passengers, to take up
a collection for the victims of the San Francisco earthquake, as if this
dignified fast ship were a Salvation Army citadel. The Captain had
refused permission until confirmation had been received. The said

Mr. Railton had led Salvation Army meetings in the stricken city on the previous Sunday. A boy at Wynberg, South Africa, would never forget that Commissioner Railton's uniform was not as splendid as his father's—who was but an Ensign—or the visitor's 'humility and gentleness'. His father wrote in his diary: 'A man of God. Filled with the Holy Spirit. Humble, Full of love. In earnest about souls. 32 seekers at the meeting.' A young man and his sweetheart remembered that, at West Hartlepool, Railton took off his overcoat and laid it down on the snow for penitents to kneel upon, and that he, a full Commissioner, carried the huge double Bb brass instrument to give the bandsman a rest.

Bramwell Booth made a generous tribute. 'I have lost a friend,' he said, and so he had, a faithful friend who, as friends must, was not afraid to be honest and candid at risk of offence. Bramwell told the story of William Booth's last words, spoken with a grim smile, 'I'm leaving you a bonnie handful. But Railton will be with you.'

War would soon break up the united Salvation Army family. The Railton boys would go as padres with the BEF to France, Mrs. Railton to the lonely, long widowhood at Margate. The Germans would return to their Fatherland soon to endure the silence, the separation and misunderstanding of war. Bramwell Booth's complex international structure would have to withstand stresses which even his statesman-like mind had not envisaged for it.

Commissioner David Rees of Canada, who paid tribute to his friend, would, in May the next year, go down, with 166 other Salvationists coming to London for the last great International Congress for fifty years, into the icy St. Lawrence River as the *Empress of Ireland* foundered. 'Commissioner Railton shaped my life,' said Rees at the Central Hall.

Yet the song theme of Railton's life was just right for the times as well as for his 'promotion'. No Salvation Army verses epitomize more closely the life of their writer. It a germinal poem of Salvationism:

> No home on earth have I,
> No nation owns my soul,
> My dwelling-place is the Most High,
> I'm under His control.
> O'er all the earth alike,
> My Father's grand domain,
> Each land and sea with Him alike
> O'er all He yet shall reign.

No place on earth I own,
No field, no house be mine;
Myself, my all I still disown,
My God, let all be Thine.
Into Thy gracious hands
My life is ever placed;
To die fulfilling Thy commands,
I march with bounding haste.

With Thee, my God, is home;
With Thee is endless joy;
With Thee in ceaseless rest I roam;
With Thee, can death destroy?
With Thee, the east, the west,
The north, the south are one;
The battle's front I love the best,
And yet: Thy will be done.

From the Mississippi River, where he had written it, to Cologne Station where he died by it, Railton had struggled heroically to live by the Christ-like aspirations of his words. Now he who had had no home on earth had a place in his Father's house.

Q

References

Chapter 1

1. *The Age of Disunity*; Epworth Press (London). By 'the Booths', Doctor Kent informed the author, he meant William and Catherine Booth.
2. *Patterns of Sectarianism*; Heinemann (London).
3. *These Fifty Years,* by Bramwell Booth; Cassell (London, 1929); p. 95.
4. *All the World,* September 1913, p. 549.
5. A notable example is Charles Terrot's highly successful TV play, *Shout aloud Salvation.* Cadman is there depicted making dramatic use of military ideas. Railton's original conceptions are not mentioned.
6. *Echoes and Memories,* by Bramwell Booth; Hodder and Stoughton (London, 1925); pp. 168, 169.
7. *The History of The Salvation Army,* by Robert Sandall; Nelson (London, 1947); vol. 1, p. 198.
8. *Echoes and Memories,* p. 192
9. Ibid. p. 194.
10. *The Age of Disunity.*
11. *The History of The Salvation Army,* vol. 1, p. 264.
12. Railton probably fathered this phrase on the Army—see page 39

Chapter 2

1. The author is grateful to Miss Margaret Allison, Rural Librarian, Douglas, Isle of Man, for information regarding Railton's parents.
2. *Commissioner Railton,* by Eileen Douglas and Mildred Duff; Salvationist Publishing and Supplies (London, 1920); p. 9.
3. The author is grateful to the present Head at Woodhouse, Dr. F. C. Pritchard, for valuable information on Railton's schooldays.
4. *Commissioner Railton,* p. 11.
5. Dr. Pritchard, in a note to the author.

6. *These Fifty Years,* p. 100.
7. But Mrs. Railton believed that Railton carried the flag during his first Christian Mission campaign in Wales, which if correct made him the first Salvationist ever to carry a flag. Bramwell Booth disagreed. From Railton papers.
8. *Commissioner Railton,* p. 21.
9. Ibid. p. 22.
10. *Methodism,* by Rupert C. Davies; Epworth Press.
11. *The Age of Disunity.*
12. *Commissioner Railton,* pp. 24, 25.
13. See *England,* 1870–1914, by Sir Robert Ensor; Oxford University Press.

Chapter 3

1. *Commissioner Railton,* p. 31.
2. Ibid. p. 30.
3. *The Christian Mission Magazine,* January 1873, p. 7.
4. *Commissioner Railton,* p. 33.
5. See *The Life of William Booth,* by Harold Begbie; Macmillan and Co. (London, 1920); vol. 1, pp. 164, 165.
6. *The History of The Salvation Army,* vol. 1, p. 210.
7. Ibid. vol. 3, p. 64.

Chapter 4

1. *The Christian Mission Magazine,* September 1873, p. 136.
2. *The History of The Salvation Army,* vol. 1, p. 167.
3. Ibid. vol. 1, p. 168.
4. Railton papers.
5. *The Christian Mission Magazine,* July 1874, p. 181.
6. *Commissioner Railton,* p. 46.
7. Ibid. p. 48.
8. *The History of The Salvation Army,* vol. 1, p. 223.
9. Railton papers.
10. Ibid.

Chapter 5

1. The manuscript of *Heathen England.*
2, 3 and 4. Railton papers.

5. Probably the origin of the well-known Salvationist term for death: 'promotion to Glory'.
6. *Commissioner Railton*, pp. 54, 55.
7. January 1873, p. 1.
8. *The Christian Mission Magazine*, December 1973, pp. 177, 178.

Chapter 6

1. *The War Cry*, February 7th, 1880.
2. *Commissioner Railton*, p. 69.
3. *All the World*, January 1912, p. 43.

Chapter 7

1. *Soldiers Without Swords*; Macmillan (New York, 1955); p. 10.
2. *The War Cry*, February 21st, 1880.

Chapter 8

1. Railton papers.
2. Three of the 'seven sisters' had returned to England being unable to endure the abnormally hot summer and Railton's arduous programme. Two, however, returned to the United States.

Chapter 9

1. *God's Soldier*, by St. John Ervine; Heinemann (London, 1934); vol. 1, p. 515.
2. Railton papers.
3. *Soldiers Without Swords*, pp. 30, 31.
4. *Life of William Booth*, vol. 2, pp. 70, 71.
5. *What Hath God Wrought?* by Arnold Brown; The Salvation Army (Toronto, 1952); p. 4.

Chapter 10

1. *God's Soldier*, vol. 1, p. 504. It is suggested that Railton had displeased William Booth by publishing the American *Salvation News* without prior permission.
2 and 3. Railton papers.
4. *The History of The Salvation Army*, vol. 2, p. 47.

5. *Commissioner Railton,* p. 94.
6. These instruments of labour—or torture—were still in use in the prisons of those days.
7. The rule that officers could marry only officers had not then been made. Until her marriage to Railton Marianne was but a sergeant. No other Salvationist has ever been promoted from sergeant to Mrs. Commissioner.

Chapter 11

1. *The War Cry,* 1884; repeated advertisements.

Chapter 12

1. It will be remembered that at this time the Union of South Africa had not been created, contemporary terms were not current and objections to the old terms had not arisen. I use the words penned by the Railtons.
2. *The History of The Salvation Army,* vol. 3, pp. 291, 292.
3. *The War Cry,* July 18th, 1885.

Chapter 13

1. Hodder and Stoughton (1964).
2. Salvationist Publishing and Supplies, Ltd. (1949).
3. This clause made his 'revolt' over The Salvation Army Assurance Society inevitable; see page 128.

Chapter 14

1. *Commissioner Railton,* p. 116.
2. Ibid. pp. 116, 117.

Chapter 15

1. Railton papers.

Chapter 16

1. *All the World,* October 1893, p. 247.
2. *God's Soldier,* vol. 2, p. 743.
3. *The Vanderbilts and Their Fortunes,* by Edwin P. Hoyt (Muller).

Chapter 17

1. From *The War Cry,* May 21st, 1892; quoted in *God's Soldier,* pp. 751, 752.

2. A reference to an illness Bramwell Booth had at the age of twenty-two. He was sent for cure to Sweden and whilst there began Salvation Army meetings which led to the Salvationist invasion of the country.

Chapter 18

1. *The History of The Salvation Army,* by Arch R. Wiggins; Nelson (London, 1964); vol. 4, p. 56.
2. *Commissioner Railton,* p. 129.
3. Ibid. pp. 129, 130.
4. *The History of The Salvation Army,* vol. 4, p. 66.
5 to 13. Railton papers.

Chapter 19

1. *Commissioner Railton,* pp. 133–135.
2. *All the World,* February 1898, p. 64.
3. Railton papers.

Chapter 20

1. *All the World,* August 1888, pp. 270, 271.
2. *Commissioner Railton,* p. 141.

Chapter 21

1. *The War Cry,* March 31st, 1900, p. 8.
   All letters quoted are from Railton papers.

Chapter 22

1. *A Scot in Zululand,* by Catherine Baird; Salvationist Publishing and Supplies Ltd. (London, 1943).
2. *Bramwell Booth,* by Catherine Bramwell-Booth; Rich and Cowan (London, 1933); p. 51.

Chapter 23

1. *Commissioner Dowdle;* The Salvation Army (London, 1901); p. 101.
2. *Commissioner Railton,* pp. 150, 151.
3. *The War Cry,* October 4th, 1902, p. 6.

Chapter 24

1. *All the World,* June 1905, p. 316.

Chapter 27

1. His view was decidedly unfavourable and time has shown that he was right. Overseas Governments continued to take Salvation Army sponsored immigrants but only into the normal labour market. Rider Haggard advocated Salvationist land colonies which had a chequered and brief existence.
2. *Commissioner Railton,* p. 160.
3. Ibid. pp. 161, 162.
4. Ibid. pp. 162, 163.
5. Ibid. p. 163.
6. Ibid. pp. 164, 165.
7. Ibid. pp. 166, 167.
8. See article on Railton by Arch R. Wiggins; *The War Cry,* February 21st, 1969.
9. Railton papers.

Chapter 28

1. *All the World,* January 1908, p. 35.
2. *Arthur James Balfour,* by Kenneth Young p. 279.
3. After Railton's death, his sons considered whether the family had a claim against the Army on the copyright of Railton's numerous books, one of which was a biography of William Booth, written in 1912. But Marianne advised against making an issue of it; she knew the copyright of all written works of serving officers is vested in The Salvation Army. She may have known that Railton helped to frame the rule, which stands to this day.

Chapter 29

1, 2 and 3. *All the World,* November 1912, pp. 603–605.
4. Ibid. p. 606.
5. The officer who had helped Junker in the training corps at Battersea had died running to catch a train.

Bibliography

BEGBIE, HAROLD, *Life of William Booth*, Macmillan.

BLACKWELL, H. BENJAMIN, *Ambassador Extraordinary*, Salvationist Publishing and Supplies, Ltd.

BLAKE, ROBERT, *Disraeli*, Eyre and Spottiswoode.

BOOTH, BRAMWELL, *Echoes and Memories*, Hodder and Stoughton. *These Fifty Years*, Cassell.

BOOTH-TUCKER, FREDERICK, *Life of Catherine Booth*, Salvationist Publishing and Supplies, Ltd.

BOOTH, CATHERINE BRAMWELL-, *Bramwell Booth*, Rich and Cowan; *Catherine Booth*, Hodder and Stoughton.

BRIGGS, ASA, *They Saw it Happen*, Oxford.

BROWN, ARNOLD, *What Hath God Wrought?* The Salvation Army, Canada.

CHESHAM, SALLIE, *Born to Battle*, Rand McNally.

CLARK, KITSON, *The Making of Victorian England*, Methuen.

COLLIER, RICHARD, *The General Next to God*, Collins.

DAVIES, RUPERT C., *Methodism*, Epworth Press.

ENSOR, R. C. K., *England*, Oxford University Press.

ERVINE, ST. JOHN, *God's Soldier*, Heinemann.

FRAZER, PETER, *Joseph Chamberlain*, Cassell.

GOUT, RAOUL, *Blanche Peyron*, Editions Altis.

HAGGARD, H. RIDER, *The Poor and the Land*, Longmans.

HALL, CLARENCE, *Samuel Logan Brengle*, The Salvation Army, New York.

HOYT, EDWIN P., *The Vanderbilts and Their Fortunes*, Frederick Muller.

KENT, JOHN, *The Age of Disunity*, Epworth Press.

KRUGER, RAYNE, *Goodbye, Dolly Gray*, Cassell.

LUNN, BRIAN, *Salvation Dynasty*, Hodge.

McKENZIE, F. A., *Booth-Tucker—Sadhu and Saint*, Hodder and Stoughton.

MORRIS, DONALD, *Washing of the Spears*, Jonathan Cape.

MORRISON AND COMMAGER, *The Growth of the American Republic,* Oxford, New York.

MURRAY, MARY, *The Salvation Army at Work in the Boer War,* The Salvation Army, London.

SANDALL, ROBERT, *The History of The Salvation Army,* vols. 1–3, Nelson.

SYMONS, JULIAN, *Buller's Campaigns,* Cresset Press.

WIGGINS, ARCH R., *The History of The Salvation Army,* vols. 4, 5, Nelson.

WILSON, P. WHITWELL, *The General, the Story of Evangeline Booth,* Hodder and Stoughton.

WISBEY, HERBERT A., *Soldiers Without Swords,* Macmillan, New York.

Index

The I.Q. Mine Field

David J. Bodycombe

BARNES
&NOBLE
BOOKS
NEW YORK

Many thanks to Chris Dickson for his many constructive criticisms of the first draft, suggesting some good puzzles, and helping me "brainstorm" for new ideas.

Thanks also go to:
Jane MacKenzie, Patrick Erwin, Daniel Connolly, and Mary Deliyannis for their cruxiverbalistic testing of The I.Q. Mine Field.
My aunt, Enid McNamara, for her help in making the book "America-friendly."
My friends for their supportive curiosity.
Nick Robinson, Jan Chamier, and Mark Crean at Robinson Publishing for their backing, scrutiny, and guidance.
My parents, Sheila and David, who have helped with testing ideas or looking up curious information for a long time.

Originally published as *The Mammoth Book of Brainstorming Puzzles, Round Two*

Text, icons, and selected diagrams copyright © 1996 by David J. Bodycombe

Copyright clipart used in this book originates from the following companies: 3G Graphics Inc., Archive Arts, BBL Typographic, Cartesia Software, Corel Corporation, Image Club Graphics Inc., Management Graphics Ltd., One Mile Up Inc., Studio Piazza Xilo M.C., Techpool Studios Inc., Totem Graphics Inc., TNT Designs.

Book Layout by David J. Bodycombe at *Labyrinth Games* using *CorelDraw! 5*, © Corel Corporation 1994. Crosswords produced with the aid of *Crossword Compiler for Windows*, © Antony Lewis 1993-5.

Word Island suggested answers checked against *Chambers English Dictionary*, 1990, edited by Catherine Schwarz *et al*.

This edition published by Barnes & Noble, Inc.,
by arrangement with Carroll & Graf Publishers, Inc.

1997 Barnes & Noble Books

ISBN 0-7607-0491-0

Printed and bound in the United States of America

98 99 00 01 M 9 8 7 6 5 4 3 2

QF

INSTRUCTIONS

#1 QUIZWORD

The first type of game in each lap is a crossword with a difference. Each clue is a trivia question, the answer to which should be entered into the grid in the usual fashion. Interlocking letters should provide you with extra clues for those questions that you cannot answer straight away.

You score 1 point for every clue you manage to complete correctly, up to a maximum of 25 points. You may NOT score more even if you have achieved higher than this. There are around 30 clues in each Quizword, so it is still possible to score full marks if you do not know some of the answers or make some mistakes.

#2 REBUS CHALLENGE

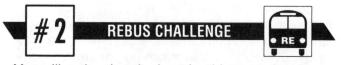

You will notice that the icon for this game is a bus with "RE" on it. In other words, it's a RE-bus. Rebus – get it? This is typical of the type of puzzle you'll be dealing with here. A rebus is a pictorial representation of a popular phrase or saying which you have to find. It won't be straightforward – the colour, positioning, shape or style of the lettering or pictures are used in clever ways to provide extra "cryptic-ness".

So, for example, suppose you were given the following rebus to solve :

BEELZEBUB C VIOLET

_____ ___ _____ ___
___ ____ ____ ___

Well, Beelzebub is another name for the Devil, and violet is a shade of blue, and there is the letter C between them. Perhaps the answer is "Between the devil and the deep blue sea" (since between the devil and the deep blue there is "C"). Notice that homophones (words that sound the same although spelled differently) are often used, so watch out for them. Also watch out for arrows – they usually point out something very important in the puzzle.

You get five points for every correctly identified rebus, there being six in each Lap, so the top score on this game is 30 points. Note that the dashes can be used to write down your answer, and also help you to see if the answer you are thinking of is the same as our answer.

2

SAFE CRACKER

The third game is *Safe Cracker*. You are presented with ten statements, a number of which are falsehoods. For each statement decide whether it is true or false. Then, for all the FALSE statements, shade in those segments in the digital display that are coded with this letter. For example, if you decide that statements A, G, H and K are all false, then shade in all segments bearing the letter A, G, H or K.

If you have done the puzzle correctly, the segments that you have shaded in will form a correct sum (as shown) and you've cracked the combination to the safe.

There are no points for doing this as such, but you are awarded two points for every statement whose truth (or otherwise) you establish correctly. Of course, if you get the sum correct it should follow on that you have all the questions correct also, thus picking up 20 points.

3

A *Logic Problem* is a puzzle asking you to deduce a situation from a number of given clues. As an example, suppose we have three children called Kath, Nicola and Brendan. They each hold a different letter on a piece of card, either N, B or K. Now suppose we are given the following :

(**1**) No child holds a card bearing the same letter as the first letter of their name.
(**2**) Nicola does not hold a card with 'B' on it.

The way you would solve this is as follows : "Nicola does not hold the 'B' (by clue 2) and she cannot hold the 'N' (by clue 1) so she must be holding the 'K'. As she has the 'K' then Brendan cannot also have it, and since he cannot have the 'B' (clue 1) he must have the 'N', hence leaving Kath with the 'B'." So the solution is :

Brendan	N
Kath	B
Nicola	K

So you get the idea that it is important to re-examine the clues repeatedly until you deduce all the information. In the real puzzles you will have as many as 20 items to place, and you get 1 point for every piece of information you put into the correct place in the answer grid.

4

The best way to demonstrate the In the Pipeline puzzles is to do an example. The rectangular grid shows both ends of three pipes.

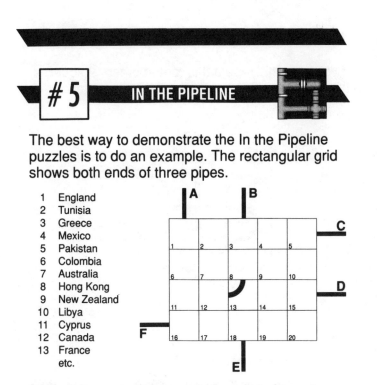

1 England
2 Tunisia
3 Greece
4 Mexico
5 Pakistan
6 Colombia
7 Australia
8 Hong Kong
9 New Zealand
10 Libya
11 Cyprus
12 Canada
13 France
   etc.

In the full puzzle there would be a list of twenty items on the left (in this case, countries) each of which uses one of the terms below to describe their unit of currency.

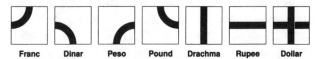

Franc   Dinar   Peso   Pound   Drachma   Rupee   Dollar

For each item in the list, draw the appropriate diagram in the numbered square. For example, if question 13 is FRANCE which has the Franc as its currency, draw the symbol corresponding to Franc in box number 13 (as shown above).

If you correctly repeat this for the other 19 squares, the diagram will show you how the pipe ends connect together.

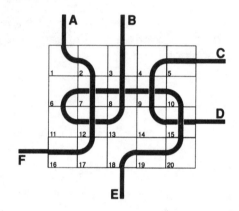

Your answer :
Pipe A connects to pipe F
Pipe B connects to pipe E
Pipe C connects to pipe D

The aim of the game is to deduce how the pipes connect up (as shown above). The three pipes never join, but may pass over other pipes via the cross-over piece. Reconsider your answers if the diagram appears to be wrong. Notice that, even if you are unable to fill in all the boxes using your general knowledge, you can use your visual intuition of the diagram to help you. I'll leave you to discover these tricks for yourself.

You get one point for every square correctly drawn into the diagram.

6   MYSTERY STORY

Here you are given a mystery story which has a question at the end. Using your powers of detection, and perhaps some logical and lateral thought in the process, it is up to you to answer the question with the right reason behind your answer. If you manage to do this, 25 points are yours.

7   WORD ISLAND

In *Word Island*, you have to form words of five letters or more by travelling from state to state around our island. For each word you may start anywhere you like, passing through touching borders to pick up the next letter (which you MUST do – skipping states isn't allowed). For example, if we were travelling around the island of Verbia shown here, then the words LETTER, TASTERS,

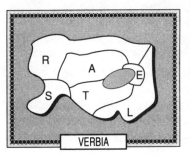

VERBIA

STARE and RATTLE are fine, but LASTS is not since you can't get from A to L. Note that double letters (picking up a letter twice when in a state) are OK, as are plurals. Proper nouns or names are out.

To help you with ten of the longest words we've provided clues, so for our example you might be given :

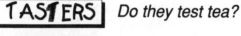

TAS1ERS   *Do they test tea?*

RA2LE   *Percussion for a snake*

After that you are on your own to find up to another 20 five letter words in a similar fashion. You score 1 point for every word you find, up to the maximum of 30, no matter whether it's one of the clued words or one you've found yourself.

#8   MISSING LINKS

Game 8, *Missing Links*, is a lateral thinking puzzle. We provide you with six clues each pointing towards a person, object, place or event. However, the clues are coded using a simple cipher. To decode, simply write down the letters next in alphabetical order to those printed. So, for example, if the clue says "CZUHC I. ANCXBNLAD" then decoded it reads "DAVID J. BODYCOMBE". Notice that Z is used to represent the letter A.

Begin by decoding the top clue. Think about what it could point towards, and if anything comes to mind write it in the right-hand box beside it, under "Guesses".

8

Now decode the second clue, and make another guess if anything different comes to mind. Continue by decoding every clue and making one guess after each clue. The following shows a game in progress, in this case to identify a famous person (shown by the WHO? banner at the top).

WHO?	GUESSES
EHUD FIVE	ENID BLYTON **12**
AZC = FNNC BAD = GOOD	**10**
BZLDQZ RGX? CAMERA SHY?	MICHAEL JACKSON **8**
LNNMVZKJ MOONWALK	**6**
ATAAKDR	**4**
SGQHKKDQ	**2**

When this player checks his answers he will find that he guessed the correct answer after three clues and thus scores 8 points (shown by the number in that box). There are four of these games in each Lap and you should add up the four scores you get, up to a maximum of 30 points. On average, you'll probably get the right answer after the fourth clue – guessing it before then is good going. (You might like to decode the last two clues in the above grid for practice.)

9

This is a quiz about numbers. The catch is... you won't know half of the answers! You are given ten questions, labelled A to K, the answer to each being a number between 1 and 500. Half of them are fairly typical general knowledge or trivia questions. However, the other half ask you to estimate the number. The challenge is to use your knowledge to make a reasonable guess at the answer. For example, if the question was :

"How many tonnes did the largest ever bell, the *Tsar Kolokol*, weigh?"

at this point you might well think 'How on earth am I supposed to know that?' The idea is – you're not. However, you might know that a family car weighs around 1000kg (a tonne) and since bells are pretty big things perhaps the answer is around 120? Actually, the answer is 202 but at least we got fairly close. Some answers are easier to ascertain – you'd probably be able to make quite accurate guesses at, say, how many inches long the average carrot is without actually knowing the answer.

Once you've got your answers, put your answer for A in the box with A in it on the right-hand page, and likewise for the other letters. Then calculate the sums in the manner demonstrated on the next page.

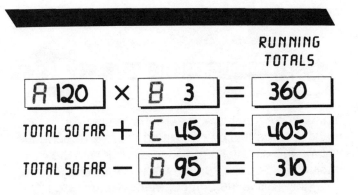

RUNNING
TOTALS

| A 120 | × | B 3 | = | 360 |

TOTAL SO FAR + | C 45 | = | 405 |

TOTAL SO FAR — | D 95 | = | 310 |

Then follow the instructions given in the puzzle to work out how far away your final answer is from the correct answer. Award yourself the number of points according to the following scheme :

HOW TO SCORE

Difference between 0 and 250 = score 25 pts
Difference between 251 and 1000 = score 20 pts
Difference between 1001 and 2500 = score 15 pts
Difference between 2501 and 5000 = score 10 pts
Difference between 5001 and 7500 = score 5 pts

NOTES

(a) Your running total should always lie between 1 and 10,000 so if you go outside this region in your calculations you might like to reconsider your answers.

(b) Figures used in this quiz come from various sources, but in all cases the latest available information has been used.

(c) Sometimes figures have been rounded to the nearest whole number.

11

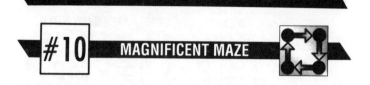
In this maze you have to earn the moves you make. You do this by answering the twelve general knowledge questions provided. Check with the back of the book to see how many answers you got right. This is the number of moves you are allowed.

Starting at either S square, use your moves to trace the path through the maze, following the arrows at all times. If you come to a dead end, that's the end of your scoring. You score the number of points that you have managed to collect using your moves (see example). Once you have visited a circle, it counts as zero on subsequent visits, as in this example :

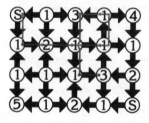

Suppose I got nine questions right. Using my nine moves as shown, I would have scored :
1+2+1+1+1+3+0+1+3
= 13 points

The following couple of pages give a summary of how to score your performance for the games in each Lap.

QUIZWORD
1 point for each clue correctly
entered into the crossword.
Maximum score – 25 points

REBUS CHALLENGE
5 points for each rebus correctly
identified.
Maximum score – 30 points

SAFE CRACKER
2 points for correctly identifying
whether each statement is true or
false.
Maximum score – 20 points

LOGIC PROBLEM
1 point for each correct piece of
information entered into the answer
grid.
Maximum score – 20 points

IN THE PIPELINE
1 point for each correct square of
the pipeline entered into the grid.
Maximum score – 20 points

CRIME STORY
Solve the mystery with the correct reason to get the points, otherwise score zero.
Maximum score – 25 points

WORD ISLAND
1 point each for words with clues; 1 point each for up to 20 more valid words found.
Maximum score – 30 points

MISSING LINKS
Score the number of points shown in the box where you first wrote the correct answer (e.g. 8 points if you guessed the answer after clue 3).
Maximum score – 30 points

NUMEROLOGY
Score the number of points shown in the table, depending on how close you were to the answer.
Maximum score – 25 points

MAGNIFICENT MAZE
Score the points you collect using the moves you have earned.
Maximum score – 25 points

LAP 1

There are no time limits on this lap.

To score each puzzle, refer to the Scoring Summary on page 13. The maximum scores available are shown below.

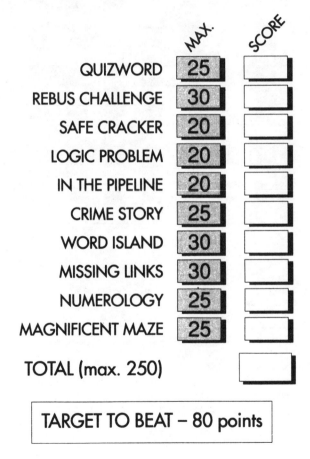

	MAX.	SCORE
QUIZWORD	25	
REBUS CHALLENGE	30	
SAFE CRACKER	20	
LOGIC PROBLEM	20	
IN THE PIPELINE	20	
CRIME STORY	25	
WORD ISLAND	30	
MISSING LINKS	30	
NUMEROLOGY	25	
MAGNIFICENT MAZE	25	
TOTAL (max. 250)		

TARGET TO BEAT – 80 points

ACROSS

1 For which 1979 Vietnam War epic did Francis Ford Coppola win an Academy award? (10,3)

8 Which ancient city of Crete was home to the Minotaur's labyrinth in Greek mythology? (7)

9 What term describes a test screening of a film designed to gauge audience reaction? (7)

11 Which tropical member of the gourd family is often used for cleaning the skin? (6)

13 Lasting a period of 365 days? (8)

15 What word describes long regions of hair found on the necks of many animals, especially horses, lions and wolves? (5)

16 Offenbach composed the operetta _____ *in the Underworld* in 1858 (7)

18 What type of church was first founded by the Englishmen Smyth and Helwys in Amsterdam in 1609? (7)

19 Which type of flesh-eating demon takes on the form of a beautiful woman? (5)

21 In psychology, this type of therapy uses a stimulus (such as electric shocks) to dissuade someone from a bad habit? (8)

23 In printing, this describes a slanted form of lettering (6)

25 What type of military settlement is stationed far from the main camp? (7)

26 What form of gliding dance, a fore-runner of the fox-trot, is set to music with two beats in the bar? (3-4)

28 Which famous Belgian detective dies in the 1975 murder mystery novel *Curtain*? (7,6)

DOWN

2 In English, which part of speech can be either personal, demonstrative, interrogative or indefinite? (7)

3 What mathematical function is the ratio of the adjacent side to the hypotenuse in a right-angled triangle? (abbrev.) (3)

4 Which computer language derives its name from the abbreviation for List Processing? (4)

5 In *Monty Python's Flying Circus* what was the collective name for the strange-talking women portrayed by the cast? (10)

6 What title is given to certain chiefs in North Africa and also all those descending from Mohammed? (5)

7 Anything portending evil is said to be this (7)

8 Which mountain, situated in Tanzania, is the highest in Africa? (11)

10 What trophy is competed for in the annual matches between women tennis players of the USA and Britain? (8,3)

12 Which Greek slave from Phrygia wrote fables in the 6th Century BC? (5)

14 In economics, what type of merger brings together firms from the same level in the production chain? (10)

17 What word for "a striking effect" derives from the French word *éclater*, meaning "to shine"? (5)

18 Which word is more commonly used to mean "respire" when pertaining to humans? (7)

20 What is the name given to someone who has a Negro parent and a Caucasian parent? (7)

22 What school of philosophy was founded in Athens by Zeno in 300 BC? (5)

24 In organ music, what mechanism is used to prevent a given row of pipes from sounding? (4)

27 What is the French word for "yes"? (3)

17

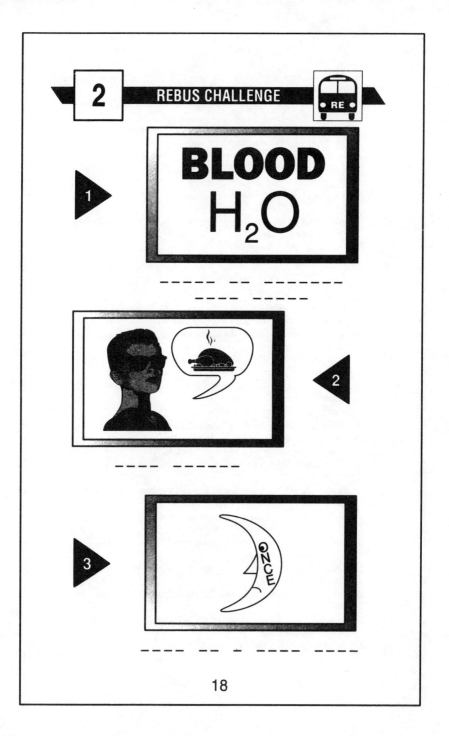

1.

_____ __ _____
____ _____

2.

____ _____

3.

____ __ _ ____ ____

Blacken out those segments on the right-hand page that are letter coded to the FALSE statements. This will form a correct mathematical sum.

		True	False
A	e.g. stands for exempli gratia	☐	☐
B	Matthias is the Apostle who replaced Judas Iscariot	☐	☐
C	Isaiah is the book of the Bible with the most chapters, at 150	☐	☐
D	The capital of the Canadian province Toronto is Ontario	☐	☐
E	The country of Burkino Faso was once also called Abyssinia	☐	☐
F	Polyhymnia was the Greek Muse of song and dance	☐	☐
G	Mount Logan is the highest mountain in Canada	☐	☐
H	St Joseph is the patron saint of travellers	☐	☐
J	The Statue of Zeus, a Wonder of the World, was situated in Athens	☐	☐
K	The first underground railway system was built in London	☐	☐

20

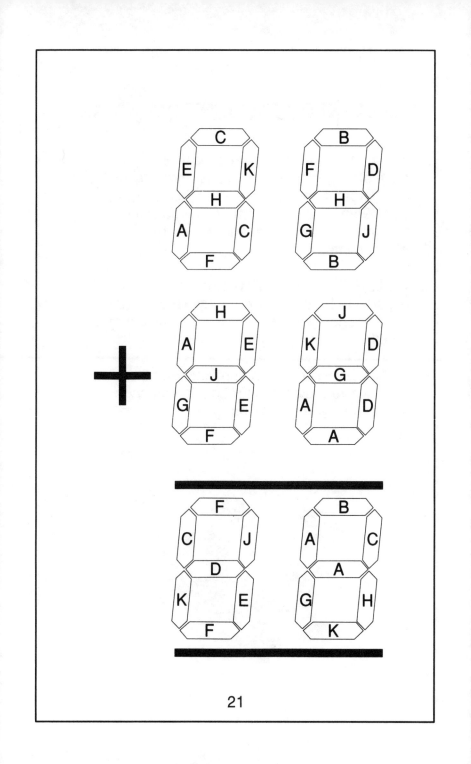

Ten men and women from a local singles club have arranged to go out this Wednesday night, at different times in the evening (either 7pm, 8pm, 9pm, 10pm or 11pm). Can you work out the dates for each man and where they went at what time?

NOTE – For these logic puzzles, if (say) David is going to Rixy's then you may assume that he is not going anywhere else, and also that no other man is going there as well.

PROBLEMS? If the starting hints (right) are no help, we've provided a full solution on page 478 to help you get the hang of these puzzles.

CLUES

1. Katherine's date will be the latest, at 11pm. It won't be with Dan, nor will it be to the cinema.

2. Mary wants to go ice skating before 8:30pm.

3. The couple who plan to go out drinking at the New Inn will do so at 7pm.

4. Patrick and Victoria will make a lovely couple on Wednesday.

5. David is off to Rixy's for a spot of clubbing.

6. Simon is going out with his date at 8pm.

7. Jane will be going out an hour before Patrick. She doesn't like videos.

8. The 11pm daters won't be watching a video either.

9. Dan and Jane are not going out together.

STARTING HINTS

a. Use clues 2, 3 and 6 to deduce when Mary went skating and with whom. Use this information together with clues 4 and 7 to see why Jane could not have gone to the New Inn at 7pm. Deduce which woman did go there. Now...

b. Use clue 2 to see when Patrick and Jane will go out.

c. Who is going out with Jill (the fifth woman)? Who is watching the video?

Man	Woman	Venue	Time
Dan			
Dave			
David			
Patrick			
Simon			

Your task is to associate each of the following scientific words with the subject with which they are most readily associated.

1 Protractor
2 Filter funnel
3 Dolomite
4 Icosahedron
5 Culture
6 Red dwarf
7 Streptococcus
8 Compiler
9 Flowchart
10 Anemometer
11 Isotherm
12 Quadratic
13 Litmus paper
14 Substratum
15 Moraine
16 Galaxy
17 ROM
18 Gamete
19 Liebig condenser
20 Feldspar

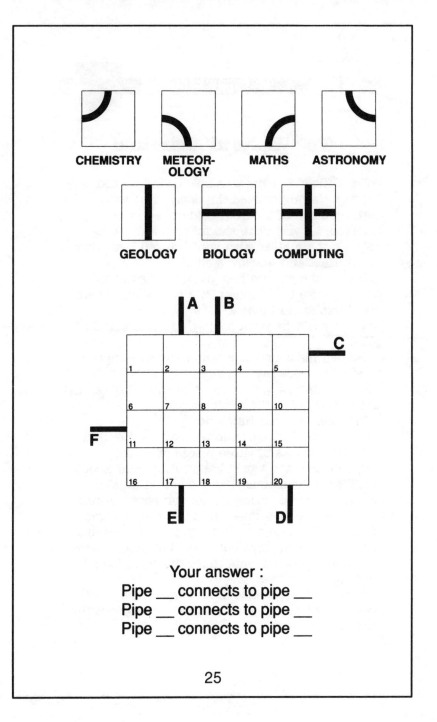

CHEMISTRY   METEOR-   MATHS   ASTRONOMY
             OLOGY

GEOLOGY   BIOLOGY   COMPUTING

Your answer :
Pipe __ connects to pipe __
Pipe __ connects to pipe __
Pipe __ connects to pipe __

The 'Helpful' Criminal

Police Officer Barlow was not having a good
Sunday. Having started the early shift with
nothing but half a cup of cold coffee in his
stomach, he wasn't in the mood for thinking.
"What's the matter with you?" asked Detective
Frank Hartland, Barlow's chief.

"One of the juniors has given me details of
some tip-offs that Smiley Pete wants us to look
into," explained Barlow.

"Why would he want to do that?" Hartland
asked.

"He has his court case tomorrow so I suppose
he wants to put word around that he's being
helpful." Barlow walked over to the filing cabinet
and pulled out Smiley Pete's file.

"Try me," offered Hartland.

Barlow shuffled through the papers. "Well, he
claims he knows of three pieces of stolen
property that the world hasn't found out about
yet. Firstly he claims that the actual musical
scores on which Irving Berlin composed 'Annie
Get Your Gun' are missing. He said that some
criminals he knows stole them from a museum
of music in New York last year, but since there
are so many documents there the theft hasn't
been discovered yet."

"Hmm. OK, what else did he say?" The
Detective began to think as Barlow read out the
second claim.

26

"He then went on to say that a criminal gang had, just yesterday, stolen the Codex of Leonardo da Vinci's inventions. He said that he's seen it personally and that the descriptions of things such as the helicopter are in clear Italian and are unmistakable. And wait for it..."

"Well, you might as well cap this lie." Hartland allowed himself a wide smile.

"He claims that his partner-in-crime sneaked into the Louvre yesterday morning before the galleries opened posing as a postman. This man is supposed to have smuggled out the 'Mona Lisa' in a rolled up postal tube! The thing is, I don't want to be the one who's ridiculed if any of these stories turn out to be true."

"I'd consider charging him for wasting police time if all those stories weren't so hopelessly funny!" chuckled Hartland.

Can you point out to Barlow the exact reason why at least two of the above stories are wrong?

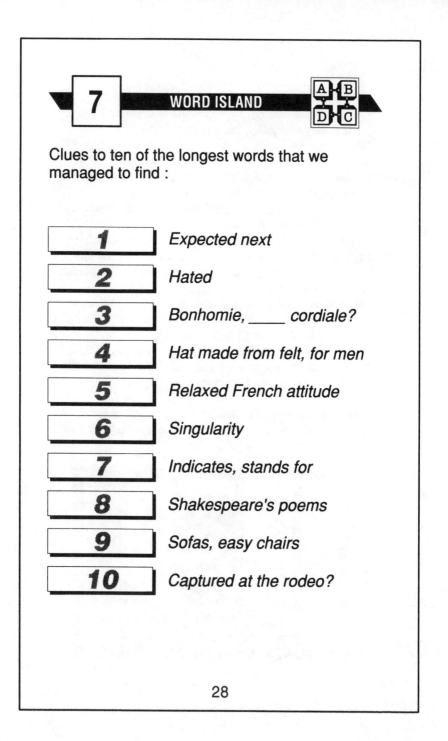

Clues to ten of the longest words that we managed to find :

1	*Expected next*
2	*Hated*
3	*Bonhomie, ____ cordiale?*
4	*Hat made from felt, for men*
5	*Relaxed French attitude*
6	*Singularity*
7	*Indicates, stands for*
8	*Shakespeare's poems*
9	*Sofas, easy chairs*
10	*Captured at the rodeo?*

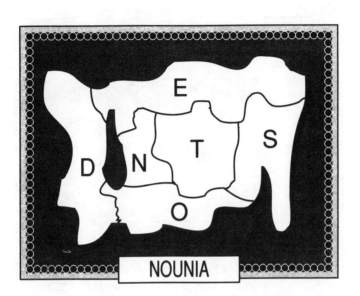

NOUNIA

Other words of five letters or more (find up to another 20) :

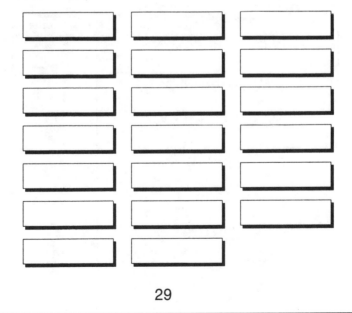

29

WHO?	GUESSES
FNKEDQ	**12**
ENQSX–EHQRS	**10**
B.H.Z.	**8**
QDOTAKHBZM	**6**
HQZMFZSD	**4**
MN LNQD SZWDR	**2**

WHAT?	GUESSES
MDV HM DHFGSX-SVN	**12**
KDZCHMF ENQLZS	**10**
SVDKUD BL CHZLDSDQ	**8**
CHFHSZK	**6**
KZRDQ KHFGS	**4**
RSNQDR LTRHB	**2**

WHERE?	GUESSES
EKZSSDRS	12
BNLOTKRNQX RTEEQZFD	10
DHFGS RSZSDR	8
MNSZAKD NODQZ UDMTD	6
RNZO NODQZ BNTMSQX	4
FQDZS AZQQHDQ QDDE	2

WHEN?	GUESSES
KDC AX QNADQS BZSDRAX	12
BNMROHQZBX AX BZSGNKHBR	10
ZSSDLOS NM IZLDR H	8
EHQDVNQJR	6
EHESG NE MNUDLADQ	4
FTX EZVJDR ZQQDRSDC	2

31

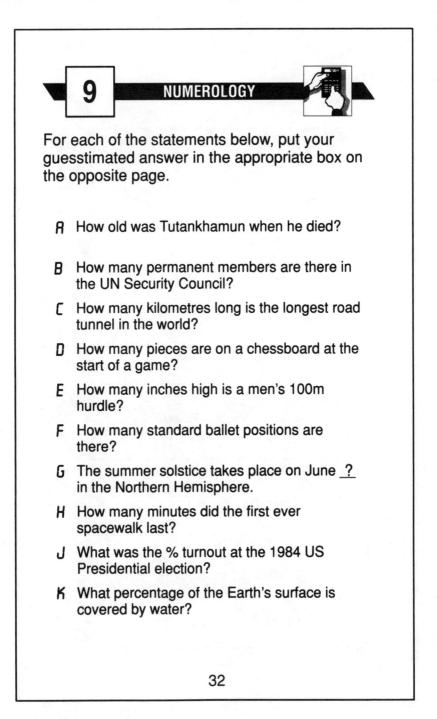

9 NUMEROLOGY

For each of the statements below, put your guesstimated answer in the appropriate box on the opposite page.

A How old was Tutankhamun when he died?

B How many permanent members are there in the UN Security Council?

C How many kilometres long is the longest road tunnel in the world?

D How many pieces are on a chessboard at the start of a game?

E How many inches high is a men's 100m hurdle?

F How many standard ballet positions are there?

G The summer solstice takes place on June ? in the Northern Hemisphere.

H How many minutes did the first ever spacewalk last?

J What was the % turnout at the 1984 US Presidential election?

K What percentage of the Earth's surface is covered by water?

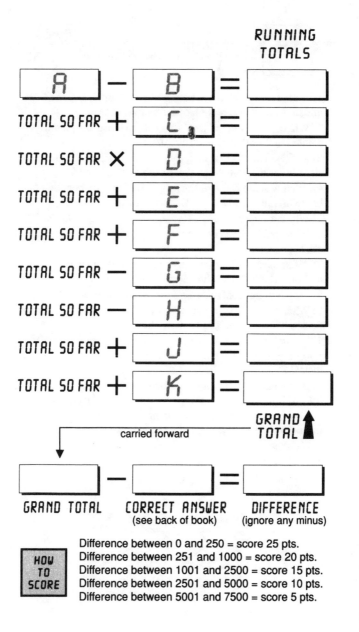

RUNNING TOTALS

$A - B =$

TOTAL SO FAR $+$ C $=$

TOTAL SO FAR $\times$ D $=$

TOTAL SO FAR $+$ E $=$

TOTAL SO FAR $+$ F $=$

TOTAL SO FAR $-$ G $=$

TOTAL SO FAR $-$ H $=$

TOTAL SO FAR $+$ J $=$

TOTAL SO FAR $+$ K $=$

carried forward   GRAND TOTAL

GRAND TOTAL $-$ CORRECT ANSWER $=$ DIFFERENCE
(see back of book)   (ignore any minus)

HOW TO SCORE

Difference between 0 and 250 = score 25 pts.
Difference between 251 and 1000 = score 20 pts.
Difference between 1001 and 2500 = score 15 pts.
Difference between 2501 and 5000 = score 10 pts.
Difference between 5001 and 7500 = score 5 pts.

33

1) Which film, with the working title of *A Boy's Life*, had three midget stars whose real faces were never seen?

2) What would you see if you looked up close at a picture painted in the style of pointillism?

3) With which other country does Jordan share a sea that contains eight times more salt than that of ordinary sea water?

4) What was the name of the original super-continent that later broke up into Laurasia and Gondwanaland?

5) Which weapon would a Roman have called his *gladius*?

6) What can basenjis not do that most other breeds of this animal can?

7) A fax machine is commonly used in modern everyday office life but what is "fax" short for?

8) Which organ contains two auricles and two ventricles?

9) What is the name of the twin sons of Zeus and Leda that are depicted in star charts as Gemini, the twins?

10) Which unit, used in metallurgy and the manufacture of jewellery, signifies the proportion of precious metal to base metal?

11) On what subject would you be expert if you most often ask for a yellow question in the Genus edition of *Trivial Pursuit*?

12) From which sport does the expression "Go for Gold" come, the aim of the sport being to hit the yellow?

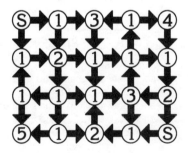

There are no time limits on this lap.

To score each puzzle, refer to the Scoring
Summary on page 13. The maximum scores
available are shown below.

	MAX.	SCORE
QUIZWORD	25	
REBUS CHALLENGE	30	
SAFE CRACKER	20	
LOGIC PROBLEM	20	
IN THE PIPELINE	20	
CRIME STORY	25	
WORD ISLAND	30	
MISSING LINKS	30	
NUMEROLOGY	25	
MAGNIFICENT MAZE	25	
TOTAL (max. 250)		

TARGET TO BEAT – 95 points

ACROSS

1 Which type of Chinese-style plate design was popularized in England by Mintons Ltd. in 1783? (6,7)

8 This word means "to reduce one's reserves" (7)

9 What, in the English language, is a statement used to express a generally accepted observation about everyday life? (7)

11 These are a type of knitted pullover, so-called due to their distinctive collar (1-5)

13 Which American missile contains a television camera which it uses to follow its target? (8)

15 A physicist might call it light amplification by stimulated emission of radiation. How is it more commonly known? (5)

16 In the field of insurance, what name is given to a regular amount of money paid to insure against possible larger losses? (7)

18 What Italian dish is made from envelopes of pasta stuffed with meat or cheese, usually served in a sauce? (7)

19 The best possible (5)

21 What geometric term is defined as "to draw a figure as large as possible inside another figure"? (8)

23 This architectural term means "to decorate with raised stone or wood work" (6)

25 What type of gas, commonly found near oil deposits, consists of a mixture of gases such as butane and propane? (7)

26 What title was given to an empress of Russia? (7)

28 What medical condition, formerly called mongolism, occurs due to the presence of three copies of chromosome 21? (5,8)

DOWN

2 Which word means "to print" and "to influence the mind"? (7)

3 The general who commanded the Confederacy during the American Civil War was Robert E. _____ (3)

4 Which small bird has the scientific name *Troglodytes troglodytes*? (4)

5 In what order is a lexicon usually arranged? (10)

6 Which demonstrative pronoun is the plural of "that"?

7 Which radioactive metallic element has the chemical symbol Re? (7)

8 In economics, what term describes the reduction of the home currency's exchange rate in the international money markets? (11)

10 What dessert is made from hot meringue filled with cold ice cream? (5,6)

12 To which Leningrad ballet company did Rudolf Nureyev belong? (5)

14 Which birds, similar to ibises, are distinguished by their flat beaks? (10)

17 What term describes a phrase particular to a given language that is a grammatical exception to normal reasoning – e.g. "a flight of stairs" doesn't fly? (5)

18 Which Italian dish is made from rice cooked with saffron, stock, meat, vegetables and/or cheese? (7)

20 What psychological condition is identified by an overuse of the word "I"? (7)

22 What word means "to repeat a radio or television broadcast" and "to repeat a race"? (5)

24 In computing, what word describes a small picture intended to represent a particular action, such as saving a file? (4)

27 What acronym is used to indicate the true interest rate, taking into account compound interest? (3)

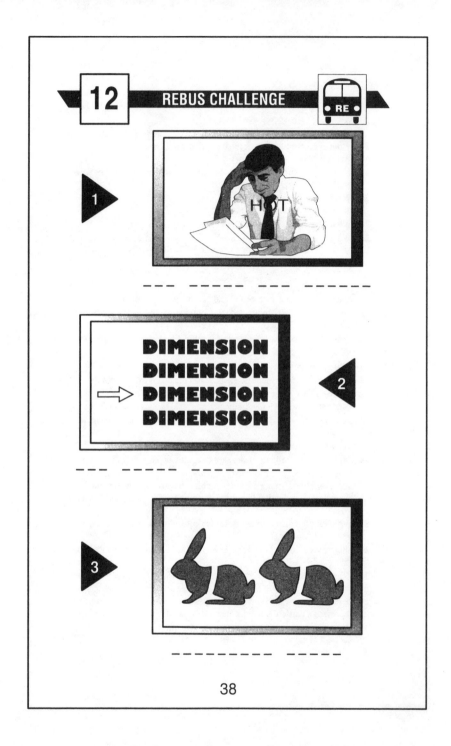

1

___ _____ ___ _____

2

___ _____ _____

3

_____ _____

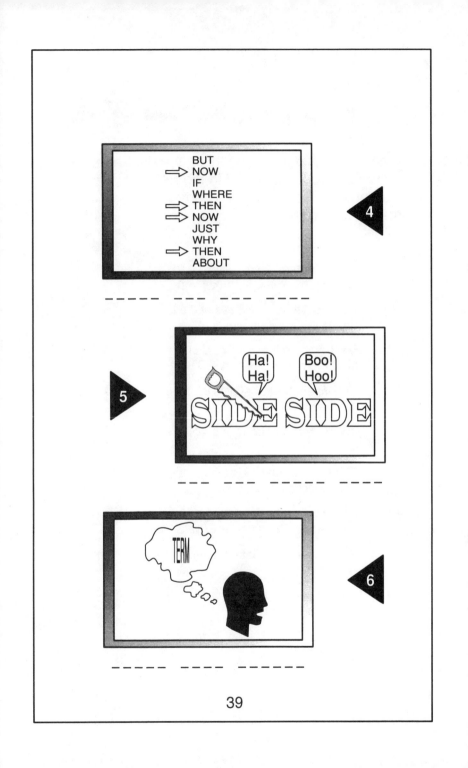

39

Blacken out those segments on the right-hand page that are letter coded to the FALSE statements. This will form a correct mathematical sum.

True False

A   Kochel numbers are assigned to classify the works of Beethoven ☐ ☐

B   Doric is the most stylized of the three orders of Greek architecture ☐ ☐

C   Macbeth, the famous Scottish king, lived in the 15th Century AD ☐ ☐

D   The Volga–Baltic canal is the longest in the world ☐ ☐

E   The currency of Chile is the Sucre ☐ ☐

F   The Roman ruler Caligula made his horse, Incitatus, a Consul ☐ ☐

G   *Sit Down You're Rocking the Boat* comes from the musical *Guys & Dolls* ☐ ☐

H   St Michael is the patron saint of tax collectors ☐ ☐

J   Shakespeare's *A Midsummer Night's Dream* is set in Rome ☐ ☐

K   Princeton is the United States' oldest university ☐ ☐

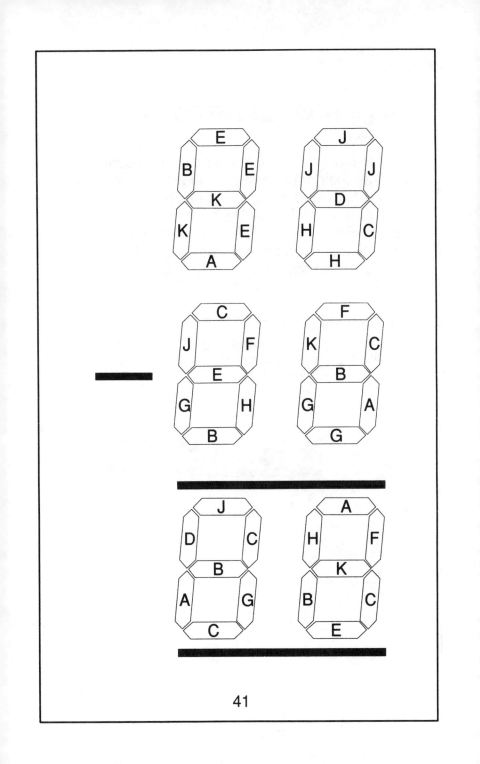

Five schoolchildren have their own individual pegs for their outdoor wear. The teacher wishes to put individual labels underneath each peg but she cannot quite remember which child uses which peg. What she can remember is shown on the right. The children's names are Adrian, Bernard, Clare, Dominic and Eve.

The pegs are numbered 1 to 5 from left to right. Can you match each peg with its owner, and the type and colour of the clothing that is usually hung upon it?

CLUES

1. Clare's anorak is somewhere to the left of the green duffel coat. However, these two garments are not directly side-by-side.

2. The clothing on peg 4 is blue, but it isn't a polo neck.

3. Eve's article of clothing is on peg 1. She does not wear the brown garment.

4. Bernard's clothing is black.

5. There is a raincoat on peg 3.

6. Adrian doesn't wear cardigans.

STARTING HINTS

a. Work out on which pegs Clare's anorak and the green duffel coat are.

b. Use the first four clues to find the colour of Eve's clothing.

c. On which peg is Bernard's black coat?

NOTES

The five articles are : an anorak, a cardigan, a duffel coat, a polo neck sweater, and a raincoat.

The five colours are : black, blue, brown, green and tan.

Peg	Child	Article	Colour
Number 1			
Number 2			
Number 3			
Number 4			
Number 5			

Your task is to put the breeds of animal below into the seven categories provided.

1 Anaconda
2 Marmoset
3 Gecko
4 Mandrill
5 Chihuahua
6 Schnauzer
7 Cariacou
8 Buzzard
9 Petrel
10 Whimbrel
11 Abyssinian
12 Iguana
13 Shrike
14 Chinchilla
15 Pomeranian
16 Palomino
17 Osprey
18 Corncrake
19 Clydesdale
20 Burmese

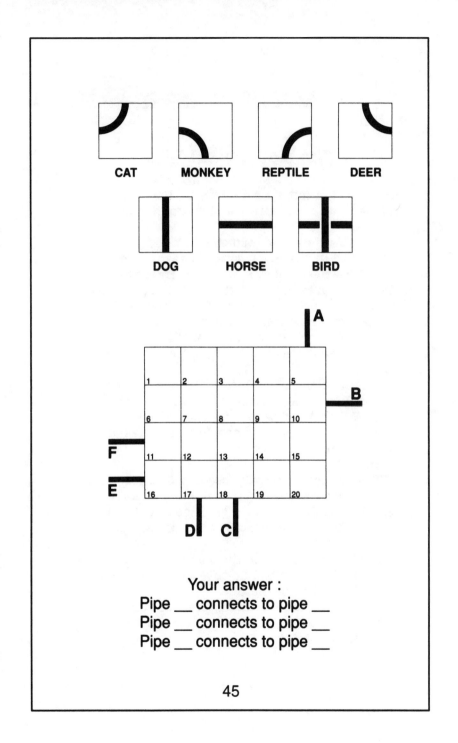

CAT   MONKEY   REPTILE   DEER

DOG   HORSE   BIRD

Your answer :
Pipe __ connects to pipe __
Pipe __ connects to pipe __
Pipe __ connects to pipe __

The Horizontal Line

In a rare ten minute coffee break, Detective Hartland was recounting a story to Officer Barlow.

"When I was on leave in the USA one year I was asked to observe a case. This was around, oh, 35 years ago now. It was very interesting. There was great concern that Russian spies had infiltrated an American site and sabotaged their equipment," recounted Hartland.

"Yes, we don't get too much of that sort of stuff now that the Cold War is over," said Barlow.

Hartland continued. "Indeed, for the best of course. I was one of a team investigating the case. We were trying to determine whether it was a case of espionage or whether it was just an unfortunate mistake."

"And...?"

"Well, we couldn't really see any foul play and it was widely suspected that it was just a mistake. We didn't have a great deal to go on anyway. Unfortunately, that one mistake cost $18 million."

"Jeez! I bet that stung the tax payers' pockets." Barlow stood up to get another cup of coffee from the percolator.

"Too right," said Hartland, "and the funniest thing was that the mistake was caused by a short, horizontal line!"

Barlow looked back at the Detective in puzzlement. "A what?" he asked.

"A short, horizontal line. Why, I don't think you need to be a great detective to work it out. There aren't too many things that are so expensive that they cost that much money to rebuild in their entirety. This certainly was an expensive job because the parts had to be made so precisely."

"Ah, so this was advanced tecchie stuff, then. Right, well I think I might have an idea of what you're on about now."

"Told you it wasn't difficult," said Hartland as he finished his coffee.

Can you guess the actual event that the Detective is referring to?

47

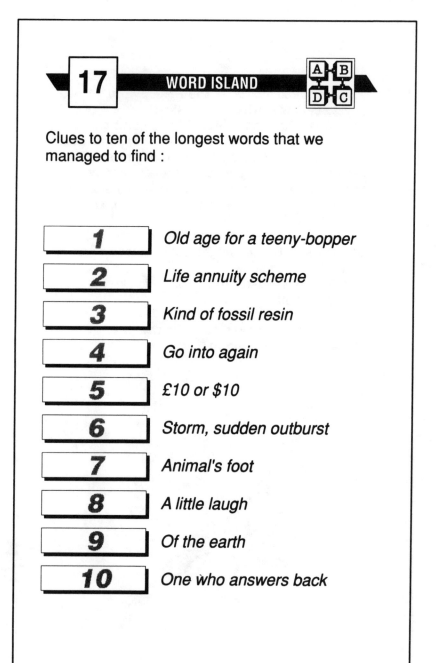

17 WORD ISLAND

Clues to ten of the longest words that we managed to find :

1	Old age for a teeny-bopper
2	Life annuity scheme
3	Kind of fossil resin
4	Go into again
5	£10 or $10
6	Storm, sudden outburst
7	Animal's foot
8	A little laugh
9	Of the earth
10	One who answers back

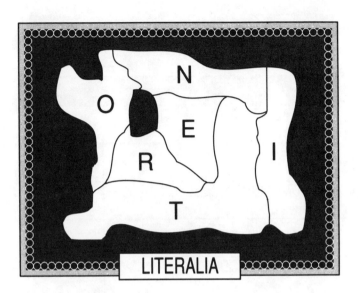

LITERALIA

Other words of five letters or more (find up to another 20) :

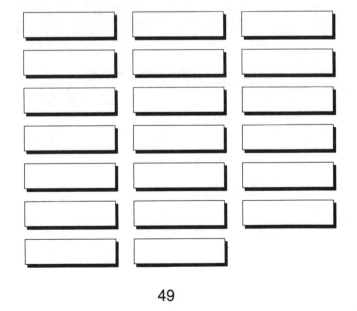

WHO?	GUESSES
BZSZOTKS CDRHFMDQ	12
RBQDV	10
SGQDD ONHMS NMD ENTQ NMD...	8
JHMFR BQNVM	6
FQDDJ	4
DTQDJZ	2

WHAT?	GUESSES
DHFGSX-DHFGS	12
PTHDS ZMC KNTC	10
GZLLDQR	8
VAVAVVAVAVAV	6
RSDHMVZX	4
KHADQZBD TRDC HS	2

WHERE?	GUESSES
QNXZK UDMTD	12
SNTQHRS ZSSQZBSHNM	10
DEEHFHDR	8
SVN ONHMS RHW LHKKHNM UHRHSNQR	6
CDZSG LZRJR	4
EQDMBG VZW VNQJR	2

WHEN?	GUESSES
SNLZGZVJ	12
SZQHP ZYHY	10
OZSQHNS	8
NHK ROHKK	6
JTVZHS	4
RZCCZL GTRRDHM	2

19 NUMEROLOGY

For each of the statements below, put your guesstimated answer in the appropriate box on the opposite page.

A How many bank holidays does Germany have each year?

B How many Wimbledon titles did Billie Jean King win?

C How many theses did Luther nail to the door of the Wittenberg Church?

D How many gallons of oil fit into a standard oil barrel?

E How many centuries made up one legion in the Roman army?

F How many feet high does the Statue of Liberty stand?

G What is the life expectancy of an average Japanese male?

H How many millions of copies of the *Los Angeles Times* are circulated each week?

J How many 1000s of words must the title role actor in *Hamlet* speak each performance?

K How many million books are there in the Library of Congress?

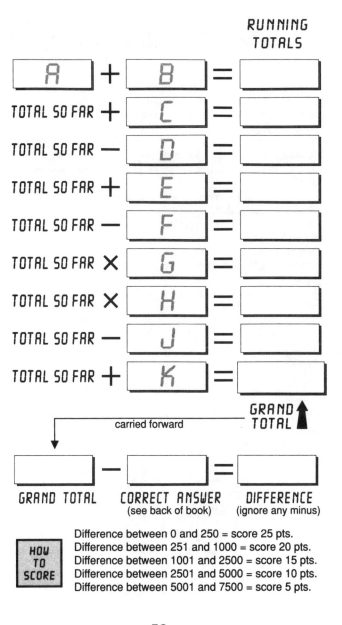

RUNNING
TOTALS

A	+	B	=	
TOTAL SO FAR	+	C	=	
TOTAL SO FAR	−	D	=	
TOTAL SO FAR	+	E	=	
TOTAL SO FAR	−	F	=	
TOTAL SO FAR	×	G	=	
TOTAL SO FAR	×	H	=	
TOTAL SO FAR	−	J	=	
TOTAL SO FAR	+	K	=	

carried forward

GRAND
TOTAL

| | − | | = | |

GRAND TOTAL   CORRECT ANSWER   DIFFERENCE
(see back of book)   (ignore any minus)

HOW TO SCORE

Difference between 0 and 250 = score 25 pts.
Difference between 251 and 1000 = score 20 pts.
Difference between 1001 and 2500 = score 15 pts.
Difference between 2501 and 5000 = score 10 pts.
Difference between 5001 and 7500 = score 5 pts.

1) Whose tomb in St Paul's Cathedral, London, bears the inscription "If you seek his monument, look around"?

2) How does the title of the French newspaper *Le Monde* translate into English?

3) Which bay, situated between Spain and France, is the site of famous ferocious seas and high tides, as detailed in a traditional song?

4) What fell for the first, and so far only, time in the Sahara Desert in 1979?

5) What name is given to flag designs such as those of Belgium, France, Germany, Holland and Italy?

6) On 7 March 1979 which planet was found to have rings like those of Saturn and Uranus from pictures relayed to Earth by *Voyager I*?

7) What yellow ingredient of fireworks and explosives was drunk in solution by Chinese emperors who believed it held the secret of long life?

8) Which is the odd one out – cone, rhombus, cuboid, pyramid, dodecahedron, sphere?

9) Called "the hall of the slain", in which place in Norse mythology could heroes' souls rest and eat with their chief, Odin?

10) In the 1960 US Presidential campaign, with which shifty occupation was Nixon mockingly connected in an anti-slogan used by his opponents?

11) What flavouring is common to the following drinks – curacao, chartreuse, Southern Comfort?

12) Who is seen clinging from the hands of a clock in his classic 1923 film Safety Last?

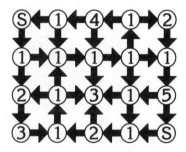

LAP 3

There are no time limits on this lap.

To score each puzzle, refer to the Scoring Summary on page 13. The maximum scores available are shown below.

	MAX.	SCORE
QUIZWORD	25	
REBUS CHALLENGE	30	
SAFE CRACKER	20	
LOGIC PROBLEM	20	
IN THE PIPELINE	20	
CRIME STORY	25	
WORD ISLAND	30	
MISSING LINKS	30	
NUMEROLOGY	25	
MAGNIFICENT MAZE	25	
TOTAL (max. 250)		

TARGET TO BEAT – 110 points

ACROSS

8 Where would milk be turned into butter and cheese products? (8)

9 What tube in the human body carries urine from the kidney to the bladder? (6)

10 What relation is your mother's husband's daughter to you if your mother's husband is not your father? (4-6)

11 In chemistry, if blue litmus paper is turned red, what does this indicate the presence of? (4)

12 In mathematics, what type of fraction has a numerator whose value is less than that of its denominator? (6)

14 Which word can be made from the letters "TORCH ICE"? (8)

15 What is a group of four performing musicians called? (7)

17 Which neurological disorder, which affects the ability to express ideas or name objects, was the subject of Sigmund Freud's first published work? (7)

20 What type of photograph is made using interference of laser light on the film to show a 3-D image? (8)

22 Which famous make of British motorcycle won the Isle of Man TT races many times in the 1940s and 50s? (6)

24 What bird is the national emblem of New Zealand? (4)

25 What European and Asian amphibian gave rise, in part, to the word "gerrymander"? (10)

27 What word describes those people who are your relatives by marriage only? (2-4)

28 What is the name of the poisonous alkaline substance found in deadly nightshade? (8)

DOWN

1 On the Moon the largest of these is "Bailly" at 180 miles wide. What type of feature is it? (6)

2 Which fish, which has an average lifespan of 30 years, has breeds including koi, leather, mirror and scale? (4)

3 Which word describes animals whose ancestors are well documented and of the same breed? (8)

4 What type of story has various fiction subgenres including detective, romantic suspense and the adventure story? (7)

5 What term describes the instructions to candidates given on the front of an examination paper? (6)

6 What leisurely form of transport involves a covered seat for one being carried on two poles? (5-5)

7 Which disease is caused by a lack of vitamin B1? (8)

13 What is a regularly produced publication containing details of new scientific research? (10)

16 What name did Thomas More give to the inhabitants of his fictional state of perfection in a 1516 book? (8)

18 What is the name of the lighter shadow, around the cone of total darkness of lunar eclipses, caused by the Earth blocking the Sun's rays? (8)

19 What adjective describes alloys which include mercury? (7)

21 If a zigzag line is seen on an electric circuit to represent an electrical component, what does that component do to the flow of current? (6)

23 Of what are there five on the Earth's surface, the Pacific being the largest? (6)

26 What is the back of the neck called? (4)

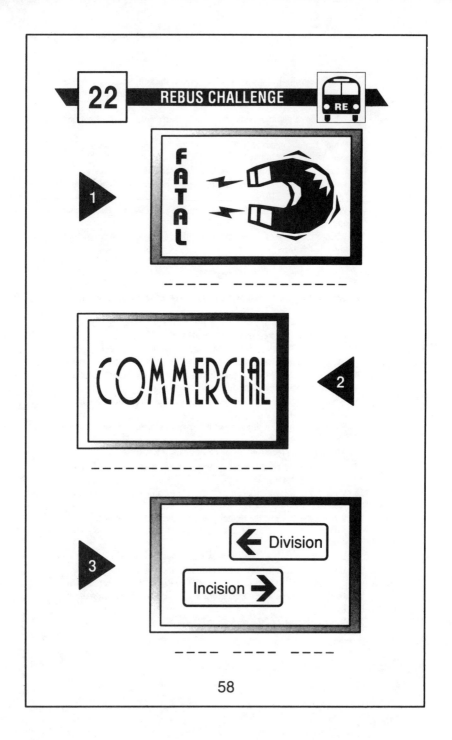

1

FATAL

_ _ _ _ _   _ _ _ _ _ _ _ _ _ _

COMMERCIAL

2

_ _ _ _ _ _ _ _ _ _   _ _ _ _ _

3

← Division

Incision →

_ _ _ _   _ _ _ _   _ _ _ _

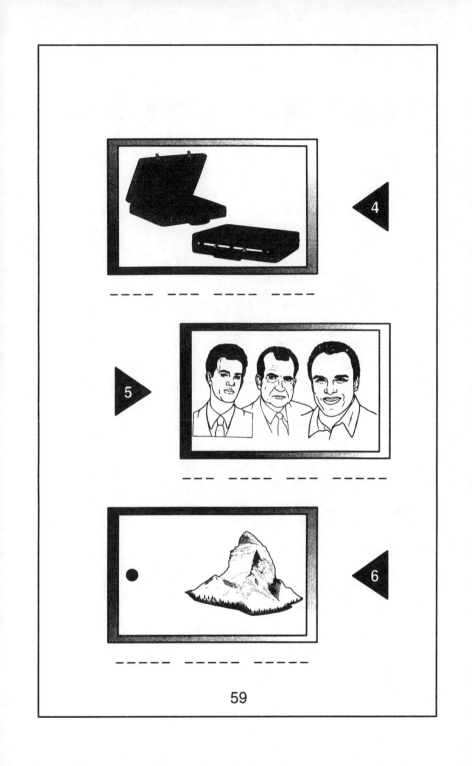

4

_ _ _ _   _ _ _   _ _ _ _   _ _ _ _

5

_ _ _   _ _ _ _   _ _ _   _ _ _ _ _

6

_ _ _ _ _   _ _ _ _ _   _ _ _ _ _

23 SAFE CRACKER

Blacken out those segments on the right-hand page that are letter coded to the FALSE statements. This will form a correct mathematical sum.

True False

A   SWAPO stands for South West Africa People's Organisation ☐ ☐

B   In architecture, a cupola is a round inlet into a church wall ☐ ☐

C   Tomas de Torquemada founded the Ku-Klux Klan ☐ ☐

D   The capital of South Korea is Seoul ☐ ☐

E   Shekels are the unit of currency in Israel ☐ ☐

F   J. R. R. Tolkien's initials stood for John Ronald Reuel ☐ ☐

G   The musical term doloroso means happily ☐ ☐

H   Ochlophobia is a fear of hearing ☐ ☐

J   The SI unit of measurement for wavelength is the Hertz (Hz) ☐ ☐

K   The International Vehicle Registration letters ZW represent Zimbabwe ☐ ☐

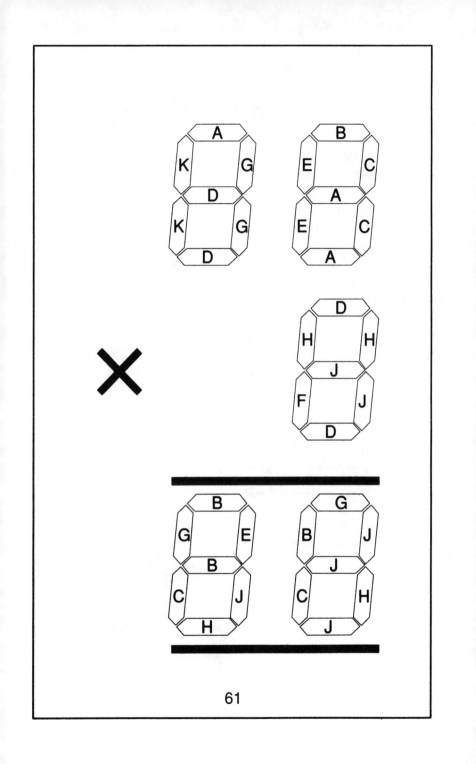

In the top-rating game show *Pick a Box*, contestants are invited to pick one of 25 boxes, although only 5 contain a card. On each card there is a question, a prize and a forfeit. If a contestant is lucky enough to choose a box containing a card, (s)he is asked the question. If they get the answer right they get the prize stated on the card, but if they get it wrong they are obliged to carry out the forfeit stated on the card.

Can you work out the positions of each card and what forfeits and rewards are on them?

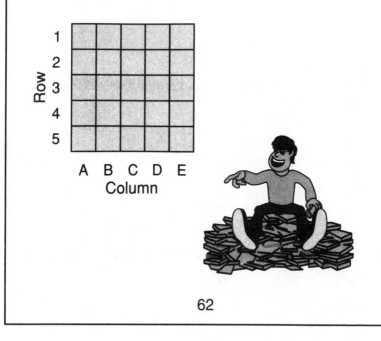

CLUES

1. Every row, column and both main diagonals all contain exactly one card.

2. The $10,000 prize is somewhere in column B.

3. The card in column E contains details of a forfeit where the contestant promptly receives a custard pie!

4. Contestants wanting the $2,000 prize also run the risk of having to donate $100 to charity if they get the question wrong.

5. The card in Row 2 says "Forfeit – you must walk the host's dogs every day for a week!"

6. The card in Row 1 has the jackpot prize of $25,000. It is not in Column A.

7. There is a prize in box 4C but not in 1E.

8. The $5,000 prize doesn't carry the custard pie forfeit nor the one where the contestant has to endure being driven round a stock car racing circuit at high speed.

9. Column A doesn't contain the forfeit asking the contestant to take part in a wrestling competition.

STARTING HINTS

a. Use clues 1, 2, 6 and 7 to deduce the whereabouts of the $25,000 jackpot prize.

b. Now consider clue 1 very carefully.

NOTE – The five prizes are : $1,000; $2,000; $5,000; $10,000; $25,000.

Card positions			
Row	Column	Forfeit	Prize
1			
2			
3			
4			
5			

63

Your task is to associate the classic films below with the actors that appeared in them.

1 *Crazy People*
2 *Return of the Jedi*
3 *Bad Day at Black Rock*
4 *A Passage to India*
5 *The Shootist*
6 *The Poseidon Adventure*
7 *Hannah and Her Sisters*
8 *Arthur*
9 *Much Ado About Nothing*
10 *The Lady Killers*
11 *Bridge on the River Kwai*
12 *It's a Mad Mad Mad Mad World*
13 *Beau Geste*
14 *Sleeper*
15 *Husbands and Wives*
16 *The Naked Gun*
17 *Anatomy of a Murder*
18 *How the West was Won*
19 *Father of the Bride*
20 *Nuts*

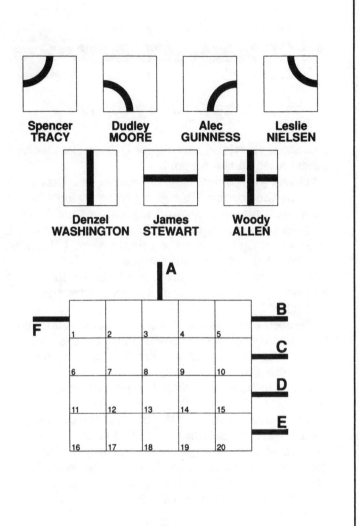

Spencer **TRACY**
Dudley **MOORE**
Alec **GUINNESS**
Leslie **NIELSEN**

Denzel **WASHINGTON**
James **STEWART**
Woody **ALLEN**

Your answer :
Pipe __ connects to pipe __
Pipe __ connects to pipe __
Pipe __ connects to pipe __

The Phoney Pilot

Detective Hartland and Police Officer Barlow had been called to the airport.

"Thank you for coming, Detective. It's that pilot over in the corner. He's going to be flying the New York plane in around an hour's time." The airport manager was slightly sweating. "I've just received a tip-off over the telephone so I thought you could check him out for me."

"Certainly. Follow me, Barlow." Hartland stepped over towards the pilot and introduced himself.

"Pleased to meet you," said the pilot, who was looking over a fold-out flight chart on the coffee table. "I'm Steven Parker. I'm just looking over the flight plan for today."

"Going to be a good trip, I hope," offered Barlow.

"Yes," said the pilot, "the control tower has advised me of the weather forecast and it looks like it's almost clear skies all the way so it's going to be a direct flight for the most part." The pilot took out a pencil and ruler from his top pocket and drew a straight line across the Atlantic.

"Is that the route you'll be taking?" asked Hartland.

"Well, not exactly, but that's our planned flight path. Of course, it's mainly down to computerised navigation and some radio contact nowadays but it helps to get an idea of the visual landmarks, just for my own peace of mind. Of course, the co-pilot helps also."

"So how long have you been a pilot, sir?" asked Barlow.

"Around 12 years now. Bit of an old hand at these transatlantic flights. I've worked for all the major companies including British Airways and American Airlines." The pilot took a sip of his coffee. "Well, I'm afraid I have to go, gentlemen, because we have to do numerous pre-flight checks before we take off. Don't want to take any risks now, do we!" he chortled.

"I'm afraid that won't be necessary, Mr Parker, because you'll be answering some questions back at the police station."

Can you spot what had particularly aroused Detective Hartland's suspicions about the "pilot"?

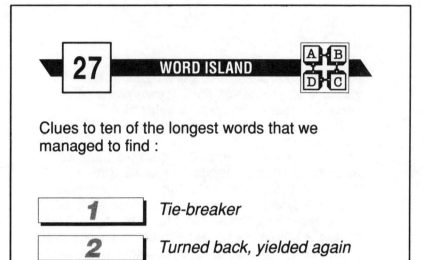

Clues to ten of the longest words that we managed to find :

1	*Tie-breaker*
2	*Turned back, yielded again*
3	*Laughed at, mocked*
4	*A judicial decision*
5	*Banished*
6	*A French posterior?*
7	*Danced in a Scottish way?*
8	*The murder of a god*
9	*Looked at lecherously*
10	*Spooky, weird*

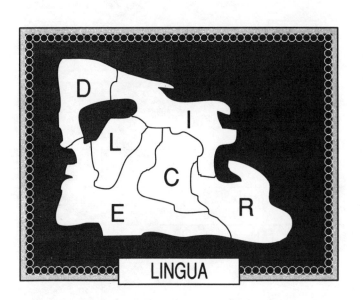

LINGUA

Other words of five letters or more (find up to another 20) :

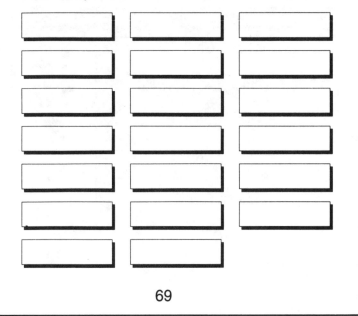

WHO?	GUESSES
RBQHAAKDQ	12
ZBSNQ	10
MZLD BGZMFD	8
FKNAD SGDZSQD	6
GZSGZVZX	4
AZQC NE ZUNM	2

WHAT?	GUESSES
SDM NM LNGR' RBZKD	12
D.F. AQHKKHZMS NQ QNRD	10
FQZOGHSD	8
ADRS EQHDMC?	6
RSZQ NE ZEQHBZ	4
BZQZS	2

WHERE?	GUESSES
MDV EQNMS	12
LDLNQHZK ENTMSZHM	10
NM SGD LZKK	8
RHW GTMCQDC QNNLR	6
QNXZK RSZMCZQC EKHDR	4
SGD FTZQC BGZMFDR SGDQD	2

WHEN?	GUESSES
DZQK VZQQDM	12
IZBJ QTAX	10
MNUDLADQ MHMDSDDM RHWSX-SGQDD	8
BNMROHQZBX?	6
RSZSD UHRHS SN CZKKZR	4
KDD GZQUDX NRVZKC	2

For each of the statements below, put your guesstimated answer in the appropriate box on the opposite page.

A How many sides does an icosahedron have?

B How many pedals does a standard musical harp have?

C How many twins appear in Shakespeare's *A Comedy of Errors*?

D How many popes have been assassinated?

E How many gold medals did Mark Spitz win in the 1968/72 Olympics?

F How many stomachs do cattle have?

G A marathon is 26 miles long plus another how many yards?

H How many locks does the Panama Canal have?

J How many million passengers use Chicago's O'Hare International Airport per annum?

K How many chromosomes does a human being have?

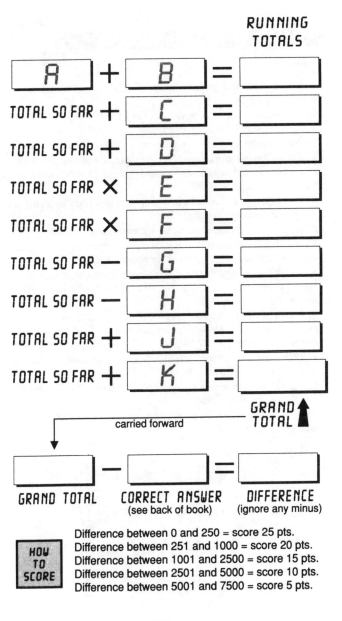

RUNNING
TOTALS

| A | + | B | = | |

TOTAL SO FAR + C =

TOTAL SO FAR + D =

TOTAL SO FAR × E =

TOTAL SO FAR × F =

TOTAL SO FAR — G =

TOTAL SO FAR — H =

TOTAL SO FAR + J =

TOTAL SO FAR + K =

GRAND
TOTAL

carried forward

GRAND TOTAL — CORRECT ANSWER (see back of book) = DIFFERENCE (ignore any minus)

HOW TO SCORE

Difference between 0 and 250 = score 25 pts.
Difference between 251 and 1000 = score 20 pts.
Difference between 1001 and 2500 = score 15 pts.
Difference between 2501 and 5000 = score 10 pts.
Difference between 5001 and 7500 = score 5 pts.

1) Who is seen clinging from the hands of a clock in his classic 1923 film Safety Last?

2) In whose honour are festivals held in Glyndebourne, UK and in his home town of Salzburg, Germany?

3) What are the most famous antipodal points on the Earth's surface?

4) Which American state has the lowest population and the most extreme male/female ratio due to the large number of men that work there?

5) Which part of an animal's body could be described as prehensile if it was especially versatile?

6) Which three chemical elements are named after planets?

7) The Greek mathematician Euclid claimed there were only five "regular" solids – what is so regular about them?

8) Which horrid mythical creatures were encountered by Jason and his Argonauts and looked like vultures but had the heads of old women?

9) Which piece of equipment is used by occultists to receive messages from the spirits, its name deriving from the French and German words for "Yes"?

10) What is the political connection between Mondale, Rockefeller, Johnson, Ford, Bush, and Quale?

11) In which game are up to six people involved in the investigation into the death of Dr Black?

12) How many events are there in the women's equivalent of the men's decathlon?

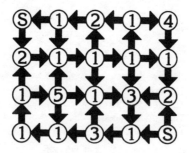

LAP 4

There are no time limits on this lap.

To score each puzzle, refer to the Scoring Summary on page 13. The maximum scores available are shown below.

	MAX.	SCORE
QUIZWORD	25	
REBUS CHALLENGE	30	
SAFE CRACKER	20	
LOGIC PROBLEM	20	
IN THE PIPELINE	20	
CRIME STORY	25	
WORD ISLAND	30	
MISSING LINKS	30	
NUMEROLOGY	25	
MAGNIFICENT MAZE	25	
TOTAL (max. 250)		

TARGET TO BEAT – 125 points

QUIZWORD

ACROSS

8 What flower is a variation of the buttercup, with smaller petals? (8)

9 What word, also used as a suffix, describes an irrational fear of a particular situation, place or object? (6)

10 What is the common name for the hyoid bone at the front of the neck, so called because of a legend in Genesis, Chapter 3? (5,5)

11 What name is given a person who comes from regions of northern Finland, Norway or Sweden? (4)

12 An emergency or state of panic (6)

14 What is the practice of giving employment to those related to you, rather than on the basis of individual merit? (8)

15 Which form of government was employed in Italy in 1922–1943? (7)

17 What classical architectural features rest on a base and are surmounted by capitals? (7)

20 What word, also meaning "concerning the head", is the name of an index concerned with various head measurements? (8)

22 Which Egyptian city was a capital of ancient Egypt and is the site of present-day Luxor and Al-Karnak? (6)

24 In astronomy, what is a large body of gases, held together by gravity, that emits radiations sometimes including visible light? (4)

25 This word means to shorten (10)

27 What alloy is primarily made from copper and tin? (6)

28 What word connects a county of New York City, a borough of London, and the main Confederate capital during the American Civil War? (8)

DOWN

1 Anyone involved in the buying and selling of goods, in particular those who use bartering (6)

2 Which of the three sporting activities in a triathlon do contestants perform first? (4)

3 Which by-product of sugar, also called treacle, was taxed in the USA by the British Parliament in the 18th Century? (8)

4 What term describes a soldier's pay, or the payment received by a parish minister in Scotland? (7)

5 The maintenance of a building or the costs involved (6)

6 Which salad vegetable comes from the second largest of the Dodecanese Islands? (3,7)

7 In music, the _____ normal is a standard set in the 1887 Vienna Conference to fix the pitch of the A above middle C (8)

13 Which powder, prepared from toluene, is 550 times sweeter than sugar in its purest state? (10)

16 Which part of a camera is a hole variable in size to alter the amount of light that falls onto the film? (8)

18 What word means "to overstretch" and "the extent of involvement of an organisation with the surrounding population"? (8)

19 What punctured five of the *Titanic*'s sixteen waterproof compartments, causing it to sink, on April 14, 1912? (7)

21 St. Peter is closely associated with the Bible story of the _____ and fishes (6)

23 What word, derived from Latin, means "to still be standing or existing"? (6)

26 What is a part of a verse consisting of an unstressed syllable followed by a stressed one? (4)

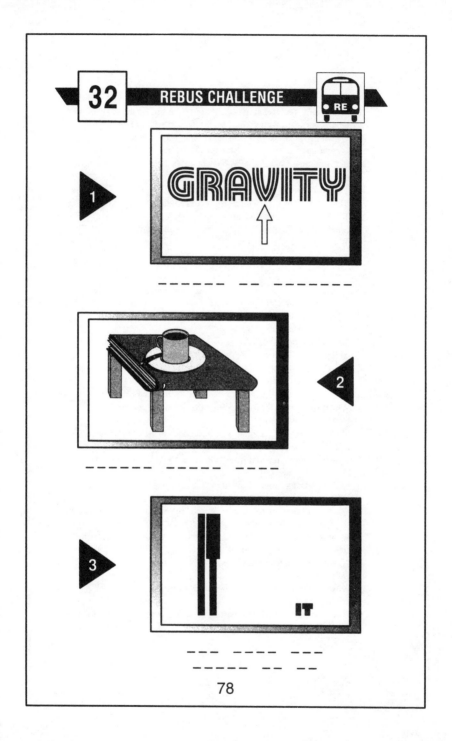

1

GRAVITY ↑

_ _ _ _ _ _   _ _   _ _ _ _ _ _

2

_ _ _ _ _ _   _ _ _ _ _   _ _ _ _

3

IT

_ _ _   _ _ _ _   _ _ _
_ _ _ _   _ _   _ _

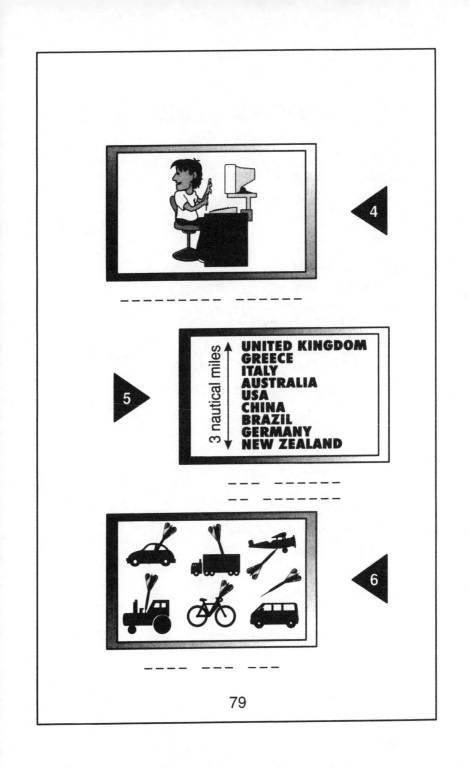

4 ◄

_ _ _ _ _ _ _ _ _   _ _ _ _ _ _

5 ►

UNITED KINGDOM
GREECE
ITALY
AUSTRALIA
USA
CHINA
BRAZIL
GERMANY
NEW ZEALAND

3 nautical miles

_ _ _   _ _ _ _ _ _
_ _   _ _ _ _ _ _ _

6 ◄

_ _ _ _   _ _ _   _ _ _

Blacken out those segments on the right-hand page that are letter coded to the FALSE statements. This will form a correct mathematical sum.

<table>
<tr><td></td><td></td><td align="center">True</td><td align="center">False</td></tr>
<tr><td>A</td><td>The Wright Brothers made the first powered flight at Kitty Hawk, NC</td><td>☐</td><td>☐</td></tr>
<tr><td>B</td><td>In a suit of armour, the gorget protects the upper arm</td><td>☐</td><td>☐</td></tr>
<tr><td>C</td><td>Yesterday was the theme song for the film On Her Majesty's Secret Service</td><td>☐</td><td>☐</td></tr>
<tr><td>D</td><td>Khartoum is the capital city of the Sudan</td><td>☐</td><td>☐</td></tr>
<tr><td>E</td><td>The Aswan High Dam is situated on the River Volga</td><td>☐</td><td>☐</td></tr>
<tr><td>F</td><td>Otis invented the lift in 1752</td><td>☐</td><td>☐</td></tr>
<tr><td>G</td><td>Ernest Hemingway never won the Nobel Prize for literature</td><td>☐</td><td>☐</td></tr>
<tr><td>H</td><td>Androphobia is a fear of electronic gadgets</td><td>☐</td><td>☐</td></tr>
<tr><td>J</td><td>In physics, the becquerel is a measure of radioactivity</td><td>☐</td><td>☐</td></tr>
<tr><td>K</td><td>Sagittarius is the zodiac sign of "the archer"</td><td>☐</td><td>☐</td></tr>
</table>

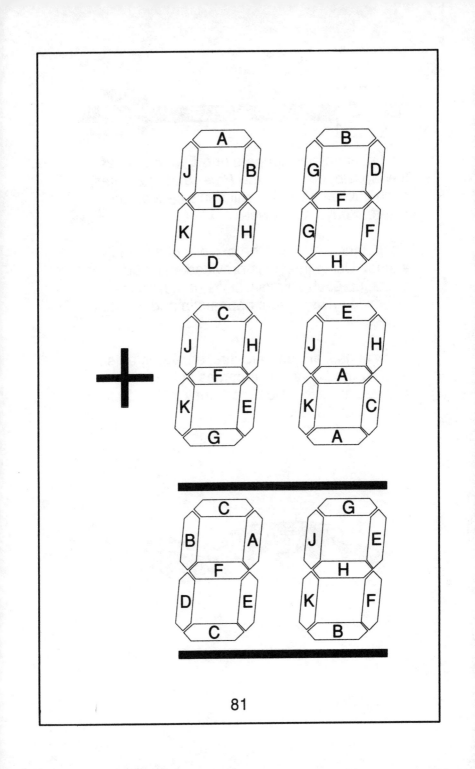

Five national newspapers (the *Evening News*, the *Gossip*, the *Post*, the *Press* and the *Times*) each publish a weekly children's cartoon on different days of the week.

Each cartoon follows the exploits of a friendly animal. Using the clues provided, can you match up each animal with its name, and tell us which newspaper it appears in and on what day?

The animals are an aardvark, a badger, a fish, a snake and a yak. The names of these animals are (in some order) Lucy, Millie, Peter, Simone and Trevor.

CLUES

1. Lucy the Snake appears two days before the *Press* runs its cartoon which features the exploits of Millie.

2. Trevor appears on Wednesdays.

3. The *Evening News* runs its children's cartoon on Fridays without fail, but it is not the paper that has Simone the Fish.

4. The aardvark appears in the *Gossip*, which doesn't have cartoons on Mondays.

5. The *Post* doesn't have cartoons on Mondays either.

6. Peter is not a yak.

STARTING HINTS

a. Bearing in mind clue 2, take a close look at clue 1. You should be able to deduce the publication days for Lucy and Millie straight away.

b. The next bit is more tricky. One possibility is to examine each animal, determine which names are possible, and also which days they could possibly come out on. You should be able to deduce the days when the aardvark and fish are printed.

NOTE – The papers only come out on Mondays through Fridays, there being no weekend editions.

Animal	Name	Paper	Day
Aardvark			
Badger			
Fish			
Snake			
Yak			

Your task is to connect the book titles below with their female authors (right).

1 *Jamaica Inn*
2 *Mansfield Park*
3 *Jane Eyre*
4 *Hollywood Wives*
5 *Whose Body?*
6 *The Five Red Herrings*
7 *The ABC Murders*
8 *The Nine Tailors*
9 *Sense and Sensibility*
10 *N or M?*
11 *A Woman of Substance*
12 *Lord Peter Views the Body*
13 *Emma*
14 *Sparkling Cyanide*
15 *Strong Poison*
16 *4.50 from Paddington*
17 *To Be the Best*
18 *The Birds*
19 *The Professor*
20 *The Pale Horse*

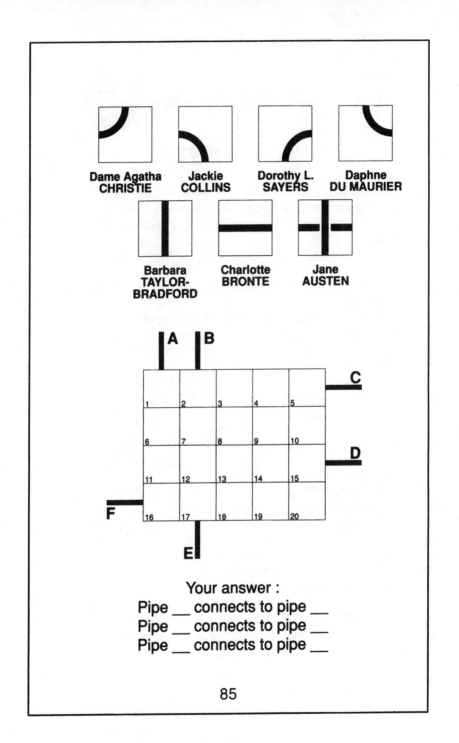

Dame Agatha CHRISTIE

Jackie COLLINS

Dorothy L. SAYERS

Daphne DU MAURIER

Barbara TAYLOR-BRADFORD

Charlotte BRONTE

Jane AUSTEN

Your answer :

Pipe __ connects to pipe __

Pipe __ connects to pipe __

Pipe __ connects to pipe __

The False Alarm

Just as the two policemen were about to leave
the airport, where their last case had been
solved, the airport manager confronted them
again.

"Here we go again," said Barlow under his
breath.

"I don't know if you could possibly..." said the
manager.

"Help you again?" suggested Hartland. "Yes, I
don't see why not. We have a special two-for-the-
price-of-one offer on today." Hartland's sarcasm
was lost on the manager.

"We have a man held in Custody Room 3. He
tried to take over the plane on a flight from
India," explained the manager. "I was wondering
if you could question him. You'd be better at it
than any of the security staff we have here."

Barlow and Hartland met the man in the room
where he was being held.

"Policemen?" asked the man. "Thank goodness.
I've been framed, I tell you. I got on the plane
and about fifteen minutes after take-off the pilot
came on to the radio to tell us the details of the
flight, like they normally do."

"Indeed. So what happened?"

The man continued. "Well, when the pilot was
speaking I thought I recognised his voice as that
of Jack Delaney, a friend of mine. You see I used
to be a pilot quite some time ago. I've been
retired for around five years now. Anyway, I

86

asked the stewardess if I could go and meet him. She said 'Yes', so I got up out of my seat and went up to the pilots' cabin, knocked on the door and said hello. At that moment, these two security goons pounced on me and within seconds I was dragged off to the back of the plane to be held there for the rest of the journey. I don't understand it."

At that moment the airport manager entered the room. "How are the investigations going, Detective?"

Hartland was puzzled. "Is it usual to have security guards aboard a plane?"

"No," said the manager, "but today's trip had a few private security guards because there were a couple of Indian film celebrities on that flight."

"Well," concluded the Detective, "I think they should be better trained. This man you are holding has done nothing wrong and this whole situation is an unfortunate mistake on the part of the security guards. They should listen more carefully."

Can you work out what the man had done unintentionally to alarm the guards so much?

Clues to ten of the longest words that we managed to find :

1	*Eastern art of knot-tying*
2	*Colloquial for 'mater'*
3	*Containing more milk?*
4	*Photographic device*
5	*School of rote learning?*
6	*A debt*
7	*More jovial*
8	*Genus of plants*
9	*Transporter of disease/virus*
10	*Caribbean percussion instrument*

ALFABETIKA

Other words of five letters or more (find up to another 20) :

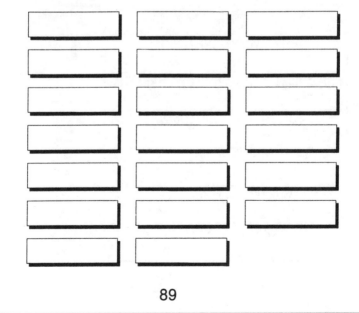

WHO?	GUESSES
PTZQQX VNQJDQ	**12**
SDM OHM ANVKDQ	**10**
EZLHKX LZM	**8**
GZMMZ AZQADQZ	**6**
ADCQNBJ	**4**
OQDGHRSNQHB	**2**

WHAT?	GUESSES
VVH NARDQUZSHNM ONRS	**12**
DHFGSDDM DHFGSX-MHMD DWGHAHSHNM	**10**
SGQDD GTMCQDC LDSQDR	**8**
BGZLO CD LZQR	**6**
CDRHFMDQ FTRSZUD...	**4**
EQDMBG KZMCLZQJ	**2**

WHERE?	GUESSES
QNXZK QDRHCDMBD	12
YHFFTQZS	10
ENTQ NQ EHUD RHCDR	8
BGDNOR	6
SNLA	4
DFXOS	2

WHEN?	GUESSES
GZVJR	12
EZM BKTA	10
ONHMCDWSDQ	8
RDBQDSZQX	6
RGQDCCDC	4
NKHUDQ MNQSG	2

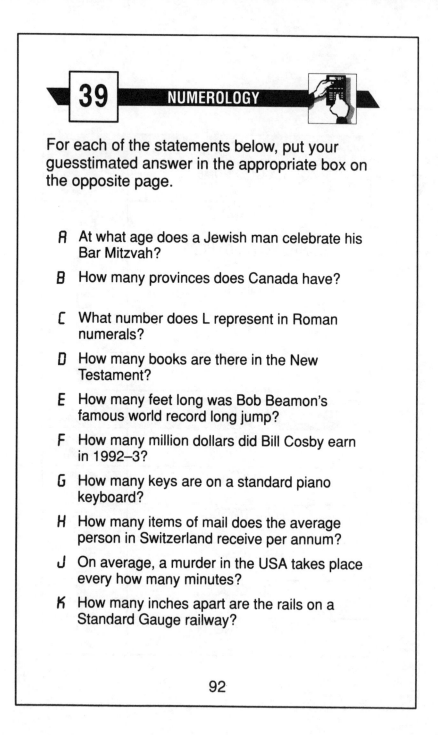

For each of the statements below, put your guesstimated answer in the appropriate box on the opposite page.

A At what age does a Jewish man celebrate his Bar Mitzvah?

B How many provinces does Canada have?

C What number does L represent in Roman numerals?

D How many books are there in the New Testament?

E How many feet long was Bob Beamon's famous world record long jump?

F How many million dollars did Bill Cosby earn in 1992–3?

G How many keys are on a standard piano keyboard?

H How many items of mail does the average person in Switzerland receive per annum?

J On average, a murder in the USA takes place every how many minutes?

K How many inches apart are the rails on a Standard Gauge railway?

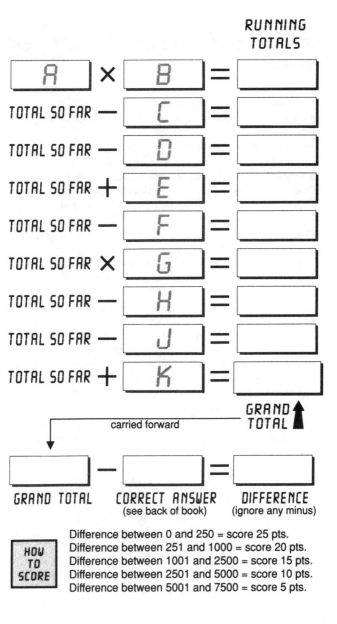

RUNNING TOTALS

$A \times B =$

TOTAL SO FAR $- C =$

TOTAL SO FAR $- D =$

TOTAL SO FAR $+ E =$

TOTAL SO FAR $- F =$

TOTAL SO FAR $\times G =$

TOTAL SO FAR $- H =$

TOTAL SO FAR $- J =$

TOTAL SO FAR $+ K =$

carried forward → GRAND TOTAL ↑

GRAND TOTAL $-$ CORRECT ANSWER $=$ DIFFERENCE
(see back of book)   (ignore any minus)

HOW TO SCORE

Difference between 0 and 250 = score 25 pts.
Difference between 251 and 1000 = score 20 pts.
Difference between 1001 and 2500 = score 15 pts.
Difference between 2501 and 5000 = score 10 pts.
Difference between 5001 and 7500 = score 5 pts.

1) Which film character uses the cover of working for the company Universal Import and Export?

2) Which of the great lakes is completely contained within the United States?

3) What is the world's second largest country?

4) Lord Tennyson's poem *The Charge of the Light Brigade* describes how 600 men on horseback rode "into the valley of Death". This was the Battle of Balaklava, during which war?

5) For what sporting purpose are ostriches, horses and camels used?

6) What general chemical term is applied to a substance created using large chains of much smaller molecules?

7) The AB blood group is called the "receive-all group" because people with it can take blood from any other group. Which group is the "donate-all" group?

8) On what fortune-telling objects would you find cups, pentacles, swords and wands in the Minor Arcana?

9) Which Italian designer's clothes were so popular, possibly due to his style of suit being worn by Richard Gere in the film *American Gigolo*, that he began designing for women as well?

10) Which game, a craze during the 1920s in the USA, requires 152 tiles divided up into 36 bamboos, 36 circles, 36 characters, 12 dragons, 16 winds, 8 jokers, and 8 flowers?

11) Which is the longest track event to use starting blocks?

12) If a chequered flag finishes a race and a yellow flag indicates "no overtaking", what does a black flag indicate?

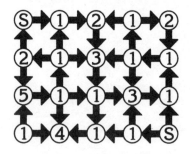

LAP 5

There are no time limits on this lap.

To score each puzzle, refer to the Scoring Summary on page 13. The maximum scores available are shown below.

	MAX.	SCORE
QUIZWORD	25	
REBUS CHALLENGE	30	
SAFE CRACKER	20	
LOGIC PROBLEM	20	
IN THE PIPELINE	20	
CRIME STORY	25	
WORD ISLAND	30	
MISSING LINKS	30	
NUMEROLOGY	25	
MAGNIFICENT MAZE	25	
TOTAL (max. 250)		

TARGET TO BEAT – 140 points

ACROSS

8   For what physical phenomenon did Sir Isaac Newton describe three laws that are still fundamental to physics today? (6)

9   Which fictitious city did the Spanish conquerors of America search for in the pursuit of its fabled golden riches? (2,6)

10   What is the simplest form of a hydraulic turbine called, as first described by the Roman architect Pollio in the 1st Century BC? (10)

11   What type of blood vessel carries deoxygenated blood from the capillaries back to the heart? (4)

12   What occurs when the sea is returning towards its lowest level? (3,4)

14   What cake is made from a long choux pastry case filled with whipped cream and topped with icing? (6)

15 This could describe the inhabitants of the land of Lilliput, in Jonathan Swift's book *Gulliver's Travels* (7)
17 In which sport is the Americas' Cup contested for? (7)
20 What title is given to the clergyman of a parish or congregation to which tithes are not payable? (6)
22 What variation of the fox-trot takes its name from the action of moving the feet with every beat of the music? (3-4)
24 In architecture, what term describes the supports of an arch, bridge or similar spanning structure? (4)
25 What practice, most often associated with the Roman Catholic church, is the act of granting penance based upon *John*, Chapter 20? (10)
27 In computing, what word describes those workers who will actually operate the finished program? (3,5)
28 Name a relative of the violin (6)

DOWN

1 Esau sold his birthright to Jacob for a bowlful of what? (6)
2 A varied assortment (5,3)
3 What crystals form around dust particles and always grow in a pattern with three lines of symmetry? (4)
4 What name is given to the official presiding over a match in sports such as lacrosse, basketball, tennis and soccer? (7)
5 Which term means "to add cheaper ingredients to make the commodity more impure with the aim of increasing profits"? (10)
6 Name the loose, rounded fragments of rock often used as a finishing material for driveways and roofs? (6)
7 Which of the four basic mathematical operations is used when computing the "sum" of some numbers? (8)
13 What are the textual and/or graphical devices used in computer programs to allow the user to tell the program what actions to perform? (10)
16 What are the people of ancient eastern and southern Spain called? (8)
18 What geometrical coordinate gives the North or South location of a place relative to the equator? (8)
19 This word means "to own" (7)
21 In physics, what type of force is induced when a turning motion results even though the resultant force may be in equilibrium? (6)
23 What type of dog has varieties including the standard, miniature and toy? (6)
26 On which side is something if it can be described as "sinister"? (4)

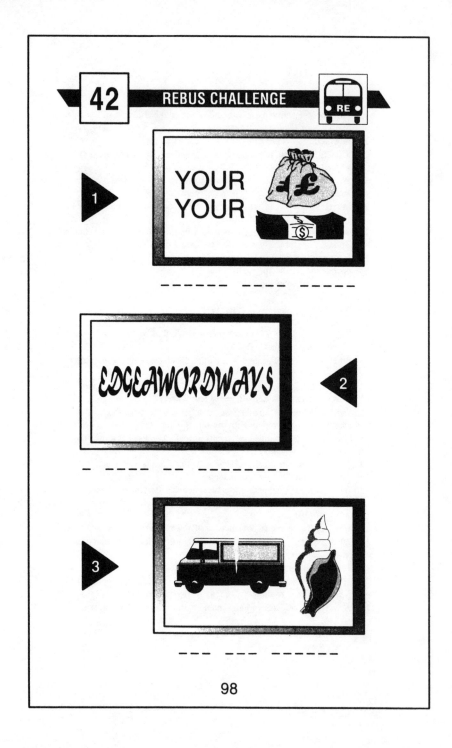

1. YOUR
   YOUR

   _____ ____ _____

2. EDGEAWORDWAYS

   _ ____ __ _____

3.

   ___ ___ _____

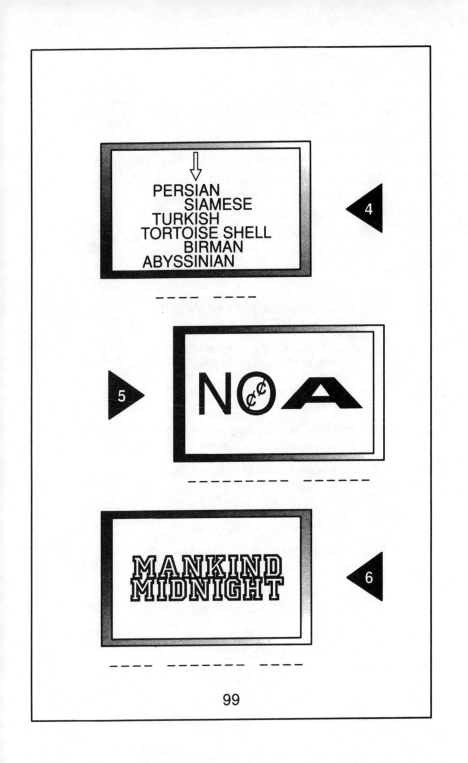

4

PERSIAN
SIAMESE
TURKISH
TORTOISE SHELL
BIRMAN
ABYSSINIAN

---- ----

5

N⊘A

------- ------

MANKIND
MIDNIGHT

6

---- ------- ----

Blacken out those segments on the right-hand page that are letter coded to the FALSE statements. This will form a correct mathematical sum.

		True	False
A	The national airline of Portugal is VARIG.	☐	☐
B	Nathuran Godse shot Mohandas K. Ghandi in 1948	☐	☐
C	A jeroboam of champagne holds a volume equivalent to 16 wine bottles	☐	☐
D	The old name for Tungsten is Wolfram	☐	☐
E	The cities in Dickens's *A Tale of Two Cities* are London and Berlin	☐	☐
F	Gutenberg invented moveable type in 1450	☐	☐
G	Paris was the first city to host the modern Olympic games twice	☐	☐
H	Phobos and Deimos are the two moons of Neptune	☐	☐
J	The clavicle is the proper name for what is called the breastbone	☐	☐
K	If you are born on August 28th, your sun sign is Taurus	☐	☐

100

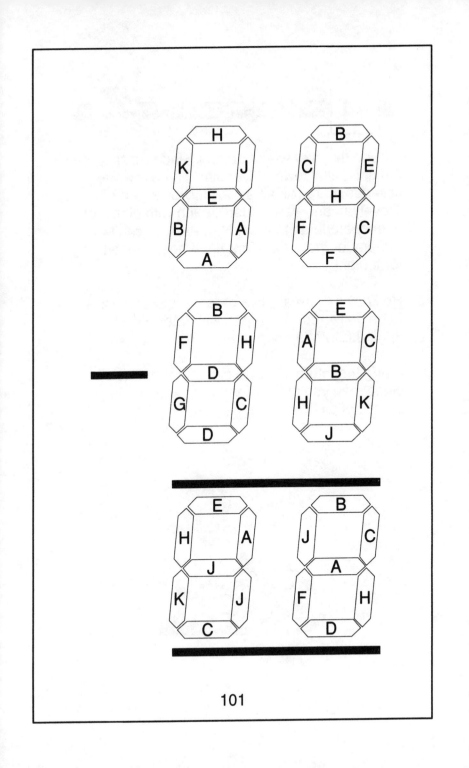

101

Alfredo the chef works at Your Kinda Pizza in the university town of Dunelm. There are five colleges there (Aidan's, Collingwood, Grey, Trevelyan and Van Mildert), each with plenty of hungry students to feed. However, he can't remember the orders that have been placed for tonight.

He knows there are five orders – the earliest is to be delivered at 7:15pm, with later orders at 8pm, 8:30pm, 9:15pm and 10:30pm.

Using the information he can remember (see clues) can you piece together the complete details of all five orders?

CLUES

1. "I remember that Martin's pizza (the exotically named Fuengerola) has to be delivered exactly 45 minutes later than the pepperoni heading for Aidan's."

2. "Oh yes, and the order for the pizza with anchovies was immediately after the Grey college order."

3. "I know Kay is in Trevelyan college because she's a regular customer. She wants a Hot & Spicy... or is it the Margherita?"

4. "The order to Collingwood needs to be there two hours before Ian wants his pizza. Actually, now I think about it, it might be a longer gap than that. I can't remember."

5. "I certainly know Heather wants her order for 8:30."

6. "Debbie's order isn't the 7:15 nor the 10:30. I know she never has the Hot & Spicy."

STARTING HINTS

a. Use clues 1, 4, 5 and 6 to work out who wants their pizzas at 7:15pm and 10:30pm.

b. Now use clues 1 and 3 to deduce the time at which the pepperoni pizza needs to be ordered.

c. From then on, it shouldn't be too difficult to deduce which student is from Collingwood college.

Name	College	Pizza	Time
Debbie			
Heather			
Ian			
Kay			
Martin			

Your task is to decide in which continents the mountains below are situated, though two of these are red herrings – for these, use the horizontal piece indicated (right).

1 Champlain
2 Everest
3 Kilimanjaro
4 Fujiyama
5 Erebus
6 Kirkpatrick
7 Stromboli
8 Mount of Olives
9 Logan
10 Popocatepetl
11 Matterhorn
12 Olympus
13 Parnassus
14 Townsend
15 Cotopaxi
16 Aconcagua
17 Sugar Loaf Mountain
18 Table Mountain
19 Titicaca
20 Cook

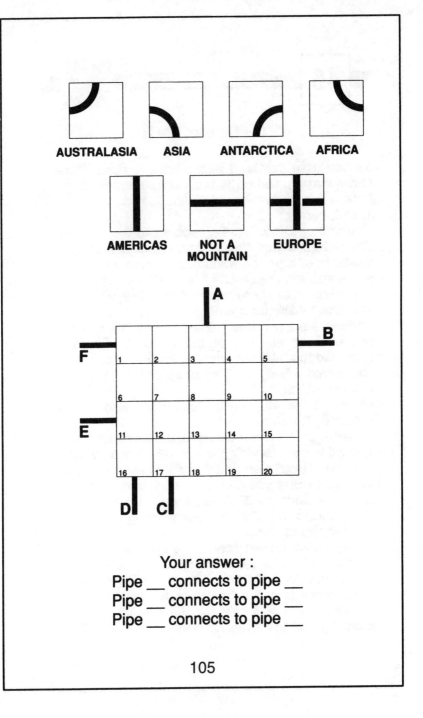

AUSTRALASIA ASIA ANTARCTICA AFRICA

AMERICAS NOT A MOUNTAIN EUROPE

Your answer :
Pipe __ connects to pipe __
Pipe __ connects to pipe __
Pipe __ connects to pipe __

105

The Great Fall

As Detective Hartland was driving towards the police station, the radio buzzed into action. The Detective returned the call signal. "Yes, go ahead, Penny."

"Morning, Detective. Can you go to the building site at Kensington Yard? Builders have found the body of a young woman. No name yet but we're still getting details," the radio crackled.

Hartland was there within five minutes. He was met by the foreman there.

"Hello, sir, my name is Pete Norris. We've got a rather nasty situation on our hands. The second shift had just started work when one of the lads discovered a body at the bottom of a long shaft in the building."

"Could I see where this shaft is?" asked Detective Hartland.

"Certainly." At that moment the foreman spotted a man leaving the site. He called over to him. "Oi! Geoff! Can you show this gentleman the same thing you showed me earlier?" He turned to address Hartland again. "Geoff will show you round. He's the one working on that floor at the moment."

The builder turned round and said "Follow me, if you would." He led Hartland up the stairs to the fourth floor of the building-to-be. "Quite a lot of the work is unfinished so watch your step. Here we are. I was here for the first shift this morning and the situation was exactly like this.

But if you look here..." The builder went to open a nearby door and pointed downwards to indicate the gaping hole in the floor. "This shaft is going to be a lift but before that's installed we use it as a hatch for a pulley system. Near the end of my shift I was raising a few planks that I wanted to bring up to this floor when I noticed this body at the very bottom."

The Detective looked down the shaft and saw the body which the builders had covered in a blanket. "Nasty. What do you reckon happened?"

The builder thought for a moment. "Well, either she was suicidal or she was just being nosy and fell without realising there wasn't a floor on the other side of the door."

"Yes, those are possibilities, but I know it was murder and so do you!"

How did the Detective know this was a murder?

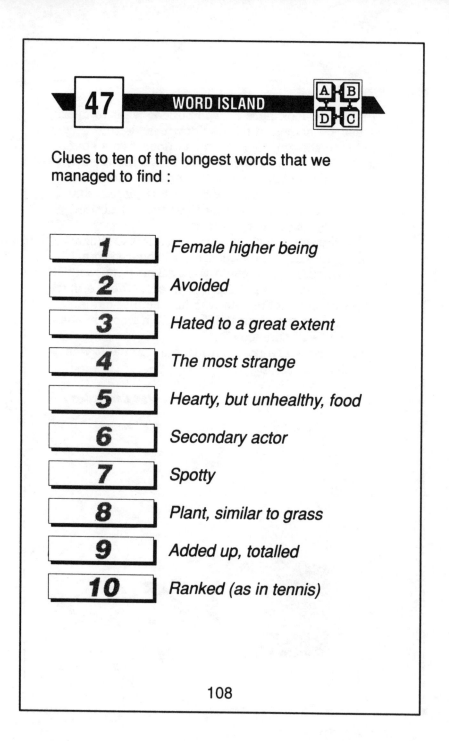

Clues to ten of the longest words that we managed to find :

1	*Female higher being*
2	*Avoided*
3	*Hated to a great extent*
4	*The most strange*
5	*Hearty, but unhealthy, food*
6	*Secondary actor*
7	*Spotty*
8	*Plant, similar to grass*
9	*Added up, totalled*
10	*Ranked (as in tennis)*

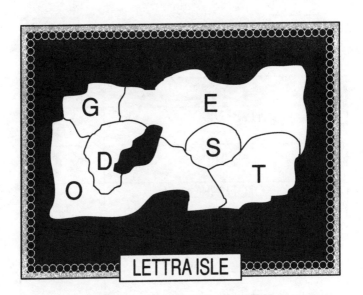

LETTRA ISLE

Other words of five letters or more (find up to another 20) :

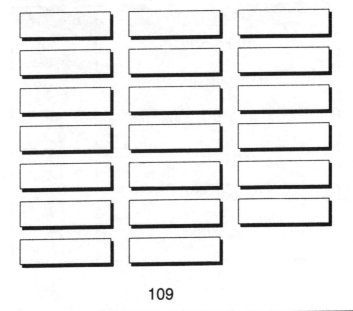

WHO?	GUESSES
JNMHFRADQF	12
RKDDODQ	10
OZQZMNHC?	8
ZLDQHBZM	6
CHZMD JDZSNM	4
ZBSR/VQHSDR/CHQDBSR	2

WHAT?	GUESSES
QDLHMFSNM	12
HAL RDUDMSX-SVN	10
BZM AD DKDBSQHB	8
BZQQHZFD	6
SZATKZSHNM	4
PVDQSXTHNO	2

110

WHERE?	GUESSES
FQDZS EHQD	12
BZOHSNKHMD	10
SQDZSHDR	8
KZYHN	6
RDUDM GHKKR	4
BNKNRRDTL	2

WHEN?	GUESSES
KNMF CHRSZMBD VZKJ	12
SDKDOGNMD BZKK	10
MHMDSDDM-RHWSX-MHMD	8
SQZMPTHKKHSX	6
DZFKD	4
ZQLRSQNMF ZMC ZKCQHM	2

For each of the statements below, put your guesstimated answer in the appropriate box on the opposite page.

A How many dice are usually provided in a backgammon set?

B How many points does a field goal score in American football?

C How many billion people are there likely to be on Earth by the year 2025?

D How many minutes long can a solar eclipse last if viewed from the Earth's surface?

E How many hours long does Wagner's *Gotterdammerung* last?

F What is the maximum number of clubs a professional golfer can carry on a round?

G What percentage of Japan is covered by forest?

H How many Nobel Prizes has the United States won to date?

J How many million miles is it from the Earth to the Sun?

K What is the average life expectancy, in years, of a man from Sierra Leone?

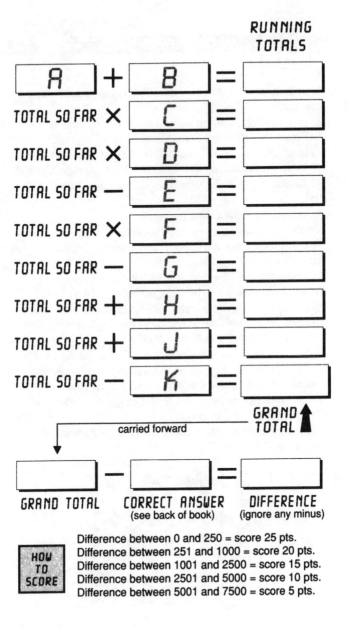

RUNNING TOTALS

A	+	B	=	
TOTAL SO FAR	×	C	=	
TOTAL SO FAR	×	D	=	
TOTAL SO FAR	—	E	=	
TOTAL SO FAR	×	F	=	
TOTAL SO FAR	—	G	=	
TOTAL SO FAR	+	H	=	
TOTAL SO FAR	+	J	=	
TOTAL SO FAR	—	K	=	

GRAND TOTAL ↑

carried forward

| | — | | = | |
| GRAND TOTAL | | CORRECT ANSWER (see back of book) | | DIFFERENCE (ignore any minus) |

HOW TO SCORE

Difference between 0 and 250 = score 25 pts.
Difference between 251 and 1000 = score 20 pts.
Difference between 1001 and 2500 = score 15 pts.
Difference between 2501 and 5000 = score 10 pts.
Difference between 5001 and 7500 = score 5 pts.

113

1) In architecture, what term describes columns supporting a handrail?

2) In which John Bunyan novel does a character called Christian attempt to get to the Celestial City?

3) In which country will you find the largest covered football stadium, the Azteca, opened in 1968 for the Olympic Games?

4) To which side of the International Date Line does Madrid lie?

5) In heraldry, what colour is azure?

6) Who provides the connection between the discoverer of the expanding universe, a telescope, and a famous number used in astronomy?

7) Seven million cubic feet of which gas ignited as the *Hindenburg* airship was hit by lightning on 6 May, 1937?

8) Perhaps contrary to popular belief, which precious stone is the most expensive despite five other materials coming after it in the list of wedding anniversary gifts?

9) Medusa was a Gorgon – how many sisters did she have?

10) What does a polygraph do that can provide (somewhat inconclusive) evidence that may be used in court cases?

11) What drink can be graded from Orange Pekoe down to Dust, depending on its quality?

12) Which athletic field event uses a piece of equipment weighing 16lbs?

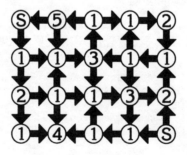

LAP 6

There are no time limits on this lap.

To score each puzzle, refer to the Scoring
Summary on page 13. The maximum scores
available are shown below.

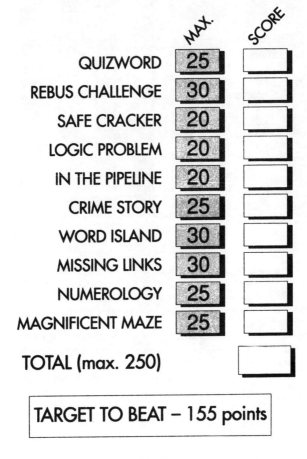

	MAX.	SCORE
QUIZWORD	25	
REBUS CHALLENGE	30	
SAFE CRACKER	20	
LOGIC PROBLEM	20	
IN THE PIPELINE	20	
CRIME STORY	25	
WORD ISLAND	30	
MISSING LINKS	30	
NUMEROLOGY	25	
MAGNIFICENT MAZE	25	
TOTAL (max. 250)		

TARGET TO BEAT – 155 points

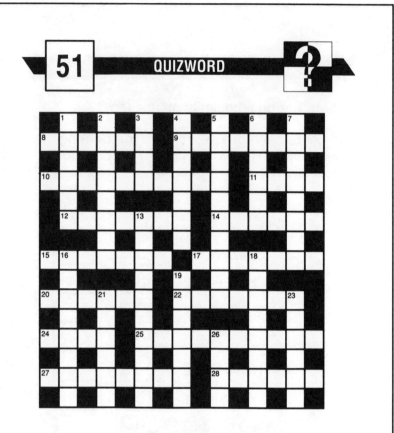

ACROSS

8 What musical term describes notes of given pitches and lengths sounding one after another to provide the "top line" of a score? (6)

9 Which animal derives its name from the Afrikaans for "earth pig"? (8)

10 Which legal term describes those rules that have been expressly enforced through legislation? (7-3)

11 Josip Broz _____, a former president of Yugoslavia, died in 1980 (4)

12 Of what are there types such as pressurised water, light water, boiling water and fast-breeder? (7)

14 What are the words that accompany the main tunes of songs called? (6)

15 Which part of the body is the most commonly pierced for cosmetic purposes? (7)

17 Which classic Activision/Atari computer game, recently re-released, invited the player to guide a character over rope swings and crocodiles? (7)

20 What is a person who practises water divining using a hazel stick called? (6)

22 What is the common name for herbs of the Ambrosia genus, noted for their small, green flowers on upright fronds? (7)

24 What was the name of the Pet Shop Boys' 1993 album, with its distinctive plastic orange CD box? (4)

25 What is the capital of Ethiopia? (5,5)

27 Which section of the Christian church takes this word of its name from the Greek word for "universal"? (8)

28 Which bird is famous for laying its eggs in the nests of other birds (although not all types do so)? (6)

DOWN

1 In mathematics, what is a line segment that has a length and a direction called? (6)

2 Which sport did the ancient Greeks call "harpaston", the Romans "harpastum" and the medieval Italians "calcio"? (8)

3 What medical term describes a sac filled with foreign matter (usually liquid)? (4)

4 What is the common name for the wild, surface-feeding duck from which the domestic duck has descended? (7)

5 Which metalwork technique uses a continuous supply of electric current to join two pieces of metal, most commonly steel? (3-7)

6 What Hindu principle, derived from Sanskrit, describes the descent of a god into the human world? (6)

7 The least amount of fissile material that sustains a nuclear chain reaction is called the _____ mass (8)

13 What type of portable hut was used by the Jews as a temple for the Ark of the Covenant whilst moving through desert land? (10)

16 In golf, what type of score is achieved by a golfer who scores a bogie or worse? (5,3)

18 What scientific term is used to explain why a speaker "whines" when a microphone is put near to it? (8)

19 What was the popular form of design for interior decor in the 1920s and 30s featuring streamlined contours? (3,4)

21 What type of blade was usually used in agriculture, said to be fixed to the wheels of Boudicca's chariot? (6)

23 In law, if a person owes a payment, and that payment is legally enforceable, then he is a _____ (6)

26 What is the usual term applied to a subdivision of one of the world's major religious divisions? (4)

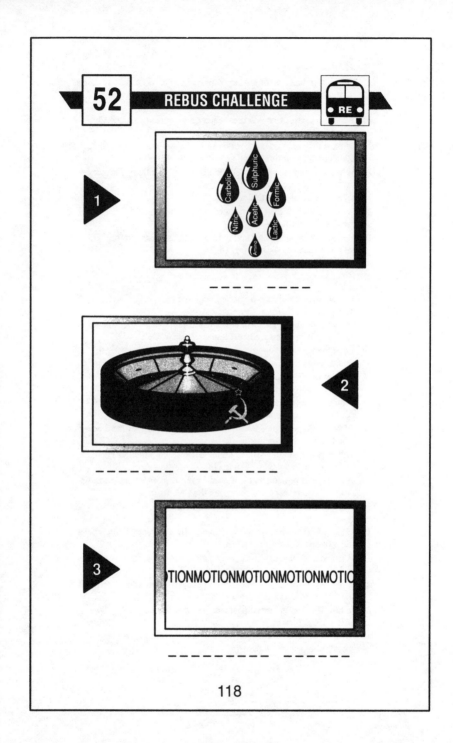

1.   ____ ____

2.   _____ _____

3.   _____ _____

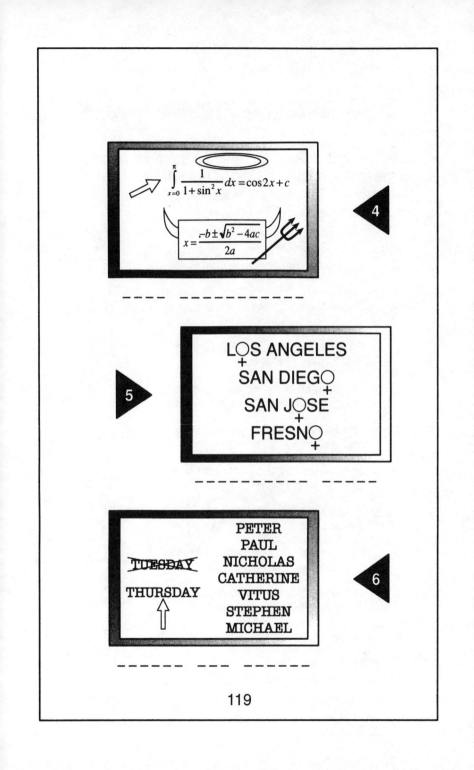

119

53 SAFE CRACKER

Blacken out those segments on the right-hand page that are letter coded to the FALSE statements. This will form a correct mathematical sum.

		True	False
A	KLM is the national airline of Belgium	☐	☐
B	There are six states of Australia	☐	☐
C	Boxer Jack Dempsey's nickname was "the Manassa Mauler"	☐	☐
D	Sublimation is the process of turning from a gas to a solid (or vice versa)	☐	☐
E	The flag of Libya is coloured black and green	☐	☐
F	Tommy Dorsey, J. J. Johnson and Glen Miller all played the oboe	☐	☐
G	Wagner's *Aida* was first performed at the opening of the Suez Canal	☐	☐
H	Neptune is the planet eighth furthest from the Sun in the Solar System	☐	☐
J	There are twenty-seven cervical vertebrae in the human neck	☐	☐
K	Halifax is the capital of the Canadian province of Nova Scotia	☐	☐

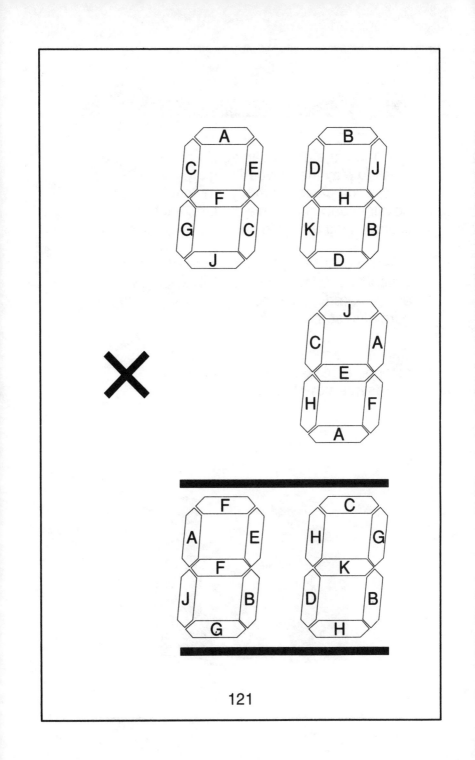

121

Five men at a board games club meet once a week to play their favourite board game *Hollywood Quest*. In this game, each space is colour coded one of five colours, each one representing a certain category of questions.

The five categories in the game are Books, Celebrities, Films, Music and Television which are coloured blue, green, grey, orange and purple (in some order).

Can you name all five men, their favourite categories of question and the colours represented by those categories?

CLUES

1. Mr Everett prefers the purple coloured squares.

2. Mr Harper likes the Films category best, which is not the blue neither the orange squares.

3. John Sanders doesn't like literature-based questions.

4. Patrick's favourite colour is the blue (this is not the colour of the TV questions).

5. The grey squares indicate the player must answer a question about Books, and you won't find Mr Erwin landing on these if he can help it.

6. Graham prefers the Celebrities category.

7. James avoids the green and orange squares.

STARTING HINTS

a. Clues 1, 2 and 5 should help you to work out the colour favoured by Mr Harper.

b. Work out John Sanders's favourite colour.

c. You should now be able to work out the colours for all five subjects. Now start matching these up to the names. (Kendal is the fifth surname.)

Forename	Surname	Colour	Category
Graham			
James			
John			
Patrick			
Paul			

55 IN THE PIPELINE

Your task is to match up the show-stopping songs below with the famous musicals that they appear in.

1 *Get Me to the Church on Time*
2 *Luck Be a Lady*
3 *Wouldn't It Be Loverly*
4 *When I Marry Mr. Snow*
5 *Sit Down, You're Rocking the Boat*
6 *Anything You Can Do*
7 *Some Enchanted Evening*
8 *If They Could See Me Now*
9 *If I Loved You*
10 *You'll Never Walk Alone*
11 *A Bushel and a Peck*
12 *There is Nothing Like a Dame*
13 *I Could Have Danced All Night*
14 *There's No Business Like Show Business*
15 *Younger Than Springtime*
16 *Rhythm of Life*
17 *Doin' What Comes Naturally*
18 *I'm Gonna Wash That Man Right Outa My Hair*
19 *Money, Money*
20 *Hey Big Spender!*

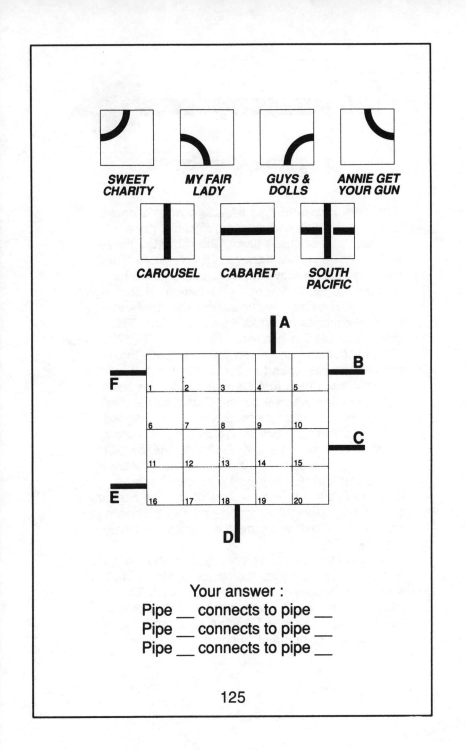

SWEET CHARITY

MY FAIR LADY

GUYS & DOLLS

ANNIE GET YOUR GUN

CAROUSEL

CABARET

SOUTH PACIFIC

Your answer :
Pipe __ connects to pipe __
Pipe __ connects to pipe __
Pipe __ connects to pipe __

125

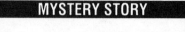

The Non-Car Crash

Detective Hartland was driving towards home. It was dark, foggy and raining. "I must get a transfer one of these days," he thought. There were some dim tail lights in the distance. They were getting nearer and nearer. He passed a stationary car in the opposite lane, and then suddenly Hartland realised that the lights in front were on a car that wasn't moving. The policeman hit the brakes.

He got out and surveyed the scene. He looked first at the car ahead of him. The driver's window was down and he saw the driver had sustained some bad injuries. Hartland reached for his radio. "Penny, you'd better get a squad car and an ambulance to Fields Lane. I have a crash driver with severe head injuries, could be fatal." As he waited, he surveyed the outside of the car to look for signs of impact. However, there didn't seem to be a scratch on the car but the engine was still running and the windscreen wipers were still working. The Detective turned the engine off.

Somewhat puzzled, he returned to the car that had been travelling in the opposite direction. It was some twenty yards down the road. The situation was much the same – the driver was badly hurt, wipers and engine still working, but no sign of any damage to the car.

At that point, a squad car turned up. "Hello sir," said the officer, "I was in the district so I thought I'd assist. Looks nasty."

"Yes," said Hartland, "not a pretty sight. I thought this was a typical crash situation. Bad weather, narrow road, all the usual characteristics. But judging by the unharmed paintwork, I'll have to think again."

The officer had an idea. "I think I know what might have happened, sir. I've heard of a couple of similar accidents happening. I bet it was a shock to them, poor souls."

Can you suggest to the Detective what the most likely explanation for this situation might be?

Clues to ten of the longest words that we managed to find :

1 Copy, impersonate

2 Hurt and mutilated

3 Turned the lights down

4 Sudden

5 Arbitrated between sides

6 Reflect upon

7 Split into halves

8 Lead chloride mineral

9 Gave out sound

10 Believed to be, thought

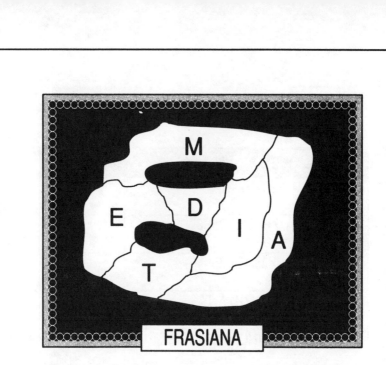

FRASIANA

Other words of five letters or more (find up to another 20) :

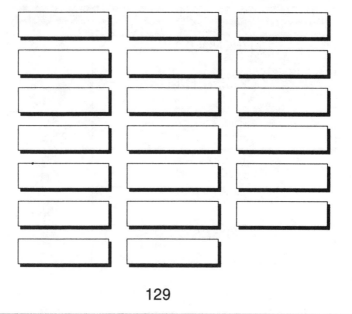

129

WHO?	GUESSES
INTQMZKHRS	12
RDQHZKHRDC ZQSHBKDR	10
UHBSNQHZM	8
MHBJMZLD ANY	6
DCVHM CQNNC CHCM'S DMC	4
BNOODQEHDKC	2

WHAT?	GUESSES
LZHK NQCDQ	12
GNROHSZK ENNC	10
RHFMZSTQD	8
BNBJDQDK	6
AQDZJEZRS	4
JDKKNFF	2

WHERE?	GUESSES
ZKLZ LZSDQ NE DQZRLTR...	12
...ZMC RHQ SGNLZR LNQD	10
GNLD NE Z CHBSHNMZQX	8
SGHQSX-EHUD BNKKDFDR	6
QGNCDR RBGNKZQRGHOR	4
NKCDRS HM AQHSZHM	2

WHEN?	GUESSES
SZWHMF HRRTD	12
DZRS HMCHZ BNLOZMX	10
ZMSH AQHSHRG	8
ONQS	6
AQDV TO SQNTAKD	4
LZC ZR Z GZSSDQ	2

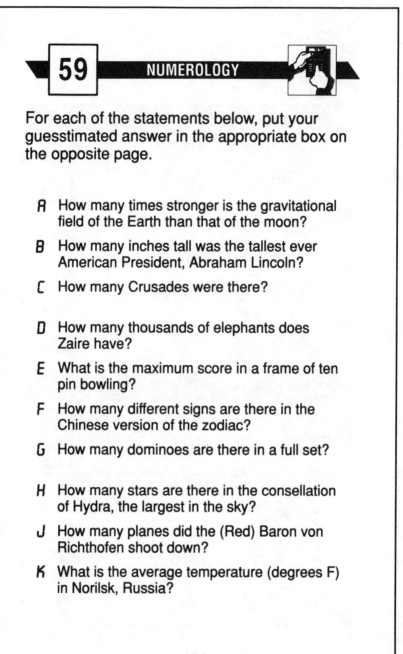
For each of the statements below, put your guesstimated answer in the appropriate box on the opposite page.

A How many times stronger is the gravitational field of the Earth than that of the moon?

B How many inches tall was the tallest ever American President, Abraham Lincoln?

C How many Crusades were there?

D How many thousands of elephants does Zaire have?

E What is the maximum score in a frame of ten pin bowling?

F How many different signs are there in the Chinese version of the zodiac?

G How many dominoes are there in a full set?

H How many stars are there in the consellation of Hydra, the largest in the sky?

J How many planes did the (Red) Baron von Richthofen shoot down?

K What is the average temperature (degrees F) in Norilsk, Russia?

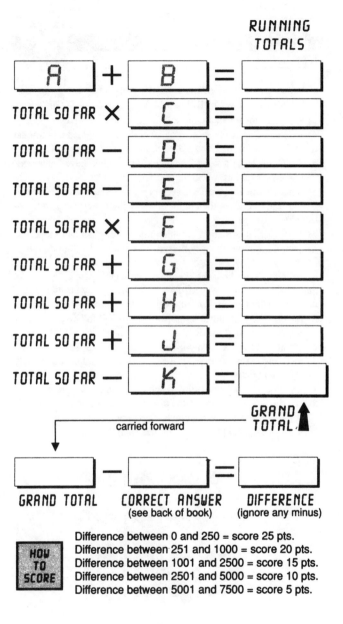

RUNNING TOTALS

A + B =

TOTAL SO FAR × C =

TOTAL SO FAR − D =

TOTAL SO FAR − E =

TOTAL SO FAR × F =

TOTAL SO FAR + G =

TOTAL SO FAR + H =

TOTAL SO FAR + J =

TOTAL SO FAR − K =

GRAND TOTAL

carried forward

GRAND TOTAL − CORRECT ANSWER = DIFFERENCE
(see back of book) (ignore any minus)

HOW TO SCORE

Difference between 0 and 250 = score 25 pts.
Difference between 251 and 1000 = score 20 pts.
Difference between 1001 and 2500 = score 15 pts.
Difference between 2501 and 5000 = score 10 pts.
Difference between 5001 and 7500 = score 5 pts.

133

1) Vampire is to wooden stake, as werewolf is to what?

2) Who is the subject of Billy Joel's hit single *Uptown Girl*?

3) Which country's name literally means Land of Silver?

4) Montego Bay is the subject of several pop songs, most famously the Number 3 hit for Bobby Bloom. In which country is it?

5) Which of the following Roman sections would have contained the most men – a cohort, a legion, or a century?

6) What chemical, which has etymological roots from the Greek word for green, gives the colour of many plants, grasses, and flowers?

7) A previous incarnation of which famous English landmark, the subject of a famous nursery rhyme, is now a tourist attraction in Lake Havasu City, Arizona?

8) Which modern household appliance uses this principle – a magnetron generates waves of a specific frequency (scattered by a fan) which excite any water molecules they come to?

9) Which (alleged) murderer did Jack Ruby kill in November 1963 saying he "did it for Jackie"?

10) Which of the six great wine-producing areas of France is further divided into many districts, of which the most famous are Medoc, St Emilion, and Graves?

11) In which field event is the women's world record greater than that of the men's because of the difference in equipment used?

12) In which sport does a game last up to 56 minutes, with up to 8 periods (or chukkas) lasting 7 minutes each?

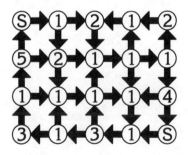

LAP 7

There are no time limits on this lap.

To score each puzzle, refer to the Scoring Summary on page 13. The maximum scores available are shown below.

	MAX.	SCORE
QUIZWORD	25	
REBUS CHALLENGE	30	
SAFE CRACKER	20	
LOGIC PROBLEM	20	
IN THE PIPELINE	20	
CRIME STORY	25	
WORD ISLAND	30	
MISSING LINKS	30	
NUMEROLOGY	25	
MAGNIFICENT MAZE	25	
TOTAL (max. 250)		

TARGET TO BEAT – 170 points

| 61 | QUIZWORD | ? |

ACROSS

1 Which river of Guyana is also the proper name of "brown" sugar? (8)

5 What is a bicycle designed to be ridden by two people called? (6)

10 Which key is usually at the top-right of the main block of keys on a standard computer keyboard? (9)

11 What type of chord is formed by playing three notes with gaps of three and four semitones between them? (5)

12 Which British writer, real name Eric Blair, wrote *Animal Farm* and *Nineteen Eighty-four*? (6)

13 In Greek mythology, who took 20 years to return home from the Trojan War, as recounted in a famous Homer epic? (8)

15 With what is a violin bow usually strung? (9)

17 In the card game pinochle, what is the lowest card value used? (4)

20 What symbol, at the beginning of a musical stave, indicates the particular range of notes used? (4)

21 What type of land, such as the Fens and the Everglades, has its water table near the surface of the ground? (9)

24 Which Indian prince, ranking above rajah, usually was in charge of his own state? (8)

25 Which period of the Christian Calendar of some four weeks prepares for Christmas? (6)

28 Which part of the body was used to indicate to a gladiator whether he should kill his defeated opponent? (5)

29 What model of motor-car, similar to a coupe, usually has two doors and a folding top? (9)

30 Which US vocalist had hits with *It Hurts So Much*, *Distant Drums* and *I Love You Because* in the 1960s? (6)

31 What Indian dish of rice, onions and spices has a European version made using rice, fish and boiled eggs? (8)

DOWN

1 One who owes money (6)

2 Which bird of the American tropics is the largest member of the parrot family? (5)

3 What word could possibly mean "fidgety" and "without stopping"? (8)

4 In the paper industry what name is usually given to a bundle of 480 sheets of paper? (4)

6 This word means "very nearly" (6)

7 Which flower takes its name from the French for "lion's tooth"? (9)

8 Wild Bill Hickok and Wyatt Earp were famous Western _____, famed for their shooting skills (8)

9 How a diver jumps into things? (4,5)

14 A travelling salesman who claims to have some amazing, too-good-to-be-true bargains (5-4)

16 A period of time, usually several hours, during which guests are particularly welcome to take hospitality (4-5)

18 What type of short sword, curved in shape and widest nearest the point, was used by the Turks? (8)

19 Which metallurgical process bonds layers of different metals together, to produce things such as rolled gold? (8)

22 If woofers provide the bass, what do tweeters provide? (6)

23 12 Across based his *Pygmalion* on the mythological character of the same name who fell in love with Galatea, a _____ (6)

26 Which Swiss mathematician was famous for solving the topological Konigsberg Bridge problem? (5)

27 Which wooden double-reed instrument has a range of over two octaves (up to a tone below middle C) using over fifteen keys? (4)

137

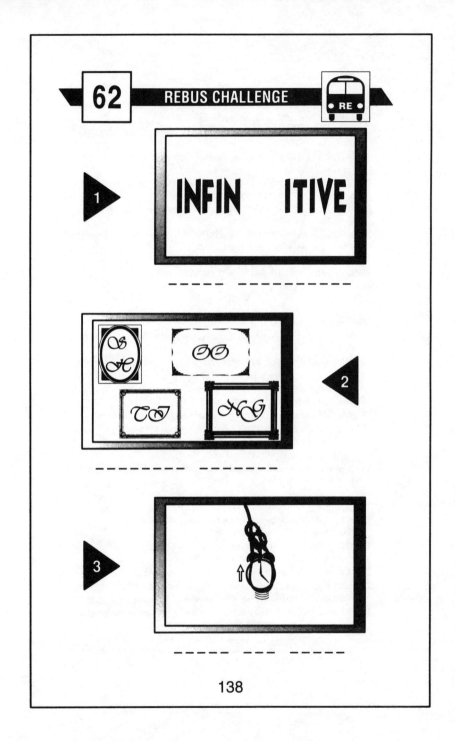

1 INFIN   ITIVE

_ _ _ _ _   _ _ _ _ _ _ _ _ _

2

_ _ _ _ _ _ _ _   _ _ _ _ _ _

3

_ _ _ _ _   _ _ _   _ _ _ _ _

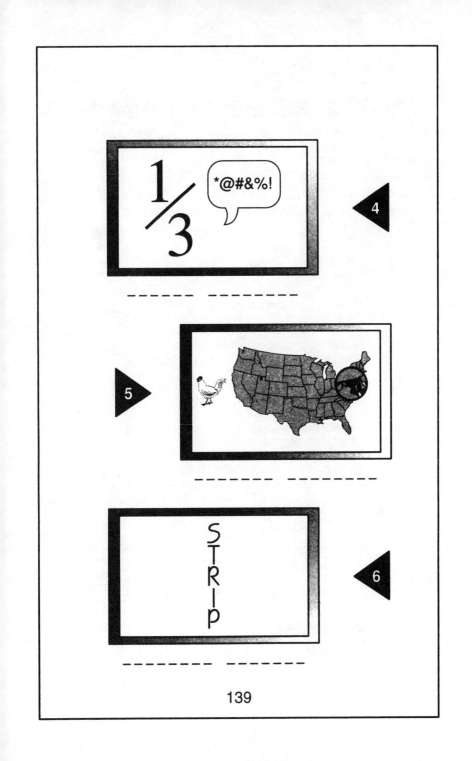

63 SAFE CRACKER

See page 263 for full instructions. Blacken out those segments on the right-hand page that are letter coded to the FALSE statements. This will form a correct mathematical sum.

True False

A   J. F. Kennedy Airport is in Dallas, Texas ☐ ☐

B   The Boston baseball team is called the White Sox ☐ ☐

C   Howard Carter discovered the sarcophagus of Tutankhamun in 1924 ☐ ☐

D   The year 2000 will be the Year of the Dragon in the Chinese calendar ☐ ☐

E   Nepal's national flag is made of two separate triangular pennants ☐ ☐

F   The liqueur Pastis is made using the blackcurrant plant ☐ ☐

G   Beethoven's second opera was *Fidelio* ☐ ☐

H   W. H. Auden wrote the famous poem *Tell Me the Truth About Love* ☐ ☐

J   The dog Laika was put into space in *Sputnik 11* in November 1957 ☐ ☐

K   A polygon can speak many languages ☐ ☐

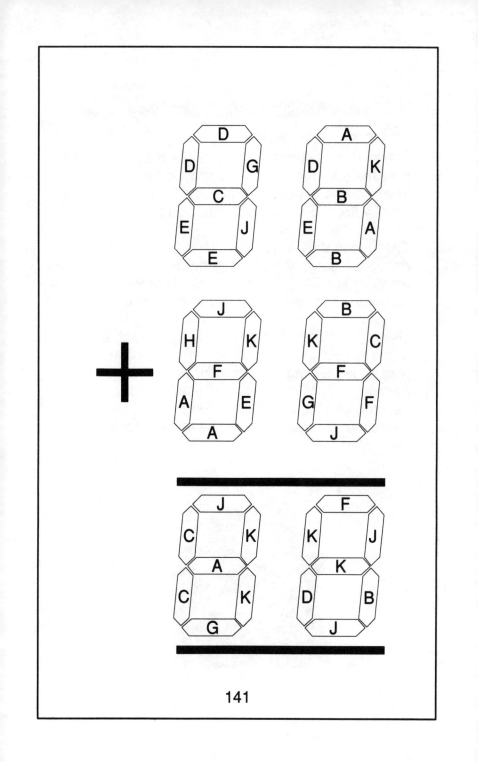

141

64   LOGIC PROBLEM

The infamous Judge Anderson has presided over the sentencing of five criminals today. Their names are Bruiser Bill, Cad Clive, Freaky Fred, Slippery Sam and Tough Tim.

The crimes they were convicted of are deception, forgery, poaching, rustling and treason. The five sentences meted out were, in no particular order, 3, 6, 7, 10 and 15 years.

Using the information given, can you match a name to each picture and say what his crime was and how long his sentence was? If a criminal says "Tim was the rustler" you may assume that the person speaking is not Tim the rustler (or else he would have said "I am the rustler").

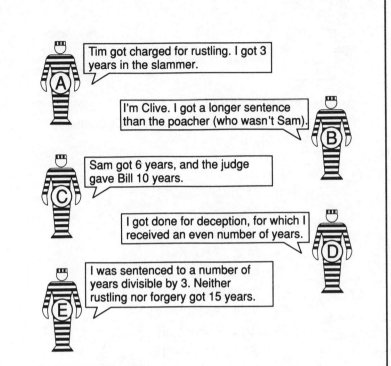

Tim got charged for rustling. I got 3 years in the slammer.

I'm Clive. I got a longer sentence than the poacher (who wasn't Sam).

Sam got 6 years, and the judge gave Bill 10 years.

I got done for deception, for which I received an even number of years.

I was sentenced to a number of years divisible by 3. Neither rustling nor forgery got 15 years.

STARTING HINTS

a. Use the information given by B, D and E to find which crime carried the longest sentence.

b. Use A, C and E's clues to work out Bill's sentence. Which picture is he?

Diagram	Name	Crime	Sentence
Picture A			
Picture B			
Picture C			
Picture D			
Picutre E			

Your task is to connect the famous sportspeople with their individual specialist sport on the right.

1 Merlene Ottey
2 Michael Stich
3 Jose Maria Olazabal
4 Mario Andretti
5 Ingrid Kristiansen
6 Sally Gunnell
7 Viktor Petrenko
8 Chris Boardman
9 Riccardo Patrese
10 Katarina Witt
11 Ben Crenshaw
12 Emerson Fittipaldi
13 Carl Lewis
14 Mats Wilander
15 Matt Biondi
16 Mark Spitz
17 Greg LeMond
18 Ben Johnson
19 Leroy Burrell
20 Hannah Mandlikova

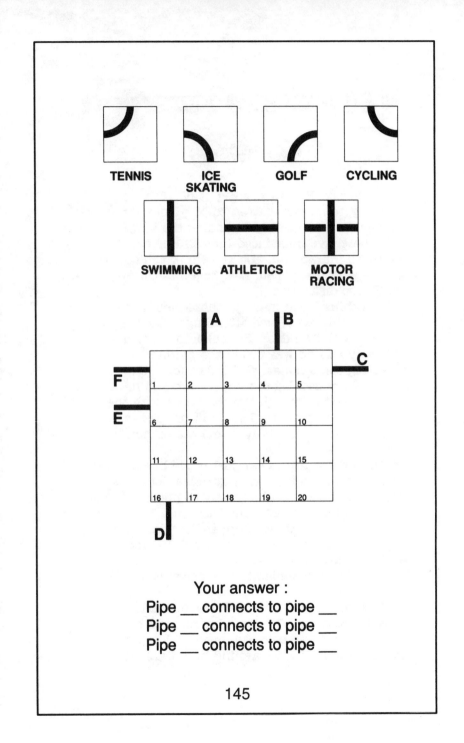

Your answer :
Pipe __ connects to pipe __
Pipe __ connects to pipe __
Pipe __ connects to pipe __

145

The Swarm

Hartland and Barlow arrived at 63, The Parkway, to meet a distressed Mrs Edge. An ambulance was already attending the scene.

The Detective introduced himself and the officer to the woman. "Do you think you could tell me what happened, Mrs Edge? Of course, if you're too distressed..."

"No, I think I can manage, thank you. Frank, that's my husband, was attending to his bees just as he always does. He looks after them regularly and he was out in the garden collecting some honey. Well today, for some reason, they decided to turn on him and he came bursting through the back door with the whole swarm in chase. I couldn't understand why after ten years they would attack him like that."

"Well, I think things can just occur like that. Nature will have it's own way." The Detective tried to find a more kindly way of putting it, but there was no point avoiding the truth. Sometimes these things happen. Hartland went to talk to the ambulance personnel, leaving Barlow to talk to the woman.

"It's such unfortunate timing as well," the woman added.

"What do mean, Mrs Edge?" asked Barlow.

"Well it was his 50th birthday just yesterday. He was looking so cheerful, opening his presents and having the family around him. Daniel and

146

Mary, our children, had just come back from six months in Malaga. He was so pleased to see them and they bought some lovely duty-free presents for Frank. We had a lovely tea and then later that day..."

"Erm, I'm sorry to interrupt you, Mrs Edge, but... Oh, here comes the Detective now."

Hartland returned to say his goodbyes. "The ambulance staff say your husband should be fine, Mrs Edge. But I must say this – spending five minutes in that ambulance has given me an idea that the action of his bees is more understandable than it first seemed!"

Can you deduce what Frank Edge did wrong to make the bees attack him?

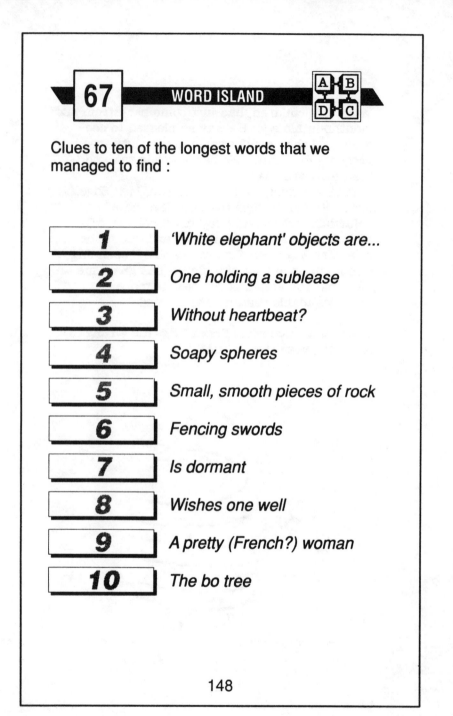

Clues to ten of the longest words that we managed to find :

1	'White elephant' objects are...
2	One holding a sublease
3	Without heartbeat?
4	Soapy spheres
5	Small, smooth pieces of rock
6	Fencing swords
7	Is dormant
8	Wishes one well
9	A pretty (French?) woman
10	The bo tree

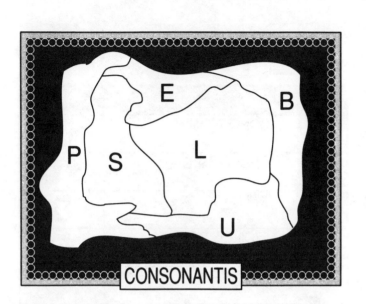

CONSONANTIS

Other words of five letters or more (find up to another 20) :

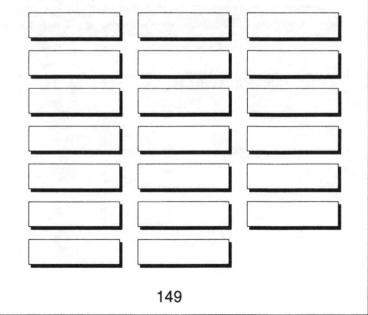

WHO?	GUESSES
LHQQNQ VQHSHMF	12
GDKHBNOSDQ	10
KZRS RTOODQ	8
ZQBGHSDBS	6
HSZKHZM	4
LNMZ KHRZ	2

WHAT?	GUESSES
LZFMDSHB	12
RHWSDDM CHFHSR	10
OHM	8
GNKNFQZL	6
DWOHQX CZSD	4
CHMDQ'R BKTA EHQRS	2

WHERE?	GUESSES
BNQCHKKDQZ	**12**
ZBNMBZFTZ	**10**
KZJD SHSHBZBZ	**8**
UNKBZMHB	**6**
BZOD GNQM	**4**
RNTSG ZLDQHBZ	**2**

WHEN?	GUESSES
QDRSZQS DHFGSDDM-MHMDSX-RHW	**12**
MNS 'RHWSDDM, 'ENQSX, 'ENQSX-ENTQ	**10**
ZTRSQZKHZ ZS RSZQS NE BDMSTQX	**8**
RSZQSR VHSG Z SNQBG	**6**
VHMSDQ UDQRHNM SNN	**4**
EHUD QHMFR	**2**

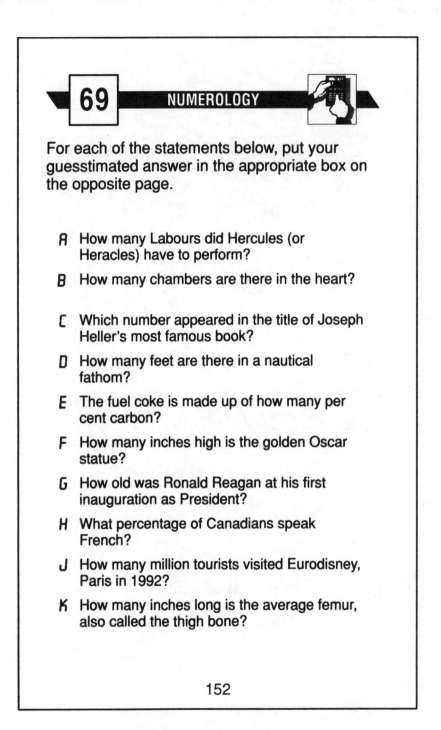

For each of the statements below, put your guesstimated answer in the appropriate box on the opposite page.

A How many Labours did Hercules (or Heracles) have to perform?

B How many chambers are there in the heart?

C Which number appeared in the title of Joseph Heller's most famous book?

D How many feet are there in a nautical fathom?

E The fuel coke is made up of how many per cent carbon?

F How many inches high is the golden Oscar statue?

G How old was Ronald Reagan at his first inauguration as President?

H What percentage of Canadians speak French?

J How many million tourists visited Eurodisney, Paris in 1992?

K How many inches long is the average femur, also called the thigh bone?

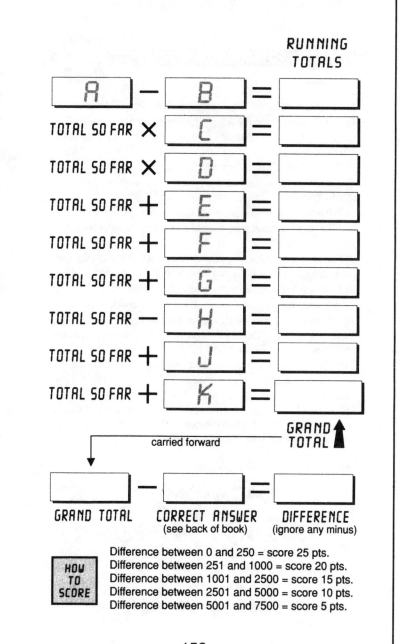

RUNNING TOTALS

A − B =

TOTAL SO FAR × C =

TOTAL SO FAR × D =

TOTAL SO FAR + E =

TOTAL SO FAR + F =

TOTAL SO FAR + G =

TOTAL SO FAR − H =

TOTAL SO FAR + J =

TOTAL SO FAR + K =

GRAND TOTAL

carried forward

GRAND TOTAL − CORRECT ANSWER = DIFFERENCE
(see back of book)   (ignore any minus)

HOW TO SCORE
Difference between 0 and 250 = score 25 pts.
Difference between 251 and 1000 = score 20 pts.
Difference between 1001 and 2500 = score 15 pts.
Difference between 2501 and 5000 = score 10 pts.
Difference between 5001 and 7500 = score 5 pts.

1) In what subject did *Alice* author Lewis Carroll lecture?

2) Which member of the *Monty Python* team had the job of delivering their catchphrase "And now for something completely different..."?

3) Why is Nepal's flag different to every other nation's?

4) Manchester, Dorchester, and Winchester were so suffixed due to which evident feature in these cities?

5) What is the British equivalent of America's Delta Force?

6) What type of connoisseur would know his muscat from his sauvignon blanc?

7) For recycling purposes, how does one tell that a drinks can is made from aluminium, rather than from less valuable steel?

8) In which layer of the atmosphere do we live?

9) What are the Avesta, Granth, Katabi Ikan and Koran?

10) What was first made by a physician from tree bark in the Venezuelan city of Ciudad Bolivar in 1824, and is an additive now used in cocktails and pink gin?

11) In basketball, how many points are scored for a basket thrown from a distance greater than 23 feet and 9 inches from the target?

12) Which 1851 trophy, originally the *Hundred Guinea Cup*, has only ever been won by two countries, the second of which only won in 1983 with John Bertram's boat *Australia II*?

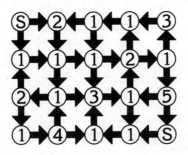

LAP 8

There are no time limits on this lap.

To score each puzzle, refer to the Scoring Summary on page 13. The maximum scores available are shown below.

	MAX.	SCORE
QUIZWORD	25	
REBUS CHALLENGE	30	
SAFE CRACKER	20	
LOGIC PROBLEM	20	
IN THE PIPELINE	20	
CRIME STORY	25	
WORD ISLAND	30	
MISSING LINKS	30	
NUMEROLOGY	25	
MAGNIFICENT MAZE	25	
TOTAL (max. 250)		

TARGET TO BEAT – 185 points

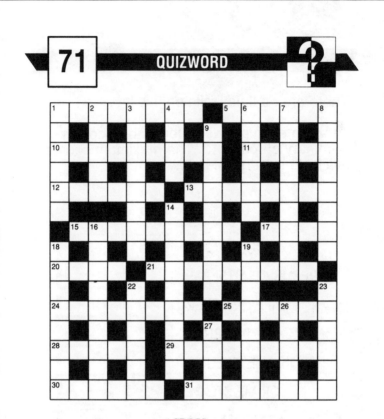

ACROSS

1 Which religious post for a cleric takes its name from *cappella*, the Latin for "short cloak"? (8)

5 What document is issued in some countries to all adults to provide proof of identity for a variety of purposes? (1,1,4)

10 Of what do humans have 20 before their adult 32 come through? (4,5)

11 What is the last letter of the Greek alphabet? (5)

12 What, in physics, is defined as "the capacity of matter to perform work"? (6)

13 In history, rib bones of animals were tied to the feet. Nowadays, we use a steel blade as an _____ _____ (3,5)

15 In what form is low-density polyethylene (or LDPE) normally sold in your local supermarket? (9)

17 In mathematics, a Mobius band is a topological shape with one side and one _____ (4)

156

20 What mathematical solid has twelve edges of equal length and six congruent faces? (4)

21 Which symbol, a five-pointed star, is one of the most significant used in witchcraft? (9)

24 What word, now the name of a car, was originally used to describe a warship smaller than a frigate with one tier of guns? (8)

25 What lizard, primarily of the Americas, lends its name to a dinosaur whose distinctive jaws have similar teeth? (6)

28 What is the French word for "school"? (5)

29 In fluid mechanics, what property measures how resistant a fluid is to flowing? (9)

30 What is the capital of Oman? (6)

31 What event occurs when the year is divisible by 4 or 400 but not by 100? (4,4)

DOWN

1 What did Athena, the Greek mythological goddess, change the rope that Arachne had attempted to hang herself with into? (6)

2 To walk at a leisurely pace (5)

3 What legal term describes one who carries out a law suit? (8)

4 What is the common name given to several species of wild Asian goat of the genus *Capra*? (4)

6 What is the general term for the medical condition of having excess fluid in the body tissue or organs? (6)

7 What is Queen Elizabeth II of England's second name? (9)

8 In mathematics, what is the maximum length for a chord of a given circle called? (8)

9 Which popular commodity was brought to Europe by Cortez, who had learnt of it from the Aztecs? (9)

14 Which word means "in operation" or "producing the effect required"? (9)

16 Requiring a lot of effort (9)

18 What frozen food is made from cream, milk, sugar and flavourings? (3,5)

19 The Australian aborigines forbid anyone to marry someone from a different _____ _____ (3,5)

22 What is the unit of currency of Spain? (6)

23 For which occupation did F. W. De Klerk, Juan Melendez, Nelson Mandela and Hillary Clinton train? (6)

26 In the books by A. A. Milne, what was the name of Christopher Robin's female companion? (5)

27 What geographical word connects Man, Royale, Wight, Presque, Belle, Ely and Pines? (4)

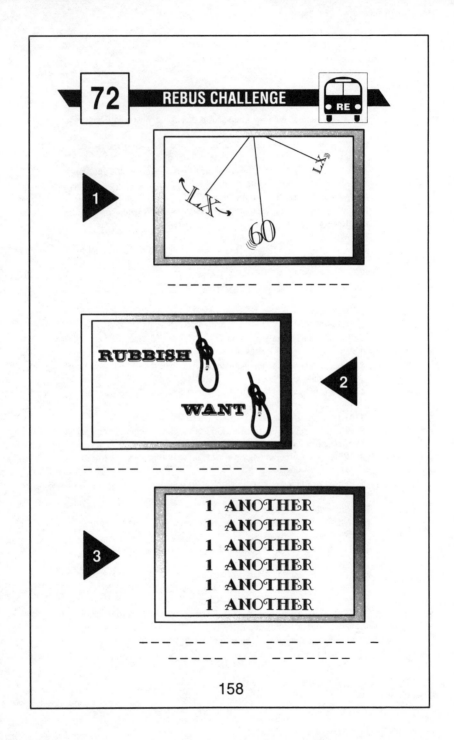

1

_ _ _ _ _ _ _ _   _ _ _ _ _ _ _

2

_ _ _ _ _   _ _ _   _ _ _ _   _ _ _

3

_ _ _   _ _   _ _ _   _ _ _   _ _ _ _   _
_ _ _ _ _   _ _   _ _ _ _ _ _ _

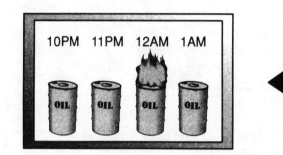

▶ 4

- - - - - - - - - - - - - - - - - - -

◀ 5 VATNIMBI

- - - - - - - - - - - - - - -

▶ 6

- - - - - - - - - - - - - - -

159

 **SAFE CRACKER**

Blacken out those segments on the right-hand page that are letter coded to the FALSE statements. This will form a correct mathematical sum.

True / False

A   Epsilon is the third letter of the Greek alphabet ☐ ☐

B   At the Battle of Rourke's Drift in 1879, 4000 British repelled 140 Zulus ☐ ☐

C   Romanian dictator Ceaucescu was assassinated on Christmas Day, 1982 ☐ ☐

D   A marguerita is made from tequila, cointreau and lemon juice ☐ ☐

E   The term 'Glasnost' means 'truth' in Russian ☐ ☐

F   Alliteration is the formation of a word that imitates the sound it represents ☐ ☐

G   Al Pacino won a '93 Academy Award for his role in *Scent of a Woman* ☐ ☐

H   No British Prime Minister has ever been assassinated ☐ ☐

J   The Walker and Curtis Cups are famous golfing trophies ☐ ☐

K   In music, *largo* means 'increase the tempo' ☐ ☐

160

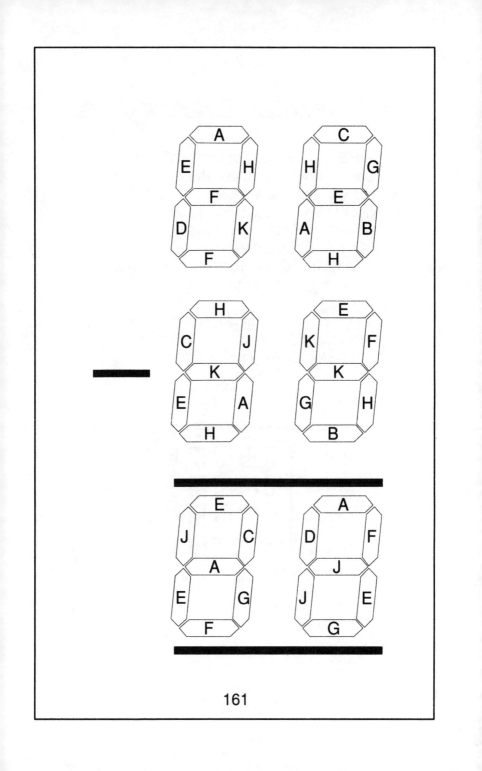

Five employees of the Labyrinth Widget Company are waiting to use the lift. **They are currently in the department in which they work**, and they wish to travel to another level in the building. Each level of the five storey building contains a different department – either Accounts, Data Processing, Marketing, Personnel or Purchasing.

Can you match each employee with their department and tell us on which level they started and where they will end up?

CLUES

1. Jonathan (who works in Data Processing) went up three levels.

2. The Purchasing department is situated on Level 2 of the building.

3. The journey that started on Level 3 was destined to go downwards.

4. Annabel (who is not from Marketing) went up one level during her journey.

5. The man from Accounts went down two levels.

6. One journey went from Level 2 to Level 1.

7. Neither Melanie nor Norman works on Level 3.

STARTING HINTS

a. Use clues 1 and 2 immediately to deduce Jonathan's level.

b. Now have a good look at the other clues, number 6 especially – can you deduce the start and end positions of all the journeys?

Worker	Dept.	From floor	To floor
Annabel			
Jonathan			
Melanie			
Norman			
Steve			

75   IN THE PIPELINE

Your task is to match the famous painters on the right with their equally famous paintings, below.

1   *The Crucifixion*
2   *Mona Lisa*
3   *Bathers*
4   *The Persistence of Memory*
5   *The Sunflowers*
6   *Ceiling of the Sistine Chapel*
7   *The Last Supper*
8   *Madonna of the Kings*
9   *Leda and the Swan*
10 *Starry Night*
11 *Le Jardinier*
12 *The Last Judgement*
13 *Wyoming*
14 *Water Lilies*
15 *Christ of St. John on the Cross*
16 *The Conversion of St. Paul*
17 *Self Portrait with Bandaged Ear*
18 *Night Cafe*
19 *Autumn Rhythm*
20 *Impression: Sunrise*

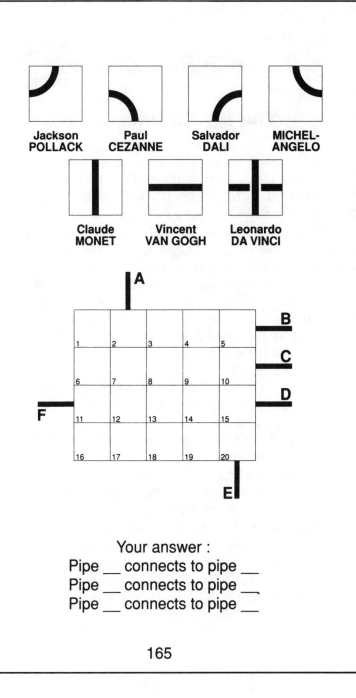

Jackson
POLLACK

Paul
CEZANNE

Salvador
DALI

MICHEL-
ANGELO

Claude
MONET

Vincent
VAN GOGH

Leonardo
DA VINCI

Your answer :
Pipe __ connects to pipe __
Pipe __ connects to pipe __
Pipe __ connects to pipe __

165

The Mysterious Coins

On the way back from their last case, Barlow struck up conversation with Hartland. "You know, Detective, there was a very strange incident I once came across when Wendy and me were on holiday. I was waiting in the car while Wendy had gone into a store for a newspaper when I noticed this man, he looked to be from the Arabian region, who was looking intently at some coins. He put the coins into this cola machine but for some reason, no matter what he tried, he couldn't get a drink out of the machine."

"Yeah, those things are always breaking down on me," commented Hartland.

"No, that was the funny thing. The chap took so long that occasionally he would have to let others use the machine and they got it to work perfectly. He started putting the coins into the machine again, and it seemed no matter what combination of coins he tried he couldn't get his can.

"So, eventually I got out of the car and went over to help him. The man held out his hand, so I took the right change from his palm and put the coins in the machine. I heard a click, I motioned to the man to make his selection, the man pressed the relevant button and out popped a can.

"Then the man said 'Thank you very much, effendi. I do not have trouble like this in other countries I go to.' We got chatting for a while. Apparently he was quite well travelled. He'd been to many different Western countries over a period of around twenty years. Yet he wasn't used to having such difficulty with such a simple task. A nice chap."

"Now I think I know where you went for your holidays," smiled Hartland.

Can you work out where Barlow was on holiday?

167

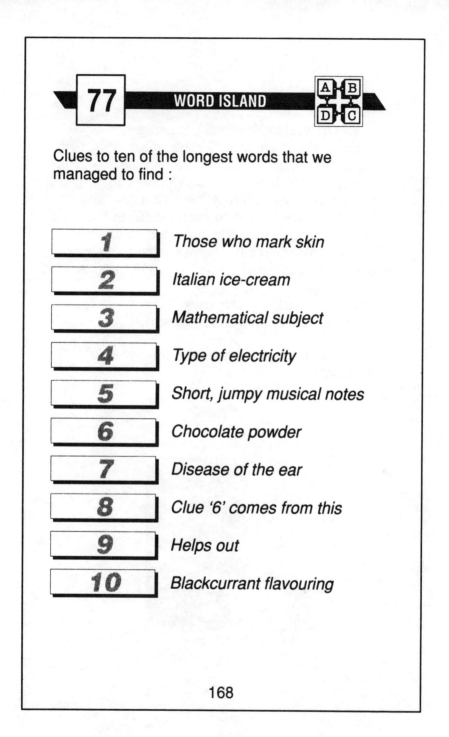

Clues to ten of the longest words that we managed to find :

1	*Those who mark skin*
2	*Italian ice-cream*
3	*Mathematical subject*
4	*Type of electricity*
5	*Short, jumpy musical notes*
6	*Chocolate powder*
7	*Disease of the ear*
8	*Clue '6' comes from this*
9	*Helps out*
10	*Blackcurrant flavouring*

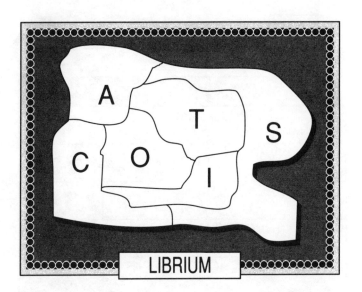

LIBRIUM

Other words of five letters or more (find up to another 20) :

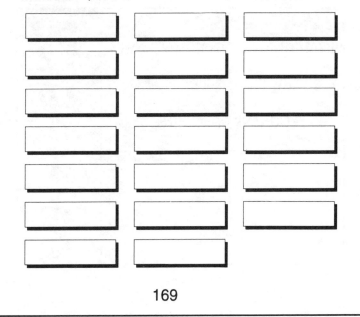

MISSING LINKS

WHO?	GUESSES
ZMSH–ONRSLDM	12
NVMDC AX ZQATBJKD	10
KZRZFMD	8
LNMCZXR ZQD AZC	6
NUDQVDHFGS ZMC OQNTC NE HS	4
BZQSNNM BZS	2

WHAT?	GUESSES
MHMDSX-EHUD ODQBDMS BZQANM CHNWHCD	12
RHW-DHFGS-RDUDM CZXR	10
OGNANR ZMC CDHLNR	8
ENTQ NE MHMD	6
BQZSDQR	4
QDC	2

WHERE?	GUESSES
GTCRNM & DZRS	12
RSZSDM HRKZMC	10
NMBD BZOHSZK	8
RSZSD SNN	6
DLOHQD RSZSD ATHKCHMF	4
AHF ZOOKD	2

WHEN?	GUESSES
AQZYHK W SGQDD	12
QHLDS	10
KZRS VZR HM TRZ	8
EHEZ	6
ENTQ XDZQR	4
ENNSAZKK	2

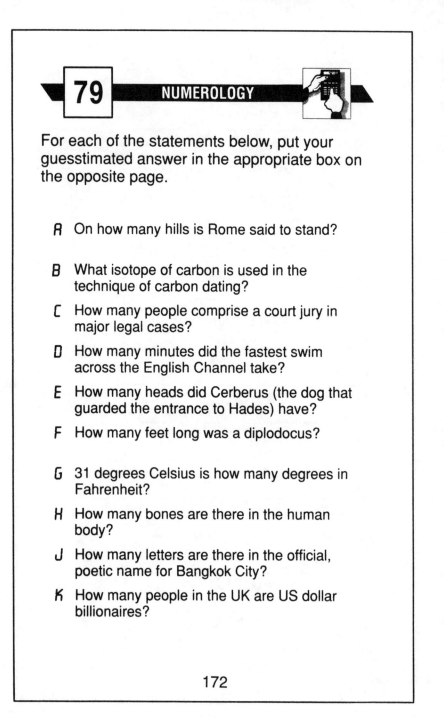

For each of the statements below, put your guesstimated answer in the appropriate box on the opposite page.

A On how many hills is Rome said to stand?

B What isotope of carbon is used in the technique of carbon dating?

C How many people comprise a court jury in major legal cases?

D How many minutes did the fastest swim across the English Channel take?

E How many heads did Cerberus (the dog that guarded the entrance to Hades) have?

F How many feet long was a diplodocus?

G 31 degrees Celsius is how many degrees in Fahrenheit?

H How many bones are there in the human body?

J How many letters are there in the official, poetic name for Bangkok City?

K How many people in the UK are US dollar billionaires?

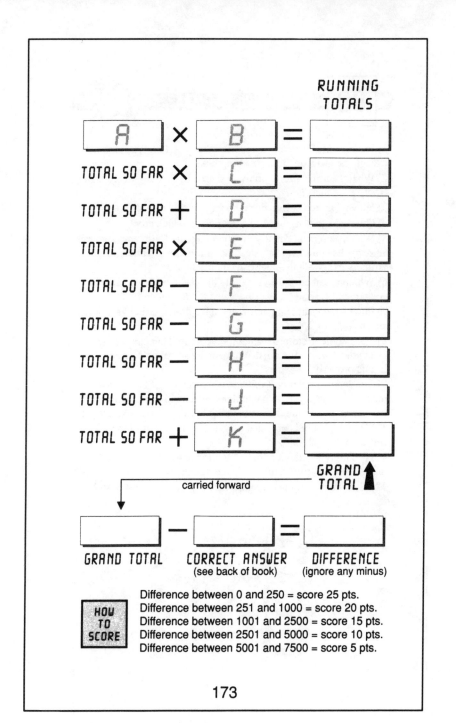

RUNNING TOTALS

$A \times B =$ ▢

TOTAL SO FAR $\times C =$ ▢

TOTAL SO FAR $+ D =$ ▢

TOTAL SO FAR $\times E =$ ▢

TOTAL SO FAR $- F =$ ▢

TOTAL SO FAR $- G =$ ▢

TOTAL SO FAR $- H =$ ▢

TOTAL SO FAR $- J =$ ▢

TOTAL SO FAR $+ K =$ ▢

GRAND TOTAL ⬆

carried forward

▢ $-$ ▢ $=$ ▢

GRAND TOTAL — CORRECT ANSWER (see back of book) — DIFFERENCE (ignore any minus)

HOW TO SCORE

Difference between 0 and 250 = score 25 pts.
Difference between 251 and 1000 = score 20 pts.
Difference between 1001 and 2500 = score 15 pts.
Difference between 2501 and 5000 = score 10 pts.
Difference between 5001 and 7500 = score 5 pts.

1) Which J.M. Barrie book provides the quotation "All children except one grow up" in its opening line?

2) What theatrical profession was shared by Hamlet's Yorick and Henry I's Rahere?

3) How many red stripes does the flag known as *Old Glory* have?

4) Queens is the largest of five districts in which city?

5) Which European country once counted the following countries amongst its colonies – Jamaica, the Philippines, Trinidad, and virtually every South American country?

6) Which member of the cat family has the alternative name of cougar, and is sometimes also termed the mountain lion?

7) In which constituent part of an engine does the fuel vapour and air mix?

8) The magnetic storms seen in the Southern Hemisphere are called the *Aurora Australis*. What are the so-called Northern Lights properly known as?

9) The *Index Librorum Prohibitorum* was a list of books that members of a certain faith could not own, read or sell under penalty of excommunication (a threat lifted in 1966). Which faith?

10) Which pepper is obtained by grinding the seeds of the capsicum berry?

11) Fromology is the term given to the hobby of collecting the labels from what foodstuff, its name derived from a French word?

12) How many umpires are used in today's cricket Test Matches?

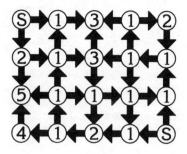

LAP 9

There are no time limits on this lap.

To score each puzzle, refer to the Scoring Summary on page 13. The maximum scores available are shown below.

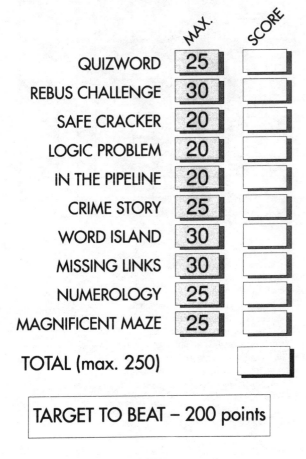

	MAX.	SCORE
QUIZWORD	25	
REBUS CHALLENGE	30	
SAFE CRACKER	20	
LOGIC PROBLEM	20	
IN THE PIPELINE	20	
CRIME STORY	25	
WORD ISLAND	30	
MISSING LINKS	30	
NUMEROLOGY	25	
MAGNIFICENT MAZE	25	
TOTAL (max. 250)		

TARGET TO BEAT – 200 points

ACROSS

9 In the brewing process, in which building are the hops or malt dried? (4-5)

10 What is the Spanish word for "friend"? (5)

11 The largest one to create a disaster so far is Chernobyl (7)

12 In gambling, what type of bet pays out upon the selected racer finishing in the top two places? (4,3)

13 What drink is made from hot beer or spirits mixed with whole egg? (6)

14 Which alcohol is a colourless, viscous liquid, obtained as a by-product of soap making, and is used in the making of plastics? (8)

16 A ritual or ceremony performed to show that a person has reached one of the key stages of life (4)

17 _____ City, in southern Kansas, was famous for having Wyatt Earp as a chief deputy marshal (5)

18 In which direction are you going if your bearing is 090? (4)

22 Which American state is south of South Dakota, west of Iowa, north of Kansas, and east of Wyoming? (8)

24 The _____ family of birds has subfamilies which include lovebirds, macaws, lories and parakeets? (6)

27 In the United States, the land upon which a foreign _____ stands actually belongs to that country (7)

28 Which city, in the Seine-Maritime Department and on the English Channel, is a main French seaport? (2,5)

29 Which English phrase for a German submarine comes from the word *Unterseeboot*? (1-4)

30 Artificial, as in the title of Philip Massinger's 1639 play *The _____ Combat* (9)

DOWN

1 What is the name of the Stock Exchange of France? (6)

2 What is the French word for "snail"? (8)

3 Which word, now used in a wider context, originally defined city regions within which all Jews must reside? (7)

4 Which golden brown powder is made from about 20 spices including ginger, fenugreek, turmeric and cumin? (5)

5 What is the study of one's ancestors, as depicted in family trees, called? (9)

6 One of Irish dramatist Sean O'Casey's most famous plays is *Juno and the _____* (7)

7 One who watches a television programme (6)

8 What word is used to describe a person who can speak many languages? (8)

15 What is another name for what is normally termed the peanut (or ground nut)? (6-3)

16 The person who came second (6-2)

19 What is the (somewhat unusual) name for the F-111 jet fighter, capable of Mach 2? (8)

20 Used for hunting and tracking small animals, which hounds are known for their superb sense of smell? (7)

21 What type of knife, with a sharp heavy blade, is often used in the jungle? (7)

23 Which type of large monkey lives in open land in Africa and Arabia? (6)

25 Which range of the musical scale does the soprano use? (6)

26 A long, thick piece of timber (5)

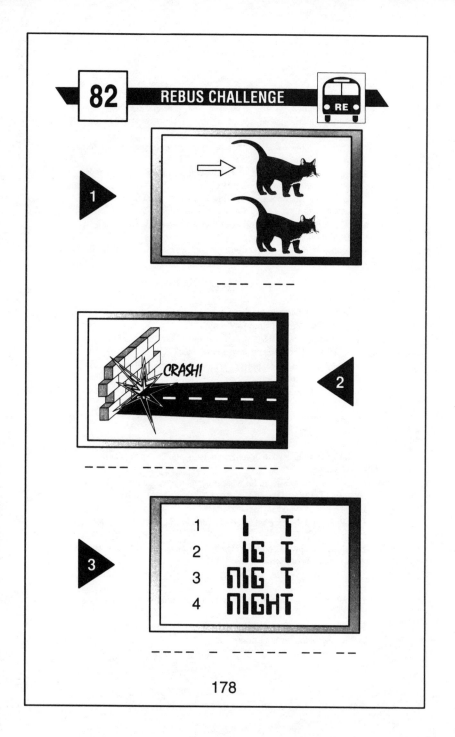

179

Blacken out those segments on the right-hand page that are letter coded to the FALSE statements. This will form a correct mathematical sum.

True | False

A   Franklin D. Roosevelt died of natural causes whilst in office as President   ☐ ☐

B   According to the Beaufort Scale, winds over 53 kph are hurricanes   ☐ ☐

C   Davy Crockett was killed at the Battle of the Alamo   ☐ ☐

D   The collective noun for owls is a 'murder'   ☐ ☐

E   The Latin name for the banana is *Ananas comosus*   ☐ ☐

F   Hyundai cars are made in Korea   ☐ ☐

G   Gauguin painted *Bathers* and *Le Jardinier*   ☐ ☐

H   The Radio Call Sign for the letter Y is Yellow   ☐ ☐

J   Symphony No. 8 in B Minor by Schubert is the Unfinished Symphony   ☐ ☐

K   Pyrographs on electric trains pick up current from an overhead power line   ☐ ☐

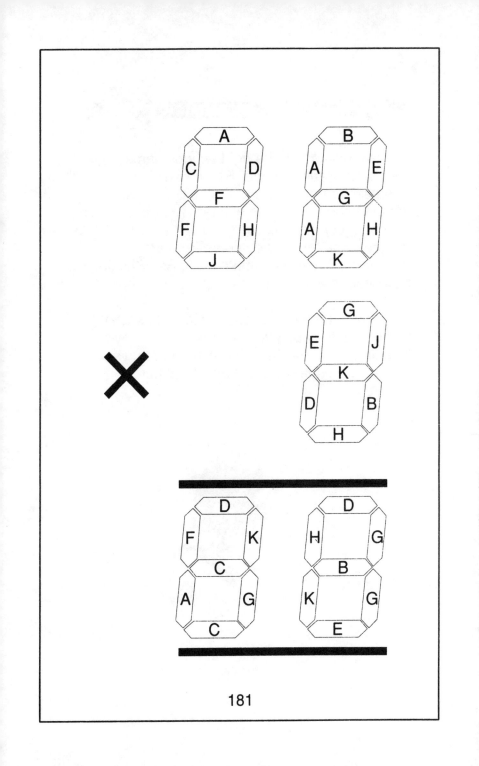

181

The five women on the right (whose names are Olivia, Paula, Rhona, Sandra and Theresa) are members of the Leicestershire Youth Orchestra. These women play the bassoon, cor anglais, flute, saxophone or trumpet. The towns they come from are Broughton Astley, Countesthorpe, Earl Shilton, Narborough and Wigston (in some order).

Can you put a name to each face, tell us what instrument they play and in which town they live? If a woman talks in the third person, you can assume she is not talking about herself.

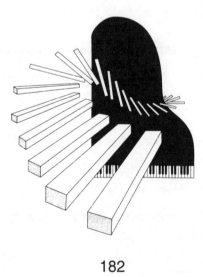

Olivia, who is not the cor anglais player, lives in Wigston.

I live in Narborough. I'm not the cor anglais player.

I don't live in Wigston. I play the trumpet. I'm not the Theresa who lives in Earl Shilton.

The saxophonist (who is not Theresa) lives in Broughton Astley.

Paula plays the flute. I'm Sandra, but I don't play cor anglais.

STARTING HINTS

a. You'll need the clues from A, B, C and E to tell you which picture is the Wigston woman.

b. Now see if you can find which pictures are the saxophonist and the cor anglais player.

Picture	Name	Home Town	Instrument
Picture A			
Picture B			
Picture C			
Picture D			
Picture E			

Your task is to connect the anatomical terms below with the area of the body in which they can be found.

1 Pituitary Gland
2 Malleus
3 Retina
4 Femur
5 Cerebrum
6 Fibula
7 Humerus
8 Tibia
9 Radius
10 Metatarsal
11 Dentine
12 Ulna
13 Phalange
14 Bicuspid
15 Hypothalamus
16 Aqueous Humour
17 Talus
18 Conjunctiva
19 Melanin
20 Cuboid

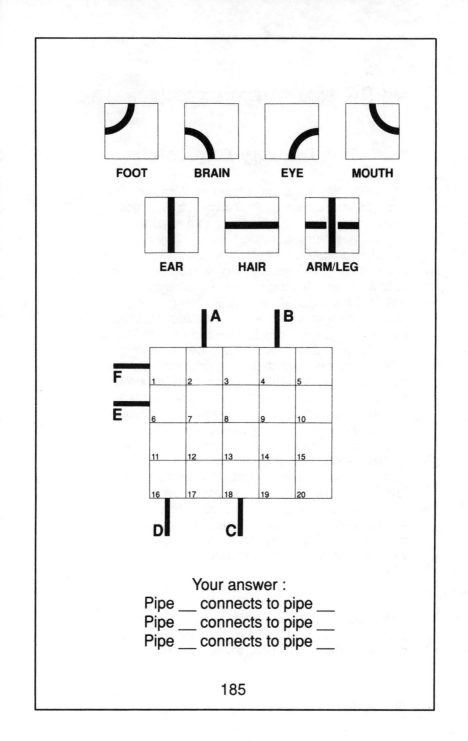

FOOT   BRAIN   EYE   MOUTH

EAR   HAIR   ARM/LEG

Your answer :
Pipe __ connects to pipe __
Pipe __ connects to pipe __
Pipe __ connects to pipe __

185

The Dummy Explosion

The radio crackled into action once more. "It's your lucky day again, Detective. That airport manager would like you to go and visit him again. Something about a woman they are holding in custody who's gone berserk."

"OK, Penny, I'm on my way there now." The Detective was getting to know the airport very well by this time. He muttered something to Barlow, who was in the car with him. "I might as well get the swines to hire me as a full time security guard. I'm practically one already!"

The policemen arrived at the airport. The now familiar airport manager came running up to them but before he could even draw breath to say anything Hartland dismissed him. "Yeah, yeah, we know. Custody Room 3."

As they entered the room, they found a doctor in attendance. The doctor turned to the policemen. "I'm sorry, gents, but she's a goner." The doctor let go of the woman's now lifeless wrist. Barlow winced. "Sir, I don't really have a good stomach for dead people. I think I'll just question the folks outside if that's all right." Hartland nodded and Barlow stepped out of the room.

Hartland began questioning the doctor. "What happened here then, Doctor...?"

"My name's Andrew Hall. Pleased to meet you," said the doctor. "Yes, apparently she came off the flight from Cuba, through customs and as

she was about to leave the airport the plastic
bag she was carrying exploded. Of course, this
caused her death almost immediately."

"Well, it's quite common nowadays, isn't it?
We'll have to see if we can persuade the airport
manager to step up security. I'll be back in a
moment. I just want to see what my colleague is
doing."

"Rightio," said Hall.

Barlow had just finished talking to the airport
manager. "Well, seems like a standard terrorist
bombing case to me," said Hartland.

Barlow put on one of his quizzical looks. "What
do you mean, sir? It's nothing of the sort. I
think you've got the wrong end of the stick..."

**Can you work out what the misunderstanding is
and thus explain what happened to cause the
woman's death?**

187

Clues to ten of the longest words that we managed to find :

1	*Mineral deposit on the teeth*
2	*Perform repeated calculations*
3	*To say again*
4	*Average over two matches*
5	*One who rues*
6	*That which is left behind*
7	*African amulet*
8	*To perform titration*
9	*Run away*
10	*Boat-racing meeting*

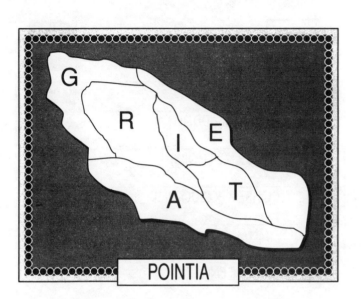

POINTIA

Other words of five letters or more (find up to another 20) :

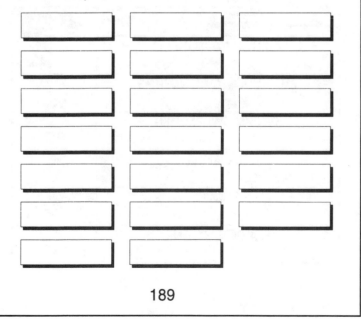

189

WHO?	GUESSES
Z FDQLZM ADDQLTF	12
RVHRR (ZS EHQRS)	10
ZLDQHBZM (KZSDQ NM)	8
MNADK OQHYD	6
EZLNTR ENQLTKZ	4
QDKZSHUHSX	2

WHAT?	GUESSES
ZTFTRSD AZQSGNKCH	12
ZMMHUDQRZQX OQDRDMS	10
SVN HM DWHRSDMBD	8
GZQANTQ	6
SNQBG	4
EQDDCNL RXLANK	2

WHERE?	GUESSES
CDOZQSLDMSR	12
LZRRHE BDMSQZK	10
NVMR FTZCDKNTOD & LZQSHMHPTD	8
QGNMD UZKKDX VHMD	6
BGZSDZTW NM SGD KNHQD	4
BGZMMDK STMMDK KHMJ	2

WHEN?	GUESSES
DCVZQC RLHSG	12
BZQOZSGHZ	10
LZHCDM	8
ZOQHK EHESDDM MHMDSDDM-SVDKUD	6
AZMC OKZXDC NM	4
HBDADQF	2

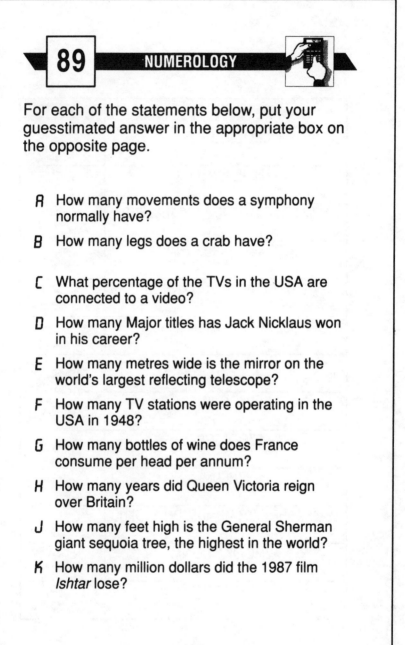
For each of the statements below, put your guesstimated answer in the appropriate box on the opposite page.

A How many movements does a symphony normally have?

B How many legs does a crab have?

C What percentage of the TVs in the USA are connected to a video?

D How many Major titles has Jack Nicklaus won in his career?

E How many metres wide is the mirror on the world's largest reflecting telescope?

F How many TV stations were operating in the USA in 1948?

G How many bottles of wine does France consume per head per annum?

H How many years did Queen Victoria reign over Britain?

J How many feet high is the General Sherman giant sequoia tree, the highest in the world?

K How many million dollars did the 1987 film *Ishtar* lose?

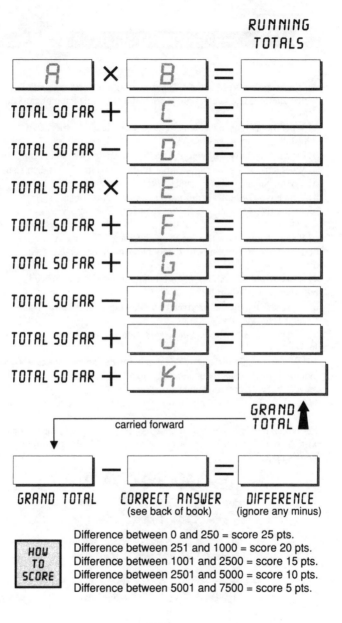

RUNNING TOTALS

A	×	B	=	
TOTAL SO FAR	+	C	=	
TOTAL SO FAR	−	D	=	
TOTAL SO FAR	×	E	=	
TOTAL SO FAR	+	F	=	
TOTAL SO FAR	+	G	=	
TOTAL SO FAR	−	H	=	
TOTAL SO FAR	+	J	=	
TOTAL SO FAR	+	K	=	

GRAND TOTAL

carried forward

| | − | | = | |

GRAND TOTAL   CORRECT ANSWER   DIFFERENCE
(see back of book)   (ignore any minus)

HOW TO SCORE

Difference between 0 and 250 = score 25 pts.
Difference between 251 and 1000 = score 20 pts.
Difference between 1001 and 2500 = score 15 pts.
Difference between 2501 and 5000 = score 10 pts.
Difference between 5001 and 7500 = score 5 pts.

1) What term derives its name from the French for "40 day period" for which animals, people, or vessels are isolated on suspicion of carrying disease?

2) What did Yorgos, a resident on the Greek island of Milos, find whilst digging in his field in 1820?

3) In which country will you find the Sierra Madre mountain range?

4) What letter starts the capital cities of these countries – Afghanistan, Malaysia, Nepal, Sudan, Uganda, Ukraine, and Zaire?

5) Which type of bullet is designed to expand upon impact and is reputedly the type with which President John F. Kennedy was assassinated?

6) You probably know that the kangaroo comes from the Aborigine for "I don't understand", but which animal's Aborigine name is "No drink"?

7) A fax machine is commonly used in modern everyday office life – but what is "fax" short for?

8) What was the nickname given to the famous neurofibromatosis sufferer John Merrick?

9) Which biblical figure had three sons named Ham, Shem, and Japheth?

10) Which vitamin is the only one that the body can manufacture itself, though is more normally obtained through liver and dairy produce, to prevent bone deformation and rickets?

11) Coming from the Greek word *nomisma*, what does a numismatist collect and study?

12) Which tennis trophy has, since 1900, been awarded to the nation with the winning men's team over a series of one doubles and four singles matches?

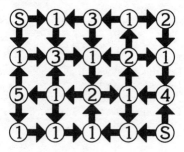

LAP 10

There are no time limits on this lap.

To score each puzzle, refer to the Scoring Summary on page 13. The maximum scores available are shown below.

	MAX.	SCORE
QUIZWORD	25	
REBUS CHALLENGE	30	
SAFE CRACKER	20	
LOGIC PROBLEM	20	
IN THE PIPELINE	20	
CRIME STORY	25	
WORD ISLAND	30	
MISSING LINKS	30	
NUMEROLOGY	25	
MAGNIFICENT MAZE	25	
TOTAL (max. 250)		

TARGET TO BEAT – 215 points

ACROSS

9 What form of soft gypsum, occurring in England and Italy, can be easily sculpted into figures? (9)

10 Which famous 1938 Evelyn Waugh novel concerned the life of a newspaper reporter? (5)

11 Which Shakespeare play of 1611 tells of a disgruntled duke banished to an island in a storm? (7)

12 What is the term for a contestant on foot taking part in a Spanish *corrida de toros*? (7)

13 In Greek mythology, which monster asked everyone who wished to enter Thebes a riddle? (6)

14 The world's first _____ with a gas light was unveiled in Pall Mall, London on January 29, 1807 (8)

16 Garlic, shallots, asparagus and chives all belong to the common family of which herbaceous flowering plant? (4)

17 What meaty word connects a 1676 rebellion in Virginia, the architect of the Lincoln Memorial, and a 16th Century English philosopher? (5)

18 Which form of Hindu philosophy emphasises the use of bodily control and discipline? (4)

22 What Russian word for "grandmother" is more often used to describe the triangular headscarf commonly worn by such women? (8)

24 To become conscious or break from sleep (4,2)

27 Which class of hunting dog has breeds such as Boston, Border, Scottish, Australian, Irish, Fox and Kerry Blue? (7)

28 Sir Jacob _____, US-born sculptor who settled in England to produce works in Rodin's style, such as *Day and Night* (7)

29 Which American city has a football team called the Dolphins? (5)

30 Which word, associated with food, can be formed from the letters of "GET BARGEE"? (9)

DOWN

1 Which plant has 17 varieties on the endangered species list, including the black-laced, Arizona hedgehog, and silver pincushion? (6)

2 Which famous 17th Century building at Agra, India was built by Shah Jahan as a mausoleum for his wife? (3,5)

3 What is a dramatic performance of an event of local historic interest acted out at a fixed place or on a float in a carnival? (7)

4 Hawaii has been known as the 50th _____ of the USA since August 21, 1959 (5)

5 What is the title of the marching leader who immediately precedes a military band? (4,5)

6 In chemistry, what term describes an atom having the same number of protons but different numbers of neutrons than another atom of the same element? (7)

7 Which Haitian religion idolises a high god called Bon Dieu? (6)

8 What type of musical drama involves a stage play consisting of light-hearted songs and dialogue? (8)

15 Which Scandinavian maidens of Odin are led by Brunhild in a 1856 Wagner opera? (9)

16 Which medical operation removes part of the brain's cortex in order to control behaviour in the patient? (8)

19 Which dish is made from fried beaten eggs usually served with a filling? (8)

20 Which drug, originally obtained from the bark of the willow, has the chemical name acetylsalicylic acid? (7)

21 In Irish legend, what female fairy wails before a family death? (7)

23 What does the "B" stand for in the acronym FBI? (6)

25 What word for a room where food and utensils are kept comes from the Latin word *panitaria*, meaning "bread room"? (6)

26 Which golf club has the largest amount of loft to help the player with shots from a bunker or heavy rough? (5)

1

_ _ _ _ _ _   _ _ _ _ _ _ _ _

2

_ _ _ _   _ _ _   _ _ _ _ _ _
_ _   _ _ _ _   _ _ _ _

3

_ _ _ _ _ _ _ _ _   _ _ _ _ _ _

--- ----- ---------

--- ---- ---- ---------
- -------- -----

--- ---- -- ---- --!

199

Blacken out those segments on the right-hand page that are letter coded to the FALSE statements. This will form a correct mathematical sum.

True   False

A   The scientific name for the vulture is *Vulpes vulpes*   ☐ ☐

B   *Romans* is the penultimate book of the New Testament   ☐ ☐

C   Thanksgiving Day in the USA falls on the first Thursday in November   ☐ ☐

D   Spiderman's *alter ego* works as a photographer for the *Daily Bugle*   ☐ ☐

E   Juno was the Roman King of the gods   ☐ ☐

F   Zodiac, Prefect and Corsair were models of Audi cars   ☐ ☐

G   Michelangelo painted the ceiling of the Sistine Chapel   ☐ ☐

H   The Marx Brothers' real surname was Cooper   ☐ ☐

J   The first Commandment is "Thou shalt not commit adultery"   ☐ ☐

K   de Morgan was a famous British mathematician   ☐ ☐

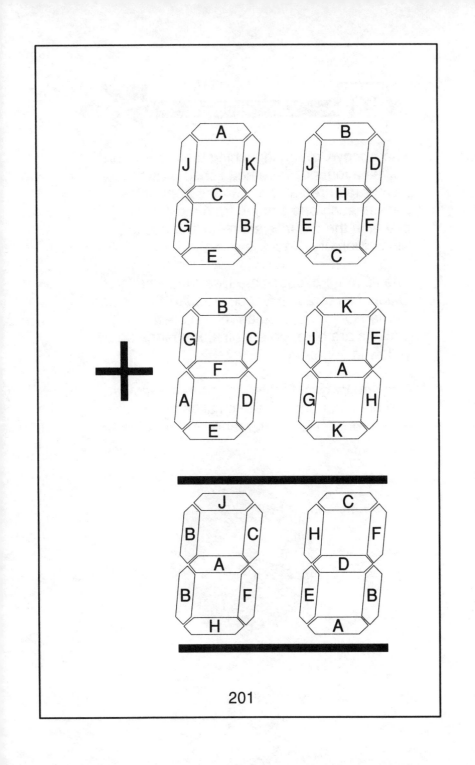

The Krispy Co. are launching their new brand – five flavours of vegetarian crisps. Each flavour features an alien on the front of the packet, each one coming from a different planet in the Solar System – either Jupiter, Mars, Mercury, Neptune or Saturn.

The flavours of crisps are Beetroot, Cheese & Onion, Horseradish Sauce, Tomato Sauce and Pickled Onion. The colour of the aliens on the packets are blue, green, pink, tangerine and yellow in some order.

Can you work out what are the name, colour and planet of origin for each alien and the flavour of crisp they appear on?

CLUES

1. Bungol is pink. He doesn't appear on the Pickled Onion crisp packet nor is he from Jupiter.

2. The Cheese & Onion packet has a blue alien on it.

3. Xippi helps to promote the delicious Horseradish Sauce flavour. He comes from a planet further away from the Sun than the blue alien.

4. Yellow monsters come from Mercury.

5. Kalok and the Tomato Sauce monster live on neighbouring planets of the Solar System.

6. Picked Onion crisps display the Neptune alien, but he is not tangerine coloured.

7. Yterb isn't green.

STARTING HINTS

a. What colour is the monster from Neptune?

b. Find the colour of Jeorj and his flavour of crisps.

c. What flavours do Kalok and Jeorj support?

d. Now look carefully at clues 3 & 5.

Alien	Flavour	Colour	Planet
Bungol			
Jeorj			
Kalok			
Xippi			
Yterb			

Your task is to match the animal characters below with the kind of animals they are. In some cases we give you the book they appear in.

1 Toto in *The Wizard of Oz*
2 Baloo
3 Black Beauty
4 Rosinante in *Don Quixote*
5 Nana in *Peter Pan*
6 Pooh
7 Justice in *Black Beauty*
8 Buck in *Call of the Wild*
9 Kaa
10 Napoleon in *Animal Farm*
11 Flicka in *My Friend Flicka*
12 The Houyhnhnms in *Gulliver's Travels*
13 Snowball
14 Mopsy
15 Polynesia in *Dr. Doolittle*
16 Nag in *The Jungle Book Stories*
17 Lassie
18 Rupert
19 Black Bess in *Rockwood*
20 General Wormwort

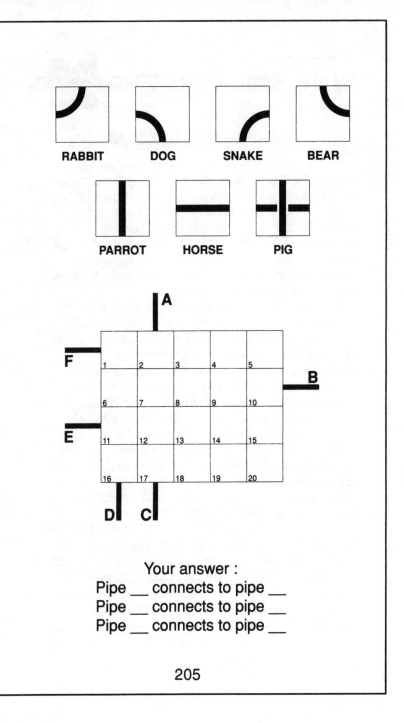

RABBIT DOG SNAKE BEAR

PARROT HORSE PIG

Your answer :
Pipe __ connects to pipe __
Pipe __ connects to pipe __
Pipe __ connects to pipe __

205

The Missing Link

Officer Barlow pulled up in his blue Ford outside the house in a depressed, industrial part of the city. Detective Hartland, an ambulance and several other police officers had been at the scene for some time. "What have you got there, sir?" he asked.

Hartland handed him the suicide note that had been found beside the dead man.

"My dear Gillian," it began. "You have been indispensible in giving my life meaning, and I hope you do not think that I have decieved you by doing this. However, you know my independant and unchangable mind is easily comitted to what I believe in, and it is my judgement that I should give up this life for a new tranquility in a separate world from here where debt is not such a burden. I hope that you understand, and that you will not feel embarassed when telling the children. I love you very much, Bennet."

Barlow put the note in a police bag. "Shame. How come he owed so much?"

The Detective filled Barlow in on the details he had found so far. "He had been unemployed for some time, ever since the Bromley News he sub-edited had folded because of falling circulation. He'd been finding it difficult to get a job and he felt he was letting the family down. She was a housewife looking after the children, sometimes helping out at the local hostel. Apart from money troubles, they were seemingly very stable, according to the neighbours I've talked to. Happy marriage, two kids, a model Catholic nuclear family."

"I thought suicide was severely frowned upon by Catholics," said Barlow.

The Detective nodded in agreement. "That's exactly what makes me suspicious. But that's not proof. I think we need something stronger to detect foul play here."

Barlow thought for a moment. "Well, thinking back to my school days, I'm fairly sure the proof is already ours."

Can you spot the exact evidence that provides the extra proof required to suspect murder?

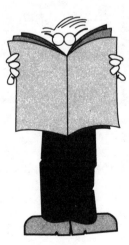

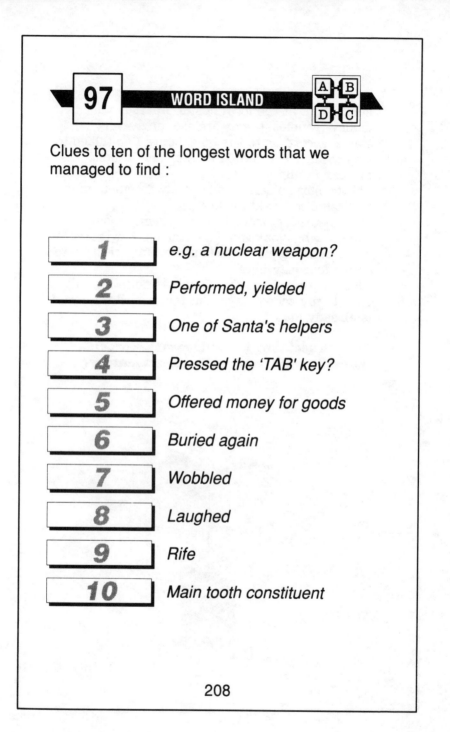

Clues to ten of the longest words that we managed to find :

1	*e.g. a nuclear weapon?*
2	*Performed, yielded*
3	*One of Santa's helpers*
4	*Pressed the 'TAB' key?*
5	*Offered money for goods*
6	*Buried again*
7	*Wobbled*
8	*Laughed*
9	*Rife*
10	*Main tooth constituent*

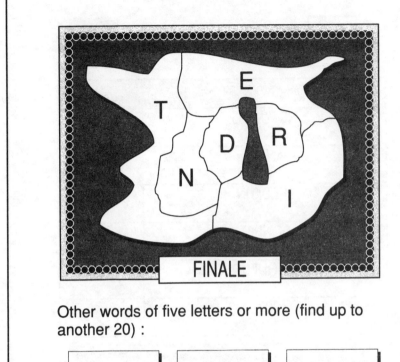

FINALE

Other words of five letters or more (find up to another 20) :

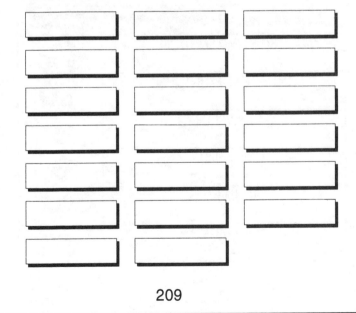

WHO?	GUESSES
NQFZMHRS	12
ANMM	10
EHCDKHN	8
DQNHBZ	6
BNLONRDQ	4
CDZE	2

WHAT?	GUESSES
Z SN E NMD SN YDQN	12
GNTMC CNF EZUNTQHSD	10
RHWSHDR	8
BGNHBD	6
BNHM RKNS	4
LTRHBZK	2

WHERE?	GUESSES
ONQS OQNCTBDQ	12
SZFTR	10
ZYNQDR	8
ZKFZQUD	6
BZOHSZK HR KHRANM	4
ROZMHRG MDHFGANTQ	2

WHEN?	GUESSES
HRKZMC QHRHMF?	12
MDV KHED	10
GNKHCZX	8
RHLMDK	6
DFFR	4
ATMMX	2

For each of the statements below, put your guesstimated answer in the appropriate box on the opposite page.

A Saturn has the largest number of moons of any planet in the Solar system – how many?

B How many Oscars did Steven Spielberg's *Schindler's List* win?

C How many million scouts are there in the USA?

D How many points are there on the Star of David?

E On average, how many people live on one square mile of the world's land?

F How long (in days) is the gestation period of the giraffe?

G How many cards are there in a standard pack of tarot cards?

H How many people died of poisoning in the USA in 1992?

J How many letters are there in the Greek alphabet?

K How old was William Pitt the Younger when he became Britain's youngest Prime Minister?

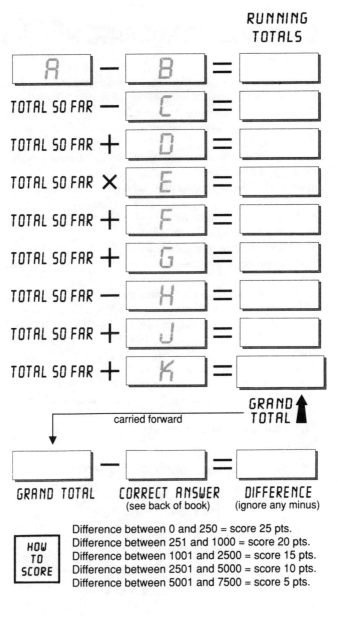

RUNNING
TOTALS

A − B =

TOTAL SO FAR − C =

TOTAL SO FAR + D =

TOTAL SO FAR × E =

TOTAL SO FAR + F =

TOTAL SO FAR + G =

TOTAL SO FAR − H =

TOTAL SO FAR + J =

TOTAL SO FAR + K =

GRAND TOTAL ↑

carried forward

GRAND TOTAL − CORRECT ANSWER = DIFFERENCE
(see back of book) (ignore any minus)

HOW
TO
SCORE

Difference between 0 and 250 = score 25 pts.
Difference between 251 and 1000 = score 20 pts.
Difference between 1001 and 2500 = score 15 pts.
Difference between 2501 and 5000 = score 10 pts.
Difference between 5001 and 7500 = score 5 pts.

213

1) Which computer company, formed by punched card pioneer Herman Hollerith, has the simple company motto "Think"?

2) *Rosencrantz and Guildenstern are Dead* is a Tom Stoppard play considering the fate of two minor characters from what Shakespeare play?

3) What connects a natural wind in the Rocky Mountains with the name of a helicopter?

4) Which famous city marks the central point of the Australian land mass?

5) What is the study, sometimes used in forensic science, of the flight of projectiles fired from a weapon?

6) Which is the only airborne mammal?

7) In computing terminology, what does the acronym VDU stand for?

8) Which two colours are most often confused by someone with Daltonism, a common form of colour-blindness?

9) Which Archbishop of Canterbury was the bishop of Bath and Wells before being consecrated in 1991?

10) What natural foodstuff is classified into monosaccharides, disaccharides, trisaccharides, and more unusually the polysaccharides such as cellulose and starch?

11) In what verbal respect are British stamps different from those of every other country in the world?

12) How many points are required to win one game of badminton?

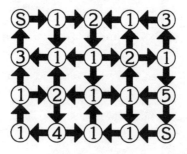

ANSWERS

TOP SECRET

NOTE — the solutions provided for the Word Island puzzles in this book are suggested lists of words that our computer found to be available. These were checked against *Chambers English Dictionary*. Depending upon where you live, there may be some words that you have found in your dictionary that are not listed herein. By all means, award yourself the points for these words.

215

ANSWERS TO LAP 1

1. **ACROSS:** 1 *Apocalypse Now*, **8** Knossos, **9** Preview, **11** Loofah, **13** Yearlong, **15** Manes, **16** Orpheus, **18** Baptist, **19** Lamia, **21** Aversion, **23** Italic, **25** Outpost, **26** Two-step, **28** Hercule Poirot.
DOWN: **2** Pronoun, **3** Cos, **4** Lisp, **5** Pepperpots, **6** Emeer, **7** Ominous, **8** Kilimanjaro, **10** Wightman Cup, **12** Aesop, **14** Horizontal, **17** Eclat, **18** Breathe, **20** Mulatto, **22** Stoic, **24** Stop, **27** Oui.

2. 1) Blood is thicker than water, 2) Talk turkey, 3) Once in a blue moon, 4) The Industrial Revolution, 5) Two left feet, 6) Third degree burn.

3. True statements are A, B, G, K. False statements (with corrections in brackets) are C (Psalms has the most), D (Ontario and Toronto are transposed), E (Upper Volta), F (Terpsichore), H (St Christopher), J (Olympia). The sum formed is 54 + 37 = 91.

4.

Dan	Jill	New Inn pub	7pm
Dave	Jane	Cinema	9pm
David	Katherine	Rixy's nightclub	11pm
Patrick	Victoria	Watched video	10pm
Simon	Mary	Ice skating	8pm

5. A connects to D; B connects to E; C connects to F.

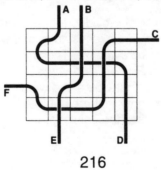

216

6. Although there are lots of ways in which the criminal's story could be false, the following are definite factual errors. Firstly, Irving Berlin could not read nor write music using scores. Second, Leonardo da Vinci wrote in mirror writing which could hardly be described as "clear Italian". Finally, the *Mona Lisa* is painted on wood, not canvas, and so could not have been rolled up into a tube. Spotting any two of these three earns the points.

7. 92 words. Clued words : soonest detested entente stetson détente oneness denotes sonnets settees noosed. Unclued words : deeded denes denned denote denoted dented dents detent détentes detents detest detests dodos donee donees donned dosed doses dossed dosses doted dotes dotted ententes needed nested nests netted nodded nodes nodose nones noose noosed nooses nosed noses noted notes oddest seeded sennet sestet sestets seton setose settee sodded sodden sones sonnet steed stenos stenosed stenoses stetted stone stoned stones stood tedded tenet tenets tenon tented tents teste tested testes tests toned tones tonne tonnes tooted toots tossed tosses toted totes totted tsetse tsetses.

8. (**These answers include notes explaining the more obscure clues**) WHO? = George Bush (who was head of the CIA before becoming the 41st President). WHAT? = Compact Disc. WHERE? = Australia (everyone is compelled to vote = "compulsory suffrage"; it is the flattest country in the world; Paul Keating is the Prime Minister, at time of writing). WHEN? = The Gunpowder Plot (the Catholic revolt against James I, led by Catesby although Fawkes was the one who was caught).

9. A=18, B=5, C=16, D=32, E=42, F=5, G=22, H=12, J=55, K=71, ANSWER=1067.

10. The correct answers are : 1) *E.T.,* 2) Little dots, 3) Israel, 4) Pangaea, 5) Sword, 6) Bark, 7) Facsimile, 8) Heart, 9) Castor and Pollux, 10) Carat, 11) History, 12) Archery.

FULL SOLUTION TO LOGIC PROBLEM, PUZZLE 255

(a) Mary went skating at 7pm or 8pm (clue 2) but the 7pm is the New Inn date (clue 3) so she must have gone at 8pm with Simon (clue 6). Jane could not have gone to the New Inn at 7pm since she went out an hour before Patrick and Victoria (clues 4 & 7) who did not go out at 8pm since we already know Mary and Simon went out then. Katherine went out at 11pm (clue 1), meaning it must have been Jill who went out to the New Inn at 7pm.

(b) Patrick and Victoria did not go out at 8pm [when we know Simon when out] or 11pm [because Katherine went out then] or 7pm [when we know Jill went out]. So they must have gone out at 9pm or 10pm. Similarly, Jane went out at 9pm or 10pm since we know Jill went out at 7pm, Mary went out at 8pm, and Katherine went out at 11pm. Using clue 7 we deduce that Jane went out at 9pm and Patrick went out at 10pm. This leaves Victoria, who must have gone out at 10pm.

(c) Dan isn't going out with Jane (clue 9), Katherine (clue 1), Mary [we know she is seeing Simon] or Victoria [who is seeing Patrick] so Dan must be with Jill.

So far the situation is :

Man	Woman	Venue	Time
Dan	Jill	New Inn pub	7pm
Dave	???	???	???
David	???	Rixy's night-club	???
Patrick	Victoria	???	10pm
Simon	Mary	Ice Skating	8pm

The video wasn't at 11pm (clue 8), 7pm (clue 3), 8pm [the ice-skating time], or 9pm [since Jane went out then but she didn't see the video by clue 7] so it must have been at 10pm with Patrick and Victoria, leaving Dave and his date to go to the cinema – the only remaining venue.

As Katherine didn't go to the cinema (clue 1), she must be the other night-clubber, and Jane must have gone to the movies with Dave at 9pm. David and Kath must have gone to Rixy's at 11pm, the only remaining time-slot. And that's all there is to it!

ANSWERS TO LAP 2

11. **ACROSS: 1** Willow pattern, **8** Deplete, **9** Proverb, **11** V-Necks, **13** Maverick, **15** Laser, **16** Premium, **18** Ravioli, **19** Ideal, **21** Inscribe, **23** Emboss, **25** Natural, **26** Czarina, **28** Down's syndrome.
DOWN: 2 Impress, **3** Lee, **4** Wren, **5** Alphabetic, **6** Those, **7** Rhenium, **8** Devaluation, **10** Baked Alaska, **12** Kirov, **14** Spoonbills, **17** Idiom, **18** Risotto, **20** Egotism, **22** Rerun, **24** Icon, **27** APR.

12. 1) Hot under the collar, 2) The third dimension, 3) Splitting hairs (sounds like "hares"), 4) Every now and then, 5) Saw the funny side, 6) Short term memory.

13. True statements are D, F, G. False statements are A (Mozart), B (Corinthian), C (11th Century), E (Peso), H (St Matthew), J (Athens), K (Harvard). The sum formed is 80 − 54 = 26.

14.

Peg 1	Eve	Polo neck	Tan
Peg 2	Clare	Anorak	Brown
Peg 3	Bernard	Raincoat	Black
Peg 4	Dominic	Cardigan	Blue
Peg 5	Adrian	Duffel coat	Green

15. A connects to E; B connects to F; C connects to D.

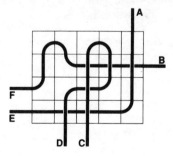

219

16. In 1962, the *Mariner I* mission was launched towards Venus. However, the rocket separated from the boosters too soon and plunged into the ocean just four minutes after take-off. The cause? A missing minus sign ("a short, horizontal line") from the computer program, caused by human error.

17. 62 words.
Clued words : nineteen tontine retinite reenter tenner torrent trotter titter terrene retorter.
Unclued words : entente enter enterer enteron error inert inner intent inter intine intone intoner intro intron ninon nitre otter renin rennet rennin renter retene retort retro rooter rotenone rotor rotten rottener rotter teeter tenet tenon tenor tenter terete terret terror tetter tinner tinter titre toner tonne tontiner tooter torte torten totter totterer treen.

18. WHO? = Archimedes (he invented the Archimedes Screw; clue 3 refers to his discovery of pi; clue 4 refers to his problem of finding out whether the king's crown was made from real gold).
WHAT? = A piano (whose full name of pianoforte means "quiet loud" in French; clue 4 lists the black and white layout of one octave; Steinway is a famous make of piano).
WHERE? = Madame Tussaud's (which is in the same building as the London Laserium).
WHEN? = The Gulf War (*Tomahawk* and *Patriot* were the principal missile systems used).

19. A=14, B=20, C=95, D=35, E=60, F=161, G=76, H=9, J=12, K=28, ANSWER=2068.

20. The answers are :
  1) Sir Christopher Wren
  2) *The World*
  3) Bay Of Biscay

4) Snow
5) Tricolours
6) Jupiter
7) Sulphur
8) Rhombus
9) Valhalla
10) (Used) Car Salesman
11) Orange
12) Harold Lloyd

ANSWERS TO LAP 3

21. **ACROSS: 8** Creamery, **9** Ureter, **10** Step-sister, **11** Acid, **12** Proper, **14** Ricochet, **15** Quartet, **17** Aphasia, **20** Hologram, **22** Norton, **24** Kiwi, **25** Salamander, **27** In-laws, **28** Atropine.
DOWN: 1 Crater, **2** Carp, **3** Pedigree, **4** Mystery, **5** Rubric, **6** Sedan-chair, **7** Beriberi, **13** Periodical, **16** Utopians, **18** Penumbra, **19** Amalgam, **21** Resist, **23** Oceans, **26** Nape.

22. 1) Fatal Attraction, 2) Commercial break, 3) Cuts both ways, 4) Open and shut case, 5) Tom, Dick and Harry (the pictures are of Tom Hanks, Richard Nixon and Harry Belafonte), 6) Point blank range (a decimal point, then a blank, then a range of mountains).

23. True statements are A, D, E, F, K. False statements are B (domed roof on a square tower), C (Spanish Inquisition), G (mournfully), H (crowds), J (frequency). The sum formed is 17 x 4 = 68.

24.

Row 1	Column D	Stock-car race	$25,000
Row 2	Column B	Dog walker	$10,000
Row 3	Column E	Custard pie	$1,000
Row 4	Column C	Wrestling	$5,000
Row 5	Column A	Donate $100	$2,000

25. A connects to B; C connects to E; D connects to F.

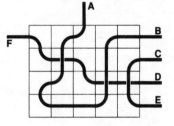

222

26. "Direct flights" between two places of different latitude over a spherical surface such as the Earth's usually look curved when projected on to flat maps. Therefore, the pilot could not have plotted the flight plan using "a pencil and ruler".

27. 54 words.
Clued words : decider receded derided decree ridded derriere reeled deicide leered eerie.
Unclued words : ceded ceiled celled cerci cered cider cirri creed creel cried crier decide decided decreed decried decrier deeded deled deride derider diced dicer dicier direr eddied eerier eider elide elided erred icier leerier lidded lieder recede redder redid reedier reeler relic relied ridder rider riled.

28. WHO? = William Shakespeare (who spelled his name many different ways; he married Anne Hathaway).
WHAT? = Diamond (the hardest naturally occuring substance at 10 on the Mohs' scale of hardness; Brilliant and Rose are cuts of diamond).
WHERE? = Buckingham Palace (it has a fountain outside it; in 1825, its front was rebuilt by John Nash; it is situated on the Mall in London).
WHEN? = Assassination of John F. Kennedy (Earl Warren was the Chief Justice who led the enquiry to investigate whether the murder was a conspiracy; Lee Harvey Oswald was killed by Jack Ruby).

29. A=20, B=7, C=4, D=26, E=9, F=4, G=385, H=6, J=64, K=46, ANSWER=1771.

30. The anwers are :
    1) Harold Lloyd
    2) Mozart
    3) North and South Poles
    4) Alaska
    5) Tail

6) Uranium, Plutonium, Mercury
7) All their sides have the same length
8) Harpies
9) Ouija Board
10) All have been vice-presidents
11) *Cluedo*
12) Seven (the Heptathlon)

31. **ACROSS: 8** Crowfoot, **9** Phobia, **10** Adam's apple, **11** Lapp, **12** Crisis, **14** Nepotism, **15** Fascism, **17** Columns, **20** Cephalic, **22** Thebes, **24** Star, **25** Abbreviate, **27** Bronze, **28** Richmond.
DOWN: 1 Trader, **2** Swim, **3** Molasses, **4** Stipend, **5** Upkeep, **6** Cos lettuce, **7** Diapason, **13** Saccharine, **16** Aperture, **18** Outreach, **19** Iceberg, **21** Loaves, **23** Extant, **26** lamb.

32. 1) Centre of gravity, 2) Coffee table book, 3) The long and short of it, 4) Shorthand typist, 5) The League of Nations, 6) Miss the bus.

33. True statements are A, D, J, K. False statements are B (throat and neck), C (All the Love in the World), E (Nile), F (1852), G (yes he did, in 1954), H (men). The sum formed is 16 + 37 = 53.

34.

Aardvark	Trevor	Gossip	Wednesday
Badger	Peter	Evening News	Friday
Fish	Simone	Times	Monday
Snake	Lucy	Post	Tuesday
Yak	Millie	Press	Thursday

35. A connects to E; B connects to F; C connects to D.

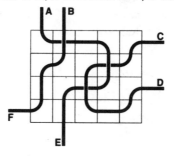

225

36. If you didn't spot this one, get ready to groan. Earlier in the story you are told that the man thought the pilot was a friend of his, Jack Delaney. When the man on the aeroplane got up, he knocked on the door and said "Hi, Jack!"...

37. 40 words.
Clued words : macramé mamma creamier camera crammer arrear merrier acacia carrier maraca.
Unclued words : acari aerie airier career carer circa cirri cream creamer creme crier crime eerie eerier emmer erica icier mammae maria marrier mimer mimic mirier racier ramie rarer reamer rearer rimae rimer.

38. WHO? = Fred Flintstone (Bedrock is his home town).
WHAT? = The Eiffel Tower (originally built on the Champ de Mars for the 1889 Paris Exhibition; in World War I, it was used as a look-out post because at the time it was one of the highest buildings in the world).
WHERE? = Pyramid (a ziggurat is a stepped-side pyramid; Cheops is buried in the Great Pyramid at Giza).
WHEN? = The Irangate affair (*Hawk* was the name of the missiles in question; other clues refer to evidence that was allegedly shredded by Oliver North's secretary).

39. A=13, B=10, C=50, D=27, E=29, F=66, G=88, H=107, J=23, K=57, ANSWER=3711.

40. The answers are :
    1) James Bond
    2) Michigan
    3) Canada
    4) Crimean War
    5) Racing
    6) Polymer
    7) The O Group
    8) Tarot Cards

9) Georgio Armani
10) Mah Jong
11) 400 metres
12) Disqualification

41. **ACROSS: 8** Motion, **9** El Dorado, **10** Waterwheel, **11** Vein, **12** Ebb tide, **14** Eclair, **15** Midgets, **17** Sailing, **20** Rector, **22** One-step, **24** Pier, **25** Absolution, **27** End users, **28** Fiddle.
DOWN: 1 Potage, **2** Mixed bag, **3** Snow, **4** Referee, **5** Adulterate, **6** Gravel, **7** Addition, **13** Interfaces, **16** Iberians, **18** Latitude, **19** Possess, **21** Torque, **23** Poodle, **26** Left.

42. 1) Double Your Money, 2) A word in edgeways, 3) Rip Van Winkle, 4) Cat's eyes, 5) Innocents Abroad, 6) Race against time.

43. True statements are B, D, F, G. False statements are A (Brazil), C (four), E (London and Paris), H (Mars), J (sternum), K (Virgo). The sum formed is 94 − 10 = 84.

44.

Debbie	Collingwood	Margherita	8pm
Heather	Aidan's	Pepperoni	8.30pm
Ian	Van Mildert	Anchovies	10.30pm
Kay	Trevelyan	Hot & Spicy	7.15pm
Martin	Grey	Fuengerola	9.15pm

45. A connects to E; B connects to D; C connects to F.

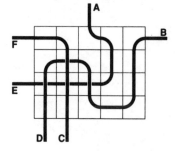

46. The builder was clearly lying. He had been "the one working on that floor", and he said himself that the scene was as the detectives first saw it. The man then· "opened the door" – impossible, since the woman could not have closed the door behind her since there was no floor on the other side.

47. 63 words.
Clued words : goddess dodged detested oddest stodge stooge dotted sedge totted seeded.
Unclued words : deeded detest detests dodge dodged dodges dodos doges dogged doggo dosed doses dossed dosses doted dotes edged edges egest egests egged geese gesso goddesses godet godets goose goosed goosegog gooses sedges sestet sestets setose settee settees sodded steed stetted stood stooges teste tested testes tests togged tooted toots tossed tosses toted totes tsetse tsetses.

48. WHO? = Woody Allen (real name Allen Konigsberg).
WHAT? = Typewriter (first commercially made by Remington before the popular IBM 72 emerged).
WHERE? = Rome (capital of the Lazio region; site of the signing of various famous treaties).
WHEN? = First Men on the Moon (clue 1 refers to the fact that the walk was a long way away!; clue 2 refers to the telephone call to President Nixon; the landing was made in the Sea of Tranquillity).

49. A=5, B=3, C=8, D=8, E=6, F=14, G=66, H=213, J=93, K=41, ANSWER=7283.

50. The answers are:
1) Balustrade
2) *Pilgrim's Progress*
3) Mexico
4) To the west

5) Blue
6) Edwin Hubble
7) Hydrogen
8) Ruby
9) Two
10) Detects lies
11) Tea
12) Hammer

51. **ACROSS: 8** Melody, **9** Aardvark, **10** Statute-law, **11** Tito, **12** Reactor, **14** Lyrics, **15** Earlobe, **17** Pitfall, **20** Dowser, **22** Ragweed, **24** *Very*, **25** Addis Ababa, **27** Catholic, **28** Cuckoo.
DOWN: 1 Vector, **2** Football, **3** Cyst, **4** Mallard, **5** Arc-welding, **6** Avatar, **7** Critical, **13** Tabernacle, **16** Above par, **18** Feedback, **19** Art Deco, **21** Scythe, **23** Debtor, **26** Sect.

52. 1) Acid rain, 2) Russian roulette, 3) Perpetual motion, 4) Pure mathematics, 5) California Girls, 6) Latter Day Saints.

53. True statements are C, D, H, K. False statements are A (Netherlands), B (seven), E (plain green rectangle), F (trombone), G (Verdi), J (seven). The sum formed is 27 x 3 = 81.

54.

Graham	Everett	Purple	Celebrities
James	Kendal	Grey	Books
John	Sanders	Orange	TV
Patrick	Erwin	Blue	Music
Paul	Harper	Green	Films

55. A connects to C; B connects to F; D connects to E.

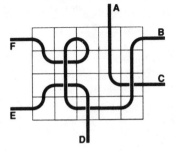

56. There were two drivers travelling in opposite directions in dense fog, which affects visibility through windscreens badly, despite the windscreen wipers. They had both put their heads out of their side windows simultaneously and their heads clashed, resulting in bad head injuries. The cars came to a gradual stop some yards later. This explains the unharmed cars still having their engines running.

57. 39 words.
Clued words : imitate maimed dimmed immediate mediated meditate dimidiate mimetite emitted deemed.
Unclued words : aided aimed amide deeded demit demitted edema edited imamate imide imitated mamma mated matte matted media mediate medii meditated meted mimed tamed tatami tatted tedded teemed tided timed timid.

58. WHO? = Charles Dickens (used pen-name of Boz; his stories were first serialised when published).
WHAT? = Cornflakes (originally designed as a food for hospital patients, it was then sold via mail order; the famous Kellogg signature is still seen on packets today).
WHERE? = Oxford University (home of the *Oxford English Dictionary*).
WHEN? = The Boston Tea Party (the tea was owned by the East India Company; clue 6 is a slightly cryptic reference to the Mad Hatter's Tea Party in *Alice in Wonderland*).

59. A=6, B=76, C=8, D=195, E=300, F=12, G=28, H=88, J=80, K=12, ANSWER=2116.

60. The answers are :
    1) Silver bullet
    2) Christine Brinkley
    3) Argentina
    4) Jamaica
    5) Legion

6) Chlorophyll
7) London Bridge
8) Microwave oven
9) Lee Harvey Oswald
10) Bordeaux
11) Discus (1kg and 2kg)
12) Polo

61. **ACROSS: 1** Demerara, **5** Tandem, **10** Backspace, **11** Minor, **12** Orwell, **13** Odysseus, **15** Horsehair, **17** Nine, **20** Clef, **21** Marshland, **24** Maharaja, **25** Advent, **28** Thumb, **29** Cabriolet, **30** Reeves, **31** Kedgeree. **DOWN: 1** Debtor, **2** Macaw, **3** Restless, **4** Ream, **6** Almost, **7** Dandelion, **8** Marksmen, **9** Head first, **14** Cheap-jack, **16** Open house, **18** Scimitar, **19** Cladding, **22** Treble, **23** Statue, **26** Euler, **27** Oboe.

62. 1) Split infinitive, 2) Shooting gallery, 3) Raise the alarm, 4) Vulgar fraction, 5) Chicken Maryland, 6) Vertical take-off.

63. True statements are C, D, E, H. False statements are A (Laz Paz), B (Red Sox), F (Anise), G (had one opera), J (Sputnik 2), K (polyglot). The sum formed is 13 + 26 = 39.

64.

Picture A	Freaky Fred	Poaching	3 years
Picture B	Cad Clive	Treason	15 years
Picture C	Tough Tim	Rustling	7 years
Picture D	Bruiser Bill	Deception	10 years
Picture E	Slippery Sam	Forgery	6 years

65. A connects to F; B connects to D; C connects to E.

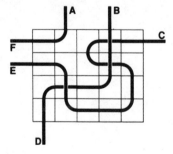

66. Among the duty-free goods the bee-keeper received was some cologne. He wore some the next day and the bees did not recognise his scent, and so they attacked the 'stranger' to their hive. When the Inspector went into the closed space of the ambulance he could smell the cologne.

67. 42 words.
Clued words : useless sublessee pulseless bubbles pebble epees sleeps blesses belle peepul.
Unclued words : beeps belles bells bleep bleeps bless bubble bulbul bulbuls bulls buses busses lessee lessees lulls lupus pebbles peels peeps pubes pules pulls pulse pulses seels seeps sells sepses sleep speel spell spells.

68. WHO? = Leonardo da Vinci (who wrote in mirror writing, as we know from Lap 26!; he painted the *Last Supper* and designed the first helicopter).
WHAT? = Cash/Credit Card (Diner's Club was the first credit card to be introduced).
WHERE? = The Andes (they are a large mountain system, or cordillera, near Cape Horn; highest peak is Aconcagua, and Titicaca is the highest lake in the world).
WHEN? = The Olympic Games (there were no Olympics in 1914, 1940 or 1944 due to wars; the flag with five rings represents the continents).

69. A=12, B=4, C=22, D=6, E=92, F=13, G=69, H=25, J=11, K=20, ANSWER=1236.

70. The answers are :
    1) Mathematics
    2) John Cleese
    3) It is not rectangular
    4) They are walled cities
    5) The SAS

6) Wine
7) Doesn't stick to a magnet
8) Troposphere
9) All are Holy Books
10) Angostura Bitters
11) Three
12) *Americas' Cup*

71. **ACROSS: 1** Chaplain, **5** I.D. card, **10** Baby teeth, **11** Omega, **12** Energy, **13** Ice skate, **15** Clingfilm, **17** Edge, **20** Cube, **21** Pentagram, **24** Corvette, **25** Iguana, **28** Ecole, **29** Viscosity, **30** Muscat, **31** Leap year. **DOWN: 1** Cobweb, **2** Amble, **3** Litigant, **4** Ibex, **6** Dropsy, **7** Alexandra, **8** Diameter, **9** Chocolate, **14** Effective, **16** Laborious, **18** Ice cream, **19** Age group, **22** Peseta, **23** Lawyer, **26** Alice, **27** Isle.

72. 1) Swinging Sixties, 2) Waste not, want not, 3) Six of one and half a dozen of another, 4) Burn the midnight oil, 5) Vitamin B complex (anagram of "Vitamin B"), 6) Peak viewing time.

73. True statements are D, G, J. False statements are A (5th), B (140 British, 4000 Zulus), C ('89), E (speaking aloud), F (onomatopoeia), H (Spencer Percival was), K (broad and slow). The sum formed is 96 − 69 = 27.

74.

Annabel	Personnel	Level 4	Level 5
Jonathan	Data Processing	Level 1	Level 4
Melanie	Purchasing	Level 2	Level 1
Norman	Accounts	Level 5	Level 3
Steve	Marketing	Level 3	Level 2

75. A connects to C; B connects to F; D connects to E.

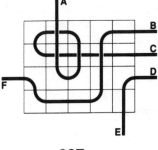

76. The man had no trouble reading the Arabic numbers (1, 2, 5, etc.) on the coins of most Western countries. However, he was currently in the United States which has words on its coins (such as TEN CENTS) which the Arab could not read. Hence, he had to guess what coins to put into the machine to make it work. It did not work if he put too much in since it accepted the exact coins only.

77. 47 words.
Clued words : tattooists cassata statistics static staccato cocoa otitis cacao assists cassis.
Unclued words : ascitic ascot ascots assist assists astatic attics casts cists coast coasts coati coatis coats cocci coots cotta iotas oasis otitic scats scoot scoots stasis statics statist statistic stats stoat stoic stoics tacit tattoo tattooist titis toast toasts.

78. WHO? = Garfield the cat.
WHAT? = The planet Mars (whose atmosphere is almost entirely made up of Carbon Dioxide; its year is 687 Earth days long; Phobos and Deimos are its moons; it is the fourth planet of the Solar System).
WHERE? = New York City (built on the junction of the Hudson and East rivers; was once capital of the USA; Staten Island is one of its boroughs).
WHEN? = The Soccer World Cup (was held in the USA in 1994; FIFA is the international ruling body; the original Jules Rimet trophy was kept by Brazil in 1970 who had it three times).

79. A=7, B=14, C=12, D=460, E=3, F=75, G=88, H=206, J=167, K=6, ANSWER=4378.

80. The answers are:
    1) *Peter Pan*
    2) Court Jesters
    3) Seven
    4) New York

5) Spain
6) Puma
7) Carburettor
8) *Aurora Borealis*
9) Roman Catholicism
10) Cayenne
11) Cheese
12) Three

81. **ACROSS: 9** Oast-house, **10** Amigo, **11** Reactor, **12** Each way, **13** Eggnog, **14** Glycerol, **16** Rite, **17** Dodge, **18** East, **22** Nebraska, **24** Parrot, **27** Embassy, **28** Le Havre, **29** U-Boat, **30** Unnatural.
DOWN: 1 Bourse, **2** Escargot, **3** Ghettos, **4** Curry, **5** Genealogy, **6** Paycock, **7** Viewer, **8** Polyglot, **15** Monkey-nut, **16** Runner-up, **19** Aardvark, **20** Bassets, **21** Machete, **23** Baboon, **25** Treble, **26** Plank.

82. 1) Top Cat, 2) Wall Street crash, 3) Make a night of it, 4) The Silence of the Lambs, 5) Foreign exchange, 6) Around the World in 80 Days.

83. True statements are A, C, F, J. False statements are B (73 mph), D (parliament), E (pineapple), G (Paul Cezanne), H (Yankee), K (pantograph). The sum formed is 13 x 6 = 78.

84.

Picture A	Theresa	Earl Shilton	Cor anglais
Picture B	Paula	Narborough	Flute
Picture C	Rhona	Countesthorpe	Trumpet
Picture D	Olivia	Wigston	Bassoon
Picture E	Sandra	Broughton Ast.	Saxophone

85. A connects to D; B connects to C; E connects to F.

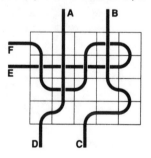

86. The Inspector had assumed the case was a typical terrorist attack and that the woman had been carrying a bomb in a plastic bag. The woman had been smuggling in drugs from Cuba. She was "carrying" a plastic bag full of drugs in her stomach. The bag burst, releasing the huge amount of drugs into her bloodstream causing her to "go berserk" (as Penny had said at the start of the story) then die.

87. 81 words.
Clued words : tartar iterate reiterate aggregate regretter arrearage greegree titrate retreat regatta.
Unclued words : aerate aerie agate agree arete arietta arrear arret artier attar attire eager eagre eatage eerie eerier egger egret errata etagere etrier garage garget garret garter getter grate grater greater greet greeter gritter grittier irate irritate rater ratite ratter rattier rearer regear reggae regrate regrater regret reiter retie retire tagger target tarrier tarter tartrate tatter tattier tearer teeter terata terete terra terrae terret terrier tetra tetter titre titter treater trier trite triter.

88. WHO? = Albert Einstein (whose name literally means "beer mug" in German).
WHAT? = The Statue of Liberty (designed by Auguste Bartholdi; one is in New York Harbour, a smaller repilca is in France).
WHERE? = France (Massif Central is a large range of mountains in France; the Loire is a famous French river).
WHEN? = The Sinking of the *Titanic* (the captain was Edward Smith; the first rescue ship to arrive was the *Carpathia*).

89. A=4, B=10, C=70, D=18, E=10, F=46, G=89, H=63, J=275, K=47, ANSWER=1314.

90. The answers are:
1) Quarantine
2) *Venus De Milo*
3) Mexico
4) K
5) Dum Dum
6) Koala
7) Facsimile
8) The Elephant Man
9) Noah
10) Vitamin D
11) Coins
12) The Davis Cup

91. **ACROSS: 9** Alabaster, **10** Scoop, **11** Tempest, **12** Matador, **13** Sphinx, **14** Lamppost, **16** Lily, **17** Bacon, **18** Yoga, **22** Babushka, **24** Wake up, **27** Terrier, **28** Epstein, **29** Miami, **30** Eggbeater.
DOWN: 1 Cactus, **2** Taj Mahal, **3** Pageant, **4** State, **5** Drum major, **6** Isotope, **7** Voodoo, **8** Operetta, **15** Valkyries, **16** Lobotomy, **19** Omelette, **20** Aspirin, **21** Banshee, **23** Bureau, **25** Pantry, **26** Wedge.

92. 1) Record breaking, 2) Burn the candle at both ends, 3) Pineapple chunks, 4) The final countdown, 5) The face that launched a thousand ships (the Queen launches Commonwealth ships) 6) Not much to look at!

93. True statements are D, G, K. False statements are A (fox), B (6th book), C (fourth), E (was Roman Queen!), F (Ford), H (it *is* Marx), J ("Thou shalt have no other gods before me"). The sum formed is 56 + 24 = 80.

94.

Bungol	Tomato sauce	Pink	Mars
Jeorj	Pickled onion	Green	Neptune
Kalok	Cheese & onion	Blue	Jupiter
Xippi	Horseradish	Tangerine	Saturn
Yterb	Beetroot	Yellow	Mercury

95. A connects to F; B connects to E; C connects to D.

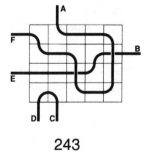

96. This was certainly murder. Although Bennet had been working as a newspaper sub-editor for many years, no less than eight words (indispensable, deceived, independent, unchangeable, committed, tranquillity, separate, embarrassed) are incorrectly spelled out on the suicide note. Obviously the murderer had tried to be more poetic than he was capable of being.

97. 118 words.
Clued words : deterrent rendered reindeer indented tendered reinterred teetered tittered ridden dentine.
Unclued words : deeded denied denier denned dented dentin deride derided derider derriere detent détente deter deterred diene dieted dieter diner dinette dinned dinner direr dited eerie eerier eider ended entente enter entered enterer entire indeed indene indent indenter inedited inner intend intended intender intent inter interred intine needed needer needier netted nineteen nittier redden reddened redder reedier reenter reentered reined reinter reiter rended render renderer renin rennet rennin rented renter retene retie retied retinite retire retired ridded ridder rider tedded tedder teenier teeter tended tender tenderer tenet tenner tented tenter terrene terret terrier terrine tetter tided tidied tidier tiered tinder tined tineid tinier tinned tinner tinnier tinted tinter tired titter.

98. WHO? = Beethoven (he became a royal organist at Bonn; composed *Eroica* and *Fidelio*).
WHAT? = Juke Box (*Hound Dog* is the most widely played track on juke boxes; clue 1 refers to the buttons).
WHERE? = Portugal (physical features include the Azores and the Tagus river; the Algarve is a famous Portguese region).
WHEN? = Easter (clue 1 refers to the Easter Rising and Easter Island; Simnel cake is eaten on Easter Sunday).

99. A=18, B=7, C=5, D=6, E=41, F=460, G=78, H=13, J=24, K=24, ANSWER=1065.

100. The answers are:
1) IBM
2) *Hamlet*
3) Chinook
4) Alice Springs
5) Ballistics
6) Bat
7) Visual Display Unit
8) Red and green
9) Dr. George Carey
10) Sugar
11) Does not give country of origin on its stamps
12) Fifteen

PROGRESS CHART

Plot your score on the chart and see if you are keeping up
with the target to beat.

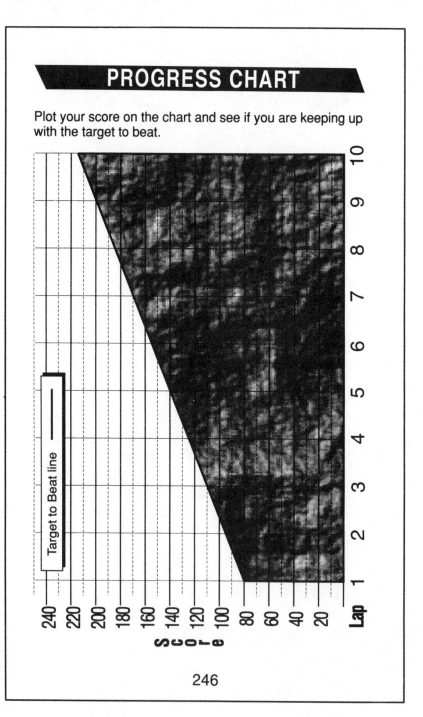